International Association for the Integrational Study of Language and Communication

2015

David Bade, Rita Harris, Charlotte Conrad. *Roy Harris and Integrational Semiology 1956-2015: A bibliography.*

2020

Sinfree Makoni. *Language in Africa. Selected papers* vol. 1
David Bade. *Efficiencies and Deficiencies: Cataloging and Communication in Libraries.*
Sinfree Makoni. *African Applied Linguistics. Selected Papers,* vol. 2
David Bade. *Integrational Linguistics for Library & Information Science: Linguistics, Philosophy, Rhetoric and Technology*
Sinfree Makoni. *Linguistic Ideologies, Sociolinguistic Myths and Discourse Strategies in Africa. Selected Papers,* vol. 3
Sinfree Makoni. *Languages and Language Planning in Zimbabwe. Selected Papers,* vol. 4
David Bade. *Making Mongolians: Linguistics, Historiography, Fiction*
Lars Taxén. *Exploring the Relation between Biomechanical and Macrosocial Factors: Integrationism meets Neuroscience and Information Systems*

2021

David Bade. *Epistemologies of Rape and Revelation*

2022

Jon Orman. *Indeterminacy and Explanation in Linguistic Inquiry: Contentious Papers 2012 – 2018*

The International Association for the Integrational Study of Language and Communication

The IAISLC was founded in 1998. It is managed by an international Executive Committee, whose members are:

Adrian Pablé (University of Hong Kong), Secretary
David Bade (University of Chicago, retired)
Charlotte Conrad (Dubai)
Stephen J. Cowley (University of Southern Denmark)
Daniel R. Davis (University of Michigan)
Dorthe Duncker (University of Copenhagen)
Jesper Hermann (University of Copenhagen)
Christopher Hutton (University of Hong Kong)
Peter Jones (Sheffield Hallam University)
Nigel Love (University of Cape Town)
Sinfree Makoni (Penn State University)
Rukmini Bhaya Nair (Indian Institute of Technology)
Talbot J. Taylor (College of William & Mary)
Michael Toolan (University of Birmingham)

Anyone wishing to join the Association can do so by email apable@hku.hk or by sending their name and address to the Secretary:

Dr Adrian Pablé
School of English
Run Run Shaw Tower
Centennial Campus
The University of Hong Kong
Hong Kong S.A.R

Jon Orman

Indeterminacy and Explanation in Linguistic Inquiry

Contentious Papers 2012 – 2018

Edited by David Bade

International Association for the Integrational Study of
Language and Communication

This collection copyright by the author 2022.
Acknowledgements:
1. Not so super: the ontology of 'supervernaculars', ©2012 *Language & Communication* Vol. 32, Issue 4, October 2012, pp. 349-357.
2. New lingualisms, same old codes, ©2013 *Language Sciences* Vol. 37, May 2013, pp. 90-98.
3. Polylanguaging, integrational linguistics and contemporary sociolinguistic theory: A commentary on Ritzau. (with Adrian Pablé), ©2016 *International Journal of Bilingual Education and Bilingualism* Vol. 19, Issue 5, pp. 592-602.
4. Linguistic diversity and language loss: a view from integrational linguistics, ©2013 *Language Sciences* Vol.40, November 2013, pp. 1-11.
5. Things people speak?: a response to Orman's 'Linguistic diversity and language loss a view from integrational linguistics' with rejoinder. (with Joshua Nash), ©2014 *Language Sciences* v. 41, Part B, Jan.2014, pp.222-226.
6. Indeterminacy in sociolinguistic and integrationist theory, ©2017 In *Critical Humanist Perspectives: The Integrational Turn in Philosophy of Language and Communication*, ed. Adrian Pablé. London: Routledge, 2017, pp.96-113.
7. A turn for the meta, a turn for the Peirce, ©2018 *Sociolinguistic Studies*, Vol. 12, No 1, pp.89-96.
8. Distributing mind, cognition and language: Exploring the (un)common ground with integrational linguistics, ©2015 *Language and Cognition*, vol. 8, issue 1, pp. 142-166.
9. Scientism and the language sciences, ©2016 *Language & Communication* Vol. 48, May 2016, pp. 28-40.
10. Explanation and theory in linguistic inquiry, ©2017 *Empedocles: European Journal for the Philosophy of Communication*, Vol. 8, No. 2, pp. 167-186.
11. Theorising the untheorisable: Notes on integrationism and the 'Mixed-Game Model', ©2018 *Language and Dialogue*, Vol. 8, Issue 1, pp. 102-117.
12. Some reflections on the uses and abuses of theory in linguistic thought. ©2018. *History & Philosophy of The Language Sciences* April 2018.
13. The linguistic thought of Ernest Gellner, ©2017 *Social Epistemology* Vol. 31, Issue 4, pp.387-399.
14. Theorised to death: Diagnosing the social pseudosciences, ©2018 *Philosophical Papers* Vol. 47, Issue 2, pp.313-332.
15. Language and 'new' African migration to South Africa, 2012 *Language Policy* Vol. 11, pp. 301–322.
16. Language policy and identity conflict in relation to Afrikaans in the post-apartheid era, ©2014 In Neville Alexander and Arnulf von Scheliha (eds.). 2014. *Language Policy and the Promotion of Peace: African and European Case Studies*. Pretoria: UNISA Press. pp.59-76.

Table of contents

Preface..7

Section I. Debunking Sociolinguistics
1. Not so super: the ontology of 'supervernaculars'....................13
2. New lingualisms, same old codes..43
3. Polylanguaging, integrational linguistics and contemporary sociolinguistic theory: A commentary on Ritzau. (with Adrian Pablé)..73
4. Linguistic diversity and language loss: a view from integrational linguistics...95
5. Things people speak?: a response to Orman's 'Linguistic diversity and language loss a view from integrational linguistics' with rejoinder. (with Joshua Nash)..............131
6. Indeterminacy in sociolinguistic and integrationist theory....147
7. A turn for the meta, a turn for the Peirce............................177

Section II. Integrationism and 'Distributed Language'
8. Distributing mind, cognition and language: Exploring the (un)common ground with integrational linguistics........191
9. Scientism and the language sciences....................................229

Section III. The Place of Theory in Linguistic Thought
10. Explanation and theory in linguistic inquiry.......................275
11. Theorising the untheorisable: Notes on integrationism and the 'Mixed-Game Model'...311
12. Some reflections on the uses and abuses of theory in linguistic thought...335
13. The linguistic thought of Ernest Gellner.............................357
14. Theorised to death: Diagnosing the social pseudosciences..391

Section IV. Language Policy in Post-Apartheid South Africa
15. Language and 'new' African migration to South Africa.....417
16. Language policy and identity conflict in relation to Afrikaans in the post-apartheid era..............................457

Preface

The papers in this volume constitute almost the entirety of my published work between 2011 and 2018. These years were spent as a precariously employed junior academic in a series of positions at the universities of Cape Town, Portsmouth and Hong Kong.

I departed academia in early 2018 having failed resoundingly to overcome the aforementioned precarity. The extent to which this failure was connected to my espousal of an integrationist position on language is an open question and not one which I intend to dwell on here at length at the risk of boring readers to whom it is no doubt of far less interest than it is to myself. Nevertheless, I mention it to broach the broader point that successful navigation within the contemporary university environment as an integrationist scholar of language is far from a straightforward affair. I remember well that the initial intellectual exhilaration that went with discovering the work of Roy Harris, Nigel Love and others was soon accompanied by the sobering realisation that it was likely going to be very difficult indeed to forge a lengthy, tenured career propounding such a line of thought. In my case, the situation was made more difficult by the fact that the departments in which I was employed were invariably dominated, numerically and intellectually, by practitioners of sociolinguistics, a field which I was always particularly interested in subjecting to an integrational critique (see Section I).

Some of the reasons why the simultaneous pursuit of an integrationist line of thought and a conventional, linear academic career are not necessarily easily reconcilable aims are touched upon at various points throughout the pieces in this collection which the editor, David Bade, has given the subtitle 'Contentious Papers'. It is hardly one I can disagree or find fault with. After all, once engaged with, integrationist ideas cannot fail to be contentious within the context of an intellectual tradition permeated by the scientism of the 'language myth' first identified and subsequently demolished by Roy Harris. This is not to say, of course, that all the papers in this collection have provoked sustained debate and counterargument. Quite often they have simply been ignored by the relevant parties or received only minimal engagement, a fate to which most integrationist authors, including Harris himself, are no doubt somewhat accustomed.

From a personal perspective, of all the papers in this collection one stands out in terms of its contentiousness. The paper *Some reflections on the uses and abuses of theory in linguistic thought* (Section III) was put together from the notes for a presentation entitled "Why theorise language?" given in the School of English at the University of Hong Kong, the department in which I was temporarily employed at the time, as part of a job application process in September 2017. To compare the reception of this paper to the proverbial lead balloon would be to render a disservice to the aeronautical capacities of the latter. I recall that my critical comments on Bakhtin, Derrida and ethnography, in particular, were met with intense hostility from more than a few of the sociolinguists and literary scholars in the audience that day. On reflection, I cannot say I regret having given the paper, however unwise a career move it may have been and awkward an occasion it may have made for. It stands as an honest account of my intellectual concerns at the time and, upon rereading, I find I am quite happy to stand by the arguments I advance in it. Whether present readers will find this paper and the others in this collection equally contentious remains to be seen.

The papers are organised thematically rather than chronologically. I should therefore make clear that the two papers in Section IV are the earliest in the collection and, as such, are not written from an explicitly integrational perspective, although keen readers may pick up on some nascent integrationist tendencies in my thinking. Anyone wishing to enter into correspondence on any matter related to the papers in this collection is welcome to contact me at orman.jon@gmail.com.

Finally, I am most grateful to David Bade, firstly for his suggestion to put together a volume such as this and secondly for his extremely diligent editorial work in bringing about its completion. He is not responsible for any errors, inaccuracies or other infelicities to be found in the pages which follow.

J.O

Worthing, February 2022

Section I.
Debunking Sociolinguistics

1.

Not so super: the ontology of 'supervernaculars'

Abstract
This article offers a critical response to Blommaert's notion of 'supervernaculars'. The discussion focuses on the tenability of the ontological assumptions which underlie its introduction. It is argued that despite the superficial terminological innovation, the concept of 'supervernaculars' rests on a quite orthodox ontology of language and communication, that is to say one which posits abstract artefactual entities existing over and above individual communicational situations and affirms a code-based view of language. Consequently, the category of the 'supervernacular' fails to provide a satisfactory theoretical framework with which to describe the types of 'mixed' language use frequently encountered in certain modern communicative practices. A more coherent and indeed prosaic account of such practices can instead be had by arguing on the basis of a Harrisian critique of orthodox linguistics.

1. Introduction

In a recent paper, Blommaert (2011) endeavours to introduce the notion of 'supervernaculars'[1] into the conceptual and terminological repository of (socio)linguistic theory. The stated motivation for doing so is to contribute towards the creation of 'a new and more accurate vocabulary for describing and understanding language in superdiversity[2]' (2011, p. 2). The main purpose of the present article, however, is to question whether the notion of supervernaculars and the ontological assumptions which underlie its introduction can actually provide a coherent basis for assisting us in this regard. The basic argument pursued is that far from representing any radical or innovative departure in linguistic theorising, the concept of supervernaculars as formulated by Blommaert is founded upon a quite traditional, orthodox and ultimately untenable ontology of language and, by implication, human communication.

In the aforementioned paper, the term 'supervernacular' is proposed as:

> a descriptor for new forms of semiotic codes emerging in the context of technology-driven globalization processes. Supervernaculars are widespread codes used in communities that do not correspond to 'traditional' sociolinguistic speech communities, but as deterritorialized and transidio-

---

[1] The term has also been used approvingly in papers by Wang and Varis (2011) and Velghe (2011).

[2] 'Super-diversity' is a term coined by Vertovec (2006; 2007) to refer to the 'diversification of diversity' which has occurred in many modern societies as a result of the ever-increasing proliferation of migration channels and varying legal statuses of immigrants. The term is one which has been enthusiastically embraced in certain linguistic circles and indeed appears to have become the pivotal foundational concept in a still embryonic yet nevertheless quite distinctive research paradigm within sociolinguistics.

matic communities that, nonetheless, appear to create a solid and normative sociolinguistic system (Blommaert, 2011, p. 2).

Supervernaculars are presented as a new type of 'sociolinguistic object' which 'when developed empirically, can lead to quite radical reformulations of cultural processes and transformations in the age of globalization and superdiversity'[3] (2011, pp. 2–3). The underlying rationale for this attempt at terminological innovation stems from the fact that certain objects posited by more traditional forms of linguistic enquiry such as the homogenous 'speech community' and named territorially bound languages or language varieties no longer appear theoretically tenable in the face of the increasingly diverse and fragmented patterns of communicative behaviour characteristic of modern-day societies subject to processes of globalisation (see also Seargeant and Tagg, 2011). The larger question of whether such concepts were indeed ever theoretically justifiable is one that can be left aside for the moment. The key point Blommaert wishes us to understand is that:

> We now observe new – or previously unnoticed – patterns of sociolinguistic distribution in which certain specific sociolinguistic resources are adopted by communities of users that share none of the traditional attributes of speech communities – territorial fixedness, physical proximity, socio-cultural sharedness and common backgrounds. People now use similar sociolinguistic resources without sharing any of the traditional features of community. And

---

[3] In a footnote, Blommaert explains that the 'super' in 'supervernacular' is to be understood differently to that in 'superdiversity'. In the latter, 'super' denotes 'hyper' while in 'supervernacular' it denotes 'trans-' and 'refers to communities and semiotic complexes whose composition and circulation transcend those of other semiotic complexes' (2011:4).

such loose, elastic, dynamic and deterritorialized communities are among the key features of superdiversity (2011, p. 3)

While one might wish to question exactly what is meant by the term 'sociolinguistic resources', the essential thrust of the preceding quotation is largely uncontroversial. Modern technological developments have indeed facilitated a proliferation in the ways in which people can communicate remotely and by consequence led to massive increases in the numbers of people able to communicate with one other and the frequencies with which they are able to do so on a local, trans-regional, international and global scale. This has also seen a concomitant increase in the global distribution and occurrence of certain recognisably similar semiotic forms and in particular forms which would ordinarily be categorised as 'English'. We can also witness highly 'mixed' instances of language use, that is to say discourse comprising elements from two or more 'languages', a phenomenon which has elsewhere been labelled as 'polylanguaging' (Jørgensen et al., 2011) or 'translanguaging' (Canagarajah, 2011). This much can be readily accepted. The question, though, is whether these interesting and novel developments in the communicative lives of such vast numbers of individuals warrant the imposition of a new meta-terminology which includes the term 'supervernacular' as conceptualised by Blommaert. As will hopefully become clear over the course of the article, the fundamental motivation for rejecting the notion lies not in the reasoning that any terminological innovation is unwelcome or unnecessary, but simply in the conviction that, in this case, it is based upon an ontology of language and implicit picture of human communication which shares a number of central and unfortunate similarities to those advanced in more traditional accounts and from which those of a Blommaertian bent conversely also seem eager to distance themselves. Thus, it seems that while the vocabulary may have changed, the ultimately flawed conceptualisation of what goes on during linguistic communication has not.

2. The ontology of the 'supervernacular'

A term which immediately strikes in Blommaert's elucidation of 'supervernaculars' is that of 'object'. As an initial observation, the positing of supervernaculars as a sort of sociolinguistic object would seem to jar with the more recent trend to move away from an 'artefactual' view of language (Seargeant, 2009).[4] Indeed, Blommaert has himself written critically of such an 'artefactualized image [. . .] as developed in modern linguistics, of language as a bounded, nameable and countable unit, often reduced to grammatical structures and vocabulary and called by names such as 'English', 'French' and so on' (2010, p. 4; see also Blommaert, 2006). However, the suspicion of a contradiction in Blommaert's thought here is suggested by his remark that supervernaculars 'have all the features we commonly attribute to "languages"' (my emphasis) (2011, p. 4). Presumably, then, these are the same features – finite stock of generative grammatical structures and vocabulary items with determinate, objectively discoverable, context-invariant meanings – which together help form the artefactual view of languages as internally systematic, bounded, countable entities. It would therefore seem that, onto-epistemologically speaking, supervernaculars are all but languages by another name. The necessary reason for the change in terminology is supposedly that 'sociolinguistically they operate in a very different way, not predicated on the traditional connections between languages and speech communities [. . .] and

---

[4] Hermann (2007), using the phrase coined by Gilbert Ryle, argues that to talk of language as a thing or object is to employ a 'systematically misleading expression'.

determined (in the strictest sense of the term) by new information and communication technologies' (Blommaert, 2011, p. 4). The essential objectness of supervernaculars is clearly not a matter of issue here for Blommaert. Instead, it is the function which the pre-theoretical object serves which constitutes the core area of focus and analysis.

The parallel between supervernaculars and languages as understood in traditional linguistic theorising is continued when we are told, in what may strike as a perplexing mixture of terminological tradition and innovation, that '[t]he important point to realise is that *supervernaculars only occur as dialects*' (Blommaert, 2011, p. 5, emphasis in original).[5] The supervernacular, then, is held to be equivalent to an imagined archetype or 'standard' language of which only dialectal or 'accented' realisations actually appear but towards which language users nevertheless orient when speaking or writing. Blommaert develops his case by citing the case of English[6]:

> [W]e never hear 'standard' English, we always hear 'English with an accent', inflected and dialected English – the 'accentless' standard is evidently an accent among others. Yet, in all the myriad actual forms assumed by 'English', we see users orienting towards an 'accentless' norm – towards the imaginary neutrality of 'normal' usage of that specific code, the 'best possible' recognizable variety (2011, p. 5)

---

[5] One is tempted to ask why the supervernaculars do not appear as 'super-dialects'.

[6] In a similar vein, Mcintosh (2010:337), in a paper on text messaging practices in Kenya, talks of the 'global medialect of condensed abbreviated English.' Note once again the postulation of an object–the medialect–of which instances of actual linguistic behaviour are held to be an instantiation.

Blommaert is clearly using the term 'accent' here in two senses, hence what may initially appear the rather confusing invocation of an accentless accent. Firstly in the sense of being distinctive of the language usage associated with some particular social group or geographical area and secondly in the sense of a form of language considered somehow inferior or with less social prestige. The term 'accentless' here might therefore better be replaced by 'prestige' or 'high-status'. However, discussion of the semantic scope of the term 'accent' represents something of a diversion and side matter. The main issue under consideration is whether there is any metatheoretical and conceptual benefit in positing particular instances of language use as dialectal realisations of an imagined (imaginary?) overarching standard, in this case the supposed supervernacular. In order to answer this question, it is first of all important to understand the theoretical assumptions and motivations underlying such an approach.

It is at this point that the notion of language codes becomes central. It is quite clear – and I doubt whether he would deny it – that Blommaert is deeply committed to a code-based view of language [7] broadly corresponding to the Saussurean doctrine of the biplanar character of the linguistic sign (Love, 1989), that is to say as constituting a determinate form-meaning combination. The language or in this case supervernacular – after all they supposedly share all of the same features – is then viewed as the totality of all possibly occurring combinations of such signs within a particular linguistic system, however that comes to be defined. As evidence of this view, we see, in a co-authored paper (Blommaert and Backus, 2011), linguistic competence defined as a 'structured inventory of units' which themselves are 'form-meaning combinations of any degree of complexity and any

---

[7] As Pablé et al. (2010:671) note, it makes little difference whether the code is seen as preceding the communicational episode or as emerging contemporaneously during it and only retaining its fixedness for its duration.

degree of simplicity' (p. 6) and in Blommaert (2011) we are on numerous occasions in-formed that supervernaculars constitute codes (semiotic codes, chat codes, gaming codes, standard codes, mobile texting codes and so on) which presumably consist of just such units. He writes for instance that '[o]ne mini-language[8] that can be described as a supervernacular is the widely used set of codes for composing mobile phone text messages' (p. 6). One might possibly counter at this juncture that too much is being read into Blommaert's frequent use of the term 'code' and that the preceding attributions do not necessarily follow. After all, the word 'code' is frequently employed, no doubt sometimes unthinkingly, in both lay and academic discourse around language and communication and its usage might even appear appropriately *zeitgeistig* given the importance which digital computer-based technologies have come to assume in many contemporary communicative exchanges. It is also not my purpose – as if it were ever possible in the first place – to attempt to impose any perduring semantic determinacy on the term, nor is it to allege any inconsistency in Blommaert's theorising by arguing that he is falsely claiming not to work with a code-based view of language. However, any doubts about Blommaert's status as a 'fixed-code theorist' (Harris, 1996, p. 151) would seem to be dispelled by his discussion of the 'linguistic rules' which are alleged to govern the production of 'mobile texting code'. Blommaert (2011, p. 8) cites the following piece of text message language with his own interpretive gloss given in parenthesis[9]:

---

[8] The term 'mini-language' is left unglossed. The 'mini-ness' is presumably a reference to the quite specific type of technological devices through which the supposed code is transmitted rather than any restriction on the range of meanings which can be thus communicated.

[9] See Velghe (2011:2) for a similar example.

'Lkn fwd 2 C U @ 4 @ Urs ☺ ('looking forward to see you at four at your place ☺ ')'

This is immediately followed by the claim that '[i]f we would change one element in this written "sentence" – if we defy the graphic rules of the mini-language, in other words – the expression becomes *meaningless* (my emphasis), as in:

*Lkn fwd 2 S̲ U @ 4 @ Urs ☺ '

This is where the difficulty of maintaining the fixed-code position starts to chafe. As an initial point, it should be understood that any decontextualised string of symbols is essentially meaningless when divorced from the circumstances of its communicational occurrence, such as is the case here. Blommaert's gloss of the text message also tells us nothing about the circumstances and context of its production and in that sense we are no more able to do anything with it in terms of assigning it any contextualised real-world import. However, let us now imagine a hypothetical situation in which such a message might conceivably be written and received. Suppose two friends are making plans to meet later in the day or one friend is reminding the other of a previous arrangement to do so. In that case, Blommaert's gloss of the message would appear an eminently reasonable one. Yet, now let us imagine that the second of the two messages is sent and received instead of the first (with the S replacing the C). This message, remember, is supposedly meaningless, but in what sense exactly? After all, it seems unlikely that it would be beyond the wit of a reasonably competent language user to make *any* sense whatsoever of such a message in such a situation. Perhaps the receiver will interpret the sender as having meant to write 'C' but having mistakenly written 'S', perhaps the 'S' will be interpreted as simply an abbreviation of the graphic form 'see', perhaps the 'S' will be interpreted as standing for some other verb, perhaps the anomalous 'S' will go unnoticed. Any number of interpretations could arise. Whatever interpretation is in reality given to the string of symbols will depend on an integrated range of contextual and circumstantial factors. One of the least plausible explanations is surely that the hypothetical recipient of the message would find it utterly devoid of meaning and unable to do anything with it. Any doubts he/she may have regarding the sender's precise intended meaning, which may of course not be the case, could be assuaged by recourse to metalinguistic glossing practices ('I take it you meant "C"?', 'Ok, C U @ 4!' or suchlike). If we extend Blommaert's reasoning to written communication more generally then it follows that any spelling mistake or typo, etc. renders the expression in which it occurs meaningless. That being the case, it is a wonder that successful written communication is able to occur as often as appears to be the case.

It is important to realise that it is Blommaert's postulation of a code-based view of language which leads him to describe the sentence as 'meaningless'. In such a view, it is the code – an inventory of determinate form-meaning combinations – which determines the value of a sign and not the use to which it is put for communicational purposes. In this case, the code postulated by Blommaert seemingly does not contain a meaning corresponding to the graphic form 'S', hence the attribution of meaninglessness to the sentence in which it occurs. Humans, however, are fortunately and necessarily somewhat more flexible in processing semiological input than computers on account of their ability to make sense of the varying range of contextual knowledge and experience available to them. This is not to say that someone would *necessarily* be able to assign a meaning to the sentence; someone (largely) unfamiliar with mobile texting practices and/or English may be quite unable to make any sense of it. The point rather is that it is the context in which a sentence (or any sign or combination of signs) occurs which will determine the value assigned to it. The ascription of meaninglessness to a decontextualised sign (or sequence of signs) only becomes a point of issue within the framework of a fixed-code semantics since it is only in such a context that meaning itself can be attributed to such a sign. However, the difficulty for those pursuing this line of thought is that human communication never takes place and could never do so on such a decontextualised basis. Communication is an inherently context-bound activity and no two contexts can ever be considered wholly 'the same', whether in terms of their temporal-spatial occurrence or in terms of the necessarily differing subjective perspectives of the participants involved. Hence, there is no question of signs having a uniform, context-free meaning stable across all occasions of their use. As Harris (2005, p. 110) notes: 'The communicational continuum is open-ended, and that is why there is no determinacy of meaning.' This open-endedness is a feature denied by the code-based view of language. Not only does the code entail determinacy of meaning, its usage is apparently also subject to strict rules. Blommaert (2011, p. 8) argues that:

> [W]hile mobile texting code appears at first sight as an infinitely creative space of practice allowing unrestricted freedom to experiment and free-wheel [. . .] it is important to see that the code is strongly *normative*; it is – like any other form of language use – a *system*, something that operates on the basis of quite rigorously applied rules, deviation of [sic] which is possible but never unlimited and always comes with a price.

So in effect we see a further layer of determinacy introduced, this time into the actual employment of the code through the mechanism of the rule-based system. While one would not wish to deny that almost all language use, even via such relatively modern technological means as text messaging, is subject to sometimes stringent normative constraints, considerations and assessments – about what constitutes correct, good, aesthetic, prestigious usage, etc. – this is not quite the same as saying it is based on systematically operating rules. The immediate question which arises is how the rules and system came into being (or into knowing) in the first place and secondly how individuals are able to select and apply such rules in the appropriate communicative circumstances. This we are not told. Blommaert claims deviation from the rules of the code is in fact possible but does not indicate which deviations are permissible. However, it is clear from the example discussed that the substitution of 'S' for 'C' in the sense of 'see' is not one such possible deviation, in which case one is led to ask why not. What sort of code is it that can tolerate some minor deviations, whatever they might be, and not others?

The postulation of rules is indeed a corollary of the postulation of the code itself. Under the terms of the code, there is a definitively correct or incorrect input (form) for obtaining a particular meaning and any impermissible deviations are consequently rendered aberrant or meaningless. It therefore appears to be the case that the obtainment of a desired meaning comes about as a result of the following of the necessary procedures or rules for doing so. If one fails to achieve the desired meaning, one clearly has not followed 'the rules'. However, as the example discussed above shows, such reasoning manifestly conflicts with our everyday linguistic experience in which apparently successful communication is frequently able to occur despite sometimes quite egregious violations of whatever codes are believed to have been instantiated.

A way out of this theoretical tangle can instead be had by abandoning the notion that what we are witnessing here is the manifestation of a hypostatised rule-based code. I would argue that what Blommaert styles as rules of usage are instead mere *conventions*, that is to say regularities or similarities in the material (graphic) instantiations of signs across multiple occasions of use. Of course, conventions may still be subject to normative constraints which in practice limit the extent of the creativity or variation individuals are *likely* to employ in producing such signs, but such constraints are of quite a different order from any supposed rules which cannot but compel observance. Might it be the case that the detection of systems and rules is itself an artefact of particular methodological and conceptual presuppositions? Fleming (1997, p. 199), in an incisive elucidation of the often unacknowledged or sometimes outright denied structuralist underpinnings of much theorising in the ethnomethodological tradition, makes some remarks pertinent to the case under discussion here, noting that according to such thought:

> [C]ommunication is situated only on the surface; abstract structures external to the particular act drive that act in a way surprisingly compatible with the orthodox structuralism that ethnomethodologists have claimed to reject [. . .]. Rather than begin, as Harris proposes, with the "individual linguistic act in its communicational setting" [they] impose on that act hypostatized invariants that exist independently of it [. . .]. The decontextualized abstractions of structuralism are thus resurrected in full force.

In this case, it is the supervernacular code and its alleged dialects that are the hypostatised invariants. Blommaert's invocation of dialects is strongly symptomatic of the concern to find invariants existing over and above the individual communicative act and also serves to buttress the code-based view of linguistic communication. As Harris (1998, p. 44) notes:

> Another common [. . .] strategy for reconciling fixed codes on the one hand with linguistic variation on the other is to appeal to the notion of 'dialects'. This makes it

more plausible – superficially, at least – to maintain that 'the same language' is spoken throughout a certain population, while admitting that it is spoken differently by different groups within that population. In short, the function of the dialect myth in orthodox linguistics is to provide theoretical support for the idea that there can be linguistic unity in diversity. The dialect is thus identified as 'the system' constituting the immediate object of the linguist's description and a language is construed (either synchronically or diachronically) as a set of dialects. It follows that a description of 'the language' simply is the description of its various dialects.

If we substitute the term 'supervernacular' for 'language' in the above passage we have what appears to be an accurate characterisation of the theoretical motivation behind Blommaert's conceptualisation of supervernaculars. A key question to determine is whether the supervernacular 'system' which Blommaert posits is really any such thing and can be seen to correspond to any coherent object of analysis. By way of further evidence to support his argument, Blommaert cites examples from two additional 'codes'. The first such example consists of text messages sent by Flemish youths in Antwerp. These include 'code symbols' such as 'W8' which is used to render the sense of the Dutch word 'wacht' (wait). Somewhat interestingly, the same form is often used by English speakers to mean 'wait' but this is the result of nothing more than a series of phonetic coincidences. The Dutch form 'L8' which gives 'lacht' (laugh) does not give a corresponding English form; it is instead normally used to mean 'late'. The only remotely contextualised example given is the following message sent from a young Antwerp girl to her boyfriend:

U R my 3 M: 'you are my dream'

This for Blommaert represents an example of so-called 'code-switching' since it contains both English and Dutch elements, the Dutch element being the '3' to be pronounced as 'drie', the Dutch for 'three', hence *drie + m = dream*. In fact, it is not so much any creativity on the part of the girl which enables the production of such a sentence but rather 'the mechanisms of the code [which] permit her to code-switch from English into Dutch and back' (2011, p. 10). Again though, it is not immediately apparent in what sense this is the case. Firstly, it is not at all clear whether we are dealing with two individual codes here which happen to be combined or with a single new code which is the product of the aforementioned combination. More importantly though, how does the fortuitous phonetic similarity, but by no means identity, between the common pronunciation of the Dutch numeral '3' and that of the initial part of the English word 'dream' become conceived as the mechanism or outcome of a prior existing code?

A similar type of example can be imagined in reverse. One can conceive of (and indeed a Google search confirms several examples) the use of the graphic form '10minste' in a number of Dutch texts. '10minste' is intended to be read as 'tenminste', the Dutch word which would typically be glossed as 'at least' in English. Here the initial numerals are to be read as the English 'ten' rather than the Dutch 'tien'. One could perhaps also imagine German speakers responding in the negative to a question with '9'. What we see here then are, from a particular perspective, kindred orthographic innovations. What is more difficult to arrive at is the view that they are in any sense the product of some system, let alone the same system – what is systematic about the pronunciation of English numerals? – and it is also not clear in what sense rules have been obeyed rather than a convention followed or a creative process initiated.

Similar considerations apply to the subsequent supervernacular examples, again fully decontextualised, offered by

Blommaert, this time from Finland and consisting of English sentences written using a characteristically Finnish orthography with Blommaert's glosses in 'standard' English orthography given in parentheses. Namely:

Lavli! Til tomorou ten! ("lovely! Till tomorrow then!")

sii juu! ("see you!!")

Häv ö seif flait tu joor nyy houm ("have a safe flight to your new home")

Häpi bööffei! ("happy birthday!") (Blommaert, 2011, p. 11)

According to Blommaert, these examples, regarding the contextual production of which we are given no information, represent 'pure dialect formation, in which the participants bring the supervernacular into the realm of Finnish spoken accent *and* orthographic conventions.' In this case, the supervernacular is clearly held to be that idealised object known as English. That said, it is nonetheless difficult to see how these examples and the others discussed above sustain the view that the 'supervernacular appears as a *system* that generates – and enables – the construction of local, 'deglobalized' dialects' (Blommaert, 2011, p. 11). Such a claim would appear to entail a considerable argumentative burden. In what sense is the production of typical English sentences using Finnish orthographic conventions the result of a system which also generates sentences such as the English/Dutch 'U R my 3 M' example above? What exactly is systematic here? It is also not apparent on what basis the examples proffered by Blommaert constitute evidence of orientations towards an 'ideological standard' and if so, which standard. In the case of the Finnish/English (Finnglish?) samples, it is surely a matter of perspective as to whether one sees them as orientations towards a Finnish standard on account of the orthography or towards an English standard on account of the structural elements or indeed towards any standard at all. After all, there would on initial view appear to be nothing particularly 'ideologically standard' about the orthographic innovation where-by English sentences are written in a characteristically Finnish style. There is after all a strong tendency in much work in the ethnographic and discourse analysis tradition to see all language use as saturated in ideological orientation. One is barely capable of opening one's mouth, putting pen to paper or finger to keypad without thereby invoking a torrent of objectively discernible (by the 'expert' theorist at least) ideological tendencies. The point to remember, however, is that the detection of ideology is the product of (sometimes quite idiosyncratic) individual contextualisation. Decontextualised utterances and written forms are not and can never be ideological in and of themselves, whatever the claims made by proponents of so-called 'critical discourse analysis' (Jones, 2007). To suppose otherwise is to be held fully captive by the 'language myth' (Harris, 1981).

3. Codes and communication

Harris (1987, p. 205) notes that 'every linguistic theory presupposes a theory of communication.' In order to appreciate the strength and persistence of the code-based view of language and meaning, it is important to grasp the theory of communication which, whether implicitly or explicitly, commonly underlies it. It is a theoretical position which has come to be known as the 'telementational', 'conduit' or 'sender–receiver' model and one which can trace its intellectual heritage as far back as Aristotle via Saussure and Locke (Harris, 1997, p. 243). In short, the telementational model holds that linguistic communication is a matter of mechanical thought transference from the mind of one person to another, essentially a process of encoding and decoding as iconically illustrated by Saussure's 'talking heads'. Pinker (1994, p. 14), for example, affirms that 'simply by making noises with our mouths, we can reliably cause new combinations of ideas to arise in each other's minds' and in the same book he goes on to note that a word is a 'shared bidirectional symbol, available to convert meaning to sound by any person when the person speaks, and sound to meaning by any person when the person listens, according to the same code' (pp. 151–2). This is not the place to reopen the debate on the merits and demerits of telementation as a theory of human communication as it is one which has been had many times before (see for example Carr, 1997; Harris, 1997, pp. 243–252; Toolan, 1997). The position adopted in this paper, however, is based firmly on the conviction that the telementational thesis represents a manifestly false and misleading account of what goes during human linguistic communication. Now, it must be conceded that at no point does Blommaert categorically advance any thesis of how linguistic communication occurs, let alone explicitly affirm the telementational model. We are therefore left to seek more implicit clues. In their discussion of 'linguistic competence', Blommaert and Backus (2011, p. 7), adopting what one might call a 'mental warehouse' position (Kravchenko, 2007, p. 658), note that if one has a particular form in one's inventory, one has 'the communicative competence to use the form in question appropriately, i.e. like other people do'. Linguistic communication therefore appears to be predicated on the shared mental possession of particular forms and the identical conceptual associations which they evoke in the minds of the interlocutors in question, a situation which would seem to coincide with the requirements of the telementational model. We can therefore see how the sender–receiver model enters into a mutually reinforcing relationship with the code-based view of communication. The model itself of course originates from a time in which the primary form of communication under consideration was of the face-to-face verbal variety between members of what was believed to be the 'same' language community. It is under such conditions that the telementational model perhaps acquires a small measure of superficial plausibility. However, it is to stretch plausibility beyond breaking point to reconcile the model with the disparate, translocal, deterritorialised communicative communities supposedly making use of supervernacular, graphic codes. We are offered no explanation whatsoever for how all these identical concepts appeared in the minds of so many people of such divergent socio-cultural backgrounds. Instead, the matter is treated as something of a pre-theoretical given or assumption in order to secure the ontological status of the fixed code. For an instructive discussion of the 'telementational fallacy' which underpins the notion of 'intersubjectivity' so central to much ethnomethodologically inspired linguistic theorising, see Taylor and Cameron (1987, pp. 161–2).

What then if we abandon the notion of fixed codes and adopt a radically indeterminate view of language, communication and meaning? Can this not perhaps provide us with a more coherent, not to mention prosaic, explanation for what can be seen to be occurring in such examples of language use?

4. Towards an alternative account of language in modern digital literacy practices

The preceding discussion has sought to show that the invocation of imagined abstract objects such as supervernaculars and their alleged dialects in order to explain the genesis of mundane examples of contemporary language usage facilitated by modern technological devices is itself the product of strongly traditional and orthodox presuppositions about language and communication. If one believes that linguistic communication occurs through the use of code-based sign systems in which each sign form has a corresponding, determinate meaning and that these meanings are similarly known to all those using the code, one is certainly more readily able to entertain notions of sociolinguistic objects such as the supervernaculars posited by Blommaert. However, if one rejects such a view and sees the making of linguistic signs as an open-ended process not subject to prior rules and systematisations in which the interpretation of the relationship between form and meaning is essentially a private matter and an element subject to constant recreation and recontextualisation, one is compelled to take seriously Harris' (1981, p. 166) suggestion that linguistic enquiry begin with the study of the 'individual linguistic act in its communication setting.' Lest it be misunderstood, such an approach need not be anti-sociological in emphasis and does not, as Jones and Collins (2006, p. 46) note, constitute:

> an empiricist's paradise; it does not at all negate the social character of communicative acts but it makes us think about their sociality in different terms. To start with, it makes us look for and try to understand communication there where it is actually taking place, where individuals are not social cyphers, sociological variables, or "mere figureheads" whose utterances display and combine elements of the "code" or "discourse type," but real historical individuals going about some business.

What such an approach would not seem to require then is the *a priori* postulation of objects, systems, codes, etc. existing in some abstract realm above and beyond the individual communicative act. As Love (2007, p. 705) notes: '[T]o envisage treating linguistic phenomena as objects is, in and of itself, to propose a distorted account of them. There are no (first-order) linguistic objects of any kind. Language is a temporally situated, ongoing *process* – the process of making and remaking signs in contextualised episodes of communicative behaviour.' With this in mind, how might we then go about describing and accounting for what is going on in the types of examples offered by Blommaert in support of his supervernacular thesis? One of the difficulties one faces in doing so is that much of what seems like the intuitively appropriate vocabulary and conceptual categories available to us are strongly predicated on a 'varieties approach' to linguistic analysis. For example, we can note that many examples of what Seargeant and Tagg (2011, p. 510) call 'vernacular practices of digital literacy' contain elements of different 'languages' but it is merely to defer the problem to claim that such examples themselves constitute the instantiation of a new variety, an explanatory manoeuvre which could theoretically continue *ad infinitum ad absurdum*. The orthodox explanation would be that such examples constitute so-called 'code-switching'. However, this becomes an entirely dud concept devoid of explanatory power once one has rejected the code-based view of language and in no way does it offer any account of why switches between the supposed codes occur. In their discussion of communication practices between Thai speakers on social networking and instant messaging services, Seargeant and Tagg (2011, pp. 510–511) insightfully note that:

> We are left with what appears to be a paradox then. We can describe the linguistic phenomena on display here by means of a terminology based around varieties – we can (mostly) identify which features belong to English or to Thai, we can match syntactic patterns with specific cultural usages [. . .] and we can identify structures and features which are often associated with online discourse. In each case, the methodology for our analysis is premised on the logic which underlies the conception of the variety: namely, we are aiming to identify what appear to be systematic regularities that can be associated with a particular community of language users [. . .]. Yet the phenomenon as a whole – the actual discourse – cannot be

subsumed under the category of a variety. It exhibits too much diversity; it does not have obviously identifiable systematic regularities and, given the variation on display it seems unlikely that one would be able to predict with consistent accuracy how shifts in style, script choice, mode and code take place. In other words it is not, in itself, an emergent 'variety'. Rather, it is a communicative act which draws on available semiotic resources in a semi-improvised way, exhibiting certain very broad regularities in terms of the constraints of the technology and the mutual competencies and orientations of its participants [. . .] We appear, then, to be at the intersection of what is regular (i.e. systematic) and what is free-flowing and possessed of a complexity which, in epistemic terms at least, evades being captured by a generalised conceptual terminology.

These comments are of acute relevance in the context of the present discussion. The *a priori* determination to identify a system underlying certain instances of communicative behaviour is likely to result in just such a presumed identification. Yet, the examples offered by Blommaert do not offer particularly impressive evidence for the existence of any system. What they do point to is the global or transnational uptake of recognisably similar or identical graphic forms (@, ☺, c u, ur, etc.) deployed using particular communications technologies. A further frequently characteristic feature of such discourse is that it can be said to be 'mixed', that is to say displaying features ordinarily associated with different 'languages', one of which is typically English, and often in what strike as unpredictable and innovative ways. It is also the case that deviations from the standard-type orthography generally encountered in more traditional and socially prestigious forms of writing abound in such language use and it is also possible to give examples of regularly occurring forms for which this is the case, as Blommaert indeed does. However, this is all quite of a different order from claiming the existence of a system which determines the production and reception of such signs. In the first place, it would seem to imply that whenever such a sign reoccurs on two or more occasions it carries the 'same' meaning. Here we again see how the alleged system supports the notion of the code. Unless the sign had the same value in all of its occurrences as is required by the code, how else could one attribute or explain any form of systematic distribution to it? After all, if it did not have an invariant value across all of its manifestations, it could hardly be said to constitute the same sign on each occasion.

What we appear to be witnessing here then is the struggle to describe and explain the new and somewhat unprecedented impact of contemporary sociological developments on certain widespread contemporary communicative processes by means of an outdated and fundamentally flawed structuralist ontological framework. The extent and complexity of the diversity of linguistic behaviour on display cannot be adequately accounted for through appeal to a prior and contrived concept of linguistic unity such as the supervernacular code. As Harris (1998, p. 46) notes in his discussion of the 'dialect myth': 'It is the concept of linguistic unity which is theoretically problematic; not the concept of linguistic diversity.' Another way of putting it might be that there is a confusion of first-order and second-order realities, or rather a misrepresentation of first-order realities through the positing of second-order conceptual categories. Hence the reason to adopt a sceptical stance towards the introduction of any further second-order categories such as that of the 'supervernacular'. Unlike the concept of 'languages', it is safe to assume that the notion of supervernaculars currently has no first-order bearing except perhaps for a very small coterie of academic linguists. Most people engaged in digital literacy practices of the type documented are certainly unlikely to regard themselves as instantiating supervernacular codes when engaging in such communicational activities or even reflect in any way upon their ontology. It is also by no means certain that the reverse necessarily applies in relation to 'languages' although it is perhaps more likely given the sociohistorical pedigree of that particular concept. In any case, the conceptual category of the supervernacular is not one which in any sense can be said to be 'lay-oriented' (Hermann, 2011), that is to say as arising from lay persons' reflection on their first-order linguistic behaviour. Levinson (1983, p. 295) writes that ethnomethodologists have traditionally adopted a 'healthy suspicion of premature theorising and *ad hoc* analytical categories', going on to note that 'as far as possible the categories of analysis should be those that participants themselves can be shown to utilise in making sense of interaction; unmotivated theoretical constructs and unsubstantiated intuitions are all to be avoided.' Blommaert's theorisation of supervernaculars would therefore seem to represent something of a break with this tradition.

5. Conclusion

There can be no 'ontologically neutral' theory of linguistic phenomena. Questions of ontology, whether addressed explicitly or not, are not an optional component of linguistic theory. They instead form the theoretical bedrock on which all subsequent analyses rest. This paper has sought to outline and question the ontological assumptions which underlie Blommaert's postulation of supervernaculars as new types of linguistic objects, the existence of which can be inferred on the basis of the inspection of isolated, decontextualised fragments of written language produced on modern communicational devices. The act of terminological creation which sees the introduction of the term 'supervernacular' is not accompanied by a departure from what can be considered a quite traditional and orthodox linguistic ontology. Supervernaculars, while apparently to be distinguished from conventional languages, are nevertheless still system-like fixed codes, albeit exclusively graphic, consisting of biplanar (form and meaning) units. It is at this level then that the fundamental objection lies. The fact these are graphic rather than verbal codes in no way circumvents the indeterminacy of meaning which is a feature of all language use (Love, 1998, p. 107). Indeed, how, for example, could one possibly go about assigning a determinate meaning to '☺', a sign which would seem to have no obviously corresponding verbal form? '☺' means 'smiley face' or something similar is hardly a satisfactory answer as it represents the beginning of a potentially infinite semantic regress. Another way out might be to deny that '☺' is a linguistic sign at all on account of its having no verbal counterpart.[10] Again though, this is also a deeply unsatisfactory position as it suggests that a clear-cut line can be drawn between the linguistic and non-linguistic elements of communication. Whether one regards the sign as having a verbal counterpart or not is very much a matter of individual perspective and meaning-making and not something which can be determined objectively by the linguistic theorist, whatever his or her level of apparent expertise.

Artefactual notions of languages as systemically-operating fixed codes provide an inadequate and fundamentally misleading account of linguistic communication. This rather bald statement applies just as much to the language created via contemporary digital literacy practices as to any other form of language. If we are to develop a more profound and nuanced understanding of the

---

[10] In a recent episode of the American comedy series Curb Your Enthusiasm, the main protagonist Larry David, playing a fictionalised version of himself, upbraids a woman, following a plea to do so from her embarrassed and exasperated husband, for repeatedly saying 'El-oh-el' (i.e. LOL) instead of laughing normally at others' jokes. This shows that what start out as graphic signs may eventually come to have a corresponding verbal representation, rather than merely the other way round.

novel aspects of language usage in the modern world, it will not do to cling onto outdated and discredited ontological frameworks however much one dresses them up in the garb of terminological innovation. One of the more interesting questions in relation to the type of language practices examined in this article, and which will hopefully be addressed with greater acuity in future research, is the sociological one of what it is about the modern world which makes such a proliferation of diversity possible and what lends it its particular and novel character. What is more, it should be quite possible to answer such a question without having to construct bogus conceptual categories in advance of our analysis.

References

Blommaert, Jan, 2006. Language ideology. In: Brown, K. (Ed.), *Encyclopaedia of Language and Linguistics*. Elsevier, Oxford, pp. 510–522.
Blommaert, Jan, 2010. *The Sociolinguistics of Globalization*. Cambridge University Press, Cambridge.
Blommaert, Jan. 2011. *Supervernaculars and their dialects*. King's College, London. (Working Papers in Urban Language & Literacies 81)
Blommaert, Jan., Backus, Ad., 2011. *Repertoires Revisited: 'Knowing language' in Superdiversity*. King's College, London. (Working Papers in Urban Language & Literacies 67)
Canagarajah, Suresh, 2011. Translanguaging in the classroom: emerging issues for research and pedagogy. *Applied Linguistics Review* 2, 1–28.
Carr, Philip, 1997. Telementation and generative linguistics. In: Wolf, George, and Love, Nigel (Eds.), *Linguistics Inside Out: Roy Harris and His Critics*. John Benjamins, Amsterdam, pp. 65–83.

Fleming, David, 1997. Is ethnomethodological conversation analysis an 'integrational' account of language? In: Wolf, George, and Love, Nigel (Eds.), *Linguistics Inside out: Roy Harris and His Critics*. John Benjamins, Amsterdam, pp. 182–207.
Harris, Roy, 1981. *The Language Myth*. Duckworth, London.
Harris, Roy, 1987. Language as social interaction: Integrationalism versus segregationalism. *Language Sciences* 9 (2), 131–143.
Harris, Roy, 1996. *Signs, Language and Communication. Integrational and Segregational Approaches*. Routledge, London.
Harris, Roy, 1997. From an integrational point of view. In: Wolf, George, and Love, Nigel (Eds.), *Linguistics Inside Out: Roy Harris and His Critics*. John Benjamins, Amsterdam, pp. 229–310.
Harris, Roy, 1998. *Introduction to Integrational Linguistics*. Pergamon, Oxford.
Harris, Roy, 2005. *The Semantics of Science*. Continuum, London.
Hermann, Jesper, 2007. The 'language' problem. *Language and Communication* 28, 93–99.
Hermann, Jesper, 2011. Integrating the persons communicating: towards a lay-oriented science of communication – defining the research agenda. *Language Sciences* 33 (4), 575–578.
Jones, Peter E., 2007. Why there is no such thing as "critical discourse analysis". *Language and Communication* 27, 337–368.
Jones, Peter E., Collins, Chik, 2006. Political analysis versus critical discourse analysis in the treatment of ideology: some implications for the study of communication. *Atlantic Journal of Communication* 14 (1–2), 28–50.

Jørgensen, JN., Karrebæk, MS., Madsen, LM., Møller, JS. 2011. Polylanguaging in superdiversity. *Diversities* 13(2), 2338.

Kravchenko, Alexander V., 2007. Essential properties of language, or, why language is not a code. *Language Sciences* 29, 650–671.

Love, Nigel, 1989. Transcending Saussure. *Poetics Today* 10 (4), 793–818.

Love, Nigel, 1998. Integrating languages. In: Harris, Roy, and Wolf, George (Eds.), *Integrational Linguistics: A First Reader*. Pergamon, Oxford, pp. 96–112.

Love, Nigel, 2007. Are languages digital codes? *Language Sciences* 29, 690–709.

Mcintosh, Janet, 2010. Mobile phones and Mipoho's prophecy: the power and dangers of flying language. *American Ethnologist* 37 (2), 337–353.

Pablé, Adrian., Haas, Marc., Christe, Noel., 2010. Language and social identity: an integrationist critique. *Language Sciences* 32, 671–676.

Pinker, Steven, 1994. *The Language Instinct*. Morrow, New York.

Seargeant, Philip, 2009. The historical ontology of language. *Language Sciences* 32, 1–13.

Seargeant, Philip, Tagg, Caroline, 2011. English on the internet and a 'post-varieties' approach to language. *World Englishes* 30 (4), 496–514.

Taylor, Talbot J., Cameron, Deborah, 1987. *Analysing Conversation: Rules and Units in the Structure of Talk*. Pergamon, Oxford.

Toolan, Michael., 1997. A few words on telementation. *Language Sciences* 19, 79–91.

Velghe, Fie. 2011. *Lessons in Textspeak from Sexychick: Super-vernacular Literacy in South African Instant and Text Messaging*. Tilburg Papers in Culture Studies, Paper 1.

Vertovec, Steven, 2006. *The emergence of superdiversity in*

Britain. ESRC Centre on Migration, Policy and Society, Working Paper WP-06-025.

Vertovec, Steven, 2007. Super-diversity and its implications. *Ethnic and Racial Studies* 29 (6), 71–83.

Wang, Xuan, Varis, Piia, 2011. Superdiversity on the internet: a case from China. *Diverse* 13 (2), 71–83.

2.

New lingualisms, same old codes

Abstract
This article seeks to highlight an example of the continued prevalence of code-based views of language and telementational accounts of communication in prominent areas of contemporary sociolinguistic theorising. Adopting a Harrisian integrationist perspective, I discuss and critique the ontological assumptions regarding language and communication which underlie the notions of 'polylingualism' and 'polylanguaging' as introduced by the Danish sociolinguist Jens Jørgensen and various co-authors. Although they reject the notion of discrete, enumerable languages as ontological realities, they nevertheless propose a method of linguistic analysis based on the identification of linguistic features in the form of units and regularities reminiscent of a Saussurean-style structuralism. I argue that the explanation for this lies in their adherence to a mythical view of language and communication, namely one which views language as consisting of coded bi-planar units and linguistic communication as involving the transfer of mental content from one mind to another.

1. Introduction

An increasingly emergent emphasis in current sociolinguistic theorising concerns the apparent need to develop a new Meta-terminology with which to better describe and account for the types of language practices considered as, if not uniquely, then strongly characteristic of the contemporary era or – to put it in terms favoured by a highly prominent new research paradigm in sociolinguistics – of the 'superdiverse' societies of 'late modernity' (e.g. Vertovec, 2007; Creese and Blackledge, 2010a; Blommaert and Rampton, 2011). This urge stems from the perceived inadequacy of more traditional concepts and categorisations to satisfactorily capture the 'mixed' or 'hybrid' nature of much modern discourse, be it verbal or the product of digital literacy practices. There appears to be a growing and one might argue belated realisation that the diversity of human linguistic behaviour ('languaging' has become a popular term) cannot be adequately described or accounted for by adopting a 'varieties approach' (Seargeant and Tagg, 2011), that is to say one involving a neat compartmentalisation based on the positing of separate 'languages' (or various 'lects' thereof) as these are seen as nothing more than abstractions and the product of a particular politico-cultural tradition. Even the traditional notion invoked to describe such 'multilingual' discourse, namely that of 'code-switching' is increasingly seen as providing insufficient analytical refinement although, as the subsequent discussion will show, this has mostly not been accompanied by the abandonment of a code-based understanding of language or an outright rejection of the notion *per se*.[1]

In recent years, various terms have been proposed as descriptors for linguistic practices exhibiting elements conventionally

---

[1] Particularly within what may be called the 'ethnomethodological' or 'ethnographic' tradition within sociolinguistics. The integrationist position, however, rejects any suggestion of language(s) as an intersubjective code.

associated with two or more 'languages'. These include 'polylingualism'/'polylanguaging' (Jørgensen et al., 2011; Møller and Jørgensen, 2012), 'translingualism'/'translanguaging' (Creese and Blackledge, 2010b; Canagarajah, 2011), 'metrolingualism' (Otsuji and Pennycook, 2010) and 'transidiomatic practices' (Jacquemet, 2005). These terms represent attempts to transcend traditional approaches which describe such language practices in terms of a pluralisation of the monolingual norm or ideal which has tended to underpin mainstream linguistic theorising, i.e. in terms of bi- or multilingualism. The extent to which they succeed in doing so is however another matter and indeed it is this question which forms the principal subject matter of this paper. I shall concern myself primarily with a discussion of the theorising underlying the introduction of just one of the four concepts, namely 'polylingualism'/'polylanguaging', although I believe that the analysis will, in some measure at least, bear upon the thought behind all four of those mentioned above since they are, in my view, all based on kindred ontological assumptions regarding language and communication. That is to say that while their proponents ostensibly reject and seek to move beyond more traditional structuralist or generative models, they are not wholly successful in doing so and fall some way short of a position consistent with integrationist thinking about language (Harris, 1981, 1996, 1998) primarily due to the retention of a code-based view of language which itself points towards the affirmation, whether implicit or explicit, of an ultimately untenable 'telementational' view of communication. Indeed, it is the integrational linguistics most closely associated with the work of its founding figure Roy Harris and briefly outlined below which will serve as the theoretical basis for the critique offered in this paper.

   Integrationism is an approach to language and semiology more generally which resists and rejects attempts to reduce human linguistic and communicative endeavours to an analysis based on the postulation of rules, objects and systems.[2] For integrationists, human communication is an irreducibly creative activity in which signs (linguistic or otherwise) are constantly being made and remade by the participants involved rather than retrieved from any pre-existing inventory. By such reckoning, humans are more accurately regarded as language makers than language users (Harris, 1980). The integrational aspect referred to in the eponymous approach is twofold. Firstly, it recognises that communication involves the integration of human activities by means of signs. Secondly, it recognises that human communication cannot be neatly segregated into autonomous domains or channels of communication, be it verbal, gestural, etc. Rather, communication is a cotemporally *integrated* process of human activity comprising various modes or types of sign-making and interpretation. To study any single mode in isolation from the others constitutes a distortion and decontextualisation of the communicative process in question.

Integrationist theory rests upon the rejection of two fundamental and mutually complementary assumptions central to canonical linguistic thought in the Western tradition, namely what it terms the 'fixed-code fallacy' and the 'fallacy of telementation' (Harris, 2007). Taken together, these two fallacies conceive of linguistic communication as involving the instantiation, in speech or writing, of underlying abstract systems of determinate biplanar (form/meaning) sign units enabling the transference of mental content (thoughts, concepts) from one mind to another. According to such thought, linguistic communication is only rendered possible due to interlocutors' shared knowledge of the same linguistic code. If two interlocutors fail to match the same mental content to particular sign forms, communication is destined to break down. The integrationist's rationale for rejecting

---

[2] For a brief introductory overview see
http://www.royharrisonline.com/integrationism.html

such assumptions is that they beg the question of intersubjectivity, that is to say how individuals come to acquire such shared mental associations and how that would even be possible in the first place given that each individual's experience of language and the world is unique. The guarantee of stability which fixed-code theory requires is simply not to be found due to the open-ended nature of human communicative encounters and purposes. Hence, for integrationists the languages, varieties and various types of lect (dialect, sociolect, idiolect, etc.) posited by mainstream linguistics are not first-order linguistic facts derived from objective, empirical observation but rather the products of a particular, culturally dependent and ultimately mythical way of thinking about language and communication (Harris, 1981). For integrationists, there are no linguistic facts prior to any communicational episode. This tallies with the integrationist view of the sign as indeterminate in both form and meaning. As Harris (1998:21) notes:

> [T]he signs that occur in first order communication are those that the participants construe as occurring, and what is signified is what the participants construe as having been signified. *There is no higher court of appeal.* (emphasis in original)

Consequently, if there are any linguistic facts to be established, it is the province of the participants in a communicational act to do so, not that of the linguistic theorist (or indeed any third party). Such a view has important methodological and philosophical implications since it brings into serious question the scientific or objective status of linguistic 'data' and the researcher's retrospective interpretation thereof (Duncker, 2011). Integrationism rejects the expert's claim to greater insight into matters linguistic and instead seeks to prioritise the elucidation of the lay experience of language and communication. One of the principal aims of integrationists has therefore been to contribute towards what they see as the necessary 'rethinking' and 'demythologising' of linguistics (Davis and Taylor, 2002).

My contention in the subsequent discussion is that the theoretical weaknesses and inconsistencies of the 'polylanguaging' framework developed by Jørgensen and various co-authors can be best brought to light through the adoption of an integrational perspective on language and communication. Whether readers come to share this view is in the end a matter for them to decide. Nevertheless, it is a perspective which would at least repay study since, even if it ultimately fails to persuade, the nature and extent of the critique which it offers ought at least to prompt more rigorous defences of the theoretical positions under scrutiny and hopefully open the way to further debate and exchange.

2. 'Polylanguaging' and linguistic features

The term 'polylingualism' seems to have made its first appearance in a 2008 paper by Jørgensen with the cognate term 'poly-languaging' being subsequently introduced by Jørgensen et al. (2011). Møller and Jørgensen (2012:1) offer the following definition:

> *Polylanguaging* is the phenomenon that speakers employ linguistic resources at their disposal which are associated with different "languages", including the cases in which the speakers know only few features associated with a given "language". This entails that speakers will not hesitate to use side by side features which are associated with different "languages".

The rash of scare quotes in the above definition makes clear the authors' scepticism concerning the ontologically real status of discrete, enumerable languages. While not necessarily denying the potency of individual languages as social constructs, the notion of polylanguaging seemingly carries with it the recognition that a more nuanced alternative is required in order to provide a satisfactory analysis of actual language practices. The difference between polylingualism and the more familiar notion of multilingualism therefore extends beyond a mere preference for a Greek prefix over a Latin one. As Jørgensen et al. (2011:34) note:

> [T]he *polylanguaging* norm [. . .] is different from the multilingualism norm [. . .] The multilingualism norm takes it for granted that the speakers have a minimum command of the involved languages. With the multilingualism norm follows the concept of "a language" which assumes that languages can be separated also in use, and in this view it is also possible to determine whether an individual "knows" a language or "has" a language. The term multilingual covers the (more or less "full") command of several languages, whereas the term polylanguaging also allows for the combination with features ascribed to other languages.

By way of example, below is an extract of a longer stretch of discourse taken from a Facebook conversation between three young girls from Copenhagen which Jørgensen et al. (2011) use as data for their discussion of polylanguaging.

> Maimuna 13:45: har købt the equipment, skal bare finde tid til at lave en spektakulær én kun tje dig morok, den skal være special med ekstra spice :p, sorry tar mig sammen denne weekend! insAllah
>
> Ayhan 15:20: gracias muchas gracias!! jeg wenter shpæændt gardash :-)) love youuu. . .
>
> Ilknur 23:37: Ohhh Maimuna, Du havde også lovet mig en skitse… Og du sagde, at det ville været efter eksamener,

men??? Still waiting like Ayhan and a promise is a promise :D :D :D

The discourse consists predominantly of what would conventionally be deemed Danish elements although we can also pick out English (*the equipment, love youuu. . .*, etc.), Spanish (*gracias muchas gracias*), Arabic (*insAllah*) and Turkish (*morok, gardash*) elements in amongst them. What makes this discourse polylingual as opposed to multilingual in the eyes of Jørgensen is that the interactants may only have a quite minimal command (maybe even just a few words) of one or more of the languages implicated. At first sight then, the notion of polylanguaging might seem to represent a favourable theoretical development insofar as it adds a degree of nuance to the analysis of language practices and does not explicitly signal the question-begging assumption inherent in the kindred notion of 'code-switching'. However, if one digs a little deeper into the theoretical justifications and ontological assumptions surrounding its introduction and subsequent discussion, a number of difficulties are encountered. In the handful of articles published thus far advancing the notions of polylanguaging and polylingualism, Jørgensen and his various co-authors argue that the analysis of language practices (or, as it turns out, the transcripts of such practices which they inevitably conceive of as 'linguistic data') should take place at the level of 'features'. After all, it is asserted that 'Speakers use features and not languages' (Jørgensen, 2008:166) and '[People] do not "learn languages". Human beings primarily learn linguistic *features*' (Møller and Jørgensen, 2012:2). On one level these may of course seem rather uncontroversial and banal truisms. However, an initial difficulty soon arrives when one stops to reflect on what is to count as a linguistic feature. However, Jørgensen and his fellow authors appear firm in their conviction that:

> Linguistic features appear in the shape of units and regularities. Units are words, expressions, sounds, even phonetic characteristics such as rounding. Regularities are traditionally called "rules", but they are not rules in the legal sense, or even the normative sense. They are regularities of how units are combined into larger units in processes through which the larger units become associated with meanings. (Jørgensen et al., 2011:30)

What is offered then is a strongly structuralist account of linguistic features and consequently of language itself. The activity of language is essentially reduced to words and the grammatical structures by which they are combined. This account of course begs various important questions relating to the determination of unit boundaries and indeed also the broader encompassing question of whether there is any universally applicable unit-based analysis to which linguistic behaviour can be reduced. As Harris (1997:269) notes: '[T]he concept "word" itself is very much the product of one particular (European) tradition of language study. The word has no status as a universally recognized linguistic unit. Nor is there any other such unit.' Consequently, the identification of discrete linguistic features/units is by no means the unproblematic or uncontroversial enterprise it may appear whether for linguists or lay people (Davis, 1997). Love (2004) argues that a unit-based analysis of an utterance is predicated upon the reification of abstract linguistic units of which the utterance is deemed to be an instantiation rather than its constituting a piece of *sui generis* discourse. Moreover, he notes that the diverse purposes of human communication are such that there appear to be no context-neutral criteria for drawing unit boundaries.

> [T]here are no obvious limits to the ways and senses in which we can employ locutions like 'the word X' or 'the

sentence Y', because the contexts in which we talk about linguistic objects in everyday metalinguistic discourse are not such as to demand consistency or systematicity, and because our use of such locutions is not controlled by the requirement that it conform to some set of objective facts. We have no purposes that necessitate a thoroughgoing, self-consistent reification of a whole language. We may be inclined vaguely to conceive of our language as made up of determinately reified linguistic entities, but this conception happily co-exists in our minds with any amount of banal evidence to the contrary. (Love, 2004:540)

A further and no less serious difficulty with the approach advocated by Jørgensen and his co-authors resides in their reduction of discourse and communication to such linguistic features (as defined by them). In the case of verbal communication, discourse is reduced to those audible elements available for retrospective inspection and subsequent conventional alphabetic transcription on the basis of audio recordings. The linguistic (as traditionally understood) element of the discourse is thereby artificially isolated and hence decontextualised from the integrated cotemporal manifestation of any extralinguistic communicationally relevant elements. For instance, the influence of any visual elements (facial expressions, gestures, positioning of interlocutors and so on) is placed beyond the scope of perception and analysis and indeed this consideration potentially applies to any of the sense modalities excluded from inquiry. In effect, this approach treats language as coterminous with verbal behaviour, thereby relegating any non-verbal responses or actions to the realm of the non- or extralinguistic. Yet as integrationists have often pointed out (e.g. Love, 2004:532), when, for example, one silently complies with (or pointedly ignores) a verbal request or command (shutting the door, passing the desired condiment, etc.) this represents just as much a manifestation of one's linguistic knowledge as if one were also to respond vocally in some way when doing so ('What did your last one die of?', 'Here you go', etc.). As such, it is a methodology which exposes itself quite blatantly to the integrationist charge of 'segregationism'[3] insofar as by limiting its focus to structural linguistic features it inevitably and necessarily leads to an incomplete and distorted account (i.e. a decontextualisation) of the communicational interactions of which those features form part.

The problem of decontextualisation engendered by segregationist methodology is, however, only superficially one of the limitations imposed by the recording methods employed. The integrationist critique extends well beyond a call for the use of video recording equipment in sociolinguistic research. It also addresses the core theoretical issue regarding the problematic manner in which supposed (socio)linguistic 'facts' are claimed to be established on the basis of the researcher's interpretation of his/her data. The rendering of a communicational episode as 'data' – that is to say its audio recording and the subsequent transcription of the assiduously isolated 'linguistic features' identified therein – already constitutes two steps in a chain of de/recontextualisation. Any resultant analysis foisted upon such data can therefore hardly hope to give a comprehensive and faithful account of the episode as experienced by the participants themselves. As Pablé et al. (2010:674) note:

---

[3] According to Harris (1998:10), the term segregationism 'alludes to the notion that linguistic and non-linguistic phenomena constitute two academically segregated domains of inquiry, and that within the former a domain pertaining to languages is to be segregated from the rest. The study of languages thus has its own autonomy within the study of language, its own methodology and programme(s) of research. It is supposedly independent of neighbouring domains: in particular, of the study of communication (to which it may contribute but on which it in no way relies).'

[T]he integrationist would like to know on what basis the sociolinguist can decide what is socially relevant among the data and what isn't. Moreover, by inspecting linguistic data exclusively, the analyst's assumption is that what is 'contained' in the tape recordings is exactly what the speakers originally had at their disposal while engaged in a conversation. Taking this stance amounts to claiming that non-linguistic components (e.g. gesture, eye gazes, appearance) are ultimately negligible when it comes to establishing what is sociolinguistically relevant. It seems [. . .] that what the sociolinguist is 'reading into' the transcripts corresponds to his/her own interpretation of a now decontextualized (or rather, recontextualized) stretch of discourse.

The elicitation of emic reflections on such data also does not circumvent the problem of de/recontextualisation as there is no way of guaranteeing that participants' subsequent interpretations and viewpoints coincide with their dispositions during the actual communicational episode in question. Such reflections themselves constitute recontextualisations. The researcher is left in the position of then having to make certain fundamental assessments regarding the participants' discourse about the communicational episode ('Is it truthful/honest/deceitful etc.?', 'Does it contain significant omissions/embellishments?', 'Has it been coloured by the researcher's own interaction with the participant?', etc.). The communicational episode itself cannot be 'got at' by the researcher as it originally occurred. Such criticism brings to light the core notion of 'intersubjectivity' much prized by conversation analysts. Intersubjectivity refers to the belief that participants in a communicational encounter share a common view of that encounter. Moreover, conversation analysts hold that it is possible for the researcher to access such shared meanings through a 'close reading' of the discourse elements, thereby 'repairing' any indeterminacies of language (see, for example, Johnstone, 1996:22 [4]). Such a position would seem to be predicated on the belief that language is coded, that is to say determinate in respect of form and meaning at some level, hence the feasibility and intuitive appropriateness of a features-based analysis. This is a point made by Taylor and Cameron (1987:162) when they note that the 'principle of intersubjectivity leads directly to a rules and units framework [and] the rules and units framework is nothing but the application of the fixed-code fallacy.'

3. Codes and telementation

It is a notable feature of much prominent contemporary theorising in sociolinguistics that the general rejection of languages or language varieties as determinate, bounded first-order entities is not generally accompanied by a renunciation of an essentially code-based view of language and meaning (Orman, 2012). While upon first consideration this may seem somewhat perplexing, it is in fact logically consistent with the maintenance of a unit-based analysis of linguistic behaviour. Indeed, the two are mutually reinforcing. As Love (2004:540) notes, 'it is hard to make sense of the idea of a code if it turns out to be impossible to identify unambiguously the operative units of which the code allegedly consists.' In the context of the present discussion, we can also turn this question around and ask whether it is possible to unambiguously identify particular features/units without reference to some determinate system which defines them and their mutual interrelationship. After all, under a structuralist (Saussurean) approach to linguistic analysis, the identification of a feature/unit is predicated upon the pairing of a determinate form (*signifiant*) with a determinate meaning (*signifié*) within the framework of a particular linguistic system, i.e. the language or *langue*. In other

---

[4] For an integrationist critique of Johnstone's approach, see Davis (2001).

words, it affirms a code-based view of language whereby the value of a sign (the so-called 'linguistic meaning') is held to be invariant across all of its manifestations in actual discourse. Such a view is in turn based upon a dubious 'telementational' picture of human communication, that is to say one which holds that communication occurs by means of the mechanical transference or 'faxing' of thoughts and concepts from one mind to another (Harris, 1981; Toolan, 1997). In the subsequent discussion, I argue that it is just such views of language and communication which motivate the 'features-based' analysis underlying the discussions of polylanguaging and polylingualism by Jørgensen and his various co-authors.

The opening line of Jørgensen's (2008) paper on 'polylingual languaging' is one which could almost have been written by Saussure[5] himself, namely: 'The uniquely human capacity of using arbitrary signs to transfer concept and experience over great distances in time and place is what we call language.'[6] Later in the same article, we are told once again that 'With language, human beings can transfer ideas over large distances in space and time' (Jørgensen, 2008:161). Elsewhere, Jørgensen et al. (2011:36) write that 'the very basis of language is that it enables us to share experience, images, etc.' and Møller and Jørgensen (2012:1) refer to the 'human capacity to acquire (or develop) arbitrary signs for creating and negotiating meanings and intentions and transferring them across great distances in time

---

[5] Saussure is of course not the originator of such a view of communication, merely one of its most renowned advocates in modern linguistic theory. Harris (1997:243–252) traces its intellectual lineage back via Locke as far as Aristotle.

[6] Although later in the same article, Jørgensen (2008:163) appears to flatly contradict himself when he states that 'Very rudimentary phenomena can be found among apes, so again we are not considering a qualitative difference between humankind and other species, but a very large quantitative difference.'

and space.' One could hardly wish for a clearer statement of a telementational view of communication.

The inevitable corollary of such a view is the affirmation of a code-based theory of language and meaning. As Harris (1997:252) writes: '[T]elementation, as a model of speech communication, will not do even in principle unless coupled with a fixed-code theory of the linguistic sign.' And indeed, we find ample evidence of just such a view in the polylanguaging literature. For example, although they speak of their 'critical view of the traditional concept of "code"' (2011:33), Jørgensen et al. do not elaborate upon it and nevertheless maintain that it is 'of course possible' to still speak of 'code-switching', despite the obvious rejoinder that the notion of code-switching is one which seems to be based very much on the 'traditional' understanding of 'code'. In effect what they seem to be rejecting is the equation of codes with conventional 'languages' since, after all, such languages do not apparently exist other than as socio-cultural constructs. However, it is evident that they are still committed to a view of language, reduced to individual structural linguistic features, as coded. The question is whether such an atomistic view of linguistic features is at all coherent under the terms of a structuralist analysis. In this connection, Harris notes that:

> Saussure goes out of his way to make the point that linguistic units are not to be thought of as a collection of independent items, a pile of bricks given in advance of the building. On the contrary, it is the whole edifice which has to be in place before there is any question of analysing its constituent parts. (Harris, 1999:61)

In other words, a coherent structuralist analysis of linguistic units presupposes that there be a language system to which those units belong. Furthermore, this system is to be conceived of as a fixed code in which each linguistic sign has a determinate form-meaning correlation as without the assignation of an inherent invariant meaning, it would not be possible to determine whether two instances of the same form constitute instantiations of the same feature or of two separate features. Indeed, the possibility of identifying features as being the 'same' across different occasions of instantiation already presupposes a code-based view of language. To quote Harris (1998:131) once again: 'Speech events are unrepeatable (even with technological aids such as gramophones or tape recorders); but what *can* be reiterated, again and again, are the linguistic signs that speech instantiates. Now the permanent possibility of that reiteration requires that the linguistic sign be determinate both in form and in meaning.' The indeterminacy of the linguistic sign as affirmed by integrationists is clearly quite unacceptable to Jørgensen for whom meaning is manifestly not the product of a creative process of context-dependent value assignment engaged in by individuals in particular communicational situations. For Jørgensen, meaning is a reified entity which both precedes and is independent of language.

> The first meaning was not constructed in production. The first meaning was there already; it combined with a sign given unintentionally, and was understood by an individual smart enough to combine the meaning with the sign. In a sense this created the linguistic meaning of the sign – but it did not create the meaning which must have been there in advance. (Jørgensen, 2008:163)

This account raises the possibility of the somewhat comic scenario of bemused humans going around producing signs without intending to or realising it until one miraculously saw fit to combine with a pre-existing meaning floating in the aether. We need not though concern ourselves here with an excursus into a debate on the origin of meaning and for good reason since as with the question of the origin of language (Taylor, 1997a), from an integrationist perspective the issue is a non-starter as there is simply no question of meanings existing prior to the production and interpretation of a sign. The key point here though is that for Jørgensen the meaning of a sign is evidently not something over which we humans have control. Meaning is determined by the fixed code which in turn enables telementation. But what form does the code take exactly? It is clearly not to be equated with those artefactual linguistic entities (English, French, German, etc.) familiar to the lay population. After all, Jørgensen's is a structuralism which explicitly focuses on *parole* while rejecting the notion of such languages as ontological realities. However, it is not one which can afford to disavow *langue* as a communal psychological reality as otherwise there would be no basis upon which to guarantee the 'linguistic stability' (Pablé et al., 2010: 673), that is to say the invariant form-meaning[7] pairings, required for a structural features-based analysis. Indeed, it is this putative intersubjective psychological reality which provides the ready-made explanation for the possibility of telementational communication.

There are several points worthy of discussion here. The first is that the distinction drawn between code-switching and polylanguaging (Jørgensen et al., 2011:33–34) operates at the level of *parole* or discourse and is more one of degree than type; it does not signal a fundamental ontological distinction. In both cases, the discourse in question is still viewed as coded, that is so say as consisting of determinate form-meaning pairings. After all, just as with code-switching, the various features by which instances of polylanguaging are identified are themselves identified through their perceived belonging to prior linguistic systems (languages) which confer their value/meaning upon them. In the

---

[7] This applies just as much to so-called indexicalities or social meanings as to 'linguistic' meanings as traditionally conceived.

examples of the mixed Danish-Turkish discourse discussed by Jørgensen (2008), the identities of the Danish features and the Turkish features are determined by reference to those postulated language systems commonly known as Danish and Turkish, and not by reference to some single *sui generis* Turko-Danish code as otherwise this would make a nonsense of the *poly*lingual aspect of the discourse. What then is the ontological status of these codes? Is it at all coherent to claim or imply the existence of a code for identifying and structurally analysing X-ish utterances while simultaneously denying the existence of X? Seargeant and Tagg (2011:504), who carried out a similar study on mixed Thai-English discourse in digital literacy practices, highlight what appears a paradoxical aspect of approaches (including their own) similar to that adopted by Jørgensen and co.:

> Feature identification uses a comparative approach between different notional systems of linguistic patterning, and so reference to different codes, varieties, styles and 'modes' is necessary despite the fact that [. . .] a central concern [. . .] is the problematisation and complexifying of just these conceptual categories.

It would seem, then, that the notion of polylanguaging could not exist without the objects its proponents claim to disbelieve in. Another notable aspect is that Jørgensen's keenness to refute delineable languages as ontologically real entities does not extend to other traditional sociolinguistic concepts such as that of *register*. Endorsing the conceptual framework developed by Agha (2007), Møller and Jørgensen (2012:3) tell us that '[w]hen speakers produce utterances they inevitably involve registers' and they then go onto define a register as 'a set of linguistic features that is associated with social practices. This means that the term [. . .] covers (or replaces) what is traditionally considered as, for instance, "languages" (such as "Standard

English" and "East Greenlandic"), but also such concepts as "business talk" ("journalist language", "academic talk", etc.), "varieties" and "argots"'. Again though, the problem is that by defining a register as a set of linguistic features which are held to co-occur in some objectively describable manner, the notion itself is unable to rise above the status of (dubious) metalinguistic abstraction. In that sense then, it no more corresponds to a discrete object of analysis and is no more able to describe a first-order linguistic reality than the notion of separate 'languages'. After all, under a traditional structuralist analysis what is a language held to be if not 'a set of linguistic features' which are regarded as belonging together in some way? There would therefore appear to be no more satisfactory criteria for distinguishing between different registers than there are between different languages. By consequence, one could logically eventually expect to witness the subsequent introduction of the notions of 'register-switching' ("Would you mind awfully slingin' yer 'ook?") followed by 'polyregistering' or 'transregistering' which, it need hardly be said, would signal very little in the way of fundamental theoretical progress. That would merely constitute the relocation of the same structuralist ontology to a different level of analysis. The idea of registers (or indeed any other Hymesean 'ways of speaking') identifiable on the basis of structural linguistic features once again presupposes a coded view of those very features.

There are also a number of other points on which one might wish to take issue with Jørgensen's linguistic theorising in his discussions of polylanguaging. One such example is the claim that 'we do not have language until an intended message is understood' (Jørgensen, 2008:162). This would of course seem to presuppose a fairly unproblematic view of both the notions of 'intention' and 'understanding'. The postulation of 'intention' as a criterion for the existence of language is problematic since it implies the possibility of arriving at a context-invariant notion of what actually constitutes intention. As Wolf (1997:364) notes 'intention itself is as fully contextualized as the rest of what gives value to the sign. Thus intention, any more than meaning, relevance, rules, or anything else, cannot be a baseline parameter in terms of which a sign is given a value, because it itself is part of the context.' As regards 'understanding', it is notable that Jørgensen does not advance any explicit criterion for determining when it is achieved. This is instead implicit in the model of communication which he and his various fellow authors endorse. Under the Saussurean[8] telementational account of communication understanding occurs when B receives and decodes the sign-concept transmitted by A in accordance with the code of which they both share knowledge. Assuming no prejudicial interference from circumstantial or 'performance' factors, understanding is essentially guaranteed in advance of any utterance through the interlocutors' sharing of a fixed code. Understanding, then, is held to be a private, mental accomplishment predicated upon the successful exchange of meaning. Such a view is squarely at odds with the integrationist and indeed the later Wittgensteinian position which holds that the criteria for successful understanding and communication must be public and observable as otherwise we could never be certain that they occur at all, which would seem an absurd conclusion for our own experience as language-users and communicators tells us that understanding and communication do regularly occur (Taylor, 1997b:74). The point is that mental understanding cannot function as a criterion for the success of a communicational act, even less so if its accomplishment is

---

[8] Saussure's conventionalist perspective on understanding can be contrasted with the more sceptical view of Locke. Although very much a telementationalist, Locke was nevertheless concerned by the 'imperfection of words' and held that one could never be certain that hearers receive exactly those thoughts or concepts intended by the speaker. For example, Locke (1812:234) writes that '[w]ords are used for recording and communicating our thoughts' but follows this by noting that 'the very nature of words makes it almost unavoidable for many of them to be doubtful and uncertain in their signification.'

deemed to involve the neat transfer and exchange of thoughts. From an integrationist perspective, the notion of what it means to understand or have understood an utterance or indeed any sign is itself inherently context-dependent and the result of individual contextualisation of a communicational situation. As Taylor (1998:206) notes: '[T]he ways in which speakers justify claims that their utterances have been understood are heavily dependent on both the contexts in which those utterances were produced as well as on the contexts in which their justifications were produced.' Viewed in this manner, it therefore appears both question-begging and highly arbitrary to make the existence of language dependent upon the achievement of understanding. If verbal misunderstandings are not language then what are they? After all, even in instances of what might commonly be termed miscommunication or misunderstanding people's activities may still be integrated with whatever signs are produced and interpreted, albeit not necessarily in line with the intentions of the participants or to any mutual cooperative benefit. The notion of understanding itself stands in need of coherent elucidation and reflection before it can serve as an assumed given upon which a subsequent theory of language and communication is to be constructed.

Jørgensen et al.'s view of understanding would also seem to underlie their claim, in stressing the social nature of language, that 'every feature we [. . .] "know" or "possess", we share with somebody else. We can not [sic] imagine a linguistic feature which is unique to one person (with the possible exception of an innovation which has still not been used by the innovator in interaction with others)' (Jørgensen et al., 2011:35). A number of interpretations are possible here depending upon what one takes them to mean by 'unique to one person'. On one reading, it could mean merely a feature never encountered (heard or read) by anyone else except for its originator, a move which has the effect of removing self-communication from the domain of the linguistic –

something which, while being consistent with Jørgensen et al.'s broader ontology of language and communication, an integrationist would doubtless call into question although this issue cannot be addressed here (see Harris, 1996, chapter 11). A second reading could take it to mean a feature which has only ever been *employed* by one person, in which case it strikes as deeply problematic. By such reckoning, any new innovation actually employed by an individual in interaction with others does not acquire linguistic status until at least two people have employed it even if it served a perfectly good communicational purpose while only being used by its originator, yet we can apparently conceive of a linguistic feature which has never been used in interaction. This places one in the absurd situation of being able to assign linguistic status to a hypothetical feature only to withdraw it upon its initial actual deployment in communication. One therefore wonders what they would have to say about the linguistic status of much of *Finnegans Wake* or *A Clockwork Orange*. It is unlikely (although not impossible) that anyone apart from Joyce has ever seriously used the terms *ouxtrador*, *oppidump* or *pftjschute* other than in discussing or reading aloud Joyce's work itself.[9] Yet

---

[9] Some of Joyce's 'invented' words from Finnegans Wake have seemingly found a place in common English usage, albeit used in quite different senses. The most commonly cited example is the sub-atomic particle known as a quark, a word apparently taken from Joyce's line 'Three quarks for Muster Mark.' However, this case is not as straightforward as it may seem. In his book The Quark and the Jaguar (2002), the physicist Murray Gell-Mann writes that he had already come up with the name for the particle, which he pronounced 'kwork', before encountering Joyce's term. Joyce's term therefore provided the graphic identity for Gell-Mann's coinage. However, Joyce's term was arguably intended to be pronounced 'kwark' so as to rhyme with the 'Mark' at the end of the line. In the light of this, Gell-Mann writes that he had to 'find an excuse' (i.e. impose an interpretation) to read Joyce's term as 'kwork'. There would seem to be no clear objective criteria for determining how many different

these are manifestly signs which Joyce has employed in (anticipated) interaction with his audience. They are not unsponsored and are clearly intended to function semiologically although how exactly may be deeply obscure, particularly to the uninitiated reader. As such, they invite broad interpretation, indeed an interpretation which is perhaps intolerably broad for the fixed-code theorist as there is simply no shared code to which they can be held to belong and there is clearly no way in which such terms could enable telementation. As Harris (2000:224) observes, in Joycian language-making 'words are freed from the constraints of any fixed code.' The only avenue left for the fixed-code theorist is the deeply unsatisfying option of having to deny that such examples constitute 'real' language or to dismiss them as highly exceptional or marginal. Now, admittedly such literary nonce words and the like may seem rather extreme cases but they illustrate a general principle of which many more mundane manifestations can be found (see for example Love's (2007:537) discussion of the now notorious phrasal verb *to sex up*). It is not impossible or even difficult to imagine linguistic features unique to one person, however ephemeral that uniqueness may be, and indeed we do not have to since there are many such examples and more are constantly being created anew. Presumably nearly all linguistic innovations start out in this manner unless devised by committee. However, it is an undertaking of the imagination out of reach for the fixed-code theorist who imposes the demand that features already form part of a shared code before they can graduate to fully-fledged linguistic status.

A further feature of Jørgensen's discussions of poly-lingualism likely to discomfort integrationists is the endorsement of what one might term a 'mental warehouse' position, that is to say the conviction that one's linguistic knowledge consists of an

---

words we are dealing with here, let alone whether Gell-Mann can even be definitively said to have taken or borrowed the term from Joyce.

inventory of features which are somehow stored in the mind patiently awaiting deployment. For example, Jørgensen et al. (2011:29) cite Blommaert and Backus approvingly when they write:

> Whether or not a particular word, combination or pattern actually exists as a unit in the linguistic knowledge of an individual speaker is dependent on its degree of *entrenchment*. 'Having' a unit in your inventory means it is entrenched in your mind. (Blommaert and Backus, 2011:6)

It barely needs spelling out how such a view tallies with a fixed-code telementational view of communication. Assuming that two interlocutors have certain common units stored in their respective minds, the fixed semantic content of those units can be conveyed from one mind to another through the physical manifestation of their corresponding forms in speech and their subsequent apprehension. Lay turns of phrase such as 'getting one's idea across' clearly assume far more than quaint metaphorical status according to such thought. Yet for integrationists, while not denying the role and importance of memory in linguistic behaviour, the whole notion of words or other units residing in mental storage is nothing more than a metaphor and a potentially highly misleading one at that (Walrod, 2008). As Love argues:

> [W]e do not proceed where language is concerned by selecting from a mental storehouse the digits or combinations of digits that have already been prepackaged for us as encoding what we want to say, or by identifying the same digits in other people's utterances and referring to the mental storehouse in order to decode them. (It may *feel* like that to some of us, sometimes, or perhaps most of us most of the time, but that is because we've been educat-

ed to think about language in that way.) Instead, I suggest, the task is to work out on the hoof what semiotic significance to confer on certain phenomena (vocal noises, marks on paper, etc.) in order to operate relevantly on the world in accordance with the requirements of the unique real-time communication situation we find ourselves in. (Love, 2007:707–708)

The notion of a stable mental fund of linguistic units can therefore be seen as an artefact of the fixed-code, telementational view of language. An alternative, as Wolf (1997:366) argues, is to adopt the view that '[t]here can be no stable, decontextualized content that [one] can reliably drawn on as *the* memory [. . .] Rather, from an integrational viewpoint we craft a memory for the current communicational purpose.'

4. Conclusion

My purpose in this paper has not been to argue against the use of the term 'polylanguaging' or any of its cognates *per se*. As pieces of potential lay metalanguage (should they catch on), they could no doubt function perfectly adequately alongside or in distinction to more familiar prefixed lingualisms such as bilingualism and multilingualism. The problem comes when such metalanguage is pressed into service as a descriptor for first-order linguistic realities. We are then forced to examine the theoretical and ontological assumptions which underlie its use. Walrod's (2008:71) observation that 'metalanguage we assume to be adequate may in fact be obscuring our understanding of linguistic reality' is of relevance here. From an integrationist perspective, any theoretical rationale behind innovations in metalanguage which propagates the notion of language as an intersubjectively shared code and a corresponding telementational view of communication does just that. Such accounts are, to recall Davis' (2001:712) neat phrase, still 'stuck in [the] segregational wheel.'

Much contemporary sociolinguistic theorising exhibits a curious characteristic. That is to say while it is readily willing to embrace what might be termed a post- or late-modern sociological perspective whereby notions such as fluidity, flux, hybridity (e.g. Otsuji and Pennycook, 2010) and so on are to the fore and there is a pervasive scepticism towards essentialist and determinate social categorisations, when it comes to linguistic analysis it all too often seeks out the comforting certainty of a traditional structuralist approach whereby the expert researcher implicitly claims to be able to read off both social and linguistic meanings from the features attested in the 'data', hence the continued reference to codes, systems, etc. The underlying ontology of language and communication remains all but unchanged. A less charitable interpretation might regard it as an attempt to have it both ways, thereby continuing to secure at least one clearly delimited field of 'scientific' expertise for the professional linguist to attend to.

What, then, are the consequences and benefits of adopting an integrational perspective? Perhaps most importantly, by allowing us to dispense with the view that linguistic communication proceeds on the basis of pre-given shared bi-planar codes or coded units, we are better able to appreciate the creative dimensions of each linguistic act. Crucially, as Joseph (2003) argues, this entails an expanded view of linguistic creativity which does not focus solely on the production of utterances, forms, etc., the chief preoccupation of Saussurean and Chomskyan theorising, but also and necessarily upon the creativity involved in their interpretation. The latter is not an option granted by the fixed-code theorist since the postulated code, revealing the inherently prescriptive character of its postulation, itself determines whether a particular interpretation is correct or not, while for integrationists judgments regarding issues of correctness of interpretation are outcomes of contextualised metalinguistic reflection on actual communicational practices. The integrationist position allows one to appreciate that any piece of discourse may be subject to open-ended creative interpretation, the exact nature of which will be a product of its unique contextualisation by whichever individual is doing the interpreting. Freed from the strictures of fixed-code semantics, one is then also able to grasp the essentially *sui generis* character of all discourse, categorisation of which in terms of codes and second-order notions of linguistic unity represents a potentially highly misleading form of de/recontextualisation.

References
Agha, Asif, 2007. *Language and Social Relations*. Cambridge University Press, Cambridge.
Blommaert, Jan; Backus, Ad, 2011. *Repertoires Revisited: 'Knowing Language' in Superdiversity*. King's College London. (Working Papers in Urban Language & Literacies, 67)
Blommaert, Jan; Rampton, Ben, 2011. *Language and Superdiversity: A Position Paper.* King's College London. (Working Papers in Urban Language and Literacies, 70)
Canagarajah, Suresh, 2011. Translanguaging in the classroom: emerging issues for research and pedagogy. *Applied Linguistics Review* 2, 1–28.
Creese, Angela; Blackledge, Adrian, 2010a. Towards a sociolinguistics of superdiversity. *Zeitschrift für Erziehungswissenschaft* 13 (4), 549–572.
Creese, Angela; Blackledge, Adrian, 2010b. Translanguaging in the bilingual classroom: a pedagogy for learning and teaching? *Modern Language Journal* 94 (1), 103–115.
Davis, Hayley G., 1997. Ordinary people's philosophy: comparing lay and professional metalinguistic knowledge. *Language Sciences* 19 (1), 33–46.
Davis, Hayley G., 2001. The linguistic individual: an integrational approach. *Language Sciences* 23, 707–713.

Davis, Hayley G.; Taylor, Talbot J. (Eds.), 2002. *Rethinking Linguistics*. Routledge, London.
Duncker, Dorthe, 2011. On the empirical challenge to integrational studies in language. *Language Sciences* 33, 533–543.
Harris, Roy, 1980. *The Language-Makers*. Duckworth, London.
Harris, Roy, 1981. *The Language Myth*. Duckworth, London.
Harris, Roy, 1996. *Signs, Language and Communication: Integrational and Segregational Approaches*. Routledge, London.
Harris, Roy, 1997. From an integrational point of view. In: Wolf, George and Love, Nigel (Eds.), *Linguistics Inside Out: Roy Harris and His Critics*. John Benjamins, Amsterdam, pp. 229–310.
Harris, Roy, 1998. *Introduction to Integrational Linguistics*. Pergamon, Oxford.
Harris, Roy, 1999. Integrational linguistics and the structuralist legacy. *Language and Communication* 19, 45–68.
Harris, Roy, 2000. *Rethinking Writing*. Athlone Press, London.
Harris, Roy, 2007. Integrational linguistics. In: Verschueren, Jef and Östman, Jan-Ola (Eds.), *Handbook of Pragmatics*. John Benjamins, Amsterdam.
Jacquemet, Marco, 2005. Transidiomatic practices: language and power in the age of globalization. *Language and Communication* 25, 257–277.
Johnstone, Barbara, 1996. *The Linguistic Individual: Self Expression in Language and Linguistics*. Oxford University Press, Oxford.
Jørgensen, Jens Normann, 2008. Polylingual languaging around and among children and adolescents. *International Journal of Multilingualism* 5 (3), 161–176.
Jørgensen, J.N.; Karrebæk, M.S.; Madsen, L.M.; Møller, J.S., 2011. Polylanguaging in superdiversity. *Diversities* 13 (2), 23–38.

Joseph, John E., 2003. Rethinking linguistic creativity. In: Davis, Hayley G. and Taylor, Talbot J. (Eds.), *Rethinking Linguistics*. Routledge, London, pp. 121–150.

Locke, John, 1812. *The Works of John Locke*, vol. 2. W. Otridge, London.

Love, Nigel, 2004. Cognition and the language myth. *Language Sciences* 26, 525–544.

Love, Nigel, 2007. Are languages digital codes? *Language Sciences* 29, 690–709.

Møller, J.S., Jørgensen, J.N., 2012. *Enregisterment among Adolescents in Superdiverse Copenhagen*. Tilburg University. (Tilburg Papers in Culture Studies, 28)

Orman, Jon, 2012. Not so super: the ontology of 'supervernaculars'. *Language and Communication* 32 (4), 349–357.

Otsuji, Emi, Pennycook, Alastair, 2010. Metrolingualism: fixity, fluidity and language in flux. *International Journal of Multilingualism* 7 (3), 240–254.

Pablé, Adrian; Haas, Marc; Christe, Noël, 2010. Language and social identity: an integrationist critique. *Language Sciences* 32, 671–676.

Seargeant, Philip; Tagg, Caroline, 2011. English on the internet and a 'post-varieties' approach to language. *World Englishes* 30 (4), 496–514.

Taylor, Talbot J., 1997a. The origin of language: why it never happened. *Language Sciences* 19 (1), 67–77.

Taylor, Talbot J., 1997b. *Theorizing Language: Analysis, Rhetoric, Normativity, History*. Pergamon, Oxford.

Taylor, Talbot J., 1998. Do you understand? Criteria of understanding in verbal interaction. In: Harris, Roy and Wolf, George (Eds.), *Integrational Linguistics: A First Reader*. Pergamon, Oxford, pp. 198–208.

Taylor, Talbot J.; Cameron, Deborah, 1987. *Analyzing Conversation: Rules and Units in the Structure of Talk*. Pergamon, Oxford.

Toolan, Michael, 1997. A few words on telementation. *Language Sciences* 19, 79–91.
Vertovec, Steven, 2007. Super-diversity and its implications. *Ethnic and Racial Studies* 29 (6), 1024–1054.
Walrod, Michael R., 2008. Language: object or event? The integration of language and life. In: Love, Nigel (Ed.), *Language and History: Integrationist Perspectives.* Routledge, London and New York, pp. 71–78.
Wolf, George, 1997. Real people doing real things in real time. *Language and Communication* 17 (4), 359–368

3.

Polylanguaging, integrational linguistics and contemporary sociolinguistic theory: A commentary on Ritzau.
(with Adrian Pablé)

Abstract
In this article, we take up and expand upon a number of issues of linguistic theory raised in Ursula Ritzau's recent article 'Learner language and polylanguaging: how language students' ideologies relate to their written language use' published in the *Journal of Bilingual Education and Bilingualism*. The present critique is informed by an integrational linguistic approach, from which perspective polylanguaging was recently discussed by one of the present authors. In the first part of this commentary we pinpoint and offer a critical analysis of some of the claims raised in Ritzau's article, providing a rationale for these claims from the perspective of the polylanguaging theorist and discussing its implications. In the second part we embark on a more general critique of polylanguaging and related branches of modern sociolinguistics by making explicit reference to an integrational semiology, showing that the linguistic philosophy of the former rests on the same mythical assumptions as the founding school they criticise (i.e. Saussurean structuralism). We also respond to some of the – in our view, inadequately grounded – criticisms that Ritzau raises in respect of integrational linguistics.

1. Introduction

In this article, we take up and expand upon a number of issues of linguistic theory raised in Ursula Ritzau's recent article 'Learner language and polylanguaging: how language students' ideologies relate to their written language use' published in the *Journal of Bilingual Education and Bilingualism* (2014). The present critique is informed by an integrational linguistic approach (e.g. Harris 1996, 1998), from which perspective polylanguaging was recently discussed by one of the present authors (Orman 2013). In the first part of this commentary we pinpoint and offer a critical analysis of some of the claims raised in Ritzau's article, providing a rationale for these claims from the perspective of the polylanguaging theorist and discussing its implications. In the second part we embark on a more general critique of polylanguaging and related branches of modern sociolinguistics by making explicit reference to an integrational semiology, showing that the linguistic philosophy of the former rests on the same mythical assumptions as the founding school they criticise (i.e. Saussurean structuralism). We also respond to some of the – in our view, inadequately grounded – criticisms that Ritzau raises in respect of integrational linguistics. These criticisms are a direct consequence of adopting an 'empiricist' attitude which, however, is founded on dubious metaphysical premises.

The integrationist position adopted and advocated by the present authors can be traced back to the seminal work of Roy Harris (Harris 1981, 1997, 1998). Harris is a thinker whose work tends either to be dismissed or ignored by the great majority of modern linguists. This is an unfortunate state of affairs although its persistence becomes less puzzling, which is not the same as pardonable, when one considers the content and emphasis of Harris' theorising on linguistic matters. After all, Harris challenges and ultimately rejects essentially the entire theoretical basis on which modern orthodox linguistics rests. In Harris' view, modern linguistics is still beholden to a 'language myth' endemic to the Western cultural tradition. This myth is composed of two interconnected and mutually supporting fallacies, namely the 'fixed-code fallacy' and the 'fallacy of telementation'. The first supposes that languages have an ontologically real existence as objectively identifiable internally structured systems of invariant units and regularities. This, in other words, is the 'grammar book plus dictionary' model of languages and linguistic knowledge (Love 2007). The second fallacy, encapsulated most memorably in Saussure's image of the 'talking heads', is the belief that linguistic communication is a matter of thought transference between the minds of people who share the same language, i.e. the same fixed code. A central element of the integrationist position is a rejection of the structuralist Saussurean sign as a biplanar pairing of a determinate form (the *signifiant*) and a determinate meaning (the *signifié*), a notion which continues to be maintained in nearly all fields of modern linguistics, including sociolinguistics. Such a view of the sign allows for a wholesale decontextualisation of language and its concomitant uncoupling from the real-world communicative processes which give rise to it. Integrationists, however, argue for a radically indeterminate view of the linguistic sign based on the conviction that signs are not decontextualised invariants which pre-exist their appearance in episodes of communication but rather the contextualised products of communication. As the subsequent discussion will attempt to show, it is this view of the sign which sets the integrational approach apart from all others in contemporary (socio)linguistics.

2. Commentary on Ritzau

What strikes us in the first place about Ritzau's case study of Swiss learners of Danish is indeed their 'commonsensical' views and expectations as regards Danish and the appraisal of their own progress in it (as expressed in their learning journals). Ritzau attributes to her students (of the first two semesters) a belief in 'language-as-system', saying of them that they 'express a structuralist view on language' (Ritzau 2014, 7). But is that the case? One student says that he/she wants to 'learn more new words' and 'study more systematically'. Another one mentions 'grammar' and the fact that he/she wants to gain a good command of the 'rules'. A third one mentions the importance of learning the language 'bit by bit' in the initial phase. Ritzau interprets the latter as saying that he/she intends to 'learn separate parts of the language consecutively', which is not what the student says. At any rate, Ritzau (2014, 8) claims that the excerpts from the learning journals show 'how the students think of language as being constituted by discrete entities such as words and grammar rules, which should be learned systematically and separately'. If so: does such an attitude reveal any 'structuralist' leanings on the part of the students? We think not. Rather it exemplifies a certain way (adult) learners approach foreign languages. In this context, it is worth mentioning three distinct strands of thinking as possible sources underlying lay linguistic theory. All of them have a long intellectual tradition and antedate early twentieth-century structuralism by far. One strand reflects a way of thinking about languages that Saussure termed *nomenclaturism* and which he strongly condemned. As language learners, especially in the context of adults acquiring a foreign language as described by Ritzau, we thus tend to treat words as surrogates of 'things' (both concrete and abstract) in the real world: 'What is the Danish equivalent of that 'thing' Germans call *Freiheit*?' This 'reocentric' surrogational doctrine of how words acquire their meaning (Harris 1980, 44) views languages as in principle intertranslatable, which is incompatible with any Saussurean structuralist views. Lay thinking on crosscultural issues will also prompt learners to endorse a surrogational stance called 'psychocentric' (Harris 1980, 44), according to which words 'stand for' ideas in people's minds. Hence the alternative, or complementary, question a German learner of Danish might ask would be: 'What idea do the Danish attach to the equivalent of

German *Freiheit*?' The third strand of thinking, often concomitant with the two semantic views identified above, is termed the 'contractual' view of how words are to be used and how they relate to each other (Harris 1980, 102), as established (or agreed on) by the native speaker community. However, what you can say in a language (because it is sanctioned by the communal linguistic contract) may be in contradiction with what you know about the 'things' that the words stand for. In fact, there is always a point where a contractual semantics turns out to be altogether incompatible with a reocentric semantics, which is typically when questions concerning the functions of a public language arise. When asked what learning a foreign language is about, it is likely that Ritzau's students would indeed express a contractualist semantic view of some sort, in relation to both lexicon and grammar: learning a foreign language is about mastering how words should be used in accordance with the agreed ways (or rules) established by the native community. However, *pace* Ritzau, it is unclear why they should hold a belief in 'language-as-system' (at least not in any strict Saussurean sense) or their comments express 'a structuralist view on language'.

Ritzau (2014) claims (8) that her students 'buy into the ideology of separate languages' and are worried about crosslinguistic interference during the Danish language acquisition process. As Ritzau tries to show, these fears turn out to be quite unwarranted: what is actually the case, according to Ritzau, is that second (or third, etc.) language learning is a matter of constantly 'reorganising one's linguistic repertoire' in terms of the linguistic resources made available by the repertoire: to the learners this might look like making headway in the acquisition of the target language, i.e. Standard Danish, but it is an illusion, Ritzau implies, generated by a belief in languages as separate entities. So polylanguaging is averse to both Saussurean structuralism and lay linguistic thinking. The features of linguistic repertoires do not belong to 'a language' as Saussure envisaged it – namely as features with a unique 'identity' in virtue of the *langue* they are an inseparable part of: the features, from a second-order perspective, can be associated with multiple 'languages', whereas on the level of first-order semiological reality, i.e. on the level of polylanguaging, speakers may know the values that features have in relation to these second-order abstractions called 'languages' and may use them purposefully for certain communicational aims (Jørgensen 2010, 145, cited in Ritzau 2014, 5). As Ritzau argues, learners of a foreign language do not possess this knowledge, and even if they should, second (or third) language learners do not purposefully 'mix' linguistic features – precisely because they (have to) cling to the myth of separate languages.

The example of *køpe* ('buy') discussed by Ritzau is a case in point. This word was produced in the journal by a learner of Danish with good knowledge of other Scandinavian languages. Ritzau practically rules out the possibility of *køpe* being a purposefully creative form. Why? Because it is unlikely that the student intentionally blended a form that would have, say, some 'Swedish' and some 'Danish' in it. Instead, what happens, according to Ritzau, is that if you have learnt 'Swedish' and 'Norwegian' and are now learning 'Danish' – then the features making up your linguistic repertoire will take that into account: this 'fact' will somehow transpire, and the researcher acquainted with the subjects' linguistic biographies will be able to spot this 'fact' in the linguistic data. What this means is that there is always a reason for learners to 'deviate' from the norm – but you have got to look in the individual's linguistic repertoire for the reason, and not consider the reason in relation to 'languages' as separate entities with an ontological status. Ritzau's (2014, 10–11) analysis of the verb *køpe* ('buy') goes as follows: the student who wrote *køpe* did not write 'Danish', for the Standard Danish form is *købe*. Ritzau knows that the student had already learnt Swedish and Norwegian, which have the respective forms *köpa* and *kjøpe/kjøpa*. At this point the linguist adopting a polylanguaging perspective seems to triumph over the Saussurean linguist, for the latter cannot possibly cope with examples like *købe*. Why? Because it is not even a 'word' (in the structuralist sense); *købe*, in fact, is 'languageless'. If the myth of separate languages is abandoned, however, *købe* no longer poses any (artificially raised) problems of an analytical nature: in fact, each letter of *købe*, we are informed by Ritzau, can be associated with respectively two and three Scandinavian 'languages'. Thus, *købe* cannot be discussed in abstract terms – it has no form and meaning in any *langue* – but still it is real (as indeed it was produced by someone). In fact, as Ritzau might argue, *købe* can only be made sense of in relation to the person who used it, i.e. in relation to that learner's personal past linguistic experience. Saussure, therefore, was wrong to believe that there can be no *parole* without *langue*. As it turns out, there is only *parole*.

Ritzau (2014, 11) concludes that since her student declared in the journal that she 'wants to learn [Danish] vocabulary in a systematic way, it is not likely that she intends to use features associated with different languages'. In other words, the student believed that *købe* is 'Danish' and the student will, presumably, find out that she was wrong. It seems to us that there is a great deal of psychologistic speculation here regarding the language user's 'intention'. Ritzau excludes the possibility that in writing *købe* the student may have had any other communicative aims than the overall task of writing a correct Standard Danish word as part of a Standard Danish sentence. She concludes this based on the background information students provided her with. This, we should like to point out, is not 'empirical'. From the learner's point of view, therefore, the form *købe* is either right or wrong. Not so for linguists who do not buy into the ideology of separate languages. Ritzau (2014, 12) tells us that the students 'use what-ever linguistic features are at their disposal'. When the student who wrote *købe* learns that this form is 'not normally associated with Standard Danish' and will write *købe* the next time, that is when she will be 'reorganising her linguistic repertoire'. Acknowledging only the reality of first-order languaging, the researcher embracing polylanguaging bans any talk of 'linguistic errors', emphasising linguistic creativity instead: this creativity manifests itself in the constant reorganising of one's linguistic repertoire. One wonders how looking up a word in a dictionary (and using it) relates to the claim that speakers 'use whatever linguistic features are at their disposal'? And is looking up a word in a dictionary also a 'creative' act?

Ritzau's article implies that the foreign language teacher who is willing to abandon mythical thinking about language will be able to exorcise the ghosts of 'authentic' or 'real' target languages haunting foreign language teaching. The proof is that Ritzau herself has managed to do this. Students, in turn, cannot afford to think like this: *qua* foreign language learners they are expected to use linguistic features associated with one language, i.e. the target language. As Ritzau argues, they are in fact 'participants in an institutional setting that propagates a corresponding ideology'. After all, taking a foreign language course is not meant to be a journey of linguistic self-discovery. Or is it? Ritzau does not tell us. At any rate, Ritzau discovers a great deal about her students. It is worth noting that she does not address the consequences that polylanguaging is supposed to have on foreign language learning. As a language 'scientist', Ritzau's concern is with 'how language students' ideologies relate to their written language use', as the title of her article makes clear. This is a recurrent *topos* in sociolinguistic theory, namely the distinction between what language users think they are doing and what they actually do. One finds it as part of the discourse of *World Englishes*, for example, which treats speakers of postcolonial varieties as undergoing a nativisation process involving 'linguistic schizophrenia'. The rationale behind postulating the language belief-language use dichotomy is, of course, to keep the academic linguist in business: it provides further justification for why sociolinguistics has to adopt the research methods of the empirical sciences. On that score, polylanguaging shares a mythical belief with proponents of other new types of 'lingualism' which have emerged in contemporary sociolinguistic theory, for example, 'translingualism/translanguaging' (Creese and Blackledge 2010; Canagarajah 2011), 'metrolingualism' (Otsuji and Pennycook 2010) and 'transidiomatic practices' (Jacquemet 2005): it insists that there are relevant facts of and truths about semiology and communication which the participants themselves cannot recover and are unaware of respectively, but to which the linguist may have miraculous access thanks to his/her refined techniques of data collection and analysis.

Polylanguaging comes across as a more 'humanistic' approach to language and communication (as opposed to Saussure's 'anti-humanism'): the signs in polylanguaging are not impersonal ones, bound to a certain linguistic system. But as it turns out, the persons have no say about their personal signs: it is the linguist who has a more direct access to their first-order semiological activities, for the learner's views are obfuscated by the ideology of institutionalised language learning itself. In fact, *køpe* is a very personal sign grounded in social reality – a reality that the person who created the word shares with others. It is not a misspelling nor the result of linguistic interference. Polylanguaging also comes across as more congenial to our modern world supposedly characterised by 'super-diversity', whereas the structuralist model of language cannot possibly cope with the communicational realities of a world gone (linguistically) global. This picture, we believe, distorts the history of human mobility and contact, but more importantly for the present discussion, theories of language and communication should not be made to fit with the latest 'social reality'. As Roy Harris (1996, 24) argues, the human 'communicational infrastructure' has not changed since *Homo sapiens* first appeared on earth. What a theory of language and communication has to do is to spell out the basic possibilities and limitations of human communication corresponding to our own basic human experiences. There are no impenetrable semiological truths hidden from lay thinking which the academic linguist can somehow bring to the fore through an analysis of linguistic 'data'. And this is essentially where integrational linguistics and polylanguaging theory differ.

3. The integrational view

Ritzau makes the tired and familiar complaint against integrational linguistics that it is 'not empirical', which she regards as a 'serious weakness'. Integrationist critiques of sociolinguistics are summarily dismissed as offering nothing more than 'philosophical discussions rather than research alternatives'. Confusingly, however, in the next breath she goes on to cite Makoni's (2011) 'empirically based' integrationist study of Facebook conversations. She could have also cited empirical integrationist studies by Wolf et al. (1998), Duncker (2011), Pablé (2009, 2010) or H. Davis (1997, 2001).[1] Now, what we believe Ritzau to be no doubt getting at, and it is a point we are happy to concede, is that integrationism does not offer a programmatic positivist methodology for the collection and analysis of linguistic 'data' as traditionally conceived by the sociolinguist. However, this is not the consequence of some oversight, omission or reluctance to get one's hands dirty 'in the field', but rather a perfectly consistent and logical entailment of the theoretical account of language and communication it offers. Yet, revealingly, Ritzau offers no criticism of integrational theory per se.

It bears (re)stating that the value of a linguistic theory does not lie in its capacity to generate empirical research programmes for linguistic researchers, as the logic of Ritzau's argu-

---

[1] See also Makoni (2014) in which he mentions polylanguaging in a discussion of integrationist critiques of several emergent concepts in contemporary sociolinguistic theorising, including 'supervernacular' and 'translanguaging'.

ment would seem to suggest. Advancing such a view might very well make one a loyal and valued member of the trade union of empirical linguists but it offers no refutation of the validity of the theoretical position concerned. A theory ought to be judged for its explanatory power in elucidating the phenomena under consideration. The fundamental problem with demanding as an apriori requirement of a linguistic theory that it be capable of generating a positivist, data-driven research programme is that to do so is to predetermine a crucial component of the content of such a theory. It is the very same skewed logic to which Saussure himself fell victim. It was Saussure's desire to set up linguistics as an autonomous 'science' distinct from potentially competing disciplines such as psychology, anthropology, etc., which led him to artificially manufacture by means of stipulative fiat its putative object of study, namely *langue*, a theoretical *cul-de-sac* from which modern orthodox linguistics has yet to fully extricate itself.

Readers may wonder at this point why we forever seem to be bringing Saussure into our discussion. After all, has not modern sociolinguistic theory moved well beyond the limitations of Saussurean structuralism and is not the notion of polylanguaging with its explicit rejection of *langue* (the language or language system) as the object of linguists' enquiry in favour of *parole* (actual language use) as the sole communicational reality a prime example of such theoretical progress? Our answer, to reiterate the point made at length in Orman (2013),[2] is that it will not do to simply reject *langue* while continuing to retain the Saussurean conception of the linguistic sign as a determinate, biplanar form-meaning combination. The reason is that the structuralist sign – as under polylanguaging theory, also conceived of as a unit – only

---

[2] Ritzau (2014, 6) dismisses the argument made in Orman (2013) as 'not entirely convincing' but interestingly offers no argument of her own to substantiate her claim.

acquires its identity and is therefore only identifiable through its belonging to the holistic linguistic system (*langue*). It has no free-floating identity of its own separate from its existence within that network of signs which constitutes the linguistic system. The result, as Harris (1999, 61) notes, is theoretical incoherence:

> Saussure goes out of his way to make the point that linguistic units are not to be thought of as a collection of independent items, a pile of bricks given in advance of the building. On the contrary, it is the whole edifice which has to be in place before there is any question of analysing its constituent parts.

In other words, what is being attempted here is to disavow the idea of a language code while at the same time retaining the notion that linguistic features are still nevertheless coded, i.e. determinate. Yet, the structuralist sign cut adrift from the linguistic system (*langue*) is no sign at all. The post-structuralist resurrection of the language as an ideological object – something which certain individuals may 'believe in' and associate particular linguistic features with – also does not rescue the manoeuvre. It does not thereby bestow the language with any ontologically *real* status in the way that Saussure claims *langue* to be a genuine socio-psychological reality by which successful linguistic communication stands or falls. An ideological object is a second-order construct, not a first-order reality. To conflate the two is a clear category mistake. Furthermore, as mentioned previously, whatever most people might believe a language to be, it is highly unlikely to be anything resembling a *langue* in the highly technical and metaphysically dubious sense in which Saussure uses the term.

In our view then, modern sociolinguistics has got things the wrong way round. It is the structuralist conception of the linguistic sign which requires rejection before one can go about rejecting or 'disinventing' the notion of individual linguistic systems/languages. As to why this is the case, one obvious answer suggests itself. The structuralist understanding of the linguistic sign as a determinate entity whose dual components (form and meaning) can be readily identified by a competent third-party observer is ideally suited to the kinds of data-driven research methodologies on which sociolinguistics relies and which have played a significant part in shaping the discipline as a whole. Indeed, to make data out of language at all, one needs a reliable source of determinacy and the structuralist sign fits the bill perfectly in this regard. In fact, sociolinguists, especially those concerned with 'super-diversity' and 'globalisation', tend to place great emphasis on studying the real (three-dimensional) world inhabited by real people with real concerns ('real-world problems', as applied linguists like to call them), without apparently realising that their linguistic theory commits them to the notion of a two-dimensional sign, i.e. the linguistic sign, which – after analysis – is projected back onto three-dimensional space and time. The integrationist, by rejecting this linguistic sign, also rejects the kind of empirical linguistic research that *only* the structuralist sign makes possible; instead the integrationist treats the sign as 'three-dimensional' (D. R. Davis 1997) and calls it the integrational sign which is neither 'linguistic' nor 'non-linguistic'. The integrational sign does not exist or has no 'residual existence' anywhere else than in the here-and-now as a consequence of someone having integrated two activities which would otherwise have remained unintegrated. The integrational sign is 'private' whether the activities integrated involve one person or more persons. In other words, when it comes to human sign-making activities, there is nothing 'shared' in any ontological sense that a linguistic researcher could have access to, as required by orthodox linguistics, i.e. a linguistics that is compatible with the empirical sciences.

As with Saussurean structuralism, the idea that linguistic signs are intersubjectively shared is also central to the theory of communication which underpins polylanguaging theory. The mechanism by which they are supposedly shared is the metaphysically recondite one of thought transference or 'telementation' (e.g. Harris 1998). Orman (2013) cites a number of examples which demonstrate Jørgensen's adherence to a telementational view of linguistic communication. Indeed, Jørgensen's view bears striking similarities with that of Saussure. For instance, we see the assertion that '[t]he uniquely human capacity of using arbitrary signs to transfer concept and experience over great distances in time and place is what we call language' and that '[w]ith language, human beings can transfer ideas over large distances in space and time' (Jørgensen 2008, 161). There can therefore be little doubt about Jørgensen's credentials as a telementationalist. Now, Ritzau barely mentions communication at all in her paper, let alone advances any theoretical view of what communication is. However, given her general approval of polylanguaging theory it is reasonable to assume that she would affirm the view of linguistic communication outlined by Jørgensen with whom, after all, this strand of sociolinguistic theorising originated. Ritzau (2014, 4) makes the observation that '[i]ndividuals do not share a fixed code, but their individual linguistic experiences must overlap to some degree to enable communication'. The problem here is that for telementation to be anything remotely resembling a credible theory of communication, it requires that individuals do indeed share a fixed code, a *langue* in the Saussurean sense. The whole rationale and logic of the telementational model falls apart if this is not the case. As Harris (1998, 40–41) observes, '[i]t makes no more sense for the fixed-code theorist to claim that fixed codes require only 'approximate' systematisation than it would for the Bank of England to declare that there are only 'approximately' one hundred pence to a pound'. To admit this, though, is to admit that individuals must share a language and therefore by consequence that languages *do* exist. Ritzau tries to avoid this unwelcome conclusion by invoking the diluted requirement that individuals' linguistic experiences only need to 'overlap to some degree'. However, unless one is willing and able to say in what way and to what extent such experiences must and do overlap, the claim is entirely vacuous and nothing more than a cop-out. If the claim is that individuals must merely share certain features or units, this still does not obviate the problem as one can then ask the question to what extent such features must be shared – is sharedness an absolute or incremental notion? – and what such sharedness consists in. The difficulty here is that there are no non-arbitrary, context-free criteria for establishing the sameness or sharedness of linguistic experience. This is a matter of individual contextualisation. What is happening here is that the absolute determinacy of the Saussurean linguistic system is being relocated to the individual features in question. The important thing is that determinacy is somehow retained at all cost since without it the sociolinguist lands in a dataless, methodological no man's land. The result of this manoeuvre is that each feature then becomes a kind of miniature fixed code in its own right. So, far from merely sharing a single holistic fixed code, individuals must now apparently be in possession of multiple atomistic fixed codes (hundreds? thousands?) for successful communication to occur. What remains obscure is how, given the irreducible individuality of linguistic experience, individuals come to share such features in the first place and bestow upon them a common determinate, context-free identity. Needless to say, multiplying fixed codes potentially ad infinitum does not rescue the telementational model of linguistic communication. Instead, it merely further highlights its manifest inadequacies and the question-begging assumptions inherent in it since, as Harris (1998, 40) notes, the move defeats the purpose of invoking the notion of a fixed code in the first place as the theorist then has to make sense of and explain how communication is possible *across* codes.

In summary, what one sees is that polylanguaging theory has taken over both the Saussurean view of the linguistic sign and the Saussurean model of communication while concurrently rejecting the ontological reality of the Saussurean linguistic system (*langue*). What we are left with, however, is not a theoretical advance, but a theoretical mess.

4. Linguistic resources

Ritzau, like many contemporary sociolinguists, sets great store by the notion of 'linguistic resources'. According to this prominent line of thought, linguistic resources are apparently what make up our linguistic repertoires and it is our linguistic repertoires which correspondingly determine our linguistic and communicative competence. It is interesting and instructive, though, to reflect on precisely what is to count as a linguistic resource as it reveals some important areas of theoretical divergence between integrationists and sociolinguists. Blommaert and Backus (2011, 7) state that linguistic resources include 'traditional linguistic elements of sound, words and patterns' but, importantly, they do go on to add that the definition of linguistic resources should not be limited to such elements and instead include 'anything that people use to communicate meaning'. To that extent, we broadly agree. However, we would like to focus here on the idea that linguistic features such as words constitute resources. According to this line of thought, linguistic features or units such as words, grammatical structures, etc., are conceived of as things which we possess, which somehow reside within us – Blommaert and Backus (2011, 6) speak of their 'entrenchment' in our minds – awaiting retrieval and subsequent deployment in real-life communicational episodes much as some tools lie dormant in a tool-box until they are taken out individually or in combination and used to some practical end. The linguistic resources at our disposal are constantly changing as one learns new features and others are forgotten or fall into disrepair. It is as if our minds were like large warehouses with a constantly changing inventory of items in stock. However, as picturesque as the metaphor might appear, we believe that it is thoroughly misleading when used as the basis for linguistic theorising.

In our view, the notion that words, structures, etc., are themselves linguistic or communicative resources is misleading and based upon reification and a failure to think in appropriate semiological terms. From an integrationist perspective, words are not things we possess, they are things we are forever creating and recreating. The fact that we may subsequently express some metalinguistic recognition of two signs as 'tokens' of the 'same' word is not the point, nor does that recognition grant an ontologically real status to the 'type' in question. What counts in semiological or communicational terms is one's ability to produce an appropriate sign at the appropriate moment in the appropriate context. Signs do not pre-exist their creation by individual signmakers. What counts in my attempt to successfully order a drink at the bar is my ability to produce the sign 'beer' or 'wine', etc., at the appropriate moment such that it results in my getting the drink I ordered. To cite my success in ordering my beer or wine as a proof that 'beer' and 'wine' are indeed *words* existing as abstractions puts the cart before the horse. So does showing them in a dictionary to anyone who doubts this. The conviction that the metalinguistic abstraction called 'word' identifies a psychologically real class of phenomena is a result of literacy and the concomitant decontextualisation of language. The mistake is on a par with supposing that what won me a particular point in a game of tennis was my possession of the tennis resource 'the backhand shot'. However, there is no such thing as '*the* backhand shot'; it is an abstraction derived from analysis of the countless actual shots which are held to resemble it to a greater or lesser degree played in tennis matches throughout history. What counts with regard to the outcome of the actual point I am engaged in is not that I know in theory what a backhand shot is, whether I believe there is such a thing, nor whether I have played one successfully or unsuccessfully in previous matches, but whether I am able to produce a winning shot at the required moment in the game in question. What I am doing if I succeed in pulling off such a shot is not reproducing an entry from my mental dictionary of tennis strokes. Rather, I am producing an irreducibly time-bound and context-bound response to an unrepeatable – because of the temporal aspect – real-world situation in which I find myself. Just as it is not possible to score the same goal twice in football, it is not possible to play the same shot twice in tennis (or cricket, badminton, ping pong, etc.). If we are to bring any notion of 'resources' into play here, the only resources in question are the biomechanical and cognitive capacities I am able to call upon which enable me to play the particular shot at the moment in question. Furthermore, there is no cast-iron guarantee that the capacities I am able to call upon in one instance will necessarily be available in any subsequent situation. The same applies, *mutatis mutandis*, to my linguistic and other sign-making abilities. The question which then arises is whether there is any point or value in conceiving of such abilities as resources. In common understanding, resources are things which pre-exist their use. Natural resources, e.g. oil or gas, are 'already there' before humans come along and extract them, process them, etc., as part of a programme of further activity. In this sense, then, one can have no difficulty in conceiving of, say, microphones, telephones or dictionaries as linguistic or communicative resources as these are not metaphysical abstractions but real-word objects which exist independently of any use made of them. The same cannot be said of words, grammatical structures or any other type of linguistic unit. Only an act of unwarranted reification can make this seem otherwise.

5. Concluding remarks

Modern sociolinguistics is certainly right in wanting to throw off and transcend the stultifying scientistic strictures of Saussurean-style structuralism. Our purpose in writing this article has been to argue that in order to avoid advancing further down any additional theoretical blind alleys, what is required is a *wholesale* rather than a selective rejection of Saussurean theory. Any such rejection must begin with the biplanar structuralist sign. Once that is rejected, the rejection of the Saussurean linguistic system (*langue*) naturally follows and without either of these two elements the 'sender-receiver' model of communication no longer stands up to serious scrutiny. All three elements are intimately connected. No single element can be retained without the other two. Unfortunately for sociolinguistics, such a wholesale rejection has rather dire methodological consequences as it destroys the rationale for the positivist, data-driven approaches on which the discipline has thrived hitherto. Hence, in our view, the widespread reluctance, typified in the polylanguaging literature, to abandon belief in the determinacy of the linguistic sign. The integrationist affirmation of the 'radical indeterminacy' of the linguistic sign (Harris 2009, 81) is regrettably often taken to imply that any form of coherent or systematic linguistic inquiry is an impossibility. We hope to have shown that this is not the case. What the integrationist position does imply, however, is a fundamental rethinking and reorientation of what passes for theoretically cogent linguistic inquiry.

References

Blommaert, Jan, and Ad. Backus. 2011. "Repertoires Revisited: 'Knowing Language' in Superdiversity." *Working Papers in Urban Languages and Literacies*, Paper 67. King's College London. www.kcl.ac.uk/ldc

Canagarajah, Suresh. 2011. "Translanguaging in the Classroom: Emerging Issues for Research and Pedagogy." *Applied Linguistics Review* 2: 1–28. doi:10.1515/9783110239331.1.

Creese, Angela, and Adrian Blackledge. 2010. "Translanguaging in the Bilingual Classroom: A Pedagogy for Learning and Teaching?" *Modern Language Journal* 94 (1): 103–115. doi:10.1111/j.1540-4781.2009.00986.x.

Davis, Daniel R. 1997. "The Three-dimensional Sign." *Language Sciences* 19(1): 23–31 doi:10.1016/0388-0001(95)00024-0

Davis, Hayley G. 1997. "Ordinary People's Philosophy: Comparing Lay and Professional Metalinguistic Knowledge." *Language Sciences* 19 (1): 33–46. doi:10.1016/0388-0001(95)00025-9.

Davis, Hayley G. 2001. "The Linguistic Individual: An Integrational Approach." *Language Sciences* 23: 707–713. doi:10.1016/S0388-0001(00)00025-5.

Duncker, Dorthe. 2011. "On the Empirical Challenge to Integrational Studies in Language." *Language Sciences* 33: 533–543. doi:10.1016/j.langsci.2011.04.013.

Harris, Roy. 1980. *The Language-makers*. London: Duckworth.

Harris, Roy. 1981. *The Language Myth*. London: Duckworth.

Harris, Roy. 1996. *Signs, Language and Communication*. London: Routledge.

Harris, Roy. 1997. "From an Integrational Point of View." In *Linguistics Inside Out: Roy Harris and His Critics*, edited by George Wolf and Nigel Love, 229–310. Amsterdam: John Benjamins.

Harris, Roy. 1998. *An Introduction to Integrational Linguistics*. Oxford: Pergamon.

Harris, Roy. 1999. "Integrational Linguistics and the Structuralist Legacy." *Language and Communication* 19: 45–68. doi:10.1016/S0271-5309(98)00017-2.

Harris, Roy. 2009. *Integrationist Notes and Papers 2006–2008*. Gamlingay: Bright Pen.
Jacquemet, Marco. 2005. "Transidiomatic Practices: Language and Power in the Age of Globalization." *Language and Communication* 25: 257–277. doi:10.1016/j.langcom.2005.05.001
Jørgensen, Jens Normann. 2008. "Polylingual Languaging Around and among Children and Adolescents." *International Journal of Multilingualism* 5 (3): 161–176.
Love, Nigel. 2007. "Are Languages Digital Codes?" *Language Sciences* 29 (5): 690–709.
Makoni, Sinfree B. 2011. "Sociolinguistics, Colonial and Postcolonial: An Integrationist Perspective." *Language Sciences* 33 (4): 680–688.
Makoni, Sinfree B. 2014. "'The Lord is My Shock Absorber'. A Sociohistorical Intergrationist Approach to Mid-twentieth Century Literacy Practices in Ghana." In *Heteroglossia as Practice and Pedagogy*, edited by Angela Creese and Adrian Blackledge, 75–98. Dordrecht: Springer.
Orman, Jon. 2013. "New Lingualisms, Same Old Codes." *Language Sciences* 37: 90–98.
Otsuji, Emi, and Alastair, Pennycook. 2010. "Metrolingualism: \ Fixity, Fluidity and Language in Flux." *International Journal of Multilingualism* 7 (3): 240–254. doi:10.1080/14790710903414331.
Pablé, Adrian. 2009. "The 'Dialect Myth' and Socio-onomastics. The Names of the Castles of Bellinzona in an Integrational Perspective." *Language & Communication* 29 (2): 152-165.
Pablé, Adrian. 2010. "Language, Knowledge and Reality: The Integrationist on Name Variation." *Language & Communication* 30 (2): 109–122.

Ritzau, Ursula. 2014. "Learner Language and Polylanguaging: How Language Students' Ideologies Relate to Their Written Language Use." *International Journal of Bilingual Education and Bilingualism.* http://dx.doi.org/10.1080/13670050.2014.936822.

Wolf, George, Michèle Bocquillon, Debbie de la Houssaye, Phyllis Krzyzek, Clifton Meynard, and Lisbeth Philip. 1998. "Pronouncing French Names in New Orleans." In *Integrational Linguistics: A First Reader*, edited by Roy Harris and George Wolf, 324–342. Oxford: Pergamon.

4.
Linguistic diversity and language loss: a view from integrational linguistics

Abstract
This article offers an integrational linguistic critique of the way in which the notions of linguistic diversity and language loss/death are theorised within orthodox linguistics. The fundamental issue concerns the ontological status of languages. While orthodox approaches take the existence of separately identifiable languages or language varieties (lects) as a foundational theoretical postulate even in the absence of any consistent definitional criteria, from an integrational perspective languages are nothing more than second-order metalinguistic abstractions from actual language practices. Consequently, any theory of first-order linguistic diversity based on the enumeration of individual languages is automatically suspect. Furthermore, since languages do not exist as ontological realia, it cannot be the case that linguistic diversity is declining due to language loss. To suppose otherwise rests on a conflation of the linguistic and the metalinguistic, a failing endemic to orthodox linguistics. The discussion concludes by offering an integrational view on some of the epistemological and language-political issues which commonly surface in discussions of linguistic diversity and language loss.

It is the concept of linguistic unity which is theoretically problematic; not the concept of linguistic diversity. – Roy Harris

As soon as one stops searching for knowledge, or if one imagines that it need not be creatively sought in the depths of the human spirit but can be assembled extensively by collecting and classifying facts, everything is irrevocably and forever lost. – Wilhlem von Humboldt

1. Introduction

In this paper, I outline an integrational linguistic perspective (Harris, 1981, 1997, 1998) on several interrelated issues which have been the subject of extensive discussion and exposition in modern linguistics and the sociology/politics of language, namely those of linguistic diversity and language loss. Despite a fairly substantial literature which has appeared since Roy Harris' seminal publications in the early 1980s, amongst the range of theoretical positions which populate the field of contemporary linguistics integrationism continues to occupy a rather peripheral place within the discipline as a whole. The foremost reason for this, perhaps combined with the sometimes bellicose rhetoric of its proponents, is that integrationism rejects the theoretical basis upon which nigh on everything which passes for contemporary linguistics rests. The response to the criticisms offered by integrational theory from within mainstream academic linguistics has, with a few exceptions, unfortunately mostly been one of silence or incomprehension. It is therefore quite probable that the present contribution will suffer the same fate.

Given the relatively low profile of integrational linguistics, a brief overview of its theoretical foundations is in order. Central to the integrational critique of what it conceives variously as 'orthodox', 'mainstream' or 'segregational' linguistics[1] is the notion of the 'language myth' (Harris, 1981). The 'language myth' refers to two interrelated fallacies which, according to integrationists, have underwritten virtually all linguistic theorising in the modern Western tradition, namely the 'fixed-code fallacy' and the 'fallacy of telementation'. The former refers to the belief that languages exist as internally structured systems of invariant units and regularities and the consequent view that the description and analysis of these systems constitute the proper subject matter of a scientifically orientated linguistics. It is the existence of such fixed codes, knowledge of which is theoretically shared by all members of the (homogenous) speech communities in question, which enables the possibility of telementation. 'Telementation' is the term used by integrationists to refer to the notion that human linguistic communication occurs through the neat transference of thoughts and concepts from the mind of one individual to another. Fundamental to the integrationist rejection of the language myth is the rejection of the Saussurean notion of the linguistic sign as a biplanar entity which pairs a determinate form (*signifiant*) with a determinate meaning (*signifié*) and which has survived virtually unscathed in nearly all mainstream approaches in modern linguistics (structuralist, poststructuralist, generativist, etc.). Integration-

---

[1] Integrationists use the designations 'orthodox', 'mainstream' or 'segregationist' to refer to any non-integrationist approaches in linguistics (structuralist, poststructuralist, generativist, etc.) which do not affirm or recognise the basic integrationist principle of the radical indeterminacy of the linguistic sign (Harris, 2007: 16). For integrationists, orthodox linguistics is 'segregationist' because it treats language and languages as autonomous objects of study, assumes that a neat dividing line can be drawn between the linguistic and non-linguistic and that language can be studied independently of the communicational context in which it occurs (Harris, 1998: 10). It is granted nevertheless that many linguists working within the aforementioned approaches would no doubt contest the attribution of such labels. I therefore employ the terms subject to this acknowledgement.

ism on the other hand adopts a *radically indeterminate* view of the linguistic sign. According to the integrationist view, signs are not decontextualised invariant items which pre-exist their manifestation in communicative episodes. To suppose otherwise is to artificially separate the material form of the sign from its semiological function which due to the open-ended nature of human communication can never be determined in advance of its deployment. Rather, signs are constantly made (and remade) by real contextualising individuals in the temporal flux of their communicative (integrating) activities. The only signs which occur in communicational episodes are those which the parties to such episodes construe as occurring, no more and no less. As Harris (1998: 21) notes, there is 'no higher court of appeal' in such matters. There is also no infallible guarantee that any two individuals involved a communicational episode will construe the 'same' signs as occurring since all signs are the products of individual contextualisation. Integrationism therefore takes a very different view of what constitutes communication. Given that the value attached to a sign is a context-dependent matter of individual contextualisation, there is no question of the intersubjective sharing of meaning which underwrites the telementational account of linguistic communication. Instead, integrationism views communication as involving the integration of human activities for which signs (linguistic or otherwise) act as interfaces. This entails a reversal of the ontological priority typically encountered in orthodox linguistics whereby communication is seen as presupposing language. Instead, from an integrationist standpoint, language presupposes communication.

The integrationist conception of the sign also entails a number of wider theoretical consequences. In particular, as Harris (1990: 45) notes, it allows one to do away with a number of commonplace assumptions, namely: '(i) that the linguistic sign is arbitrary; (ii) that the linguistic sign is linear; (iii) that words have meanings; (iv) that grammar has rules; and (v) that there are languages.'

Now, given that integrationism denies both the existence of languages as first-order linguistic realia as well as the possibility of providing objective criteria for the analysis of linguistic structure, the issues of linguistic diversity and language loss/death might not initially seem particularly promising candidates for an integrationist treatment, or at least one which is anything but relentlessly negative or critical in emphasis. However, while a critique of the orthodox account necessarily forms a central component, this paper attempts to challenge this view by showing that an alternative perspective on such phenomena is possible. The primary focus is on the ontological and epistemological issues thrown up by discourses on linguistic diversity and language loss/death from within mainstream linguistic approaches. The paper begins by outlining an integrationist view of linguistic diversity and language loss/death. My main contention in doing so, drawing on Harris' (1981) identification and deconstruction of the two-pronged 'language myth', is that there are no first-order linguistic phenomena which provide justification for the manner in which these phenomena are theorised and conceptualised in mainstream accounts. This alone is a controversial enough claim for the orthodox linguist to entertain. In fact, echoing the quotation from Roy Harris which stands as an epigraph to this paper,[2] I would even push the claim a little further and argue that while orthodox linguistics necessarily requires a theory of linguistic diversity – indeed Nichols (1989: 231) in her monumental study of worldwide typological diversity makes this very claim – as a corollary to its primary concern for the theorisation of components of linguistic unity, integrationism

---

[2] Of course, however, as I shall argue in this paper, the concept of linguistic diversity does become problematic when founded upon theoretically dubious components of linguistic unity or invariance.

requires no such corresponding theory at the first-order level. After all, if, as integrationists maintain, the linguistic sign is not the instantiation of an abstract invariant but rather always the product of an act of context-bound creation, language is an important sense inherently and irredeemably diverse and any supplementary notions of linguistic diversity or difference can only be the product of metalinguistic reflexive practices, rather than objective-empirical accounts of actual states of affairs. Indeed, a central thrust of my argument is that orthodox accounts of linguistic diversity and language loss/death rest upon a confusion or a failure to draw the appropriate line between the *linguistic* and the *metalinguistic*, as a result of which we have what from an integrationist perspective are essentially post-hoc second-order accounts posing as first-order descriptions. In point of fact, one might more accurately describe language loss/death as a *meta*–metalinguistic occurrence given that the notion of 'a language' is itself a metalinguistic construct. An important initial task for the integrationist then is to attempt to provide an account of the types of events which lead to the postulation of instances of language loss without invoking what are seen as the dubious, question-begging theoretical constructs of orthodox linguistics and confusing first- and second-order objects of analysis.

Also discussed are some of the epistemological questions linked to mainstream discourses about language loss and endangerment. In particular, I argue that an integrationist standpoint requires one to take issue with the commonly rehearsed (or implied) argument that languages are in themselves repositories of knowledge and that their loss represents a consequent and irretrievable loss of knowledge to mankind. Such arguments are based on the (untenable) assumption that languages are surrogationalist fixed codes which allow for context-free forms of knowledge. In contrast, I outline the integrationist position which views knowledge as arising from human beings' creative engagement in sign-making activities and therefore as something which cannot be decontextualised. In addition, I argue that discipline-internal claims from within linguistics that language death constitutes a tragic loss of potential data sources for research into linguistic universals also do not carry any weight from an integrationist perspective.

In addition to this inevitable and necessary critical engagement with orthodox theory, I am also keen to introduce into the discussion a reflexive component for proponents of integrational linguistics to take onboard by exploring some of the practical and rhetorical challenges integrationism itself faces in engaging with questions pertaining to linguistic diversity and language loss. In particular, I address the question of whether integrational theory provides any basis or pointers for taking up a certain stance as regards the politics or ethics of such issues. Or does integrationism, given its ontological and epistemic implications, merely imply a form of political agnosticism? If so, what can integrationism hope to offer those with any form of vested interest in maintaining an orthodox-style discourse on such issues? To illustrate the foregoing point, what the integrationist regards as a legitimate, if perhaps somewhat provocative, rhetorical question – for example 'how can languages be lost or die if they do not exist in the first place?' – may well strike those with little or no interest in the finer points of academic linguistic theory as both absurd and irrelevant. After all, it will likely be of little comfort and indeed make little sense to communities undergoing what they perceive as language shift/loss to be informed that their languages are mythical constructs that never really existed to begin with.[3] Furthermore, given the very real socio-

---

[3] Owen (2009: 163) makes a similar point in relation to the integrationist/ Harrisian view of traditional approaches to language teaching: 'Fulminating that teachers are teaching a myth conjured up by the institutionalised practices of pedagogy is probably not going to win many converts to integrationism.'

cultural, political and ethical concerns amongst both 'experts' and lay persons which may accompany the discussion of such matters, does it count as a satisfactory response for integrationists to simply wash their hands of them and dismiss them as based on myth and misconceptualisation? On this level then, there is a challenge of *engagement* for proponents of integrational linguistics to contend with due in no small part to the fact that most of the moral and political claims made on all sides of the debate surrounding linguistic diversity and language loss tend to gain their force from ontological and epistemological assumptions derived from the 'language myth'.

2. The ontology of linguistic diversity – an integrationist view

The highlighting and discussion of instances of language loss/ death or endangerment often tends to be underpinned by a more general concern for worldwide linguistic diversity and an accompanying alarm at its accelerating decline (e.g. Nettle and Romaine, 2000; Skutnabb-Kangas, 2000; Crystal, 2002). The reasons for this concern may be diverse but most 'enlightened' linguists at least would appear to be in broad agreement that linguistic diversity is, in the main, a 'good thing' and merits some form of promotion or protection via targeted policy and planning measures.[4] But what is this linguistic diversity exactly and how are we to go about assessing it? A prominent feature of much of the mainstream literature on the subject has been the quest to arrive at an objective 'scientific' basis for the definition and quan-

---

[4] Why this should be the case is an interesting and complex question in its own right although it would no doubt be somewhat gratuitous and overly cynical to explain such a consensus solely in terms of orthodox linguists' obvious vested interests. Clearly, there are wider influential (liberal) ideological and political discourses in operation which promote interest in and respect for all kinds of manifestations of human cultural diversity and which naturally dovetail with the rhetoric and aims of those seeking to defend linguistic diversity.

tification of linguistic diversity. This is only to be expected of course given orthodox linguistics' more general claim or aspiration to be a scientific discipline. A notable feature of this quest, however, is the absence hitherto of any vigorous consensus in response to the matter, with numerous alternatives having been proposed. Moreover, such approaches are not necessarily conflictual or antagonistic, an indicator of the diverse perspectives from which linguistic phenomena may be conceptualised and categorised and thereby perhaps suggesting the futility of hoping to arrive at a single uncontested definition. What is of interest however, and indeed deeply problematic, from an integrationist perspective is that almost all conceptualisations of linguistic diversity and the resultant socio-political discourses which they inform are based upon theoretically suspect 'segregationist' notions of language. In all cases, a measure of diversity is arrived through an enumeration of holistic units of some kind, be it individual language systems which essentially reduce to language or lect names or, in more technically sophisticated accounts (e.g. Nichols, 1989), particular typological or 'genetic' features. What unites such methods is their presupposition of the possibility of establishing objective criteria for determining the sameness or difference of linguistic phenomena. Indeed, if there were no such criteria, as integrationists argue, linguistics' claim to be a scientific discipline would be on shaky ground. As Mühlhäusler (2004: 286) notes: 'A science needs to meet the minimal requirement of having reliable criteria for demonstrating that two things are the same or different and criteria for saying whether one is dealing with one or two objects.' Orthodox approaches to defining and quantifying linguistic diversity[5] are infused by what Harris (2012:

---

[5] The term 'language diversity' is also often used in relation to measurements of diversity arrived at purely through the counting of 'languages' (e.g. Nettle, 1996). Needless to say, from an integrationist point of view, this term begs the very question under consideration here.

119) refers to as the 'denumerability doctrine', that is to say the seemingly unwavering conviction that there are actually discrete languages or language varieties 'out there' waiting to be identified and counted, which itself also entails the possibility of unambiguously identifying the structural components of which they consist. Such approaches still operate very much on the Saussurean assumption that '[p]our la linguistique, c'est bien le fait primordial que la diversité des langues'.[6] The fact that nobody, let alone linguists, is able to tell us with any certainty or great conviction exactly how many languages there are in a given area or in the world as a whole tends to be seen more as the consequence of a lack of methodological consensus or inadequate data rather than as an indicator of the fundamental futility of the question itself since, as Harris (2012: 124) notes, to admit the latter would be to 'undermine at the outset the academic standing of [the] discipline'. Such theoretical intransigence is even more curious in view of the fact that some linguists even go so far as to admit that they cannot provide unambiguous criteria for defining what constitutes a language. For instance, having stated that '[l]anguages are today being killed and linguistic diversity is disappearing at a much faster pace than ever before in human history' (2000: ix), Skutnabb-Kangas (2000: 6) goes on to make the extraordinary claim that '[t]he number of "languages" in the world [. . .] *cannot* actually be known' (my emphasis) since 'we don't even properly know what "a language" is.' As a declaration of theoretical incoherence, this is hard to beat. It is certainly difficult to imagine any parallel claims being entertained with any seriousness in the hard sciences: 'Gold deposits are being exhausted faster than ever although where exactly and at what rate we don't know and never will because we can't actually tell

---

[6] 'As far as linguistics is concerned, the diversity of languages is indeed the fundamental fact' (Komatsu and Harris, 1993: 12).

you what gold is. Nevertheless, we are certain that gold exists.'[7] Such mystical claims would be laughed out of the scientific court. This is not a facile attempt to play to the gallery on my part here. If one cannot say with any conviction what a language is or if the criteria for distinguishing between languages vary arbitrarily from case to case – the 'hocus-pocus' approach to language definition – it is a nonsense to maintain that such entities nevertheless exist. One cannot have it both ways. Nor are the claims of linguists exempt from the burden of proof.

It is quite remarkable how steadfastly some linguists cling to their faith in the denumerability doctrine in the face of any amount of compromising evidence. For example, Nettle and Romaine note that:

> Another problem in deciding precisely how many languages there are in the world arises from the fact that many have no special names. The Sare people of the Sepik region of Papua New Guinea, for example, call their language Sare, but this means simply "to speak or talk." The Gitksan people of British Columbia have no conventional native name for their language which sets it apart from other varieties such as Nisgha and Tsimshian. The Gitksan generally refer to their own language as *Sim'algax*, "the real or true language," but the Nigsha and Tsimshian people do the same. (Nettle and Romaine, 2000: 27–28)

It would seem apparent, then, that such groups do not possess the Eurocentric concept of discrete languages as shared by Nettle and Romaine who nevertheless still seek to impose it upon them

---

[7] The analogy is perhaps not completely satisfactory since gold, unlike a language, is a physical object. Nevertheless, even abstract objects require consistent definitional criteria.

despite its manifest irrelevance to their cultural self-conceptualisation. They do not draw the integrationist conclusion that there might actually be something ontologically dubious about the category 'a language' and their subsequent attempt to construct a theory of linguistic diversity based upon it.[8] Elsewhere, Austin and Sallabank (2011: 4) speak of the 'paradox' of the 'mutual incomprehensibility of Chinese "dialects" compared to the mutual comprehensibility of mainland Scandinavian languages.' An alternative view would be that this is not so much a paradox as evidence that the notions of 'a dialect' and 'a language' are poorly defined and indeed indefinable according to anything other than arbitrary (i.e. non-linguistic) criteria.

The cultural specificity of the notion of countable named languages is also a point made by Makoni (2011) in the Southern African context who argues that the presence of the concept of named objects known as 'languages' in the region was a product of 'colonial imaginings' and the transplantation of European linguistic ideologies. He notes, for example, that:

> The naming of languages produced puzzling questions such as 'What languages do you speak?', as opposed to the typical African language question 'do you speak?', which on its own suggests that names of languages are not part of the lexicon of speakers of these languages. This indicates that language among lowly literate Africans is conceptualized without necessarily positing the existence of languages as spatially or ethnically bounded entities, or

---

[8] Yet, in a previous work, Romaine (1994: 12) affirms a position which seems to tally with the integrationist view when she writes that 'The very concept of discrete languages is probably a European cultural artefact fostered by processes such as literacy and standardization. Any attempt to count distinct languages will be an artefact of classificatory procedures rather than a reflection of communicational practices.'

without cutting language up into different languages or constituent parts such as verbs, nouns, etc. (Makoni, 2011: 683)

Whatever concept(s) pre-colonial Africans may have had of linguistic diversity or linguistic difference, it would clearly not have been based on the denumeration of separate object-like entities corresponding to the Eurocentric notion of 'languages'. It would appear then, somewhat ironically, that the hubristic colonial enterprise of identifying and inventing languages where previously there were none has found continuation in even the most 'politically-correct' of contemporary mainstream linguistic approaches with their enduring adherence to the denumerability doctrine. For integrationists, the supposed 'problem' of how to go about identifying and counting discrete languages is itself bogus since there are no non-arbitrary criteria for doing so. As Harris (2012: 127) notes: 'The problem of counting languages will not 'go away' until more linguists realize, as integrationists do, that ontologically there are no languages to be counted.' What, then, explains this puzzling disinclination to disbelieve in the ontological reality of discrete languages while simultaneously being unable to provide any non-arbitrary or unambiguous criteria for their identification? One candidate explanation is a belief in what integrationists refer to as a reocentric semantics (Harris, 2005: 3), that is to say the (mistaken) view that words acquire their meanings by standing for things/objects existing in the 'real world'. If we have the linguistic expression 'a language', so the reasoning goes, there must be something tangible 'out there' to which it corresponds.[9] All one would therefore seem to need to do to bring a new language into being is to name it, a point made by Makoni and Pennycook (2005: 143) who note that languages do not pre-

---

[9] For an in-depth discussion and critique of reocentric semantics from an integrationist viewpoint, see Pablé (2011).

exist their naming, rather it is the act of naming which performatively calls them 'into being'.

The key point then in the context of this discussion is that from an integrational perspective a notion of linguistic diversity based on the counting of languages, or what in the end turn out to be nothing more than language names, is an ontological fiction founded upon abstraction and reification. Consequently, the idea that linguistic diversity is declining because languages are disappearing is similarly mythical and indeed collapses into incoherence. The whole discourse of language death and endangerment is a good illustration of the inadequacy of certain lay metalinguistic concepts as theoretical bases for academic enquiry into language issues. For integrational linguists, a starting point for an exploration of themes such as 'language death' or 'language revival' would be to examine why language is talked of in such terms at all. What is it that gives rise to the cultural belief that the human linguistic behaviour can be explained in terms of the instantiation of discrete object-like entities (languages) each possessing the potential for vitality, mortality, illness (sometimes terminal) and even in some miraculous cases resurrection, qualities in terms of which the general faculty itself is generally not discussed, except perhaps in certain pathological cases? To take the vitality and mortality of languages as pre-theoretical givens is therefore to beg fundamental questions and confuse *explicanda* with *explicantia*. The anthropomorphosised notion of languages as mortal entities can also be regarded as 'systematically misleading' (Hermann, 2007) insofar as it contributes towards the propagation of a range of derivative terminology predicated upon the ontological possibility of language death, for example 'killer languages', 'linguicide', 'language murder', 'linguistic genocide', 'language extinction', etc. From an integrational point of view, such terms merely serve to muddy the theoretical waters even further.

It ought to be stressed at this point that the failure to embrace such emotive terminology and the corresponding political discourses is by no means limited to integrationists. Non-integrationist authors such as De Swaan (2004) and Mufwene (2005) have rejected language preservation efforts as 'linguistic sentimentalism' and written of the 'myth of killer languages' respectively. However, unlike integrationists these authors do not tend to call into question the fundamental ontological possibility of language loss/death since the ontological status of 'languages' is itself not seriously disputed. The whole debate regarding the politics of language endangerment therefore mostly continues to take place on the basis of segregationist assumptions about language whereas integrationism calls into question the very basis of the debate itself.

To recap some of the key claims advanced thus far. What orthodox approaches see as linguistic diversity is, from an integrational viewpoint, really a form of metalinguistic diversity, a diversity of metalinguistic classifications, based upon a theoretically problematic notion of the linguistic sign and, by consequence, of languages themselves. Orthodox linguistics appears unable to theorise linguistic diversity without recourse to the postulation of discrete languages or lects/varieties. Even those approaches which place emphasis on the diversity of structural-typological features rather than simply counting language names are still committed to an ontology of language which affirms the existence of discrete languages since, as Saussure was at pains to stress, structural features are only identifiable within the framework of their belonging to a self-contained system – *la langue*. It is on this score that, as I have argued elsewhere (Orman, 2012, 2013), certain prominent poststructuralist or postmodernist sociolinguistic approaches come theoretically unstuck and reveal an internal inconsistency. It is all very well expressing scepticism about or even denying the ontological discreteness of languages and varieties as conceived within more traditional sociolinguistic approaches, but it makes little sense to do so if one does not alter one's fundamental theory of the linguistic sign. One cannot retain the Saussurean notion of the determinate biplanar (form/meaning) sign in the absence of the linguistic system (language) which confers its identity upon it. This is the theoretical incoherence at the heart of approaches which profess to focus on linguistic features, still conceived as coded units and regularities, at the expense of languages or lects (e.g. Jørgensen, 2008; Jørgensen et al., 2011). Such approaches are rendered all the more problematic by their simultaneous affirmation of traditional sociolinguistic categories such as 'registers', 'genres' and 'styles' which, just like 'languages', are held to be identifiable and distinguishable (and thus countable) through the co-occurrence of particular linguistic features. Blommaert (2011), who is quite explicit about his commitment to a code-based view of language, has even gone so far as to proclaim the existence of a new type of 'sociolinguistic object', namely 'supervernaculars',[10] which nevertheless 'have all the features we commonly attribute to "languages"' (p. 4). The point here is that from an integrationist perspective any approach which fails to call into question the validity of the determinate biplanar linguistic sign can provide no coherent basis for the construction of a viable theory of first-order linguistic diversity. The postmodernist project of 'disinventing' languages and lects (Makoni and Pennycook, 2005) is in itself not sufficient; it is the even more foundational notion of the linguistic sign which also requires rethinking. A rethinking of the linguistic sign along integrationist lines – i.e. as something which is radically indeterminate and does not pre-exist its instantiation and recognition in real-time communication – must necessarily lead one to reject the possibility of arriving at an objective or scientific conception of the linguistic sign and therefore of linguistic diversity. Any retrospective 'third-party' interpretive account of linguistic pheno-

---

[10] For an integrationist critique of the notion, see Orman (2012).

mena constitutes an act of re/decontextualisation and distortion. No 'linguistic facts' can be recovered by such means. As Duncker (2012: 403) observes: 'No episode of communication can be observed from the outside or collected and subsequently studied as a specimen in the laboratory. The "view from nowhere" only admits a third person perspective which differs radically from the view of the situated participants involved in first-order communication.' 'Linguistic diversity' is also not a conceptual item in any surrogationalist fixed code and what counts as linguistic diversity is a question which must therefore be left open as it will always be the product of particular contextualisations performed by individuals with particular communicative (integrational) purposes in mind.

3. Making integrational sense of language loss/death

What are we to take it to mean when it is said, for instance, that the Gothic or Ubykh languages are dead or extinct? Of course, from a certain lay perspective this may seem a rather banal question with an all-too-obvious answer, namely that nobody speaks (and perhaps writes) them anymore. Viewed in this manner then, the question of what it means for a language to be dead or have disappeared seems a perfectly reasonable one to which a sensible and satisfactory answer can ordinarily be given. What is less certain from an integrational perspective is whether it is the sort of question, taken at face value, which ought to form the basis of linguists' theoretical enquiries since it begs a crucial question from the outset, namely that of whether ontologically speaking there is any such thing as the Gothic or Ubykh language. As the question stands, a certain type of affirmative answer is almost preordained, namely that there is indeed something which has been lost or has disappeared and the task is simply to find out what it is. For the integrationist, this is an unacceptable premise upon which to launch one's enquiries for if languages are held to be what structuralist or generative theory claims or implies, namely fixed codes of bi-planar sign units which through their material instantiation in speech enable the neat transfer of mental content from one mind to another, then there are clearly no such things.

How, then, would an integrationist make sense of the notion that language X is no more? Is it possible to provide an account of the type of first-order events which lead to the positing of language loss/death? One possible answer would be that there has been a discontinuation of verbal sign-making practices which give rise to a metalinguistically expressed belief in the existence of something called language X. A response of this type crucially relocates the notion to the metalinguistic level, that is to say to a reflexive domain of discourse *about* language, rather than its constituting a description of any first-order linguistic state of affairs. This is in line with Harris' (2009a: 41–42) observation that '[a] "language" is [. . .] metalinguistic extrapolation that has become attached to a particular language name.' It is noteworthy in this regard that all that would seem to be necessary to ensure the continued existence of a language is the survival of the language name. The diachronic integrity of a language is assured by little more than the retention of the metalinguistic label. A new language can be brought into being and a new historical meta-linguistic narrative inaugurated through the simple act of relabeling, as was the case in South Africa when what was formerly 'Dutch' became 'Afrikaans' (officially in 1923). Conversely, cases of language 'revival' or 'resuscitation' can be viewed as the resumption of such narratives. A language is deemed to have undergone revival when a particular metalinguistic label which had ceased to refer to any extant linguistic practices is once again used in order to do so. Had Modern Hebrew instead become widely known as 'Israeli' or by some other name,[11] it is doubtful

---

[11] Indeed, such a name change has been recommended, somewhat ironically by the language revival activist Ghil'ad Zuckermann (Zuckermann, 2008), on

whether there would have been so much talk of the language's alleged 'revival' – we would most probably expect to encounter discourses proclaiming the birth or making of a 'new' language. Latin is widely considered a 'dead' language but the grounds for making such a claim are strongly metalinguistic. Certainly no time and place of death has ever been specified.[12] Latin is deemed dead because nobody now engages in vernacular language practices labelled as 'Latin' despite the fact that it 'survives' in the form of the modern Romance 'languages'. Latin is therefore in the curious existential position of being, in a certain sense, linguistically extant but metalinguistically dead insofar it is rarely discussed *as if* it were still a going concern.

For the integrationist, in using terms such as 'language death' or 'language loss' we are not and indeed cannot be describing any first-order reality. The failure to recognise this rests upon a prior failure to realise that a language is nothing more than a metalinguistic abstraction from actual linguistic practices. It has no ontological existence of its own beyond the metalinguistic discourses in which it is invoked. However, even if one accepts the integrationist position thus far, one might counter at this point by claiming that the fact that languages are frequently such potent objects of belief amongst ordinary people and deemed capable of death or disappearance is itself sufficient to justify discourses which talk in such terms. After all, isn't integrationism supposedly 'lay-orientated'? This is a rejoinder which cannot be dismissed out of hand. Yet, as Harris (2009a: 43) notes, 'a linguistic fiction is still a fiction.' One would therefore first question the extent to which it is appropriate or helpful for academic linguists, many of

---

account of the fact that there is no continuous chain of native speakers linking modern and older forms of Hebrew.

[12] Unlike in the case of the Ubykh language which apparently died on 7th October 1992 with the death of its last 'native speaker', Tevfik Esenç. (http://languagesoftheworld.info/geolinguistics/obituary-the-ubykh-language.html)

whom would no doubt regard themselves as 'scientific' researchers, to collaborate in the propagation of such fictions. For integrationists, one of the purposes of linguistic enquiry is to understand and raise awareness of why lay people hold particular mythical beliefs about language and communication, not to abet them in maintaining such beliefs. This is of course not to idealise the concept of 'lay speaker' beyond necessity as clearly no neat dividing line can be drawn. How much linguistics education must one have had to no longer count as a lay speaker (Pablé et al., 2013: 42)? The question is unanswerable in anything other than arbitrary terms. Don't experts also sometimes talk about linguistic matters in unconsciously lay terms? What sense are we then to make of Harris' (1998: 20) dictum that 'everybody is a linguist'? The historical symbiosis of 'expert' and lay beliefs about language should also be emphasised. Hutton (1997: 54), for instance, notes that '[t]he views of the academic linguist and those of the public are connected not least through the education system, where ideas gradually trickle down from specialist disciplines to university students who become teachers to schoolchildren.' Yet conversely, as integrationists have often pointed out, many of the concepts in which professional linguists trade and erect as fundamental theoretical postulates in their work originate in lay discourse about language and communication. Indeed, as Love (2004: 528) notes, modern mainstream linguistics constitutes an attempt at the 'scientisation' of a lay 'commonsense' discourse about language whereby the 'most fundamental idea is that the domain of language (mass-noun) has crucially to be understood in terms of the concept of *a* language (i.e. 'language' as a count-noun).' On this view then, prominent lay and professional conceptions of language may be seen as engaged in something of a self-reinforcing cycle of myth elaboration and consolidation. The role which integrational theory can assume in this regard is to subject such discourses to demythologisation. The aim, as Harris (1996: 148) has argued, is not to undertake the

Sisyphean task of reforming lay metalanguage, but rather to raise awareness of the linguistic illusions which such metalanguage may generate and prevent such illusions being erected as theoretical foundations for serious enquiry into questions of language and communication.

4. Language(s) and knowledge

One of the more interesting and controversial questions raised by the phenomenon of language loss is that of what else, in addition to the language itself, is deemed to have been lost. My particular focus in this section is on the epistemic implications of language loss and the question of why it is generally held to be such an impoverishing phenomenon that ought to be resisted through active intervention. There are several commonly advanced arguments from within orthodox linguistic circles and it seems that these too are ones with which an integrationist must take issue.

The first argument, advanced in all seriousness in some quarters and reflecting orthodox linguistics' rather self-serving preoccupation with its own disciplinary survival, is that language loss constitutes an irretrievable loss of data sources for linguists' research into typological variation and language universals, thereby rendering the task of generative grammarians even more arduous. Krauss (1992: 10), for example, warns of the danger of linguistics 'go[ing] down in history as the only science that has presided obliviously over the disappearance of 90% of the very field to which it is dedicated.' Needless to say, these are hardly concerns with which integrationists can have much sympathy given their wholesale rejection of the basis upon which universal grammar theory is founded (see Harris 1997: 302-303). However, even if one is sympathetic to the generative position, one might also point out that the fact that in the course of human history thousands of languages—the typological features of most of which are utterly unknown—have perished undocumented has rendered the generative exercise futile from the very beginning.

Consequently, any claims to universality which might be advanced on behalf of particular typological features are wholly unverifiable and unable to achieve anything other than an eternally provisional status. It is therefore not clear what fundamental difference the loss of a few more thousand languages is going to make to the generative enterprise.

It would seem, then, that by ensuring the survival of languages, we would also be helping to ensure the survival of linguistics as an autonomous academic/scientific discipline. The question is whether this is a valid concern for anyone other than those linguists with a vested professional interest in doing so. An *a priori* commitment to the maintenance of academic linguistics in its current guise is not an unbiased basis upon which to found one's subsequent enquiries since it is overwhelmingly likely to produce only research which reaffirms the theoretical assumptions on which the predefined discipline rests. Such attitudes therefore endow the discipline with something of an in-built survival mechanism. However, an approach such as integrationism offers no such guarantees. By problematising those aforementioned theoretical assumptions – for example by arguing that to assert that the study of 'languages' is the proper concern of linguistics is to beg fundamental ontological questions – it calls into question, without passing prior judgment on, the very validity of the discipline itself.

Probably the most frequently heard claim in lamentations for the loss of linguistic diversity is one which, being of a more fundamental epistemological nature, extends well beyond the discipline-internal concerns of linguistic science. It is common to encounter the claim, often formulated in quite hyperbolic terms, that the loss of languages represents an irretrievable loss of knowledge to mankind, particularly in relation to the natural world. For example, Hinton (2001: 5) claims that 'the loss of language is part of the loss of ... knowledge systems' as a result of which 'the world stands to lose an important part of the sum of human knowledge whenever a language stops being used.' Harrison (2008: 3) in his book *The Extinction of the World's Languages and the Erosion of Human Knowledge* writes that when languages die, we lose 'an immense edifice of human knowledge, painstakingly assembled over millennia by countless minds [...] vanishing into oblivion.' Elsewhere, we read that language diversity constitutes 'one of the treasures of humanity' (Zepeda and Hill, 1992: 135). It is noteworthy that the speakers of such languages generally figure only peripherally in such accounts. Instead, it is the languages themselves which are held to be repositories of knowledge and therefore form the prime object of linguists' concerns. For example, the fact that speakers of many 'indigenous' languages are able to name more elements of the natural environment – plants, animals, geographical features, etc. – or draw greater degrees of distinction in describing such objects is construed as a fact about the knowledge contained within their languages rather than a reflection of the typical activities those individuals may seek to integrate linguistically. The language is thereby reified as a 'container' of knowledge and so if the language is lost, the knowledge which inheres in it also supposedly disappears. It is perhaps also worth raising the no doubt provocative issue of whether such a fetishisation of languages over and above individual speakers comprises quite the humanitarian enterprise some language preservationists/revivalists would have us believe. By any measure, the relegation of individuals to the status of mere vehicles for the survival or revival of a language can hardly be said to constitute a form of linguistics in the humanistic tradition.

It is at this point that one is compelled to reflect upon the ontological and epistemological assumptions supporting the view that languages can and indeed do contain knowledge. Firstly, it is clear that such a view must necessarily conceive of languages as fixed codes, that is to say as structured inventories of units or features which are determinate in respect of both form and meaning, knowledge of which is, in theory at least, shared by all members of the linguistic community. Indeed, it is commonly claimed that languages 'encode' knowledge. For instance, Skutnabb-Kangas (2004: 2) writes that '[m]uch of the knowledge about (necessary) elements of integrated ecosystems and the relations between these elements and about how to maintain biodiversity is encoded in small local languages.' Similarly, Grenoble (2011: 37) mentions the 'kinds of world knowledge which languages encode.' How is it that words (and other lexical items) can become conceived as items of knowledge in themselves? What does one know when one knows a word, other than, trivially, the material form of the word itself? From an orthodox linguistic perspective, the answer to such a question again lies in the affirmation of a surrogational-ist semantics, the notion that words stand for objects in the external world. Knowing the word 'haddock' therefore entails knowing what haddock 'really' is. Here the word, there the fish. Nettle and Romaine (2000: 69), for example, nail their surrogationalist colours firmly to the mast when they write that:

> [S]cience is all about naming and categorizing the things we find in the world around us and constructing theories to explain them. Because language does the same sort of thing, we can think of each language as a way of coming to grips with the external world and developing a symbolism to represent it so that it can be talked and thought about.

A language then is thought of essentially as a vast resource for labelling and describing aspects of the external world. Different languages may label the world differently and with greater or lesser degrees of accuracy and distinction, but they nevertheless constitute forms of knowledge of that world. What would be an integrationist response to such arguments? One would begin by pointing out that words are not and cannot be coherently conceived as items of knowledge in themselves. To do so is to treat them as decontextualised abstractions and divorce them from any communicational contexts in which they occur. From an integrationist perspective, 'knowing' a word entails knowing what to do with it, that is to say how to integrate it – whether as the producing or the interpreting party – into a communicational process. Harris (2009b: 162) makes the point that knowledge is not a matter of gaining access to something outside of oneself but is instead generated by the internal, individual human capacity for sign-making, a capacity which is manifestly not predicated on the mental possession of a language in the sense in which it is construed by orthodox linguistics. On the integrationist view, knowledge is a capacity for action and arises from human beings' creative attempts to integrate their various activities via the medium of signs, linguistic or otherwise. It does not reside in the lexicon or grammatical structure of an abstract fixed code which faithfully represents states of affairs in the external world or conceptual schemata in the minds of speakers. Put more succinctly, the integrational theory of the radical indeterminacy of the sign entails that there can be no such thing as decontextualised knowledge. To suppose otherwise is to confuse the sign with its reified physical embodiment and to conflate information and knowledge. As Harris (2009b: 80) notes: 'Just as every sign presupposes a context, every item of knowledge presupposes a context. There are no free-floating, contextless items of knowledge. There are no processes of knowing that exist independently of what is known.' To take an example, the encyclopaedia is not in itself a container of knowledge. Rather, it is a source of information which may give rise to knowledge – in this case a collection of visible marks printed on paper or appearing on a digital screen which may be construed as signs by contextualising humans engaged in some particular integrative sequence of activities. The kinds of activities which are integrated and hence the knowledge which is generated are, however, wholly context dependent. If the print is too small for me to read adequately and it is written in Finnish, the kinds of activities I am able to integrate as a result will be far more limited than a native of Helsinki with better eyesight. The point this trivial example is intended to serve is merely that all knowledge requires contextualisation by an individual knower. Knowledge can therefore be regarded as something which may be generated on the basis of information, information being any elements which have the potential to be 'made signs of'.

To accept the premise that languages themselves contain knowledge necessarily involves conceiving of them as surrogationalist fixed codes which itself involves an act of abstraction and reification. The uniformity of interpretation of their constituent signs across all of their instantiations has to be somehow guaranteed in advance. Knowledge must be coded in the language or else how could it reside there at all? The integrationist answer is that it does not reside there since 'the language' is not a fixed code, a fact which itself calls into serious doubt the ontological status of 'the language' itself. Written metalinguistic documents such as the dictionary and grammar book may foster the idea of the language as a determinate system of form-meaning correspondences and contain information about the putative object, but that does not endow it with any ontologically real status of its own. It merely propagates a metalinguistic illusion.

5. Integrationism and the politics of language

In this section, I consider briefly what role integrational theory might assume, if any, in language-political debates concerning issues such as language loss and linguistic diversity. The matter is far from straightforward. Hutton and Pablé (2013: 36–37) are without doubt correct when they note that integrationism offers no clear 'party line' on issues in the politics of language. It is also certainly difficult to detect any clear political leanings – apart from perhaps a strain of individual libertarianism and a high prioritisation of freedom of speech – let alone specific agenda in the profuse writings of Roy Harris.[13] Nevertheless, it hardly sits comfortably to say that integrationism is apolitical, offering as it does a thoroughgoing ontological critique and deconstruction of the Western 'language myth', a complex of beliefs about language and communication with clear political characteristics and affordances (Hutton, 2011); witness, for example, debates about the role of Standard English, 'global' English, national and minority languages, so-called 'linguistic imperialism', etc., all of which from an integrationist perspective have generally taken place on the basis of the questionable assumption that languages and linguistic communities exist as discrete, identifiable ontological realities. So at least in this rather negative sense then, integrationism obviously has highly political implications through its promotion of intellectual and moral liberation from the language myth. What it does not offer is a specific alternative model of language and society to the one based on the language myth. It is also true that integrational theorists have generally not shown much interest in issues of ethnicity, identity and other abstract categories of social classification which have featured prominently in more mainstream language-political discussions both within and beyond academia.

Could it be that in attacking the language myth so comprehensively integrationism thereby ensures its own peripheral status in language-political debates? Does the adoption of an integra-

---

[13] One exception is Harris' controversial inaugural lecture on taking up his professorship at the University of Hong Kong (Harris, 1989) in which he directly addresses language-political issues concerning the role of English in Hong Kong and surprisingly even advocates the establishment of a Language Planning Centre, although he is quick to reject any suggestion of its being a prescriptive enterprise.

tionist position force one to stand outside of such debates? If one takes the example of linguistic diversity and language loss, it would seem that integrationism and the ontological and epistemological arguments which it advances offer little in the way of succour to vested interests on any side of the mainstream debate in relation to these issues; that is to say, broadly speaking, the related questions of whether linguistic diversity constitutes in itself a positive or negative phenomenon and what, if any, measures should be taken to promote or counter it. The difficulty for integrationism here resides in the fact that the language myth may be just as politically and strategically convenient a fiction – although it is rarely acknowledged as such – for both polity-led homogenising, centralising forces as it is for endangered and minority language movements. Indeed, the latter gain much of their perceived moral force from arguments derived from the language myth; for example, the notion that the loss of a language entails the loss of an associated identity, cultural tradition or repository of irreplaceable knowledge. In this sense then, the language myth also appears to be an opportune emotive peg on which to hang certain 'politically correct' discourses about indigenous communities. Moreover, once communities become defined linguistically (i.e. on the basis of 'a language') and achieve some form of political representation or participation on that basis, it is hardly in their own self-interest to effectively renounce their existence by showing their language (and those of other communities) to be an ontological fiction.

Once the core assumptions of the language myth are accepted as valid on opposing sides of the debate, any approach which calls into question those assumptions can easily be dismissed as irrelevant to the debate, thereby precluding the possibility of mutually engaged discussion and any form of meaningful dialogue. This would appear to resemble the kind of rhetorical impasse in which integrationism finds itself here. With its emphasis on the demythologisation of much prominent Western thinking about language (which brings into question such politically-charged and cherished notions as native speakers, mother tongues, multilingualism, language rights, etc.), the role of individuals as responsibility-bearing language 'makers' as opposed to language 'users' and the importance of lay conceptualisations of language vis-à-vis 'expert' theorising, integrationism might instead be seen as envisaging the basis or at least clearing the theoretical ground for an alternative politics of language.[14] Hutton (2010: 646) makes a similar point, noting that integrationism 'might better be considered as a "metapolitics", in that it opens up the politics of metalanguage, directing our attention to issues of fictionality, reification, and issues of language expertise, ownership and control'. Such a view chimes with the point often made by Roy Harris that integrational linguistics does not represent an attempt to merely patch up the orthodox approach and seek some form of theoretical compromise by ridding it of its more obviously implausible claims, but rather that it represents a fundamentally different and ultimately incompatible perspective on language and its role in human affairs. Does this then ultimately leave the integrationist with nothing consequential to say qua integrationist on the politics of such 'segregational' issues as language endangerment/loss? This might well be the case although it would perhaps be more in line with integrational thinking to leave the question open based on the recognition that each instance of language endangerment/loss will be embedded in a unique mesh of contextualising factors, thus rendering the advancement of any blanket formula to such issues an unwarrantedly essentialist and decontextualised approach. To some this might seem a rather

---

[14] Challenging the common view of integrationism as relentlessly negative in outlook and emphasis, Hutton (2011: 509) detects what he terms 'idealistic – even utopian – tendencies' in the Harrisian/integrationist view of language and society.

unsatisfactory response, a non-committal cop-out, but it is in fact entirely consistent with integrationism's wider scepticism in relation to the locus of expertise in linguistic matters and consequent reluctance to embrace any kind of prescriptive model. As Hutton and Pablé (2013: 37) note:

> [I]ntegrationism is fundamentally suspicious of claims to academic expertise in linguistics being played as a trump card in political debate. It questions the linguist's claim to special authority or scientific expertise, regarding it primarily as an act of self-authentication. In stressing the complexity and intricacy of situated action integrationism would reject any global formula or framework for the politics of language. Of course that rejection is also a political position, paradoxically grounded in a form of 'counter-expertise' about linguistics. Further, integrationism's stress on individual agency, responsibility and experience inevitably takes on a political dimension in particular contexts and rejects what has been called the 'morally purged view of language which orthodox linguistics has given to the world'.

6. Conclusion

The main purpose of the preceding discussion has been to call into question the status and usefulness of the notions of linguistic diversity and language loss/death as descriptive and explanatory concepts in linguistic theory. In terms of a theoretical framework which takes the existence of separate, discretely identifiable linguistic systems (languages, varieties, dialects, other types of 'lect', etc.) as a foundational postulate, such concepts fulfil a self-evident role. A measure of linguistic diversity can (theoretically) be ascertained simply by counting the number of systems identified or determining the degree and type of structural variation within and between such systems. The possibility of identifying elements of linguistic difference is essentially a matter of empirical investigation. A case of language loss/death can then be said to have occurred when any previously identified linguistic system is no longer actively used as a means of communication.

However, as far as an integrational theory of language is concerned, the concepts of linguistic diversity and language loss/death have no role to play. Language, for the integrationist, is inherently diverse and necessarily so since first-order linguistic communication involves the constant creation of contextualised signs and not the deployment of a pre-existing inventory of invariant signs (the fixed code). The notion of first-order linguistic diversity therefore amounts to nothing more than a banal truism. Furthermore, languages cannot be lost or die since ontologically speaking there are no such entities to begin with. Does this mean that all talk of linguistic diversity and language loss/death should be abandoned? No, not necessarily. At least not in lay discourse where it may make perfectly good communicative sense to talk in such terms. What is important though is that the meta-linguistic nature of such concepts is appreciated. As such, they are concepts which are themselves in need of explanation rather than ones which can be deployed as a theoretical basis for explaining actual linguistic phenomena. It is the failure to realise this point which haunts orthodox linguistic theorising on such issues.

Acknowledgements
My thanks to Adrian Pablé and Nigel Love for comments on an earlier version.

References
Austin, Peter K., Sallabank, Julia, 2011. Introduction. In: Austin, Peter K., Sallabank, Julia (Eds.), *The Cambridge Handbook of Endangered Languages.* Cambridge University Press, Cambridge, pp. 1–24.

Blommaert, Jan, 2011. *Supervernaculars and Their Dialects*. King's College London. (*Working Papers in Urban Language and Literacies,* 81)

Crystal, David, 2002. *Language Death*. Cambridge University Press, Cambridge.

De Swaan, Abram, 2004. Endangered languages, sociolinguistics, and linguistic sentimentalism. *European Review* 12 (4), 567–580.

Duncker, Dorthe, 2012. Conventionalization, glossing practices and linguistic (in)determinacy. *Language and Communication* 32, 400–419.

Grenoble, Lenore A., 2011. Language ecology and endangerment. In: Austin, Peter K., Sallabank, Julia (Eds.), *The Cambridge Handbook of Endangered Languages*. Cambridge University Press, Cambridge, pp. 27–44.

Harris, Roy, 1981. *The Language Myth*. Duckworth, London.

Harris, Roy, 1989. 'The worst English in the world?': an inaugural lecture. *University of Hong Kong, Supplement to the Gazette* 16 (1), 37–46.

Harris, Roy, 1990. On redefining linguistics. In: Davis, Hayley G., Taylor, Talbot J. (Eds.), *Redefining Linguistics*. Routledge, London, pp. 18–52.

Harris, Roy, 1996. *The Language Connection: Philosophy and Linguistics*. Thoemmes, Bristol.

Harris, Roy, 1997. From an integrational point of view. In: Love, Nigel, Wolf, George (Eds.), *Linguistics Inside Out: Roy Harris and His Critics*. John Benjamins, Amsterdam, pp. 229–318.

Harris, Roy, 1998. *Introduction to Integrational Linguistics*. Pergamon, Oxford.

Harris, Roy, 2005. *The Semantics of Science*. Continuum, London

Harris, Roy, 2007. Integrational linguistics. In: Verschueren, Jef, Östman, Jan-Ola (Eds.), *Handbook of Pragmatics*. John Benjamins, Amsterdam.

Harris, Roy, 2009a. Implicit and explicit language teaching. In: Toolan, Michael (Ed.), *Language Teaching: Integrational Linguistic Approaches*. Routledge, London, pp. 24–46.
Harris, Roy, 2009b. *After Epistemology*. Gamlingay, Bright Pen.
Harris, Roy, 2012. *Integrating Reality*. Gamlingay, Bright Pen.
Harrison, K. David, 2008. *When Languages Die: The Extinction of the World's Languages and the Erosion of Human Knowledge*. Oxford University Press, Oxford.
Hermann, Jesper, 2007. The 'language' problem. *Language and Communication* 28, 93–99.
Hinton, Leanne, 2001. Language revitalization: an overview. In: Hinton, Leanne, Hale, Ken (Eds.), *The Green Book of Language Revitalization in Practice*. Academic Press, New York, pp. 3–18.
Hutton, Christopher., 1997. The 'dictator of taste': rules. regularities and responsibilities. *Language Sciences* 19, 47–55.
Hutton, Christopher, 2010. Who owns language? Mother tongues as intellectual property and the conceptualization of human linguistic diversity. *Language Sciences* 32, 638–647.
Hutton, Christopher, 2011. The politics of the language myth: reflections on the writings of Roy Harris. *Language Sciences* 33, 503–510.
Jørgensen, Jens Normann, 2008. Polylingual languaging around and among children and adolescents. *International Journal of Multilingualism* 5 (3), 161–176.
Jørgensen, J.N., Karrebæk, M.S., Madsen, L.M., Møller, J.S., 2011. Polylanguaging in superdiversity. *Diversities* 13 (2), 23–38.
Komatsu, Eisuke, Harris, Roy (Eds.), 1993. F. de Saussure. *Troisième Cours de Linguistique Générale (1910–1911)*. Pergamon, Oxford.

Krauss, Michael, 1992. The world's languages in crisis. *Language* 68, 4–10.
Love, Nigel, 2004. Cognition and the language myth. *Language Sciences* 26, 525–544.
Makoni, Sinfree B., 2011. Sociolinguistics, colonial and postcolonial: an integrationist perspective. *Language Sciences* 33 (4), 680–688.
Makoni, Sinfree B., Pennycook, Alastair, 2005. Disinventing and (re)constituting languages. *Critical Inquiry in Language Studies* 2 (3), 137–156.
Mufwene, Salikoko S., 2005. Globalization and the myth of killer languages. In: Huggan, Graham, Klasen, Stephan (Eds.), *Perspectives on Endangerment*. Georg Olms Verlag, Hildesheim/New York, pp. 19–48.
Mühlhäusler, Peter, 2004. Review of Harris, Roy (Ed.), 2002. *The Language Myth in Western Culture*. Curzon Press, London, pp. 227. *Language in Society* 33, 285–288.
Nettle, Daniel, 1996. Language diversity in West Africa: an ecological approach. *Journal of Anthropological Archaeology* 15, 403–438.
Nettle, Daniel, Romaine, Suzanne, 2000. *Vanishing Voices: The Extinction of the World's Languages*. Oxford University Press, Oxford.
Nichols, Johanna, 1989. *Linguistic Diversity in Space and Time*. University of Chicago Press, Chicago.
Orman, Jon, 2012. Not so super: the ontology of 'supervernaculars'. *Language and Communication* 32 (4), 349–357.
Orman, Jon, 2013. New lingualisms, same old codes. *Language Sciences* 37, 90–98.
Owen, Charles, 2009. Integrational linguistics and language teaching. In: Toolan, Michael (Ed.), *Language Teaching: Integrational Linguistic Approaches*. Routledge, London, pp. 156–176.

Pablé, Adrian, 2011. Integrating the 'real'. *Language Sciences* 33 (1), 20–29.
Pablé, Adrian & Chris Hutton. 2013. *Signs, Meaning and Experience. Integrational Approaches to Linguistics and Semiotics.* Berlin: Mouton de Gruyter. (Semiotics, Communication and Cognition, 15)
Romaine, Suzanne, 1994. *Language in Society: An Introduction to Sociolinguistics.* Oxford University Press, Oxford.
Skutnabb-Kangas, Tove, 2000. *Linguistic Genocide in Education, or Worldwide Diversity and Human Rights?* Laurence Erlbaum Associates, Mahwah, NJ.
Skutnabb-Kangas, Tove, 2004. *On Biolinguistic Diversity – Linking Language, Culture and (Traditional) Ecological Knowledge.* Invited Plenary lecture at Department of Linguistics and Philosophy, Universidad Autónoma de Madrid and Cosmocaixa.
Zepeda, Ofelia, Hill, Jane H., 1992. The condition of Native American languages in the United States. In: Robins, Robert H., Uhlenbeck, Eugene M. (Eds.), *Endangered Languages.* Berg, Oxford, pp. 135–156.

גלעד צוקרמן. ישראלית שפה יפה. עם עובד

Zuckermann, Ghil'ad, 2008. [Israelit Safa Yafa (Israeli – A Beautiful Language. Hebrew as Myth)]. Am Oved, Tel Aviv

5.

Things people speak?: a response to Orman's 'Linguistic diversity and language loss a view from integrational linguistics' with rejoinder.
(with Joshua Nash)*

Abstract
This article is presented in two parts. The first is a response to Orman's integrationist critique of orthodox theorising of linguistic diversity and language loss. It asks how integrationist claims might be empiricised and translated into a practical research programme. A discussion of the ontology of Norf'k and the pitfalls of employing metalinguistic terminology is followed by the second part: an argument claiming an integrationist investigation of language loss/death is possible if conceived as a lay-oriented enquiry.

*This article is a response to the immediately preceding essay in this volume.

Joshua Nash[1]

I read with interest Orman's article on linguistic diversity, language loss/death, and integrational linguistics in a recent number of *Language Sciences* (2013, 40). He offers a clear explication of what Harrisian integrationism is in terms of modern linguistic theory and how it deals with its own critique of mainstream linguistics and indeed modern approaches to language documentation and 'saving languages'. However, Orman offers few clues as to what integrationism can do for *things people speak*[2] and any other reified or non-reified ideation of language, or whatever linguists or others choose to label as their "first-order" research object.

While I agree with much of his critique of the mainstream linguistic diversity and language loss/death literature, by focusing on the *not* in his argument (what integrational linguistics is not), I believe Orman has avoided the *is* of his defence. By taking a strongly theoretical and philosophical approach to a historical fiercely practical discipline like linguistic diversity studies and language documentation, it appears he may have thrown out the baby (saving languages and understanding ways of speaking and first-order phenomena) with the bathwater (integrationism's rejecting of the possibility of 'language' and 'a language'; the claim that metalinguistics cannot be culture neutral).

Orman can of course be excused for this – it was not a part of his brief. What remains, and what I was left wondering was:

---

[1] Joshua Nash is the 2013 Bill Cowan Barr Smith Library Fellow at the University of Adelaide. He acknowledges the generous financial support of a Sir Mark Mitchell Research Foundation grant and a J.M. Coetzee Centre for Crea-tive Practice small grant for 2013.

[2] By using this rather inelegant expression, I am avoiding a connection to any Hymsean use of 'ways of speaking' (e.g. Hymes, 1974).

What would a practical and empirical integrationist perspective look like when considering the ontological basis of language and its relationship to aspects of modern language documentation and revival, if indeed such a perspective is congruous or possible? As a linguist with some training in integrational approaches to language (though not necessarily Harrisian integrational linguistics) and ecolinguistics, the empiricisation and description of a few of Orman's integrationist claims would certainly help me, and I would hope other linguists and other scientists, in approaching their 'first-order' object of study. I also hope these descriptions could and would be able to exist aside from any metalinguistic terminology one attaches to these first-order phenomena. My piece will be exploratory and consider the 'things people speak' or 'what people speak' instead of using language or 'way of speaking' to make sense of Orman's argument and a possible empiricisation of integrationism vis-à-vis studies in linguistic diversity and language loss.

Norf'k is what the descendants of the *Bounty* mutineers speak on Norfolk Island, South Pacific (see Mühlhäusler, 2011 for historical and linguistic details). What Norf'k is, whether it is an indigenous language, or indeed a language at all is far from clear. Whatever it may be, it has been recognised as an endangered language by UNESCO (2007). I have worked on Norfolk Island and Norf'k for more than 7 years. I have heard people speak Norf'k, a 'thing people speak' distinctly different from other 'things people speak' in Australia, New Zealand, and New Caledonia, the closest inhabited neighbours to Norfolk Island. Norf'k has had many names, many positive and negative interpretations, and which only seem to make sense when spoken in the ecology where it was introduced and continued to develop – Norfolk Island. I have recently published a documentary account of Norfolk Island placenames (Nash, 2013), wherein I describe how arriving at an understanding of the situatedness and ecological embeddedness of Norfolk toponyms is crucial to appreciating not necessarily what the Norf'k *is*, or how Norf'k can be characterised, but more so how important toponyms are to understanding the *nature* of what Norf'k is and how Norf'k *works* linguistically, socially, and ecologically.

While I do not label my approach to this understanding of toponymy and language documentation integrationist by any means, an ecolinguistic analysis of toponyms and other linguistic and non-linguistic artefacts (words, expressions, other verbal and non-verbal behaviours) considers the elements (and even non-elements) of the contextualisations of things people speak which integrational linguists like Harris and Orman espouse. My collection, analysis, and interpretation of Norfolk toponyms in terms of Norf'k and English on Norfolk Island have, in a similar way to Orman, led me to conclude:

> Does this then ultimately leave the integrationist with nothing consequential to say qua integrationist on the politics of such 'segregational' issues as language endangerment/ loss? This might well be the case although it would perhaps be more in line with integrational thinking to leave the question open based on the recognition that each instance of language endangerment/loss will be embedded in a unique mesh of contextualising factors, thus rendering the advancement of any blanket formula to such issues an unwarrantedly essentialist and decontextualised approach. (Orman, 2013: 9)

The Norf'k situation is a single case and possibly not applicable to other situations. My Norfolk research has led me to two scientific and personal realisations:

1. "What Norf'k is typologically does not affect how Norf'k is used in Norfolk toponymy" (Nash, 2013: 24).

2. There is a strong requirement to look at the role of singular cases in measuring and theorising about how people speak rather than striving to arrive at universalist or generalisable claims about the nature of language, ways of speaking, and human communication and/in context, whatever these concepts may mean or how they are managed.

Such an approach may be 'conclusion poor' but it may actually get us closer to understanding and approaching what our research object, way of speaking, or language we are observing (or partici-pating in, or are a part of, or contextualising through our meta-linguistic terminology) actually is.

Before inviting Orman to respond I would like to reflect on some of his claims to speculate about an answer myself. What are linguists (or anyone) to do to avoid a "non-committal cop-out" (Orman, 2013: 9), regardless of whether action is "entirely consistent with integrationism's wider scepticism in relation to the locus of expertise in linguistic matters and consequent reluctance to embrace any kind of prescriptive model"? Orman is clear about what integrationism's position is on the politics of language: "What it does not offer is a specific alternative model of language and society to the one based on the language myth". He also concedes "integrational theorists have generally not shown much interest in issues of ethnicity, identity and other abstract categories of social classification which have featured prominently in more mainstream language-political discussions both within and beyond academia".

It is essential for us to ask a few clear questions regarding linguistic diversity and language loss. First, do we speak (or communicate or make utterances or open our mouths)? If yes, do we also agree there are many varieties of how people speak (or what-ever an integrationist would call them)? If yes, what are we to do with them, especially if people have political, social, and emotional motivation to continue speaking these things? Does it really matter whether we use the labels language, a language, ways of speaking, codes, or modes of communication when there is 'language work' to be done, however this is to be conceived or perceived philosophically? Despite the structuralist or any of the other –ist/–ism tendencies of most linguists engaging in language documentation and theorising about language loss as Orman claims, some language (or things people speak?) work is being done. Only time will tell whether such methods and theoretical outcomes are good or bad, successful or unsuccessful, and applicable to linguistic theory and language philosophy or not. My question to Orman is, and I ask not in a hostile tone rather with a spirit of optimism and an invitation for a response: How can integrational linguistics contribute to practical and empirical work into maintaining linguistic diversity? If it does not contribute in any tangible way, this would appear as good place as any to make this explicit. I wish to invite Orman to explicate, at least briefly, what in his terms an integrationist empiricisation of the claims he presented in his paper dealing with linguistic diversity and language loss may be. Orman gives some hints at what his answer would be:

> Does this mean that all talk of linguistic diversity and language loss/death should be abandoned? No, not necessarily. At least not in lay discourse where it may make perfectly good communicative sense to talk in such terms.

I am interested to know what a practical answer to this question 'at most' instead of 'at least' is or would be and indeed what it may, might, or should necessarily entail. No doubt metalinguistic terminology is always inadequate to talk about and describe the varied 'first-order things people speak' or 'speaking continua' (or whatever integrationists wish to call them) which exist on our planet. If we appreciate and concede that we are always restricted by our metalinguistic terminology and notions of 'language' and 'a language', then what can integrational linguistics qua Harris and Orman offer our understanding and appreciation that people want to 'preserve' or 'continue' how they speak and what they speak?

In offering an integrationist position, Orman notes an important point for the ontology of any scientific discipline:

> A science needs to meet the minimal requirement of having reliable criteria for demonstrating that two things are the same or different and criteria for saying whether one is dealing with one or two objects. (Mühlhäusler 2004: 286)

While I believe Orman has reliably demonstrated how integrationism and traditional approaches to linguistic diversity and language loss are different, he has not adequately shown how the traditional approach and any integrational approach is or would be a new approach (i.e. there would now be two approaches instead of one).

References
Hymes, Dell, 1974. Ways of speaking. In: Bauman, R., Sherzer, J. (Eds.), *Explorations in the Ethnography of Speaking*. Cambridge University Press, Cambridge, pp. 433–451.
Mühlhäusler, Peter, 2011. Some notes on the ontology of Norf'k. *Language Sciences* 33 (4), 673–679.
Mühlhäusler, Peter, 2004. Review of Harris, Roy, (Ed.), 2002, *The language myth in western culture*. *Language in Society* 33, 285–288.
Nash, Joshua, 2013. *Insular Toponymies: Place-naming on Norfolk Island, South Pacific and Dudley Peninsula, Kangaroo Island*. John Benjamins, Amsterdam & Philadelphia.
Orman, Jon, 2013. Linguistic diversity and language loss: a view from integrational linguistics. *Language Sciences* 40, 1-11.
UNESCO, 2007. *Degree of Endangerment of the Norf'k Language (Norfolk Island, South Pacific)*. Ms.

Reply to Nash
Jon Orman

Nash's amicable and welcome response to my article raises a familiar complaint levelled against integrational linguistics, namely that it fails to provide an alternative empirical and practical research programme to the orthodox approaches which it subjects to such thoroughgoing theoretical critique (see, for example, Fleming, 1997). I am quite happy to concede that my paper neglects to do this since, as Nash is good enough to point out, it was not my primary purpose. He therefore invites me to spell out how integrationist claims might be empiricised in order to investigate linguistic diversity and instances of language loss. Now, although I do believe there is a way in which such issues can be approached from an integrationist perspective, I am not convinced that Nash is going to find what I have to say in this regard altogether satisfactory. In particular, I am not sure he will find the approach I propose sufficiently empirical or data-oriented and I will certainly stop short of providing the kind of positivist methodology he seems to be seeking, the reasons for which I will set out in due course.

Firstly, however, I would like to comment on a number of other points raised in Nash's response. Nash wonders what a practical and empirical integrationist approach to language documentation and language revival might look like. The short answer is that there is no such approach. From an integrationist perspective, the notions of language documentation or language description already beg fundamental theoretical questions, namely that there are such ontologically real entities as languages which can be neatly circumscribed and described. Language documentation is therefore not merely the 'fiercely practical' discipline he describes it as. The whole enterprise comes with a series of in-built and deeply problematic segregationist theoretical assumptions and indeed its products (descriptions of languages) are nothing more than an artefact of those assumptions. Just as there is no integrational syntax, phonology, morphology or semantics to rival orthodox approaches, there is also no integrational language documentation. This inevitably follows from the integrationist conception of the linguistic sign as radically indeterminate. No determinate sign, no determinate system of signs. What an integrationist perspective instead offers is the possibility of an alternative understanding of what is going on when 'a language' is documented, namely a form of metalinguistic systematisation rather than a description of some empirical first-order linguistic reality. Now, this is not to deny that there may be some viable or useful purposes (e.g. pedagogical) for producing metalinguistic systematisations. The integrationist point however is that those engaged in such initiatives ought at least to understand the nature of the activity they are undertaking and this cannot be achieved on the basis of an adherence to a segregational view of language and communication.

    In relation to his own research on Norfolk Island, it is apparent that Nash agonises somewhat over the ontological status of his object of study, Norf'k. He is reluctant to affirm Norf'k as a language or even a variety and settles on describing it as a 'thing people speak'. The initial concern here is that labelling Norf'k as a 'thing' suggests we are dealing with some kind of real-world object or reified entity. From the point of view of integrational theory, however, there are no linguistic objects. Consequently, the term 'way of speaking' may be preferable on this count, although Nash is quite right in wanting to avoid any association with the Hymsean notion of 'ways of speaking' which is still very much based on a segregationist conception of the linguistic sign. Whatever formulation one decides on, the next and more important question which then arises is what kind of theoretical load one is to attach to it. If it is held to refer to some determinate phenomenon objectively identifiable by the linguist on the basis of structural criteria, then it would seem to have little more to recommend it than the term 'a language'. The indeterminacy of what Norf'k is (or indeed any language, dialect, way of speaking, etc.) is a simple corollary of the indeterminacy of the linguistic sign, which is the foundational principle of an integrational philosophy of language. One can certainly accept that Norf'k may be recognised by both islanders and outsiders as a thing that is spoken or a way of speaking, etc. For the integrationist, however, the key point is that what that thing actually constitutes is a question which must be left open-ended since it will always be subject to varying contextualisation by different individuals in different circumstances. There is consequently no guarantee of absolute consensus on the matter. As Mühlhäusler (2011: 678) has noted:

> There is little agreement as to what the language actually is. It has proven very difficult for linguists to draw a boundary between Norf'k and colloquial English and Norfolk Islanders are often unsure whether an expression such as *jump dar fence* 'to have extramarital relations' is an English expression or a Norf'k one.

This, from an integrationist viewpoint, is just what one would expect. It is only in the idealised homogenous speech community postulated by orthodox linguistics that one would expect to find absolute consensus about what belongs to the language and what does not. However, no such communities exist and the linguist is in no position to supply a better or more correct answer to the question of what actually constitutes any community's language, even less so one would imagine in those cases where the community in question can hardly even be said to possess the concept of 'a language'. To loosely paraphrase Roy Harris' famous remark from *The Language Makers*, one could say that Norfolk Islanders have the only concept of Norf'k worth having, which is not to say that all islanders have the same concept of Norf'k. Now, what that concept is, how that concept varies between islanders, how that concept varies circumstantially and over time and whether there are even some islanders who lack such a concept are all matters for empirical investigation which can be conducted without succumbing to any segregational assumptions. As Roy Harris states on his personal website[3]:

> What particular language (or variety of a language) individuals regard themselves or others as speaking is a question open to empirical research. This is research into the popular use of language-names and descriptions (such as English, Glaswegian, Cockney, slang, etc.). The answer will vary in different cases. It cannot be answered in advance by postulating that every such designation corresponds to some specific system of linguistic 'rules', of which the speakers themselves may be only dimly or unconsciously aware. That is neither a 'scientific' nor even a plausible assumption.

In other words, an integrationist approach to the issue will seek to discover how individual speakers construe and make sense of their own linguistic experience in terms of the metalinguistic labels and categories they apply. As far as language loss/death, language shift or linguistic diversity are concerned, any integrationist study must also take place on the same basis, that is to say as an investigation into the extent to which and the manner in which such notions are a reality for lay speakers and the consequences thereof. Certainly, no integrationist would seek to deny that many individuals and communities do indeed find themselves in situations in which they articulate experiences of and thoroughgoing concerns about language loss and language death. However from an integrationist point of view the notions of language loss/ death and language shift, like language change, are not empirical

---

[3] http://www.royharrisonline.com

phenomena in the way they uncontroversially are for the structural linguist. They are instead explanatory attempts to account for certain perceived differences in macrosocial linguistic behaviour over time. As Harris (2003: 50) notes, the mistake of orthodox linguistics is to treat such notions as theoretical postulates when they are instead themselves in need of explanation, i.e. confusing an *explicans* with an *explicandum*. This has the result of obscuring from view the communicational processes which give rise to those notions in the first place.

An integrational approach to such segregationist topics as linguistic diversity and language loss is therefore possible if conceived as a lay-oriented enquiry. As for a research programme and methodology, this I am reluctant to supply and believe it is a question best left open and up to the individual researcher. As Harris (1997: 304) observes, in stipulating a precise methodology one risks merely producing an analysis which reveals and confirms nothing more than theoretical assumptions built into the methodological procedure. However, for an example of how an integrationist study of lay metalinguistic knowledge might be conducted, see Davis (1997).

Nash asks whether integrational linguistics can make any contribution to practical and empirical work into maintaining linguistic diversity. It is important to remind oneself that the notion of linguistic diversity plays no role in an integrationist account of first-order linguistic behaviour. The kind of linguistic diversity Nash has in mind is, as I explain in the article, for the integrationist a form of *meta*linguistic diversity predicated upon the use of different language names. An integrationist in flippant mood might say that if Norfolk Islanders wish to ensure the survival of Norf'k they should continue to insist that whatever they speak is Norf'k and just is different from Colloquial English or Standard English, etc. After all, from an integrationist perspective, who is the linguist or indeed any outsider to argue? The metalinguistic diversity will thereby be preserved. Obviously, such an argument is not likely to prove particularly satisfactory to anyone concerned but it highlights the theoretical point that the survival of a language ultimately depends on the survival of its metalinguistic label. Can integrationism provide any sort of methodology or practical programme in order to ensure the continuation of linguistic practices which give rise to the use of particular metalinguistic labels? No, I rather doubt it and indeed it would seem well beyond its theoretical remit to do so. It must be remembered that integrationism is at base a semiological theory offering an alternative account of what goes on in first-order communication. It offers an opportunity for understanding and the demythologisation of the metalinguistic practices of both lay people and 'expert' linguists. Whether one ultimately comes to accept or reject the integrationist account is another matter.

Nash wonders whether all this theorising and philosophising is really necessary or helpful when there is apparently so much 'language work' to be done. My answer is that it is unavoidable if a fuller understanding of the relevant issues is to be achieved. After all, there is no ontologically neutral language work. Any account one gives of linguistic phenomena implies a certain view of language and of languages. To take up Nash's question, I would therefore argue that it does matter in what terms we, as linguists, choose to describe linguistic phenomena. Certainly, from an integrationist perspective there is no theoretical justification for using such positively misleading terms as 'code'. The theoretical dimension of linguists' work 'in the field' is inherent and inescapable however practically-minded it may appear for the simple fact that there is no objective vantage point from which linguistic facts can be established. Eventually, the language revivalist or documenter must be confronted with the question of what exactly it is that s/he is attempting to revive or document. A determinate, real-world, empirically verifiable object or a meta-linguistic extrapolation from a language name? For integrationists, the answer is clear. One wonders though whether language revival or preservation activists would espouse their cause with quite such fervency if they believed all they were seeking to secure was the continued use of a metalinguistic label. It is therefore unsurprising that they would appear to count very few integrationists amongst their number.

An integrationist might also wonder whether all this 'language work' (documentation, revival, preservation, etc.) deemed so necessary is anything more than a mere artefact of the theoretical assumptions of the orthodox linguist. This is of course not to deny that communities may wish to document and preserve what they regard as their language, dialect, way of speaking, etc and undertake endeavours to do so. The question is what role the linguist ought to assume vis-à-vis such activities. Should the linguist be an active participant in such initiatives or merely an observer? This inevitably raises questions of politics, morality and responsibility. Harris (1997: 309) makes the following pertinent and provocative observation:

> As some linguists have learned to their cost, "collecting data" and "writing grammars of the local language" are not always regarded by suspicious foreign governments or populations as the innocent occupations those bland descriptions suggest. But the fact that missionary linguists sometimes end up in tribal cooking pots is no more surprising than the fact that even well-trained troops end up as casualties. This is simply the sharp end of a reminder to the effect that there is no such thing as a socially neutral professional linguistics, any more than there is a socially neutral professional militarism.

In talking of tribal cooking pots Harris' is obviously playing a strong rhetorical card but his point is nevertheless valid. Who decides what 'language work' is to be done and for what purpose? The orthodox linguist on the basis of his/her prior theoretical, methodological and socio-political assumptions or the communities and individuals concerned? If the linguist is to avoid polluting his/her subsequent account with such assumptions, then s/he has no option but to base it on the manner in which such communities and individuals articulate their linguistic experience through the deployment of their own metalinguistic terminology and categorisations. In other words, adopting an integrational approach requires the linguist to take the seemingly paradoxical and perhaps unwelcome step of renouncing his/her *a priori* claim to expertise in matters linguistic.

References

Davis, Hayley, 1997. Ordinary people's philosophy: comparing lay and professional metalinguistic knowledge. *Language Sciences* 19 (1), 33–46.

Fleming, David, 1997. Is ethnomethodological conversational analysis an 'integrational' account of language? In: Wolf, George, Love, Nigel (Eds.), *Linguistics Inside Out: Roy Harris and His Critics*. John Benjamins, Amsterdam, pp. 182–207.

Harris, Roy, 1997. From an integrational point of view. In: Wolf, George, Love, Nigel (Eds.), *Linguistics Inside Out: Roy Harris and His Critics*. John Benjamins, Amsterdam, pp. 229–318.

Harris, Roy, 2003. On redefining linguistics. In: Davis, Hayley G., Taylor, Talbot J. (Eds.), *Redefining Linguistics*. Routledge, London, pp. 17–68.

Mühlhäusler, Peter, 2011. Some notes on the ontology of Norf'k. *Language Sciences* 33, 673–679.

6.

Indeterminacy in sociolinguistic and integrationist theory

Introduction

In this chapter, I discuss and contrast the manner in which the notion of *indeterminacy* is theorised in contemporary sociolinguistics and integrational linguistics. It is an exercise which reveals some telling theoretical differences, most notably with regard to the respective approaches' appraisal of and reliance upon traditional structuralist-descriptive linguistics. While integrational linguistics' recognition of the radical indeterminacy of language (i.e. indeterminacy of form *and* meaning) entails an emphatic and unambiguous rejection of the theoretical basis of orthodox linguistics, as well as an acceptance that such recognition makes any form of data-driven empirical enquiry into language highly problematic, modern sociolinguistics' readiness to acknowledge only a much weaker form of indeterminacy also enables it to claim rhetorical and methodological reconciliation, symbiosis even, with linguistics. Indeed, my claim is that despite ostensibly rejecting some of its fundamental assumptions, contemporary sociolinguistic approaches (which may be labelled variously as 'postmodern', 'poststructuralist' or 'ethnographic') actually need traditional linguistics, or at least certain principles and techniques derived from it, far more than some of their proponents are willing to acknowledge. The basic reason is that linguistics provides an essential source of determinacy in data description and analysis which enables sociolinguistics to maintain its historical disciplinary identity as a positivist-empirical form of enquiry. Forms of linguistic enquiry with such an *a priori* methodological commitment cannot in practice afford to countenance the integrationist principle of the radical indeterminacy of the linguistic sign. However, as I shall argue, in attempting to cherry-pick from orthodox linguistics only what it requires to sustain itself methodologically, contemporary sociolinguistics ends up in a theoretical morass of its own making.

(In)determinacy and linguistic science
Historically linguistics has had an uneasy time reconciling itself to any suggestion of indeterminacy in linguistic phenomena. This is in no small measure a result of the specific circumstances surrounding its rise and self-perpetuation as a modern academic discipline. From Saussure onwards, the dominant assumption that it is both desirable and necessary for linguistics to be a science of language has largely overridden any tendencies towards sustained reflection and scepticism on the question of whether language is actually amenable to scientific investigation (Wittgenstein's later work, especially that of the *Philosophical Investigations*, may be seen as a notable exception to this tendency). This has had inevitable consequences for the types of definition of language adopted since the perceived necessity to establish a science could only permit definitions of a certain sort. Language, it should be

remembered, is a concept which far pre-dates that of science and as the history of linguistic thought both ancient and modern has shown, it is also a notoriously heterogeneous and mutable one. However, if one was to have a genuine science of language, it could no longer continue to be conceptualised and defined in a vague, open-ended manner. To render language suitable for scientific enquiry, the concept would have to be scientised, i.e. rendered determinate (and ahistorical), since a science of indeterminate phenomena borders on the oxymoronic. Enter Saussure and synchronic structuralism. Indeed, one can observe as the defining feature of structuralism as a theory of language its postulation of absolute determinacy in the putative object of investigation, a move which has been an important ingredient in lending whatever plausibility there has ever been deemed to be in modern linguistics' rhetorical self-presentation as a genuine 'science of language'. Any threat to the determinacy of language would seem to be a threat to the very status of linguistics as a science. For structuralist linguistics therefore, whether in its Saussurean, behaviourist or Chomskyan guise, any acknowledgment of indeterminacy in the make-up of the linguistic sign or the language system has been theoretically inadmissible.

An important point to emphasise, however, is that the postulation of objective determinacy in language is in the end nothing more than a theoretical artifact. As Harris (1983:x) points out, Saussure himself readily acknowledged that an all-encompassing science of language that incorporated physiological, psychological, sociological and philosophical aspects was an unwieldy impossibility. He also recognised that there were no linguistic objects out there in the world awaiting discovery which could go on to form the self-evident focus of a science of language, hence the famous dictum that in linguistics 'it is the viewpoint adopted which creates the object'. However, this did not lead Saussure to conclude that a science of language was a non-starter but merely that a science of language could not produce a comprehensive account of all of language (whatever that might turn out to be) with its many different and disparate aspects which were beyond the purview of a single discipline. The object of linguistic science, then, would have to receive a pared-down, technical definition which would produce a determinate and manageable object of study and that object was to be linguistic structure or *langue* since 'linguistic structure seems to be the one thing that is independently definable and provides something our minds can satisfactorily grasp' (Saussure, 1983:9). For Saussure *langue* was an internally structured system or network of determinate bi-planar signs and the only proper subject matter of a scientifically-oriented linguistics. Yet he was also quick to point out that linguistic structure is not isomorphic with language, rather it is 'only one part of language, even though it is an essential part'. The legitimacy of this theoretical move by Saussure rests on the validity of his contention that linguistic structure is independently definable (i.e. objectively identifiable) and graspable as such by the human mind. If this turns out not to be the case, the prospects for a *bona fide* science of language based on the analysis of linguistic structure look dire indeed. Saussure, however, does not trouble himself to argue a case for the alleged independently definable nature of linguistic structure. Rather, he simply postulates it and insists upon it. However, as integrationists and many others have repeatedly argued, it is a highly questionable postulate based on the ultimately untenable notion that linguistic structure is a communal fixed code determinate in respect of both form and meaning, a position which is an inevitable corollary of adopting an equally ill-founded telementational view of communication (Toolan, 1997). Saussure's object for his science of language is not a product or finding of science or even of common-or-garden observation but one conjured up through speculative metaphysics, partly in an attempt to rectify the fallacy of nomenclaturism in linguistic theory. The object thus conjured does not belong to the realm of ontological *realia* but is instead a reification ensuing from an *a priori* commitment to a particular epistemological framework and methodology.

Saussure was at least open about what he was up to in removing the term 'language' from its everyday use and assigning it a specialised, reduced, technical definition: 'Our definition of a language assumes that we disregard everything which does not belong to its structure as a system; in short everything that is designated by the term "external linguistics"' (Saussure, 1983: 21). Saussure's scientism also stops short of regarding those aspects which fall outside the bounds of his narrowly defined linguistic science as unworthy of the scholar's consideration. He notes for instance that '[e]xternal linguistics is none the less concerned with important matters, and these demand attention when one approaches the study of language' (Saussure, 1983:21) and goes on to discuss the various kinds of political, social, cultural and institutional issues with which an external linguistics might concern itself. In this respect at least, it could be argued that Saussure's theorising is well in advance of his generativist successors whose conception of language, at least in its earliest incarnations, barely permitted any acknowledgement that there might be any linguistic phenomena of interest beyond their own hypothetical, idealised accounts of abstract syntactic structure.

Saussure's view of language and the goal of linguistics was to prove highly influential on so-called 'first wave' sociolinguistics and especially the work of Labov. Figueroa (1994:75) rightly notes that 'Labovian sociolinguistics may be defined as conforming strongly to a particular reading of Saussure'. As she goes on to clarify, this reading consists in the affirmation of the idea that 'the locus of language is in the community and that *langue* is a social fact which determines/constrains language behaviour.' Furthermore, for Labov the ultimate purpose of linguistics is to identify and describe the linguistic facts which make up the *langue* of the speech community in question. The epistemological and methodological consequence of this commitment is signalled by his assertion that 'the general program of all linguists begins with the search for invariants' (Labov, 1975: 7). In other words, even in a sociolinguistics ostensibly interested in making sense of the observable truism of variation and difference in language, the primary aim is still to uncover the fixed system or set of features believed to underlie said variation. Indeed, Labov's greatest – and arguably insurmountable – theoretical challenge is still the same one which besets sociolinguistics today. The more interesting metatheoretical question is whether it is a challenge which needs to be taken seriously in the first place.

Contemporary sociolinguistics and orthodox linguistic theory: a relationship of critical (inter)dependence?
The nature of the relationship between traditional structuralist linguistics and contemporary ethnographically-inspired sociolinguistics is an intriguing, complex and perhaps even contentious one. Given the size and diversity of the field of modern sociolinguistics in terms of both practitioners and topical focus, it is perhaps unwise and also unproductive to formulate too many catch-all generalisations about the discipline. However, certain generalisations are possible at the level of fundamental theory. For example, it is, I think, uncontroversial to assert that, unlike integrational linguistics, sociolinguistics in any of its current guises does not amount to an all-out rejection of the structuralism of traditional linguistics. Whatever it is, poststructuralism is most definitely not anti-structuralism. Indeed, in what amounts to an explicit acknowledgement of modern sociolinguistics' continuing reliance on certain of the methods and assumptions of traditional descriptive linguistics, Rampton et al. (2014:2-3) note that:

> - it is possible to isolate and abstract structural patterns in the ways in which people communicate, and that many of

these patterns are relatively stable, recurrent and socially shared [...]
- there is a wide range of quite well-established procedures for isolating and identifying these structures
- that the description and analysis of these patterns benefits from the use of technical vocabularies and
- that although there is certainly much more involved in human communication, these technical vocabularies can make a valuable contribution to our understanding of the highly intricate processes involved when people talk, sign, read, write or otherwise communicate.

For those unsure of where the key theoretical differences lie between modern sociolinguistics and integrationism, the above passage and indeed Rampton et al.'s paper as a whole makes for instructive and illuminating reading (assuming one has a basic grasp of integrationism). Of particular interest in the present context is the self-serving manner in which they present their view of the relationship between traditional linguistics and their own brand of sociolinguistic ethnography. Despite previous magnanimous talk of 'tying ethnography down and opening linguistics up' (Rampton et al., 2004), on reading the 2014 paper one comes away with the strong impression that it is only through its subordinate incorporation into ethnography that orthodox linguistics can possibly find redemption and salvation from the increasingly acknowledged implausibility of its scientific claims to analytical objectivity and explanatory adequacy. They note, for example, that:

> Before, ethnography could simply be seen as an additional method of data-collection, supplementing the otherwise standard procedures of elicitation and analysis in linguistic science. But as we become more conscious of the social and historical particularity of knowledge, ethnography

gains foundational weight as a way of seeing, building on dialogue and on a reflexive recognition of the researcher's own positioning. Instead, it is linguistics that becomes the operational resource, prized for its capacity to spotlight even the very smallest moves in the practical negotiation of social relations, but no longer revered as the path from interpretation to objective science. At the same time, perhaps somewhat paradoxically, this decline in the epistemological authority of linguistics opens the door to fuller interdisciplinary engagement. (Rampton et al., 2014:5)

Linguistics, it would seem, needs to know its new place in the new epistemological order and that place is in the service of – what appears an admittedly benevolent – prior ethnography. Such claims are likely to leave most unreformed linguists of the old school for whom ethnography only ever figured dimly, if at all, on the disciplinary horizon either bemused or unmoved, perhaps both. This would clearly include most 'first-wave' sociolinguists who were never particularly interested in documenting the 'very smallest moves' in social relations anyway. There is, after all, the possibility of an alternative take on this issue, namely that the relationship of dependence postulated by Rampton et al. is in fact quite the reverse of what they claim it to be. In other words, it is ethnography, or at least linguistic ethnography, which actually needs traditional linguistics rather than the other way round. Some evidence for this claim might seem to be found in the remarkably strong continuity of conceptual terminology between the latest wave of sociolinguistics and previous, more traditional forms. It is interesting to note that alongside some of the much-hyped terminological innovations such as *superdiversity, supervernaculars, crossing, late modernity, polylanguaging, translanguaging* etc. one still encounters frequent reference to and important emphasis laid upon concepts such as *register, genre, indexicality, style, dialect, variety, (total) linguistic facts, linguis-*

tic features, units, languages and, perhaps most unforgivably, *code(-switching)* (see Orman, 2012; 2013; Orman and Pablé, 2015, for discussions). One obvious question which arises in this context is that of just how theoretically progressive or revolutionary all this new, shinily packaged sociolinguistic work actually is (see Pavlenko, 2018, for an uncompromising and incisive critique). Another is the question of why it is that so much of this work continues to rely heavily on traditional structural linguistics when it comes to the analysis of data. The following passage from Creese (2010:139) offers a highly revealing insight in this regard:

> Linguistic ethnography conjoins two fields of study arguing that there is more to be gained in their unison than in their separation. Ethnography is said to be enhanced by the detailed technical analysis which linguistic [sic] brings, while linguistics is said to be enhanced by attention to context. Ethnography offers linguistics a non-deterministic perspective on data, while linguistics offers ethnography a range of established procedures for identifying discursive structures […] [L]inguistics provides an authoritative analysis of language use not typically available through participant observation and the taking of fieldnotes.

In other words, while ethnography purportedly offers linguistics something it has arguably never wanted – indeed modern linguistics only ever took the form it did by taking a resolutely deterministic perspective on data – linguistics provides ethnography with exactly what it requires in order to establish its credentials as a data-driven form of empirical enquiry, namely a source of determinacy or rather a set of procedures for establishing determinacy of structure in its data, the very same data which at the same time somehow apparently also offers linguistics a source of indeterminacy. Without the determinacy provided by linguistics, the desired methodology and epistemological framework of sociolinguistic ethnography, *qua* positivist-empirical investigation into language, collapses. The most remarkable aspect of Creese's statement, however, is her claim that linguistics offers an authoritative, by which she presumably also means comprehensive, account of both language structure *and* language use. This will no doubt come as a surprise to all those linguists who were only ever concerned with analyzing linguistic structure and cared little or not at all for how language was actually used in real-life communication. However, Creese also seems to be saying that linguistics can account for language *use* without any attention to context since it is apparently the job of ethnography to provide any contextual reading going. Linguistics, then, would at best seem to provide an analysis of decontextualised language use. Unfortunately, the problem is that there is no such thing as decontextualised language *use*. One is therefore forced to conclude either (i) that linguistics cannot offer any account of language in context in which case it would seem to be of very little help in understanding communication or (ii) that context is not really so important after all. Neither conclusion is a particularly attractive option for the sociolinguistic ethnographer.

However, if, for the sake of argument, we grant Creese's claim regarding linguistics, one is then compelled to raise the awkward question of what exactly the point or use is of ethnography in elucidating language use. If participant observation and fieldnotes cannot, as Creese clearly seems to recognise, tell us anything substantive about language beyond the researcher's own – no doubt theoretically motivated – interpretations, why do *linguistic* ethnography at all? If linguistics provides us with an exhaustive account of both linguistic structure and use, does not ethnography become a superfluous irrelevance or, at best, mere window-dressing? Far from linguistics needing ethnography, sociolinguistic ethnography, it seems, cannot do without linguistics. Why is this the case? A great deal seems to hang on the assumption that linguistics somehow has the tools and onto-epistemological framework to offer an objective account of what is going on in particular interactions. There appears to be a recognition of the brutal fact that no amount of increasingly 'thick' ethnographic description can ever overcome the subjectivity of the researcher. This is clearly not a happy state of affairs for a discipline which wants to conduct empirical investigations based on real-world data. Hammersley (2007:693) acknowledges this point directly when he writes that 'without linguistics, ethnographic accounts will be speculative'. Sociolinguistics clearly aspires to be something more than an exercise in ethnographic hermeneutics.

So can linguistics rescue ethnography from mere impressionistic anecdotism and speculative interpretation by providing an epistemologically authoritative analysis of determinate linguistic data? Needless to say, from an integrationist perspective to subscribe to the view that it can is to fall victim hook, line and sinker to the 'language myth' (Harris, 1981). However, it also points to some crucial internal inconsistencies in the sociolinguistic-ethnographic position, in particular with respect to the ontological status of languages. Now, if linguistics takes anything at all for granted it is that languages exist. This is fully in line with Saussure's original, discipline-founding dictum that '[p]our la linguistique, c'est bien le fait primordial que la diversité des langues'. The descriptions offered by linguistics are therefore descriptions of languages conceived of as ontologically-real, first-order structural systems. These are points which immediately put any such descriptive linguistics squarely at odds with those numerous contemporary sociolinguists who claim that there really are no such thing as languages *qua* ontological realia (e.g. Makoni and Pennycook, 2005; Pennycook, 2007). If it is the case, then, that descriptive linguists are describing things which literally do not exist, one wonders why so many sociolinguists are still nevertheless anxious to recognise linguistics' capacity to offer authoritative accounts of linguistic structure and use. There is surely more to it than a perverse admiration for the ability to describe theoretically misleading metalinguistic abstractions using an arcane terminology. Something here does not quite add up. Some might retort here by arguing that, rather than describing languages, linguistics is of great use in describing and analyzing the individual 'bits of languages' (Blommaert, 2010:106) or the free-floating, 'languageless' structures and features which appear in socio-linguists' data (see Jørgensen et al., 2011, for such an argument). However, this is a theoretical move which fails utterly. As far as the descriptive linguist is concerned, there are no languageless linguistic features. Such features are irredeemably language-bound in a structural-systemic sense, not merely index-ically or ideologically. Indeed, the fact that languages may also be 'ideological objects' insofar as people may believe they exist is, strictly speaking, irrelevant to the concerns of a descriptive linguistics. What sociolinguistics does not adequately explain, however, is why it is that linguistic features and structures are apparently real and a worthy object of description but languages (linguistic systems) are not since from the point of view of descriptive linguistics the two are inseparable. One cannot have one without the other. They stand or fall together. From an integrational perspective, the idea of determinate linguistic features with a stable, situation-transcending identity is no less an illusion of structuralist linguistics than that of the determinate linguistic systems to which they allegedly belong. They too are metalinguistic abstractions. In the same way as there are no such things as languages, there are also no such things as linguistic features. As Pablé and Hutton (2015:24) put it: 'Communication is not the contextual deployment of abstractions'.

Contemporary sociolinguistics is therefore in the curious and ultimately incoherent position of denying the fundamental postulate of linguistics while simultaneously lauding its ability to provide authoritative analyses of linguistic data. However much one finesses it, this is ultimately a case of trying to have things both ways and suggests a fundamental theoretical crisis at the core of the discipline. Yet it is one which goes all but unacknowledged. The crisis is compounded by the fact that, as far as an objective and authoritative analysis of contextualized acts of linguistic communication is concerned, traditional descriptive linguistics can offer ethnography nothing of the sort. The objectivity it claims to offer is a spurious one based on an untenable view of languages as communal fixed codes. The attraction of this view, however, is that it offers a reliable and prestigious method for manufacturing determinacy in linguists' data, a determinacy which helps salvage an empirical methodology which in turn serves to salvage the linguist's professional identity as some kind of expert with a mastery of the tools of the trade. For this reason, orthodox linguistics is far more useful to modern sociolinguistics alive than dead. This becomes all the more apparent when one considers explicit attempts from within sociolinguistics to theorise *indeterminacy* in language.

Indeterminacy in sociolinguistic theory
The most explicit account of the role played by the notion of indeterminacy in contemporary sociolinguistic theory can be found in Jaffe (2009). Indeterminacy, claims Jaffe (p.229), is both a 'fundamental property of social life' and a 'fundamental principle of sociolinguistic variables'. She goes on to suggest that 'it is productive to ground sociolinguistic research and analysis on a premise of inherent indeterminacy, both as a defining feature of sociolinguistic data and as a baseline for our understanding of social action through language' (p.230-231). It is telling here that Jaffe refers to *socio*linguistic variables and data since it is apparent that nowhere does she entertain the more radical notion of indeterminacy in purely linguistic data, i.e. at the level of linguistic structure. Her sociolinguistic indeterminacy is therefore one which sits on a bedrock of linguistic determinacy, hence the apparent ease with which she is able to discuss indeterminacy

alongside talk of decidedly determinate, traditional structuralist notions such as *code*. Indeed, far from any indeterminacy undermining the ontological status of the code, Jaffe notes that the code itself can be a sociolinguistic variable, a claim which necessarily presupposes the determinacy of the code as an identifiable entity.

What is immediately apparent, then, is that the kind of indeterminacy Jaffe has in mind is not one which compromises or questions the fundamental identity of the sociolinguistic variable. We are not dealing with any indeterminacy of (socio)linguistic form. After all, this would leave the empirical sociolinguist dataless. For Jaffe, the indeterminacy of linguistic variables resides primarily in their alleged social or indexical meaning. From a Saussurean point of view, this form of indeterminacy is an irrelevance since it resides outside of the linguistic code, i.e. *langue*, and therefore can only be a concern for an 'external' linguistics. Nevertheless, it is an indeterminacy which would not be identifiable without the determinacy of form offered by the linguistic code. However, it also soon becomes clear that such indeterminacy is not of the radically open-ended type but rather merely a form of a far weaker ambiguity.

> One element of this indeterminacy has to do with the permeable and potentially fuzzy boundaries between codes. This means that a given utterance may be formally ambiguous – and thus bi- or polyvalent. Social interaction may preserve ambiguity or multiplicity of meaning, or conversely, may exhibit regularizing tendencies and define an utterance as having one clear code/category membership. The analytical focus thus has to be on these processes: if, how, by whom (and with what sources of authority) the essential indeterminacy of formally ambiguous language is undercut. (Jaffe, 2009:233)

There are several points worthy of comment in this passage. The first is what sense to make of the suggestion of fuzzy boundaries between codes. An initial question is whether this fuzziness is to be conceived as a purely observational indeterminability stemming from the linguist's inadequate data, methodology or analysis or whether it is taken to be a fundamental ontological property of the codes themselves. If the latter, it should be noted that from a linguistic point of view the notion is theoretically incoherent. Sociolinguists have often tended to present the fact that they are unable in practice to clearly demarcate one linguistic system – that is to say one code - from another as an interesting or quirky puzzle when it is in fact symptomatic of a basic theoretical blunder which calls into question the very notion of linguistic codes (i.e. discrete languages, dialects, varieties etc.) altogether. Integrationists have long railed against the postulation of 'fixed codes' in linguistic theory but the 'fixed' part of that description is largely superfluous since the notion of an unfixed, i.e. indeterminate, code undermines the original theoretical purpose which the postulation of the code was designed to serve, namely to guarantee intersubjectivity in linguistic communication. To claim that it is only some penumbral part of the code which is indeterminate merely defers the issue as one then has to identify which features belong to that part and those which do not, a task for which there appear to be no determinate criteria. A code in the Saussurean sense is a strictly determinate, bounded phenomenon. It is a holistic, internally structured synchronic network or system of determinate signs (form-meaning combinations). It has no blurry edges and cannot leak. Such sign forms only acquire their identities through their belonging to the determinate system. It is the code which identifies them, not vice-versa. It therefore follows from this that a sign unit cannot belong to more than one code. A sign is not the same as a linguistic form. What the linguist takes to be the same form may well be deemed to belong to more than one code but it is a different linguistic sign in each case.

Now Jaffe's concern is obviously not with the finer points of Saussurean theory. Her chief purpose is to make some kind of theoretical sense of the sociolinguistic phenomenon whereby, due to the use of so-called 'bivalent' forms (Woolard, 1998), people may sometimes be unsure what language, dialect or other linguistic variety is being spoken or situations where the use of what participants take to be a particular language, or certain forms belonging to that language, may generate conflicting, uncertain or ambiguous indexical associations. The main example Jaffe gives is from her research in Corsica. Her particular interest centres on the variability or lack of stability in what she terms the 'meaning of speaking Corsican'. While observing that the predominant use of Corsican (as opposed to French) between elders as a language of familiarity and solidarity no longer automatically carries over to relationships between elders and younger people since French has now penetrated the sphere of intimate relations, she also notes that Corsican has encroached into areas of public life that were previously dominated by French. The result is apparently an ambiguity in the social significance of the two 'codes'.

> Speaking Corsican today, even with other elders, does not have the same meaning as speaking Corsican in an era where it was more or less unmarked, and spoken by everyone. Today, it is not just opposed to French as a language of status, power and distance, but to French as a language of intimacy. By the same token, the introduction of Corsican as a language of instruction in school has not just raised the status of Corsican and left the rest of the system of oppositions intact. The use of Corsican in education has also reconfigured the sociolinguistic landscape and people's experiences in and through language. A new generation of Corsican children is now accruing expe-

riences of institutional life in Corsican, where it is both part of an adult regime to which they have no choice but to submit and where it is explicitly promoted as a language of personal identity and unique cultural heritage. Both of these experiences of Corsican are far removed from the experiences of their parents' and grandparents' generations. Adapting Corsican to a new domain of practice, the school, has also changed the code itself, and created new kinds of awareness of variation *within* Corsican, including the variation associated with 'new' linguistic forms whose authority is anchored in the institution vs. 'old/traditional' forms whose authority derives from 'authentic' elderly speakers. The meaning of the sociolinguistic variable in this context – whether it is using Corsican or a particular kind of Corsican – is thus fundamentally indeterminate in the sense that it simultaneously brings into play multiple social and historical fields of reference [...] the tension between, in this case, power and solidarity is an enduring, and irresolvable feature of what it means to speak Corsican: in short, indeterminacy is built into this kind of sociolinguistic context. (Jaffe, 2009:235-236)

For Jaffe, it seems that the indeterminacy of what it means to speak Corsican essentially reduces to an uncertainty or ambiguity as regards which of a determinate range of pre-given social meanings are being invoked or indexed; a kind of determinate indeterminacy in effect. There is no admission of the possibility of the sort of open-ended indeterminacy which would allow 'speaking Corsican' to mean whatever participants in a particular communicative episode might in context take it to mean, if they take it to mean anything, i.e. grant it any communicational significance, at all. Jaffe also does not entertain the question of whether there is/are any such thing(s) as 'the meaning(s) of speaking Corsican' but simply assumes it to be the case. What is it then for sociolinguistic variables to have social meanings, how are we to identify them and what tools or techniques does the sociolinguist have at his/her disposal to help us do so? These are abstract, i.e. decontextualised, questions which invite abstract answers. One answer Jaffe (p.234) supplies is that linguistic forms and social meanings somehow 'map onto' one another and that 'meanings accrue to linguistic variables from diverse domains of practice'. If more than one social meaning attaches to a linguistic variable, we have a case of sociolinguistic indeterminacy. Such meanings then, while they may be invoked in specific contexts, are not the localised products or outcomes of specific communicative episodes but somehow exist over and above them and would furthermore appear to have a determining effect on them. They are, in short, reified abstractions. Nowhere in Jaffe's account is there any suggestion of indeterminacy in what Corsican (or French) actually is. After all, the linguist needs to be sure that it is Corsican, French etc. which is being spoken in order to be able to attribute the correct indexical meanings to it. If one is unsure what is being spoken, that is to say uncertain as to which sociolinguistic variable is in play, one has no way of knowing what is being indexed. For sociolinguistic variables to have indeterminacy of social meaning, they must be determinately identifiable – i.e. have determinacy of form – otherwise it would not be possible to map any meanings onto them. As long as there is determinacy of form, the sociolinguist has some kind of data. However, this necessarily involves setting up the sociolinguistic variable as a decontextualised abstraction, the result of which is that linguistic communication inevitably becomes reduced to the supposed instantiation of such abstractions.

Sociolinguists sometimes claim to have refuted the charge of working with a code-based view of language by invoking the variability or indeterminacy of social meaning/indexicality (see, for instance, Buchholtz and Hall, 2004). However, it is a move which does not succeed. Firstly, it presupposes the highly problematic notion that meaning can be neatly divided into a linguistic and indexical component. This is already to adopt a highly segregationist view of communication. The effect of this separation of linguistic and indexical meaning is to leave the code, qua structural linguistic entity, fully intact. So while it may be the case that the social meaning of the code is itself not coded, i.e. fully determinate, the linguistic meaning certainly is because if it were not, it would not be possible to identify the code in the first place. In other words, in addition to reifying the alleged social meanings, nothing is done to call into question the basic ontology of the code and it is at this fundamental level that the integrationist critique of code-based views of language applies. From an integrationist point of view, all meaning is equally indeterminate, linguistic no less than indexical.

Radical indeterminacy
For integrationists, the recognition of indeterminacy in language goes far beyond the acknowledgement of any ambiguity in the indexical meanings of determinate sociolinguistic variables and begins instead by contemplating the ontological make-up of the linguistic sign itself. This is the crucial difference. Harris (1998: 131) writes that '[t]he indeterminacy of the linguistic sign is the central doctrine of integrationism'. This recognition gives rise to the notion of 'radical indeterminacy' which according to Harris and Hutton (2007:201-223):

> questions the notion of semantic determinacy altogether. In integrational semiology, the sign does not 'have' its own meaning: it is 'made to mean' whatever the circumstances require. And may be made to mean different things by different individuals on the same occasion. More exactly, the contextualization that makes a sign mean something is simultaneously what establishes its identity

as a sign. So *even if* by some miracle human beings woke up tomorrow equipped with those concepts with 'sharp boundaries' that Frege longed for, [...] radical indeterminacy would still be the order of the day. For there would still be no guarantee that A's system of determinate concepts matched B's. In other words, once integrationist premises are adopted, the notion of semantic determinacy is theoretically superfluous to requirements.

However, semantic indeterminacy is not all. An integrationist semiology also entails the arguably more challenging notion – and one which manifestly does not even appear on the horizon in sociolinguistics – of the indeterminacy of form. Love (1990:105-106) presents this idea as follows:

> No viable descriptive science of spoken language can be based on the idea that utterances are to be understood as the outward manifestation of members of a determinate set of underlying abstractions [...] [T]he descriptive scientist has no basis for disengaging from the incessant flux of speech the recurrent invariants he is seeking [...] *Language is radically indeterminate as regards both what is meant and what is said* [my emphasis]. The use of spoken language involves an incessant process of guesswork as to the significance of the vocal noises we hear one another make, against the background of such general ideas as we may entertain as to the sort of creatures we are and what, in given circumstances, our behaviour is likely to be. We communicate successfully by means of language to the extent that we achieve whatever may have been the purposes for which, on a particular occasion, we used it.

The idea that there are determinate formal entities underlying our use of language is, as far as integrationists are concerned, one of the cardinal errors of modern orthodox linguistics and derives chiefly from the decontextualisation and reification of language made possible by writing (Harris, 2000; Love, 1990, 2007). As Love (1990:112) observes: 'Writing […] eliminates the indeterminacy of spoken language, but only in the very general sense of eliminating, for a literate individual at least, doubts as to what abstractions he is supposed to refer what he says and hears to'. The misconception of determinacy of form is, for instance, encapsulated in the popular sociolinguistic notion of 'linguistic resources'. It is only by assuming the determinacy of form made possible by an act of literacy-facilitated abstraction that the idea that individuals somehow already possess the signs *qua* resources (words, structures, sounds etc.) which they deploy in actual communication can get off the ground at all in anything but the most metaphorical of senses.

However, can we at least not say that we are nevertheless (nearly) always *perceiving* determinate forms in speech? While it obviously cannot literally be the case, is it not in some sense true that as members of a hyper-literate culture we typically *experience* speech as if it involved determinate word forms pouring forth from the mouths of speakers, in other words almost as a kind of spoken writing? Certainly, when we reflect on episodes in our own linguistic experience we may well be inclined to conceive of things in such a manner. After all, writing provides an ideal source of formal determinacy to ground and order any meta-linguistic discussions and reflections. Yet even this conviction appears fairly easy to shake and, in the end, it would seem to be the result of the very same form of decontextualisation, albeit at one onto-phenomenological remove. Indeed, on further reflection, it is not a claim which stands up to any serious scrutiny since, if it were granted, it would seem to suggest that the speech of literates is fundamentally different from that of non-literates. Yet, we need only reflect on the uncontroversial observation that literate and non-literate members of the same linguistic community are able to produce speech which may be all-but indistinguishable in terms of verbal fluency. But what conclusion is to be drawn from it?

Nigel Love (personal communication) tells of a severely dyslexic individual of his acquaintance who has great difficulty navigating his way around the London Underground network due to his inability to read the names on the platform station signs. However, one would not glimpse any such difficulties by merely talking to him. His conversation is apparently 'perfectly fluent'. Love notes that '[h]is problem is his inability to attach semiological significance to configurations of marks on a surface, let alone to make any connection between such visible marks and speech. But that in no way affects his ability to talk like anyone else. Spoken language, it seems, has *nothing to do with writing*'. This would suggest that while familiarity with writing *may* shape our perception of what speech involves and *may* be an important factor in the articulation of linguistic experience, it cannot in any way *explain* the human ability underlying spoken language. For hyper-literate persons, it is nigh-on impossible to empathise with the linguistic experience of non-literates. Perhaps the nearest we can get is when we encounter 'new' words or forms for which we have never encountered a graphic form and which exist only in spoken language. However, even though we have never encountered graphic forms for these words, as literate persons we still have available the possibility of somehow writing them down and reducing them to a determinate visual form. We can still 'imagine' them as written even if we never actually get around to writing them down.

Continuing on the underground transport theme, when travelling on the Hong Kong MTR I hear multiple times each day an announcement in Cantonese which, as someone speaking and understanding virtually no Cantonese and unable to read or write

Chinese script, I would venture to write as something like *Zeng mut kau gun ter mun*. This is more or less what it 'sounds like' to me. The only reason I have any idea what this phrase means is that it is followed immediately by the English announcement 'Please stand back from the train doors'. Whether the English version is a 'literal' or accurate translation of the Cantonese I do not know. Despite a vague notion that what I write as *mun* might mean 'door' or 'doors' (I have the idea that there are generally no differentiated singular and plural forms in Cantonese), I am unable to parse the sentence any further. The reason I have written it as six separate 'words' is my tentative belief that most Cantonese words tend to be monosyllabic. The English announcement is followed by the same instruction in Mandarin (Putonghua) which even after several months in Hong Kong and having heard it many hundreds of times I find I am unable to render or imagine in anything like an approximate written form with any degree of conviction. I still cannot 'see' any sufficiently determinate abstract pattern in it which would enable me to put it down in writing. Although I recognise the announcement in context, I cannot 'visualise' what is being said and therefore also do not feel able to make any credible attempt to repeat it verbally. I literally would not know what sounds to make. It would almost be like trying to write down birdsong. My poor ear for Chinese aside, I could of course quite easily resolve all this uncertainty by, for example, looking up the announcement online and seeing how it is written in Pinyin or asking a Mandarin speaker to slowly repeat what is said so that I can attempt to imitate it and thereby assign it an imaginary written form of my own devising. However, the simple fact is that I have yet to do so. Now, the point of all of this is that even though I am completely illiterate in Chinese, my immediate instinct is to still try to make sense of my aural experience of the language via the dominant form of literacy available to me, i.e. alphabetic writing in the Roman script. I cannot experience it as a non-literate *tout court*. Of course, in writing *Zeng mut kau gun ter mun* I am invoking abstract units very much of my own creation (and no doubt also exposing myself to the possibility of ridicule from those who know better). The extent to which my second-order abstractions may or may not correspond to those which Cantonese speakers might employ to write the same announcement is irrelevant because I do not know any Cantonese. *My* phenomenologically perceived abstractions have no social or cultural history. However, it is important to note that my abstractions are revisable. If I start learning Cantonese, if I ask a Cantonese speaker what is 'actually' being said in the announcement or if I hear something in the announcement I didn't previously perceive, I will no doubt entertain the idea of some quite different set of abstractions underlying it and indeed the same potentially applies, *mutatis mutandis*, to all instances of spoken language I may encounter whether they involve languages with which I am familiar or those which I am wholly ignorant of. For example, widely available written evidence clearly suggests variation amongst 'native' English speakers (at least in Britain) as regards the perceived abstractions underlying the formation of what grammarians would call the conditional perfect tense, i.e. *would of* + past participle vs *would have* + past participle. Those who persistently write *would of* are of course quite likely to be invited by some concerned party, and sooner rather than later, to entertain the possibility of the alternative abstraction. The point, though, is that such issues cannot even arise without the availability of writing.

The problem here, as Love (1990:108) notes, 'is not the idea of abstractions underlying speech, but the idea of *determinate systems* of abstractions underlying speech'. Both non-literates and literates are clearly able to entertain the notion of abstractions underlying their spoken language. The capacity for abstraction *per se* is not conditional upon the possession of literacy. It is one which stems from nothing more than the mundane ability to repeat what has been said. However, non-literates have no enduring medium at hand in order to ground the determinacy of form required to set up determinate systems of abstractions. This is the crucial change brought about by the availability of writing. However, the availability of writing which makes it possible to set up systems of determinate forms does not thereby mean that the abstractions underlying speech become determinate for literate persons even if they may be inclined to perceive that as being the case under certain circumstances. It is also in this sense, then, that we can make sense of the proposition that speech has nothing to do with writing.

There is more to be said, however. While we may very often regard instances of spoken language as involving the instantiation of particular abstractions, it need not necessarily be the case. As Love (1990:100) notes: 'Perceiving utterances as manifestations of underlying "sames" is not a necessary condition of any use of language whatever. It must be at least possible to understand an utterance without relating it to an antecedently given underlying abstraction.' New or nonce words and expressions could never be coined if this were not the case. Yet, as Love (1990:100) immediately goes on to observe, 'once one has understood an utterance for the first time, one will entertain the possibility of repeating it. This involves *deciding* what would constitute repeating it.' It is only once we start writing down these repetitions that we are able to engage in a process of metalinguistic abstraction which generates in us the illusion of determinacy of form in speech. From that scriptist illusion, there arises modern linguistics, including sociolinguistics. The adoption of an integrational perspective at least offers a way of seeing that illusion for what it is.

Conclusion
Failure to acknowledge the radical indeterminacy of language and take onboard the theoretical and methodological implications which that acknowledgement entails would seem to lead

inevitably, somewhere along the line, to the invocation of abstractions as *explanantia*. Yet, abstractions explain nothing and are instead themselves in need of explanation. The limited measure of linguistic indeterminacy recognised by modern sociolinguistic theory is built upon a foundation of just such abstractions. One way of weakening those foundations would be to drop the pretence that orthodox linguistics has anything meaningful to contribute to the understanding of human communication and instead come to the view that linguistics is actually primarily a severe *hindrance* to that endeavour. This would require a fundamental rethinking of sociolinguistics in terms of both theory and method. It seems unlikely to happen any time soon.

Readers might at this point wonder what relevance the seemingly arid and perhaps even abstruse theoretical focus of this chapter has for the overall theme of the volume. In other words, what has the indeterminacy of language got to do with the (non-) adoption of a humanist perspective on communication? There is, I think, a reasonably short and straightforward answer to this question. One concept commonly invoked as the antipode of humanism is scientism. Scientism is anti-humanism and from an integrationist perspective orthodox linguistics represents a form of scientism *par excellence* (see Harris, 1987; Orman, 2016). The scientism of orthodox linguistics is largely a consequence of its refusal or inability to recognise the radical indeterminacy of the linguistic sign. Despite any theoretical differences one might discern between the various approaches which integrationists would categorise as belonging to orthodox linguistics, there is an underlying unity insofar as all of them can be said to postulate a source of objective invariance/determinacy in language somewhere along the line. As I have attempted to show, sociolinguistics, in any of its modern or postmodern guises, is no exception here. However, any such determinacy is a spurious fabrication, nothing more than a methodological artifact. By failing to reject orthodox linguistics and indeed by actively seeking compromise and alliance with it, modern sociolinguistic approaches continue to partake of and propagate its scientism. Now, pointing out the scientism of orthodox linguistics does not automatically make any approach opposed to it humanistic. Integrationism clearly has a heavier argumentative burden than that in order to establish its own humanist credentials, a challenge taken on by several of the other contributions to this volume. However, a first, necessary step in taking on that challenge is to acknowledge the radical indeterminacy of language for the semiological reality that it is.

References
Blommaert, Jan. 2010. *The Sociolinguistics of Globalization.* Cambridge. CUP.
Bucholtz, Mary and Hall, Kira. 2004. Theorizing identity in language and sexuality research. *Language in Society* 33(4): 469-515.
Creese, Angela. 2010. Linguistic ethnography. In Lia Litosseliti (Ed.) *Research Methods in Linguistics.* London. Bloomsbury. 138-154.
Figueroa, Esther. 1994. *Sociolinguistic Metatheory.* Oxford. Pergamon.
Hammersley, Martyn. 2007. Reflections on linguistic ethnography. *Journal of Sociolinguistics,* 11 (5): 689-695.
Harris, Roy. 1981. *The Language Myth.* London. Duckworth.
Harris, Roy. 1983. Translator's Introduction. In Ferdinand de Saussure, *Course in General Linguistics* (translator R. Harris). ix-xvi. London. Duckworth.
Harris, Roy. 1987. *The Language Machine.* Ithaca. Cornell University Press.
Harris, Roy. 1998. *Introduction to Integrational Linguistics.* Oxford. Pergamon Press.
Harris, Roy. 2000. *Rethinking Writing.* London. Continuum Press.
Harris, Roy and Hutton, Christopher. 2007. *Definition in Theory*

and Practice. *Language, Lexicography and the Law.* London. Continuum Press.

Jaffe, Alexandra M. 2009. Indeterminacy and regularization: a process-based approach to the study of sociolinguistic variation and language ideologies. *Sociolinguistic Studies,* 3 (2): 229-251.

Jørgensen, J.N., Karrebæk, M.S., Madsen, L.M., Møller, J.S., 2011. Polylanguaging in superdiversity. *Diversities,* 13 (2), 23–38.

Labov, William. 1975. *What is a Linguistic Fact?* Lisse. Peter de Ridder.

Love, Nigel. 1990. The locus of languages in a redefined linguistics. In Hayley G. Davis and Talbot J. Taylor (eds.) *Redefining Linguistics.* 53-117. London. Routledge.

Love, Nigel. 2007. Are languages digital codes? *Language Sciences,* 29: 690-709.

Makoni, Sinfree B. and Pennycook, Alastair. 2005. Disinventing and (Re)constituting languages. *Critical Inquiry In Language Studies* 2 (3): 137-156.

Orman, Jon. 2016. Scientism in the language sciences. *Language and Communication,* 48. 28-40.

Orman, Jon and Pablé, Adrian. 2015. Polylanguaging, integrational linguistics and contemporary sociolinguistic theory. A commentary on Ritzau. *International Journal of Bilingual Education and Bilingualism.* **DOI:** 10.1080/13670050.2015.1024606

Pablé, Adrian and Hutton, Christopher. 2015. *Signs, Meaning and Experience: Integrational Approaches to Linguistics and Semiotics.* Berlin. Mouton De Gruyter.

Pavlenko, Aneta. 2018. Superdiversity and why it's not. In Barbara Schmenk, Stephan Breidbach, Lutz Küster (eds.), *Sloganizations in Language Education Discourse : Conceptual Thinking in the Age of Academic Marketization.* 142-168. Bristol. Multilingual Matters.

Pennycook, A. 2007. The myth of English as an international language. In S. Makoni & A. Pennycook (Eds.), *Disinventing and Reconstituting Languages*. 90–115. Clevedon: Multilingual Matters.

Rampton, Ben, Tusting, K., Maybin, J., Barwell, R., Creese, A., and Lytra, V. 2004. UK linguistic ethnography: a discussion paper. Unpublished. www.ling-ethnog.org.uk.

Rampton, Ben, Maybin, Janet & Roberts, Celia. 2014. *Methodological foundations in linguistic ethnography*. Tilburg. Tilburg University, Culture Studies Department. (*Tilburg Papers in Culture Studies,* paper 102)

Saussure, Ferdinand De. *Course in General Linguistics* (translator R. Harris). London. Duckworth.

Toolan, Michael. 1997. A few words on telementation. *Language Sciences,* 19 (1): 79-91.

Woolard, Kathryn A. 1998. Simultaneity and bivalency as strategies in bilingualism. *Journal of Linguistic Anthropology,* 8 (1): 3-29.

7.

A turn for the meta, a turn for the Peirce.

Anyone seeking a guide to the state of contemporary sociolinguistic theory straight from the horse's mouth need look no further for the time being. Editor Nikolas Coupland has done a good job in bringing together eighteen contributions addressing a broad sweep of concerns from some of the most prominent and prolific scholars in the field. Accordingly, the book ought to be required reading for any serious student of the discipline albeit subject to the proviso that this is very definitely not an introductory tome. Readers unfamiliar or on nodding terms only with the more theoretically ambitious sociolinguistic literature are likely to find much of the volume heavy-going. However, there is a great deal here to keep more advanced scholars engaged in reflection and argument. The book should also provide some excellent discussion material for graduate seminars, sociolinguistic reading groups and the like.

The invited contributions, which are bookended by two lengthy chapters from the editor, are grouped thematically into six parts entitled (i) *Theorising social meaning*, (ii) *Language, markets and materiality*, (iii) *Sociolinguistics, place and mobility*, (iv) *Power, mediation and critical sociolinguistics*, (v) *Sociolinguistics, contexts and impact*, and (vi) *The evolution of sociolinguistic theory*. There is not space here to comment at length on each of the contributions individually so the focus of my comments will necessarily be somewhat selective.

In his scene-setting introductory chapter, Coupland makes a welcome and arguably long overdue call for sociolinguistics to return to a 'reflexive contemplation' of *meta*theoretical questions. It is pleasing to see his reference to Figueroa's excellent and unpardonably neglected book *Sociolinguistic Metatheory* (1994) but it is equally disappointing that no other contribution makes any further mention of it. Coupland goes on to provide a brief but useful state-of-the-art summary of different trends in modern sociolinguistic research followed by a more extensive overview of the various contributions in which he comments on many of the most pertinent thematic continuities and, just as importantly, areas of theoretical tension.

So what is the current state of sociolinguistic theory? It has become something of an axiom in the field to claim that the contemporary sociolinguistic landscape is a complex, messy, chaotic, sometimes even 'baffling' affair which is nevertheless at the same time underpinned by some deep-seated, ethnographically discernible form of order. Upon reading this volume, readers may be inclined towards the view that a similar description could be applied to sociolinguistic theory itself. On the surface, one encounters a proliferation of differently packaged and partly over-lapping perspectives each exhibiting divergent levels of interdisciplinary focus, historical sensibility and what for all but the most conversant members of the sociolinguistics 'discourse community' can seem a bewildering and intimidating arsenal of metalinguistic terms of art defined and frequently redefined with varying degrees of rigour and clarity. Beneath this surface dishevelment, however, one can identify a number of important areas of common ground, most significantly an unwavering ideological and, it must be said, professionally self-serving commitment to empirical-positivist, data-driven studies and a quite traditional metaphysics of communication predicated on the requirement of intersubjectively shared sign forms.

Part 1 begins – appropriately enough given his influence on the field at present – with Michael Silverstein's contribution. Displaying an acquaintance with the history of linguistic thought unrivalled by any of the other contributions, Silverstein traces the emergence of the now commonplace sociolinguistics concepts of *enregisterment, register* and *indexicality* and tries to show how they have served to challenge traditional 'sound-law' explanations of change in historical linguistics. I suspect, however, that Silverstein's chapter is also the one less well-versed readers in particular are most likely to skip over and leave for another day so frequently difficult and dense is his prose. This would be a pity, though, since anyone wanting to understand how sociolinguistic theory has got to the point where it is at present needs to make good sense of Silverstein's not inconsiderable contribution. Difficult writing is not necessarily bad writing of course but if it is to travel well outside of the often quite narrow disciplinary niches from which it originates, it requires a degree of lucidity and felicity of exposition which is sometimes lacking from certain of the contributions to the present volume. Reading this collection prompts one to ask what exactly the language of contemporary sociolinguistics is itself indexical of. This would be an interesting question for a truly meta sociolinguistics of sociolinguistics to consider but perhaps there is only so much reflexivity the discipline can comfortably tolerate.

Silverstein's chapter is followed by contributions from Penelope Eckert, Alexandra Jaffe and Susan Gal all of whom take up the indexicality baton in various ways which will be familiar to those already acquainted with their work. Eckert's more reflective chapter is particularly notable for its discussion of Peircean semiotics. Gal also mentions Peirce although neither she nor Eckert make any sustained argument as to why exactly a Peircean model of the sign is to be preferred above others. One therefore has the sense that a Peircean semiotics has been inherited some-what uncritically and sometimes even unknowingly into modern sociolinguistics more on account of its usefulness in opening up the field of ideology and indexicality studies than as the result of any thoroughgoing interrogation of the plausibility of Peirce's overall philosophical and theoretical framework. In one of his characteristically mordant discussions of ethnomethodology, Ernest Gellner (1975:431) once wrote that 'consciousness [...] is all over the place, there is no end of it, it's coming out of everyone's ears. It is indeed not entirely clear whether *anything else* exists.' If he were alive to read this volume, one suspects that he might reach a similar conclusion about sociolinguistics and indexicality. There really does seem to be an awful lot of it about. The more interesting question is why all the burgeoning interest *now* given that signs have presumably always been indexical and Peirce himself has been dead for over a century. If indexicality is truly where it's at sociolinguistically speaking, one wonders why the discipline as a whole has taken such an age to realise it. As with the current explosion of interest in Bakhtin – another old name which features regularly in the present volume – one sometimes has the impression of a certain degree of fashion-conscious 'theory shopping' in sociolinguistics.

Part 2 addresses the theme of 'markets and materiality' and kicks off with Monica Heller and Alexandre Duchêne's discussion of linguistic commodification, followed by Helen Kelly-Holmes on theorisations of 'the market' in sociolinguistics and Mary Bucholtz and Kira Hall's discussion of embodiment. Of all the chapters in the volume, Heller and Duchêne's piece is a theoretical debate in the best sense of the term insofar as it openly engages in good faith and temper with critiques of previous work by the authors. It therefore represents one of the more stimulating contributions. As one would expect, Bourdieu figures prominently in this section although Kelly-Holmes casts her gaze wider to consider alternative approaches to marketisation, in particular Norman Fairclough's brand of Critical Discourse Analysis, and does well to draw out some of the main differences between them. Bucholtz and Hall's plea for an 'embodied sociolinguistics' is simultaneously both sensible and perplexing. They make the rather obvious point that the human body frequently plays an extremely important role in linguistic interaction or the 'production of meaning' as they put it and they rightly castigate most previous sociolinguistic work for ignoring the corporeal dimension entirely, describing it quite accurately as a 'disembodied undertaking'. I therefore find it puzzling that they display no familiarity with the extremely rich theoretical and empirical work in fields such as embodied and extended cognition, distributed cognition, distributed language and the biology of cognition, all of which make a serious fist of attempting to describe and explain the integration of linguistic and corporeal aspects in episodes of human interactivity. However, whether those more naturalistic approaches could ever be reconciled with a sociolinguistics seemingly fixated on linguistic and other semiotic *forms* is open to question.

Part 3 is arguably the keynote section of the volume. If anything has characterised the much-vaunted 'paradigm shift' in recent sociolinguistic theory, it is the now seemingly ubiquitous emphasis on mobility. Jan Blommaert's typically forthright contribution constitutes another rigorously argued and theoretically ambitious attempt to justify such lofty claims. Blommaert's name is of course all but synonymous with the sociolinguistic study of 'superdiversity' and his piece consolidates his prolific work of recent years. It is therefore slightly odd that his chapter is placed after those of Alastair Pennycook and David Britain both of whom are somewhat more circumspect in their appraisal and embrace of the conceptual and terminological developments ushered in under the aegis of the new 'sociolinguistics of mobility'. Britain's sober and balanced chapter on 'Sedantarism and nomadism in dialect' contains a thoughtful antidote to some of the more breathless, mobility-fetishising claims advanced on behalf of the new paradigm with which he does though on the whole seem broadly sympathetic. However, he explicitly singles out work on 'superdiversity' and wonders whether it is not in fact an approach which 'romanticises the mobile in ways that smack of orientalism [and] presents mobility rather than the academic recognition of that mobility as new' (p. 231). These are pertinent observations which should provide grist for much further debate. It is unfortunate, however, that some other recent strongly worded and penetrating critiques of the rhetorical manoeuvres driving the superdiversity paradigm (especially Pavlenko, 2018) came too late for the possibility of any mention or discussion in the present volume.

The most revealing chapter of the entire book and an indicator that all is not necessarily as well and as progressive with modern sociolinguistic theory as some would have it is Alastair Pennycook's discussion of what he calls the 'trans-super-poly-metro movement'. Pennycook sees that despite an abundance of often quite hyperbolic terminological innovation there is something suspect and quite unrevolutionary about recent attempts to escape traditional structuralist understandings of language(s) and multilingual practices by way of notions such as *translanguaging*, *polylanguaging* and *supervernacular*. With their frequent employment of traditional terminology and talk of 'mixing' languages, Pennycook notes that such frameworks 'struggle to escape the linguistics that still defines the objects of critique' (p. 208). He therefore wonders whether and seems to have some sympathy with the view that these developments represent little more than 'old wine in new bottles' (p. 201). However, by the end of the chapter one is left with the distinct impression that this might just be how Pennycook prefers his wine for want of anything more palatable on offer. Unusually for a sociolinguist, Pennycook is at least prepared to openly sample the distinctive but by no means new wine of integrational linguistics and he glimpses that it might offer a potential *theoretical* solution to his dilemma. He also makes the important and often overlooked point that integrationists – notably Roy Harris – were arguing that there are no such thing as languages *qua* ontologically-real, bounded, code-like entities long before the notion appeared as a revolutionary insight on the horizon of poststructuralist sociolinguistic orthodoxy. On reading some of the contributions to this volume, one comes away with the feeling that structuralism in linguistics is only now seen as descriptively and explanatorily inadequate as the result of a certain set of historically quite recent sociological and technological developments. The fact is that it does not and indeed never did take any familiarity with the diverse communicative practices of so-called 'late modernity' to see that the entire theoretical edifice of linguistic structuralism was based on dubious metaphysical abstraction and an implausible model of communication (insofar as certain strands of structuralism had one at all). Ultimately, though, it seems that integrationist wine is also not quite to Pennycook's liking with the unwelcome methodological implications which he alludes to when noting – not entirely correctly – its 'lack of empirical work' (p. 212) perhaps leaving a rather sour taste in the mouth. Pennycook hedges his bets by claiming that translanguaging and polylingual approaches share a number of characteristics with integrational linguistics. This may well be true but it is a pity he does not explore further the more thoroughgoing incompatibilities of the two strands of thought, for instance their clearly distinct theories of the sign. In the end, Pennycook appears to side with the new sociolinguistic orthodoxy by settling on the bland conclusion that 'speakers draw on repertoires of semiotic resources and that language is best understood in terms of social practices' (p. 212).

Pennycook does, however, raise an important point in respect of the twin notions of *linguistic repertoires* and *linguistic resources* both of which have come to assume an absolutely central role in modern sociolinguistic theory. The idea that individuals communicate not via languages or any other bounded systems but by instead deploying the linguistic resources which constitute their linguistic repertoires is now an article of faith in poststructuralist sociolinguistics. Yet Pennycook rightly notes that these concepts have received far less scrutiny and critique than one might expect given the extremely heavy theoretical load they are required to bear. This can perhaps be explained to some degree in terms of self-preservation for, if having first been denied separate languages and other types of lect as first-order *realia*, it were then deprived of the notion of linguistic resources, the threat to sociolinguistics as a discipline, which, as Coupland makes clear in his introduction (p. 6), prides itself on what it sees as its resolutely empirical approach to linguistic data, would be of existential proportions. The sociolinguistic notion of linguistic resources is essentially a repackaging of an old instrumentalist view of the linguistic sign most famously evoked by Wittgenstein's 'tool-box' metaphor. Like Wittgenstein's tools, our linguistic resources are what we supposedly deploy in order to achieve particular communicative outcomes and effects in episodes of linguistic interaction. The difficulty for a sociolinguistics eager to avoid reification and embrace indeterminacy is that the notion of linguistic resources, which has none of the metaphorical lustre of Wittgenstein's toolbox, is absolutely dependent on a reified and abstract view of the linguistic sign because such signs must logically already be in existence prior to their use or else there is no coherent sense in which they can be conceived of as resources. This allows such 'resources' to be envisaged as circulating and leading a life of their own beyond the control of the individuals who deploy them. Furthermore, it also requires that the linguistic sign have determinacy of form for if it did not there could be no question of individuals sharing or using the 'same' resources on different occasions. Yet sociolinguists have so far shown little appetite for addressing the vexed theoretical question of why it is that linguistic signs can somehow exhibit indeterminacy of meaning (whether denotational or indexical) yet remain resolutely determinate in respect of form. The great difficulty of course for the sociolinguistic researcher is that as soon as indeterminacy of form is conceded, s/he has no – or at least a very different type of – data with which to work.

Parts 4 and 5 both contain a rather eclectic collection of chapters addressing topics such as rhizomatic discourses, mediatisation, governmentality, language policy, sign language and sociolinguistics and the law. As one might imagine when the discussion turns explicitly 'critical' and concerned with 'power' in the abstract, the postmodernese tends to be ramped up and Part 4 does not disappoint in this regard. The chapters by Sari Pietkäinen and Ben Rampton at times make for particularly challenging reading but they will no doubt engage those with a well-developed interest in areas such as CDA, Foucault, Gumperz and the theorisation of power relations more generally. However, I must confess I found this section to be the least compelling of the volume.

Lionel Wee's astute discussion in Part 5 of so-called 'zombie categories' in language policy is, however, one of the highlights of book. Displaying a commendable sensitivity to the historical development of language policy scholarship, Wee makes the important point that essentialist understandings of language and languages are very much still 'alive and kicking' (p. 335), which is to say socially and politically relevant, when it comes to language policy and planning. Invoking Giddens' notion of the 'double hermeneutic', Wee sensibly warns against disregarding the power of often highly essentialist lay conceptions of language to drive and inform language policy purely on account of their increasing academic and theoretical obsolescence.

Devotees of sociolinguistics are especially likely to appreciate the two contributions by Alan Bell and Barbara Johnstone in Part 6. Editors of the *Journal of Sociolinguistics* and *Language in Society* respectively, they each provide a reflective and at times critical commentary on the development of sociolinguistic theory as borne witness to in the pages of their journals. Both acknowledge the discipline's crucial theoretical debts to thinkers such as Labov and Hymes, while at the same time drawing attention to the ever-increasing diversification of the field. Bell makes an especially pertinent observation when he notes that '[s]ociolinguists do not raise the question "What is language?" often enough compared with the frequently debated "what is a language?"' One might also add that before one can feasibly ask 'what is language?' one must first pose the even more foundational question 'what is communication?' since how one goes about answering that particular question will go a long way to determining the nature of one's answers to all those subsequent ontological questions regarding language and languages. It is only by returning to this most basic of metatheoretical questions and coming up with a genuinely alternative answer that one will truly be able to speak of a paradigm shift in sociolinguistic theory.

In summary, by signalling and partly constituting the discipline's renewed interest in (meta)theory, this volume is certainly a valuable addition to the sociolinguistic literature. However, if any single lesson is to be drawn from it, it is that there remain more debates to be had. Whether inquiry into the social life of language really requires an ever-increasing proliferation of theory or might instead benefit from a good deal less of it is one meta question upon which such debates might usefully focus.

References
Figueroa, E. (1994) *Sociolinguistic metatheory.* Oxford: Pergamon.
Gellner, E. (1975) Ethnomethodology: The re-enchantment industry or the Californian way of subjectivity. *Philosophy of the Social Sciences* 5: 431–450.
Pavlenko, A. (2018) Superdiversity and why it's not. In S. Breidbach, L. Küster and B. Schmenk (eds) *Sloganizations in Language Education Discourse*. Bristol: Multilingual Matters.

Section II.
Integrationism and
'Distributed Language'

8.
Distributing mind, cognition and language: Exploring the (un)common ground with integrational linguistics.

Abstract
While acknowledging that they have many points of theoretical agreement, the discussion deliberately focuses on areas of incompatibility between integrational and 'distributed' approaches to mind, cognition, and language in the light of Roy Harris' claim that the notion of a 'distributed mind' comprises a category mistake. Harris' position is based on his affirmation of a 'vulgar concept of mind' which contrasts sharply with certain accounts of mind originating from within cognitive science. The tension between lay and scientific understandings of mind and language forms a key point of discord between the two approaches. I discuss Harris' argument that the category mistake inherent in the notion of 'distributed mind' can be dissolved by replacing it with the notion of an 'integrated' or 'integrating' mind. I then consider the derived notion of 'distributed language' and its theoretical and explanatory value from an integrational perspective. Finally, I conclude by arguing that although they share many important insights, the differences of perspective which exist between the integrational and distributed approaches are such as likely to prevent the emergence of anything resembling a unified movement.

1. Introduction: integrational linguistics and distributed cognition

Proponents of integrational linguistics are notably short of allies in the field of traditional academic linguistics. However, in recent years a seemingly willing dialogue partner has emerged from within cognitive science, cognitive anthropology, and the philosophy of mind in the form of various advocates of distributed cognition/mind.[1] The grounds for potentially fruitful exchange and collaboration between integrationists and distributors (for short) have been mooted on a number of occasions and the issue has even formed the subject matter of a number of conferences and special journal editions. Although authors on both sides have been quick to point to certain areas of incompatibility between the two research programmes,[2] a measure of reciprocal interest has

---

* I am grateful to Nigel Love for many discussions on the questions addressed in this paper and comments on an earlier draft. Thanks also to Adrian Pablé. I am also grateful to the two anonymous reviewers for their comments, criticisms and suggestions

[1] It should be emphasized that distributed cognition by no means presents as a homogenous movement, incorporating, for instance, a range of views on language, some of which are manifestly irreconcilable with an integrational approach, while others are far more compatible. Harris (2004, p. 728) notes that positions associated with the expressions *distributed mind* and *distributed cognition* "appear to have as the highest common factor an insistence that we should not think of the mind just as something in the head, or as goings-on in the head, but as something, or as goings-on, in the body and the local environment too". Proponents of distributed cognition are wont to talk of the 'leakiness' of the mind but, as Steffensen (2009, p. 678) observes, this is perhaps not the most felicitous metaphor for their purposes since it suggests a kind of degeneracy and that the mind really ought to be found in the head.

[2] Love (2004), for example, notes that a number of distributors, including Andy Clark, continue to adhere to code-based views of language and communication. Harris (2004) also convicts various distributors of subscribing to one or other version of the 'language myth'. On the other side, Sutton (2004) regards the

been expressed. Love (2004, p. 526), an integrationist, notes for example that:

> The distributed cognitionist and the integrational linguist have a lot to learn from each other and a lot to gain from acknowledging each other's ideas. The former needs the non-mythic account of language which [...] is provided by the latter; while integrationism, currently seen within linguistics as scarcely more than a bundle of sceptical attitudes to various orthodoxies, may have an interest in associating itself with – indeed, incorporating itself into – a positive movement within cognitive science.

Of the distributors, Sutton (2004, p. 503) has stated that "Distributed Cognition and Integrational Linguistics have much in common. Both approaches see communicative activity and intelligent behaviour in general as strongly context-dependent and action-oriented, and brains as permeated by history." Cowley (2004, p. 587) pushes things a little further and claims that integrational linguistics in fact needs to incorporate a theory of distributed cognition if it is to avoid remaining "locked into a critical tradition that neither illuminates semiogenesis nor the many ways in which multimodal activities are orchestrated". Cowley is also a leading advocate of the derived view that language is itself 'distributed', although quite what this claim amounts to in onto-epistemological terms is not always clear. I shall return to this question later on.

The most notable exception to the circumspect enthusiasm which has attended the prospect of incorporating insights from distributed cognition into integrational linguistics has been, perhaps unsurprisingly, the latter's founding and central figure, Roy

---

integrationist position on language as too extreme and as making any form of empirical enquiry nigh on impossible.

Harris. Harris argues that in endorsing the proposition 'the mind is distributed' the distributors are the perpetrators of a 'category mistake'[3] in the sense of the term used by Ryle (1949) in his attack on Descartes' classical view of mind, a view which the distributors are themselves seeking to demolish. The irony of this is not lost on Harris (2004, p. 730) who asks: "Having got rid of one category mistake [...] why set up another in its place?" Harris (2004, pp. 728–729) sets out a characteristically strong rhetorical stall by invoking a number of examples intended to bring into focus what he sees as the oddness or absurdity of the distributors' position.

> When, for instance, I use a pocket calculator I feel no temptation to say 'Ah! The machine is doing my thinking for me'. Or: 'Part of my mind is now in the machine'. Because it patently isn't the case. How do I know? Because whatever is going on inside the machine, it is not part of *me* . [...] I am no more convinced that using my pocket calculator is an extended form of thinking than that riding a bicycle is an extended form of walking, or driving a motor car an extended form of riding on horseback. Thinking by proxy makes no more sense than being happy or sad by proxy. The black tie I wear at the funeral isn't doing my grieving for me. Nor is it a bit of grief that somehow escaped from inside me and got distributed.

Just as a tie or any other item of clothing simply does not fall into that category of things or entities capable of grieving or harbouring grief, for Harris "the mind – or mind, if you prefer it without the article – just isn't the kind of thing that can get

---

[3] A category mistake is a kind of ontological fallacy committed when "things of one kind are presented as if they belonged to another" (Blackburn, 1994 , p. 58), or something is ascribed a quality which it could not possibly possess.

distributed. I live in a world in which there is in practice no alternative to treating my mental activity as *sui generis*" (2004, p. 729). It is clear that for Harris the term 'distributed mind' is to be treated as synonymous with 'extended mind' as used by Clark and others, although it should be pointed out that 'distributed mind' is not a term Clark himself uses, nor in general do advocates of socially distributed cognition (see below). In any case, 'distributed mind' is certainly a notion which has become widely associated with Clark in particular. Whether Harris can be said to have coined the term himself is a matter of debate.[4] Now, terminological matters aside, it would be unfair to dismiss the kind of examples Harris mentions above as rhetorical cheap shots on his part, for some distributors have explicitly endorsed quite such notions. In the famous case of the senile Otto trying to find his way to the museum, Clark and Chalmers (1998), wielding a metaphysical Occam's Razor, do not make the intuitive common-sense claim that Otto's notebook functions as an aide-mémoire and that Otto believes that it can tell him where the museum is, but rather that the notebook actually is the repository of his memory and belief as to the museum's location. Elsewhere, Chalmers (2008, p. ix) writes of his recently purchased iPhone that:

> [It] has already taken over some of the central functions of my brain. It has replaced part of my memory, storing phone numbers and addresses that I once would have taxed my brain with. It harbours my desires: I call up a memo with the names of my favourite dishes when I need to order at a local restaurant. I use it to calculate, when I need to figure out bills and tips. [...] Friends joke that I should get the iPhone implanted into my brain. But [...]

---

[4] That Harris did indeed coin the term 'distributed mind' is certainly the view of one of the anonymous referees.

all this would do is speed up the processing and free up my hands. The iPhone is part of my mind already. [...] Parts of it have become parts of me.

One might instead ask whether Chalmers' iPhone has not merely taken over the 'central functions' of any previous address-recording or number-calculating technologies he may have possessed (address book, pocket calculator, abacus, etc.) rather than those of his brain. Chalmers' position logically entails that he would also be willing to regard anything from a wall calendar to a copy of the Yellow Pages as part of himself and his mind under the right circumstances. Can minds also extend into one another? Suppose I ask another person to remember a piece of information for me (telephone number, address, etc.) and I then subsequently ask him/her to relate it to me. In doing so does that person, however ephemerally, become part of my mind, part of me? It would seem so given that that person is effectively performing the same function as my address book, and in their seminal paper Clark and Chalmers (1998) make an explicit appeal to such explanatory simplicity in justifying their extended mind thesis. Any other type of explanation would, in their words, be 'needlessly complex'. Now, if the distributed answer to the fore-going questions is indeed affirmative, it clearly torpedoes common-sense understandings of both mind and individual self-hood and furthermore points to a deep divide between the distributed position and that of Harris. The divide can perhaps best be regarded as ensuing from a conflict between a theory which makes a virtue of terminological innovation in pursuit of a particular kind of scientific rationality and one which seems to favour a common-sense or lay discourse about the mind and mental acts.

For Harris, it is not so much the case that talk of a distributed or extended mind and the assigning of cognitive status to inanimate material objects is straightforwardly false, but rather that in his view it does not make sense to talk in such terms. Harris (2004, p. 727) declares his "extreme diffidence" in using the terms "distributed mind" and "distributed cognition" because, as he puts it, "I do not know what meaning to attach to them". In essence then, Harris appears to be advancing an 'Ordinary Language' argument against the notion of distributed/extended mind. Indeed, his position is strongly reminiscent of that of Bennett and Hacker (2003) in their criticism of cognitive neuroscience and the habit of certain authors – Daniel Dennett is a particular target of their displeasure – of ascribing psychological attributes to the brain rather than to the human being as a whole. For Bennett and Hacker, to say that the brain feels, thinks, decides, believes, etc. is to commit the mereological fallacy and to simply not make sense, as in their view such psychological notions can only be sensically predicated of individual persons. In support of their position, they cite Wittgenstein's remark from the *Philosophical Investigations* that "Only of a human being and what resembles (behaves like) a living human being can one say: it has sensations; it sees, is blind; hears, is deaf; is conscious or unconscious." Harris, however, encounters a difficulty here, and the force of his argument is somewhat drained by his own philosophy of language. Bennett and Hacker – clearly in thrall to the 'language myth' (Harris, 1981) and the idea of a language as a fixed code shared by all members of the linguistic community – base much of their argument on an appeal to the supposed rules of linguistic usage, claiming that "nonsense is generated when an expression is used contrary to the rules for its use" and that nonsense ensues from the use of "a form of words that is excluded from the language" (Bennet & Hacker, 2003, p. 6). Now, as an integrationist, Harris cannot appeal to such arguments based on norms of discourse since there simply are no rules for the use of expressions, and ontologically there is no language from which words or expressions can be excluded. For integrationists, it is individual language-makers who determine the meaning of words and expressions, not the language to which they allegedly belong. As a consequence, it would seem at most that Harris is only able to invoke this kind of ordinary language argument in respect of himself, and that talk of a distributed or extended mind makes no sense FOR HIM PERSONALLY. This has the effect of depriving his category mistake allegation of much of its rhetorical and philosophical potency, since there clearly are many – intelligent – people for whom talk of a distributed mind and any related or derived claims are reasonable and do make good sense.

A retrospectively notable and unfortunate aspect of Harris' conceptual critique of distributed cognition, particularly in view of the discussion of 'distributed language' below, is the failure to distinguish between the view of the individually distributed or extended mind as advanced most notably by Clark and Chalmers (see also Menary's edited volume, 2010a) and the notion of a socially distributed cognitive system, the seminal account of which can be found in the work of Hutchins and his study of the collective cognitive tasks performed by the crew in the navigation of a US Navy warship (1995a, 1995b). In fact, unlike the extended/distributed mind view, the distributed cognition perspective does not focus on mental activity at all, but rather on how practical tasks are accomplished through social interaction. And indeed, Harris does not address the latter. This, however, is largely understandable, since at the time of his article in the 2004 *Language Sciences Special Issue* on 'Distributed Cognition and Integrational Linguistics', what was to become the distributed language view still drew heavily on Clark's individual-centred account of cognition. However, following the formation of the Distributed Language Group in 2005, the influence of Clark appears to have waned considerably, due in part to his problematic views on language and continuing adherence to a 'naïve realist' position (Steffensen, 2011). In fact, Harris (2004, p. 733) had already identified Clark as a "reocentric surrogationist", the pinnacle of integrationist condemnation (see also Wheeler, 2004, for another representationalist or code-based view of language). Challenging appeals to an individual language faculty, the current distributed language movement instead promotes a social, collective view of language and human interactivity (see Cowley & Vallee-Tourangeau, 2013) in which individual beings and actions are not the primary units of analysis, and it therefore owes far more to Hutchins' concept of socially distributed cognition. The ontological status or importance assigned to individual minds within this strand of theorizing is not altogether clear, although one can note affirmative references to the notions of 'distributed mind' or 'extended mind' from authors who would otherwise also advocate social, ecological, or dialogical views of language and cognition, notably Cowley and Spurrett (2003), Linell (2009), Ross (2007), and Menary (2010b). Indeed, Menary (2010b, p. 227) notes that the "extended-mind-style arguments" of Clark and Chalmers are "allied" to those of distributed and embodied cognition associated with, amongst others, Hutchins (1995a) and also Gallagher (2005).[5] Hutchins (2000, p. 4) himself has also written that "the cognition of an individual is distributed cognition too".

2. Harris and the 'vulgar concept of mind'

Harris' principal objection to the notion of distributed or extended mind is that it conflicts with and indeed appears to involve a significant reconceptualization away from a "vulgar concept of mind" (Hampshire, 1971, p. 20). Such a concept is underwritten by what Harris (2008, pp. 1–5) terms 'vulgar mindspeak' – a province of 'ordinary language' which serves common-sense or

---

[5] See also Sinha and Jensen de López (2000) for another 'extended' approach to cognition, namely 'extended embodiment'. This approach builds on work in the cognitive linguistics tradition and therefore encompasses a theoretically quite distinct view of language from the integrationist or distributed language approaches.

folk-psychological intuitions about the mind and mental activities. Such language comprises the everyday use of verbs such as *think, intend, believe, imagine, remember* and nouns such as *idea, belief, memory*, etc., and according to Harris (2008, p. 2) "allows one to talk, in short, as if there were no doubt whatever that human beings had minds, and that minds were where most of human thinking was done". Harris contrasts vulgar mindspeak with what he mischievously refers to as 'cognobabble' – what he regards as the arcane and obfuscatory jargon employed in many discussions of the mind and particularly from within the field of cognitive science. According to Harris (2008 p. 4):

> Cognobabble does introduce theoretical terms, and many of them. It avoids the use of vulgar words such as *thought* and *idea*, preferring to speak of *mental states* and *mental representations*. In cognobabble, we also hear not of *beliefs* but of *propositional attitudes* and *intentional contents*. I mention this because in current discussions of the mind one striking feature is that the initial questions are formulated in vulgar mindspeak (to make them readily intelligible) and the answers given in cognobabble (which is often not).

Harris' support for the vulgar concept of mind has found little favour amongst the distributors, and indeed is the source of some impatience and bewilderment. Spurrett (2004, pp. 500–501), for example, is deeply suspicious of appeals to common sense over and above the claims of scientific enquiry.

> It seems to me that one useful way of organising much of the history of science is as a series of disconfirmations of common sense, adding up to a powerful inductive argument that if there's some way things generally seem to us folk, then there's a good chance that we're wrong. [...]

[E]ither we think science *can* tell us that we're wrong about how things are with us (so that our distinctive personal psychology really *can't* inhabit a teapot no matter what possibilities we are able to entertain), even to the extent of showing our common sense, or vulgar, self-conception to be deeply mistaken, or common sense is holding some sort of trump that means it always beats science, or even that it never has to pay attention to science. Most cognitive science goes down the one branch, and it seems like Harris is committed to the other.

Spurrett would seem to be implying that Harris' appeal to a lay notion of mind is on a par with, say, the privileging of folk theories of medicine at the expense of the empirically tested claims of medical science. However, it is important to appreciate certain subtleties in Harris' position here. His point is not that vulgar mindspeak represents some kind of "transcendental wisdom about mental activities", and he acknowledges that "it can be thoroughly misleading when its distinctions are promoted to the status of theoretical truths" (2008, p. 148). His main target here is clearly theorists, including certain proponents of distributed cognition, who promote erroneous telementational accounts of communication. For Harris (2004, p. 729), such accounts in part find their origin in theorists taking too seriously idiomatic lay expressions such as *conveying one's thoughts* . It is not the case then that vulgar mindspeak provides an infallible theory of mind or shows conclusively what (and where) the mind really is. Indeed, it might even be questioned whether vulgar mindspeak can actually be said to imply or constitute a theory of mind at all, let alone a coherent or consistent one. This is the view of Melser (2004, p. 184), who writes that:

> [T]he properties by which lay folk characterize the mind are by no means easy to elucidate. Even when you have

> isolated some plausible ones, you can't press them too hard. You can't say whether folk really *believe* this or that about the mind or whether it's just their way of talking. [...] There really is no lay concept of mind, only a way of talking.

Melser makes a compelling point here, although one might respond by arguing that vulgar mindspeak at least provides some basis for an implicit theory of what the mind is not or cannot be, which would presumably include something which can be located outside the human body in material artefacts or any other elements of the local environment. However, for Harris, the category mistake which he attributes to the distributors would seem to lie not so much in their locating the mind outside the skull or the body, but in their seeking to locate it at all. As such, the issue of whether the mind and cognition is distributed or not is itself misconceived. For Harris, the question of location therefore simply does not or ought not to arise.

> Those who saw (rightly) that there was something amiss in sealing the mind hermetically inside the head leapt to the erroneous conclusion that it might be somewhere *else*, i.e. outside the cranium. They failed to see that the concept of *location* itself was the root of the problem. You do not solve it by dividing the mind generously between all available locations. (Harris, 2008, p. 63)

Set against this is the fact that vulgar mindspeak, which often overlaps and intersects with vulgar brainspeak, would intuitively appear to locate the mind in the head, and indeed Harris is quick to warn against investing any 'blind faith' in the vocabulary of vulgar mindspeak. Yet, at the same, he still "cannot see it ever being replaced by a better or more 'scientific' one" (2008, p. 148). Here we come to the crux of the matter. The question is then whether the distributors are able, as they implicitly claim, to offer a viable scientific account of mind and mental phenomena which improves upon lay or common-sense conceptions. Harris is deeply sceptical about theories of mind constructed under the banner of 'cognitive science'. Indeed, his position would seem to question whether there can be any such thing as a viable 'science of the mind', or at least one which in his view does not simply involve a gratuitous stipulative redefinition of what counts as either 'mental' or 'scientific'. He notes of such theories that:

> At bottom, they always turn out to be unverifiable speculation founded on analogies between mind and machine. The machine currently in favour as the model for such speculation is the computer. The basic reason why these enterprises are in vain is that in the mental world there is nothing that corresponds to enhanced observation in the natural sciences. We cannot construct the mental counterparts of telescopes and microscopes. We cannot make microphones to hear the mind talking to itself (if that is what it does). Brain scans can reveal part of what is going in the cerebral cortex, but a brain scan does not reveal the thoughts of the patient. (Harris, 2008, pp. 155–156)

Harris here touches upon an important and powerful argument for proponents of distributed cognition to contend with, and which bears similarities to that advanced by Button (2008), who also levels the charge of non-verifiability. Button notes, rightly, that certain proponents of distributed cognition draw conclusions about inner computational-type processing in the brain on the basis of publicly observable behavioural data. Yet such internal processing is not observable or measurable. Instead, it is simply postulated as the result of an a priori adherence to a computational model of mind.

> Champions of 'distributed cognition' argue that people are engaged in doing computational processing as they undertake the doing of their actions and interactions, and that this processing and conduct goes on as part of a cognitive system. However, while they can say this they cannot actually show this to be the case. All they can do is *infer* that processing is going on as conduct is engaged in. They can only *read out* of the data observed in the setting what is going on in the brain, they cannot actually show that processing is going on. In this respect, all they have – at the very best – is just a hypothesis that there is data being processed in the brain. But it is a hypothesis that can never be checked out for they just do not have access to this posited brain processing. (Button, 2008, p. 100)

It is not necessary to accept every prong of Button's argument against distributed cognition to see that he raises a crucial issue here. In fact, the linguistic strand of his argument, which takes as its inspiration Wittgenstein's rejection of the possibility of a private language in order to question the validity of an inner world/outer world dichotomy, is unlikely to hold much appeal for the integrationist, the reason being that the denial of such a dichotomy would seem to conflict sharply with the individual's own lived experience. As Harris (2008, p. 158) notes, "there is no single, common, undivided world that 'we all' live in. I don't even know who 'we all' are." Moreover, for Harris it is the role of vulgar mindspeak to articulate the connections and integrations between these inner and outer worlds. It would therefore be misplaced to criticize distributed cognition on account of its affirmation of an inner realm. The difficulty instead arises in relation to the kind of claims which are made as to the nature of that inner realm and what can be known about it.

Interestingly, Harris is not the only author to explicitly accuse distributed cognition of comprising a category mistake.

Nardi (2002), for instance, detects a 'major category error' in distributed cognition's ascription of cognitive status to non-human elements and artefacts.[6] She argues that to talk of 'non-human cognitive agents' is to pervert the meaning of cognition beyond recognition and usefulness by eradicating from its definition certain key elements which are central to human cognition and cannot be shared by non-human elements. She notes that "[a]s far as I know, distributed cognition does not attribute awareness and judgment to 'non-human cognitive agents.' A theory of cognition that deletes awareness and judgment from the meaning of cognition has reduced its scope to the point of changing the very meaning of the word" (Nardi, 2002, p. 274). This echoes the point made by Harris that whatever is going on inside the machines and artefacts with which a person interacts, such objects and their operations do not thereby constitute part of that person. Perhaps, granted a certain degree of metaphorical licence, it might seem reasonable to talk of one's smartphone or calculator as being part of oneself and one's mind, but, *pace* the distributors, one cannot say that it just simply is the case. Again, though, Nardi's ordinary-language-style category mistake argument falls down, or rather fails to hit home, on precisely the same grounds as the one advanced by Harris. That is to say that there is simply no such thing that is the meaning of the word 'cognition' and no language-immanent rules for its use which have been or indeed can be violated. In fact, there seems to be a striking lack of unanimity as to the question of precisely what is meant by 'cognition' and many of its derived terms and notions, as is starkly illustrated by Menary's (2010b, p. 230) observation that there is "no real agreement in the cognitive science community on

---

[6] See, for example, Sutton's (2004, p. 506) contention that "[i]n certain circumstances, artefacts and other external structures are literally cognitive […] in certain circumstances, along with body and brain interacting with them, they are the mind".

a definition of what a cognitive process is nor of what the vehicles of cognition are". It is interesting, however, that this failure to agree on a common definition has not led more cognitive scientists to question the scientific status of their discipline. We would certainly be surprised and no doubt disturbed if neuroscientists were to cheerily announce that they were unable to reach any sort of consensus on what the brain is or what constituted a neural process. After all, it is precisely an analogous difficulty which has led integrationists to question the self-proclaimed scientific status of modern orthodox linguistics, i.e., its failure to satisfactorily and non-arbitrarily identify and define its purported objects of study, namely individual languages. Even Saussure recognised that the failure to define the object of study was a mortal threat to modern linguistics' claim to be a science, although his solution to the problem was ultimately an unsatisfactory one.

3. Harris' (integrated) mind

Given that distributed cognition is unable to show (as opposed to infer) what – and hence also where – the mind is or might be, does Harris have a more compelling positive (as opposed to positivist) account of mind on offer? This is a matter open to debate, although one can concede that it is an account unlikely to win many converts from within cognitive science. First, it should be made clear that Harris has little truck with eliminativist theories of mind, and is quite clear in stating that he believes himself (and presumably other people) to have a mind (Harris, 2008, p. 155). However, he immediately adds the disclaimer that this belief is not based on any arguments or evidence and that he finds it unlikely that he will "ever find much more about it than [he] can gather from the humdrum experiences of daily life". Harris' argument for the existence of his mind is essentially a linguistic one based on the affordances of English vulgar mindspeak. He admits as much, noting that "the mind I think I have is largely a linguistic construct […] I can imagine that if I had been brought up to speak a quite different language, I might have learnt quite different ways of talking about my inner and outer worlds – perhaps it might have been a language in which there was no word for *mind* at all" (Harris, 2008, p. 158). Indeed, he even expresses a measure of empathy with the view that the existence of mental activities does not logically commit one to the postulation of a mind in which those activities occur. Yet, for Harris, such a view nevertheless constitutes a "verbal cop-out" since the "way vulgar mind-speak works in practice hardly allows us to admit to mental activities and in the same breath deny that we have minds".

Harris' reasoning here is, however, perhaps not especially compelling, and he could be equally vulnerable to accusations of a 'cop-out', since his position suggests that vulgar mindspeak is or ought to be beyond any possibility of revision or reform (see below). However, the question remains as to whether mental activities necessarily need a mind in which to occur, and it is one which cannot be answered by any analysis of linguistic usage, ordinary or otherwise. It is essential not to conflate the semantics of the word *mind* with questions of ontology. Whether we are actually in possession of real-world things which we might call minds is independent of any linguistic conventions which may make reference to them.

Harris' standpoint would seem somewhat tantalizing and probably also deeply unsatisfactory for some, for in effect it amounts to saying that "yes, there may really be no such thing as *the* mind, but ordinary language (in English at least) gives us little option other than to talk as if there were such a thing". Is Harris skirting close to a deterministic position here? It is perhaps significant that Harris' account is largely in the first person. If his point is merely that our ordinary language used to refer to our mental activities is so permeated with terms and expressions implying that there are such entities as minds that he himself is willing to go along with it for the most part – all the while conceding that his mind to which he refers is largely a linguistic construct – there would appear few grounds for dispute. However, given that Harris regards his mind – and presumably those of others – as an essentially linguistic construct, one might counter by arguing that, this being the case, one is therefore free to define and construct it as one chooses and that consequently his attribution of a category mistake to those who choose to construct it differently falls down. What linguistic grounds are there for discouraging one from constructing the mind such that it extends beyond the skull and body of the individual? If you choose to regard certain exosomatic objects as part of you and your mind for particular purposes, who am I to argue? To parry this objection, however, one could question what sense it makes to talk of the location of linguistic constructs given that they are – almost by definition – not real-world objects or entities which occupy physical space. When viewed in this way – i.e., as a linguistic construct – *mind* would seem to belong to the same order of such concepts as *personality* or *identity* . Now, the question 'Where is your personality/identity located?' seems an odd one and I find that, upon personal reflection at least, I have no particular view on the matter and indeed have trouble making sense of the question. One might respond here by claiming that if my mind or personality must, as Harris would maintain, be PART OF me, it must in some sense also be IN me. But in what sense exactly? Again, here no clear answer emerges. Perhaps figuratively or metaphorically, but as Harris (2008, p. 63) himself has noted, it is far from clear that the distributors are indulging in metaphor. The question then is whether reference to the distributed or extended mind is anything more than just a rhetorical device, a 'way of talking' to attract attention to the wider research programme, or whether they are claiming that the mind is something more than a linguistic construct and really is distributed or extended.

What Harris is in effect doing is denying the possibility of a 'real definition' of mind, that is to say a definition which states the essence of the thing 'mind' and which pre-exists its naming. Providing a real definition of mind is therefore not to be regarded as a parallel enterprise to giving such a definition of a natural substance like *salt* or *copper*, for there is no equivalent empirical enquiry which can be conducted into the matter. If a definition is to be provided for some particular purpose then it must be of the word *mind*, which requires one to look at and select from the multiplicity of ways in which it is used. But is a definition of *mind* even necessary other than for the purposes of academic theorizing or compiling dictionaries? After all, lay speakers are presumably able to successfully integrate the term *mind* and its various cognates into patterns of communicative behaviour without having any firm conviction as to what 'the mind' actually is, for there is rarely cause to reflect on the matter. Does the question of whether humans have minds, let alone where they might be located, even crop up in lay discourse? When I tell someone that some matter or other has been "on my mind all week", I would be surprised to say the least if I received a reply along the lines of "well, can you be sure that you even have a mind and if so, where is it?" After all, *mind* is manifestly a term which originates in ordinary, lay language, much like its conventional translation equivalents in other European languages – *Geist, geest, esprit*, etc. Use of the term does not presuppose a scientific account or theory of mind. An instructive analogy can here be made with the integrational critique of orthodox linguistics, a central thrust of which is that mainstream academic linguistics represents the attempted (and indeed ultimately futile) scientization of the lay concept of 'a language' (Love, 2004 , pp. 528–529). A similar accusation could be made against attempts from within cognitive science to define the mind on a more 'scientific' (i.e., surrogationalist) basis. After all, from an integrationist perspective, the semantic footing of 'scientific' language is no more (or less) secure than any other form of discourse, i.e., meaning is equally indeterminate (Harris, 1990, 2005).

Just as Harris (1996a, p. 148) sees no prospect of or point in reforming lay metalanguage in order to do away with the various mythical assumptions about language it may harbour, he also has no ambition to do likewise with vulgar mindspeak, regarding "anyone who has such an agenda [...] as a quack prescribing linguistic pills for philosophical ills' (Harris, 2008, p. 158). Such a position will clearly prove utterly unacceptable for anyone seeking to define the mind on a reocentric basis, whereby the use of a term is validated through its correspondence to an object in the external world. For anyone so inclined, it would consequently be quite intolerable to talk as if one had a mind purely as a consequence of lay linguistic convention. For Harris, however, the challenge is rather to avoid becoming captive to language and to see the myths and misconceptions which it engenders for what they are. Nevertheless, it is interesting to speculate – since he does not address the question directly – on the extent to which Harris would be prepared to go in the direction of favouring vulgar mindspeak over any rival mindspeaks, given its inconsistency. How about religiously or mystically tinged vulgar mindspeak?[7] Would he be willing to sanction talk of the 'soul' or 'spirit' in the same way he does 'mind'? Given the indeterminacy and open-endedness of what could be deemed to constitute vulgar mind-speak, it is by no means clear where one is to draw the line.

I should perhaps again make it clear at this point, if it was not already so, that my purpose here is not to call into question or undermine the entire programme of research which goes under the banner of distributed cognition. My limited objective has been merely to examine, from an integrationist perspective, the theoretical cogency and explanatory utility of the proposition that the mind is or can be distributed. However, this leads on to another important point raised by Harris, namely that of whether the

---

[7] Thanks to an anonymous reviewer for raising this question.

distributors' adherence to the metaphysical contention that the mind is distributed is actually necessary in the context of their wider programme of research. Harris clearly believes not, describing it as a "self-inflicted injury" and "masochistic" (2004, p. 730), and proposes instead to talk of an 'integrating' or 'integrated' mind.

> I think all the essential progress that distributors would like to achieve in understanding language would be furthered if they sacrificed talk of 'distribution' and talked instead of an 'integrating' and 'integrated' mind. That might remove some of the potential misunderstandings and obstacles to co-operation. For the notion that one's mental activities are indeed *jointly* integrated with one's bodily activities and one's environment is at the core of the integrationist approach. […] If we speak of an 'integrating mind', the rationale of the term *integrating* is that in order to explain how different types of sign are created we have to attribute to the mind the ability to integrate a whole range of biomechanically, macrosocially and circumstantially diverse activities. If we speak of an 'integrated mind', the rationale of the term *integrated* is that we conceive of our mental activities as part and parcel of being a creature with a body as well as a mind, functioning biomechanically, macrosocially and circumstantially in the context of a range of local environments. (Harris, 2004, p. 738)

This is not just minor terminological quibbling on Harris' part. As he sees it, the advantage of talking of an integrated/integrating mind rather than a distributed mind is that the former makes no claim about the location of the mind and hence does not commit the category mistake which he identifies in the latter. Furthermore, it would also not seem to require one to abandon the vulgar or lay concept of mind, which the notion of distributed mind clearly does. As such, it is consistent with integrational linguistics' wider concern to be a lay-oriented form of enquiry. This, of course, is not likely to prove a particularly attractive argument for the distributors, whose approach is manifestly not lay-oriented and may even be said to be hostile to such an orientation. Sutton (2004, p. 517), for example, sees the avowed 'lay orientation' of integrational linguistics as a serious obstacle to the advancement of a viable research programme, noting that "Harris's restriction of linguistics to (suitably purified versions of) common-sense understandings threatens to paralyze enquiry". This hostility to a lay-oriented approach is revealed perhaps most starkly in the jargonistic terminology frequently employed by the distributors. For example, instead of 'people' or 'individuals' we find terms such as 'embodied brains', 'brains-bodies', and a pervasive predilection for what Harris terms 'computational rhetoric'. Indeed, it is the peculiar idiom employed in much of the distributed literature which constitutes one of its most inaccessible features from an integrationist point of view. Button (2008) – not an integrationist, although making a point with which Harris would likely sympathize – argues against distributed cognition on the grounds that it gratuitously redescribes the socio-cultural world in the 'arcane language' of cognitive science (see also Jones, 2010). Yet this language of cognitive science itself often draws heavily from the language of computer science, and so what we in effect see is the socio-cultural world described at double remove in a kind of second-hand computerese. It would be an interesting exercise to see whether the distributors would be able to reformulate the full gamut of their claims in something resembling 'ordinary language' and eschewing any computational jargon. Whether they would be inclined to do so is another matter. Spurrett (2004) makes a telling observation when he notes that integrational linguistics' aversion to computational talk in relation to the study of language and the mind points to a 'deep divide' with distributed cognition and scientific approaches more generally. If, as Spurrett claims, acceptance of a computational model of mind is indeed an "admission criterion for the distributor club" one is unlikely to see too many integrationists filling out membership forms.

A more promising candidate for reconciliation with Harris' idea of an integrated mind might – on initial inspection at least – be found in the notion of 'cognitive integration' advanced by Menary (2007, 2010b). Rejecting more traditional internalist and connectionist accounts of cognition, Menary emphasizes the interplay and integration of an organism's body and bodily processes with certain features of its environment in accomplishing cognitive tasks. For Menary (2007, p. 13) a cognitive task includes such acts as "perceiving the world, remembering things about the world and employing things remembered in making inferences, problem solving and the like". Menary (2010b, pp. 229–230) writes that "the primary motivation for cognitive integration is the brute fact of our embodiment, especially our bodily manipulation of environmental vehicles". A chief concern of Menary is to establish that the bounds of cognition and hence the mind lie beyond the brain and body, in contrast to the view of internalists such as Adams and Aizawa (2010), for whom the mind is very definitely 'in the head'. Again, there is a focus on locating cognition and the mind in spatial terms. Harris rejects the validity of debates on the location of the mind altogether, so it is important that by questioning externalism he is not immediately categorized as an internalist alongside Adams and Aizawa. Indeed, Harris explicitly rejects the view that the mind is bounded by the brain, The one area in which Menary's and Harris' otherwise quite kindred notions of 'integration' perhaps do not quite coincide is in regard to which elements of a process either is prepared, for the sake of argumentation, to regard as cognitive. However, given the quite vague agreement on what the term means, this is ultimately a minor matter given the more important shared insight, namely that of the body's and brain's necessary and unavoidable integration with elements of the external physical environment in performing a wide range of contextualized human activities.

4. Integrational linguistics and distributed language

An outgrowth of the increasing reciprocal interest between advocates of distributed cognition and certain researchers in the language sciences has been the emergence of a would-be research paradigm centred upon the notion of 'distributed language'.[8] Like integrationists, proponents of distributed language are seeking to combat the code-based view of language and languages all but ubiquitous in mainstream linguistic theorizing, as well as traditional approaches to linguistic cognition founded upon notions of inner symbolic representation. Distributed language research typically focuses on how individuals coordinate their interactions with each other and the local environment in first-order communication or 'languaging'. According to Thibault (2011, p. 5), the rationale behind the use of the term 'languaging' as opposed to the more common 'language' or 'language use' is that "what we habitually and unthinkingly call 'language' is an open-ended meshwork of interlinked functioning components founded on material dynamics that know no single stable state based on abstract forms. If we assume that language is a stable synchronic state, we end up with the idea that people 'use' a stable language system and its concomitant that individual persons are 'language users'." Here we see a reformulation of the integrationist insight that humans are more properly regarded as 'language-makers' (Harris, 1980) rather than users. Admittedly, this is little or no mention of the term 'languaging' in the integrationist literature, but there is clearly a great deal of common

---

[8] It is worth mentioning that Roy Harris has not discussed the notion of 'distributed language' in any publications to date.

ground here based on the rejection of a Saussurean-type linguistics concerned with the description and analysis of form-based abstracta.

What, though, are we to make of the proposition that language is distributed, and what theoretical status are we to assign to it? While Linell (2013) is quite prepared to talk of Distributed Language Theory, the position statement of the Distributed Language Group[9] makes the claim that "[t]here can, we believe, be no theory of distributed language", which itself of course is very much a theoretical proposition. What then is the motivation for viewing language as distributed? According to Rączaszek-Leonardi (2009, p. 670), "Far from being reducible to a system 'in the brain', language must be viewed as radically heterogeneous and as spread across space, time and bodies", while Steffensen (2009, p. 684) similarly claims that "language is a heterogeneous set of physical, cognitive and social activities that unfold in real-time on many time-scales. It arises as we adjust to each other and coordinate our life worlds with each other, behaviourally and cognitively." The key point of emphasis then in the distributed account would seem to be the non-local or, as Linell (2013) would prefer it, the nonlocalizable character of language.[10] The parallels with the notion of the distributed mind are clear. If language is not just to be found in the brain and about the body, it must be therefore be seen as extending into the local environment and incorporating or co-opting non-human elements of it. This non-localizability leads Cowley (2014, p. 68) to claim enigmatically that language is both "nowhere and everywhere". The immediate suspicion which again arises though, from a Harrisian perspective at least, is whether the same kind of cate-

---

[9] Online: < http://www.psy.herts.ac.uk/dlg/index.html >.
[10] Nevertheless, elsewhere Linell (2009, p. 151) talks of meanings being located in an 'interworld', a rather mystical metaphysical proposition if ever there was one, and also surprising given that 'meaning' is not a first-order concept.

gory mistake is not once again being made. While an integrationist would certainly agree that linguistic communication involves the interaction of mind, body, and environment, does this warrant the conclusion that language is itself distributed? Does non-localizability entail distributedness? Do the questions 'Where is language?' or 'Where does language take place?' even make sense? They are certainly not the sorts of questions one can envisage cropping up in lay discourse.

What does not emerge especially clearly from the distributed language literature is a unified sense of what 'language' is or is taken to be. Perhaps the most succinct definition is that offered by Thibault (2011, p. 7) who states that "[f]irst-order languaging [...] is whole-body sense-making activity that enables persons to engage with each other in forms of coactions and to integrate themselves with and to take part in social activities that may be performed either solo or together with other agents". This is a definition with which an integrationist, although unlikely to put it in quite those terms, could not find too much fault, as it highlights the important integrationist point that language is not limitable to mere verbal output and that no definitive dividing line can be drawn between the linguistic and non-linguistic components of a communicational episode. To this extent, the distributed and integrational approaches to language would seem to largely coincide as regards their views of what first-order linguistic activity actually involves. The more contentious issue would seem to centre more upon the terms and concepts invoked in its description and analysis. As with the notion of distributed mind, an integrationist will again be inclined to pose the question of what benefit there is to be gained from describing language as distributed as opposed to integrated. After all, for integrationists the term 'language' refers chiefly to the human faculty or capacity for verbal sign-making which comprises both the physical production and interpretation of signs. In first-order communication, this capacity is integrated with other biomechanical and cognitive capacities as well as with features of the local environment. This much is uncontroversial. However, to accept the view that language is distributed would seem to require something of a redefinition away from this view of language, since it hardly makes sense to say that my capacity to create signs extends beyond my brain and body, beyond me in effect. According to Cowley (2009, p. 497), "language emerges as bodies engage with both each other and the world". The thing is, though, almost any form of human (inter)activity could be described in this way – cricket emerges as bodies engage with each other and bat and ball, fishing emerges as bodies engage with rod and line, etc. Are cricket and fishing also distributed? If so, it is not especially clear what is to be gained from describing them thus. What would it contribute to our understanding to say that cricket is distributed across players, balls, stumps, etc.? What such activities manifestly are though is INTEGRATED and INTEGRATING. From the distributed perspective then, it seems language is not merely to be equated with human sign-making but expanded to also include the material artefacts and products which may facilitate and result from such sign-making.[11] Is there any temptation for the Harrisian integrationist to view language in this way? It seems doubtful, since the notion of integrated language alone performs the necessary theoretical task – i.e., that of emphasizing the interaction of mental, physical, and environmental phenomena – without requiring one to subscribe to the rather arcane metaphysics inherent in the distributed view. If we are to regard language as a form of semiologically driven behaviour or activity, it is surely a category mistake to assign linguistic status to non-human material artefacts. To do so is to confuse their material form with their semiological function, and in order to function semiologically they require the presence of a sign/language-maker, that is to say some-

---

[11] From the Distributed Language Group website: "The term 'language' applies to a heterogeneous bundle of events, activities and material artefacts."

one who integrates them into a pattern of activity. Viewed in this way, the question of the location of the sign as a semiological phenomenon – be it localized or distributed – is a red herring and just does not arise.

A more substantial and, in my view, potent integrationist objection to the distributed language approach might run as follows. As a self-avowed 'scientific' approach to human interaction, the distributed language approach needs a determinate, objective object of analysis. Indeed, a unit of analysis. In passing, one can note the rather rich irony of Harris' integrational linguistics serving as a theoretical 'springboard' (Steffensen, 2011, p. 204) for a supposedly scientific approach to human interaction, given his repeated contestation of linguistics' claim to scientific status. Clearly, in seeking to identify such a unit of analysis, the phenomenological Saussurean dictum that, as far as language is concerned, it is the point of view which creates the object, will not do in this regard. Now, of course, by endorsing an integrationist view of language and communication which denies the linguistic sign any sort of determinacy, one is forced to seek determinacy elsewhere. The distributed language view does so by locating it in the postulated distributed socio-cognitive system or 'extended ecology', which it sees as responsible for producing human interactional behaviour. Steffensen's (2011, p. 205) remark that "in order to fully grasp the complexities of human interaction and cognition, the entire extended ecology will have to become our unit of analysis" is highly revealing in this regard. The "entire extended ecology" is clearly held to be a determinate entity. This may well be the case, of course, if it amounts to nothing more than the claim that the workings of the universe are fundamentally determinate and regular. Integrational linguistics also has no place for magic or mystification. The more important question is whether this "entire extended ecology" is in any realistic or practical sense DETERMINABLE, especially when it includes, as it must surely do, a temporal dimension (Uryu,

Steffensen, & Kramsch, 2014). How does one go about determining all the events and arrangements of matter which have contributed to an episode of human interaction? How does one identify and rank relevant causality within that process? It is rather like retrospectively explaining the weather. How far back does one go? How can one be sure one has all relevant data? Explanations of everything come to an end somewhere. Different human purposes call for different levels of explanation, different units of analysis. The problem with the "entire extended ecology" is that it is so unwieldy a notion as to be barely credible or operable when conceived of as a unit. The notion of a unit implies countability, and therefore also discreteness. How does one go about identifying the boundaries of and between different extended ecologies? If there are none, or it cannot practically be done, then we can hardly be said to be dealing with a unit in any recognizable sense of the term. Just as Saussure was never actually able to identify with any conviction any actual, real-world examples of a *langue* in his technical sense of the term as an ontologically real social unit of the human language faculty, it seems as if a similar difficulty may attach to the extended ecologies of the distributors. What is interesting in both cases is that a communal social system, admittedly of a quite different type and emphasis, is posited to which the individual person appears wholly subordinate. Under both the Saussurean and distributed models, it is the system which ultimately determines an individual's behaviour as well as his/her phenomenological experience. Hence Steffensen's (2011, p. 205) remark that "in an extended ecology [...] biology and phenomenology cease to be individual". Now, of course, pointing out similarities between Saussure and the distributed language approach may be seen as a provocative manoeuvre, given the latter's wholesale rejection of the former. However, it seems clear that under both approaches the individual *qua* individual is required to fall out of view in order to establish a determinate, albeit highly abstract, unit/object of analysis.

From an integrationist viewpoint, in seeking to understand human communication, the solution to the quandary thrown up by the indeterminacy of the linguistic sign is not merely to relocate determinacy or to go and seek it elsewhere. The only SEMIOLOGICAL determinacy an integrationist is willing to recognize is a phenomenological one based on the individual's own experience. This is not to affirm the view that individuals are merely doing and saying what they claim to be doing and saying, although this subjective dimension is clearly lost sight of to a considerable extent in the distributed language view. Lay (meta)linguistic knowledge does not hold a trump card in this sense. The point rather is that the semiological dimension of a communicative encounter cannot be 'got at' from a third-party, outsider perspective other than through an essentially and ultimately inadequate behaviouristic account. While the distributed view sees the integrationist preoccupation with the individual's private semiological experience as unduly narrow, one might counter by asking to what extent viewing language naturalistically as socially coordinated whole-body sense-making activity underplays the role of individuals' second-order metacommunicative beliefs and conceptualizations in shaping their interactional behaviour (dynamics vs. symbols). Once again, though, one is left faced with the seemingly intractable problem of how to go about investigating such a question empirically.

Distributed language claims to be concerned with human interactivity in its broadest sense. An important point to consider, however, is that not all human interactivity is semiological activity. Not all integrations involve contextualized sign-making activity. The most obvious examples here are purely sensory experiences and the biomechanical responses they draw forth (Harris, 1996b, pp. 176–178). Now, in claiming that "language is real-time metabolic activity" and that "language functions as airborne synapses" (2011, p. 205), Steffensen would seem effectively to be eradicating any distinction between the semiological and non-semiological. Language certainly would not be possible without metabolic activity, but it is altogether another matter to claim that language is metabolic activity. Playing the piano is also not possible without metabolic activity, but it hardly advances our understanding of what it involves and requires of individuals to say that it just is metabolic activity. A conception of language removed from semiology and which is theoretically unable or unwilling to acknowledge the distinction between those forms of interaction mediated by the real-time contextualization of signs by individual sign-makers and those which do not is an impoverished one and explanatorily inadequate. Language is in a very important sense then not like breathing or thermoregulation.

5. Conclusion

As to the question of whether the notion of 'distributed/extended mind' comprises a category mistake, there can be no conclusive answer. As I have argued, if one accepts an integrationist view of language, traditional ordinary language arguments which purport to separate sense from nonsense can only hold in respect of the individuals advancing them, and even then are always subject to the possibility of revision. They cannot apply in any timeless, fact-of-the-matter sense to all the individuals of the postulated linguistic community. This is not to say, of course, that individuals cannot be persuaded by such arguments and come to hold similar views. It is, more importantly, to say that sense and nonsense do not reside in a language and the structures and sentences into which its constituent units may be combined. Rather, attributions of sense and nonsense are the product of an individual's own sign-making activities, however much they are embedded in a social world. If, as Harris (2004, p. 729) claims, we find ourselves in agreement that we have no viable choice other than to regard the mental activities which constitute our 'inner world' as *sui generis*, one might be more inclined to answer the question in the affirmative. However, if, as the distributed position suggests, there is nothing especially significant about the internal-external distinction in terms of the capacities which individuals possess for integrating their activities with their environment, then Harris' contention would perhaps appear less persuasive.

What, then, of language? While it is important not to lose sight of the fact that the integrational and distributed approaches to language and cognition do indeed share a number of crucial theoretical insights which set them apart from the great majority of approaches in contemporary linguistics, the inevitable question which emerges is to what degree the differences which exist between them act as a barrier to further, sustained cooperation and incorporation of respective insights. The (Harrisian) integrationist difficulty with talk of distribution as outlined thus far ought not to be interpreted as a fundamental rejection of the entire theoretical basis of the distributed programme, which in any case is far from homogenous, although there are undoubtedly also other points on which an integrationist may take issue with it. The limited claim made here is that the notion of distribution brings very little of theoretical benefit to the table, and is instead a source of potential confusion and obscuration. In other words, it is a notion which is dispensable and better replaced by the notion of INTEGRATION, and it is noticeable that certain distributors do indeed frequently talk of integration in a manner broadly consistent with the integrationist position. Not everything therefore stands or falls on the issue of distribution since so little seems to actually depend on it. Sutton (2004, pp. 514–515) is probably closer to the mark when he notes that a more fundamental difference between the two approaches is the level of analysis and explanation at which they operate.

> Integrational Linguistics is about embodied agents, not their components. Where machines compute [...] living

bodies contextualize. Not brains, but conscious human bodies are masters of symbolic reference and the tasks those bodies engage in are separate from the neural instruments used. Integrational Linguistics, then, is to operate at the personal level of explanation, which is autonomous from and irreducible to any subpersonal processes and mechanisms: this personal level, however, is not to be understood psychologically, but as the level of ordinary integrative agency in the natural and social world.

Is it simply the case that we are just dealing with different, but not necessarily conflicting perspectives? Is it that the personal level of explanation sought by the integrationist points towards a quite different form of philosophical-epistemological enquiry to the naturalistic, organic-holistic perspective adopted by the distributors? Harris (2013, p. 56) has stated that "Philosophically, integrationism is a form of existentialism [...] in the Sartrian sense", which clearly speaks of a commitment to the view that there are such things as individual minded agents which, although they interact with each other, nevertheless retain their individuality. Whatever distributed cognition or language is, it is quite manifestly not a form of existentialism in the Sartrian or any other sense. That said, I am far from certain that all card-carrying integrationists would necessarily embrace Harris' idea of integrationism as an existentialist philosophy of language with any great enthusiasm. In any case though, from the distributed perspective, the integrationist perspective is likely to be seen as entailing an unwarrantedly solipsistic view, whereas for the integrationist it is essential to understanding the HUMAN dimension of linguistic communication – which includes issues of individual agency, morality, and responsibility – as opposed to merely the anatomical or bio-cognitive aspects.

Sutton (2004, p. 520) does point to an area of more significant theoretical tension though, when he goes on to state that "the possibility of developing a shared vision for Integrational Linguistics and distributed cognition depends on the integrationists dropping some more extreme glosses on their important insights". These "extreme glosses" include the rejection of a scientific approach to linguistics, which manifests as an unflinching lay orientation and a dogmatic attention to context and contextualization which in Sutton's view rules out any attempts at explanatory generalization. An integrationist might reply here in a (later) Wittgensteinian spirit that the drawing of general conclusions is not the primary concern. Instead, the focus ought to be on elucidating the hitherto unappreciated diversity in human communicative behaviour and the dissolving of pathological, category-mistake-invoking questions – in the case of the present discussion, questions concerning location. This fundamentally philosophical therapeutic conception of enquiry into language and cognition is of course less likely to appeal to the scientifically minded researcher and perhaps points to a more unbridgeable divide in outlook and method.

A useful question to consider is whether the distributed language approach actually needs the concept of 'language' at all. It is doubtful whether it does, and indeed this point seems to be openly acknowledged in Steffensen's (2011, p. 204) dictum "If you want to learn about language, forget about language!" It is perhaps in this light then that we can best understand Cowley's previously mentioned claim that there can be no theory of distributed language given that there is no single, unitary phenomenon in the natural world that is language. If distributed language is not or cannot actually be a theory of language, it seems to me that it can only promote conceptual confusion to nevertheless continuously refer to 'distributed language' and affirm the proposition that 'language is distributed'. It is a case of trying to make an ordinary lay term do too much. Language is neither distributed nor not distributed. Of course, it may appear that I am simply setting out my own 'ordinary language' argument in respect of distributed language which is subject to precisely the same criticism as I have applied to the arguments of Harris and Nardi above, and this is indeed largely the case. My purpose here is primarily to persuade and, in doing so, seek some form of useful agreement on the meaning of terms in the hope that conceptual coherence and theoretical understanding of the relevant phenomena may be advanced. Whether I succeed in doing so is another matter and one for individual readers to decide.

Finally, it seems then that integrationism might need to pay a double price for incorporation into the distributed movement. Not only would it have to moderate some of its central theoretical claims, it would also have to accept, or at least turn a blind eye to, talk of distribution. Hence the "compromise position" which Harris (2004, p. 730) accuses Cowley of occupying – "a bit of integration plus a bit of distribution". As with asking the distributors to abandon talk of distribution – an improbable act of self-refutation – for integrationists this may be too high a theoretical price to pay. It is therefore probably too rash or optimistic to talk of incorporating either of the approaches into the other. Theoretically and conceptually important differences remain.

REFERENCES

Adams, F. , & Aizawa, K. (2010). Defending the bounds of cognition . In Richard Menary (Ed.), *The extended mind* (pp. 67 – 80). Cambridge, MA : MIT Press.

Bennett, M., & Hacker, P. (2003). *Philosophical foundations of neuroscience*. Oxford : Blackwell.

Blackburn, S. (1994). *The Oxford dictionary of philosophy*. Oxford : Oxford University Press .

Button, G. (2008). Against 'distributed cognition'. *Theory, Culture & Society*, **25**(2), 87 – 104.

Chalmers, D. (2008). Foreword. In A. Clark, *Supersizing the*

mind: embodiment, action and cognitive extension (pp. ix
– xvi). Oxford : Oxford University Press.
Clark, A., & Chalmers, D. (1998). The extended mind. *Analysis*,
58(1), 7 – 19.
Cowley, S. J. (2004). Contextualizing bodies: human infants and
distributed cognition. *Language Sciences* , **26**, 565 – 591.
Cowley, S. J. (2009). Introduction: distributed language and
dynamics. *Pragmatics & Cognition*, **17**(3), 495 – 507.
Cowley, S. J. (2014). Bio-ecology and language: a necessary
unity. *Language Sciences*, **41** (Part A), 60 – 70.
Cowley, S. J. , & Spurrett, D. (2003) 'Putting apes (body and
language) together again', a review article of S. Savage-
Rumbaugh, T. J. Taylor, & S. G. Shanker, *Apes, language,
and the human mind* (Oxford: 1999) and A. Clark *Being
there: putting brain, body, and world together again*
(MIT: 1997). *Language Sciences*, **25** (3), 289 – 318.
Cowley, S. J. , & Vallee-Tourangeau , F. (Eds.) (2013).
*Cognition beyond the brain: computation, interactivity
and human artifice*. Springer-Verlag : Berlin.
Gallagher, S. (2005). *How the body shapes the mind*. Oxford :
Oxford University Press.
Hampshire, S. (1971). Critical review of 'The Concept of Mind '.
In O. P. Wood & G. Pitcher (Eds.), *Ryle* (pp. 17 – 44).
London : Macmillan.
Harris, R. (1980). *The language-makers*. London : Duckworth.
Harris, R. (1981). *The language myth*. London : Duckworth.
Harris, R. (1990). The scientist as *homo loquens*. In R. Bhaskar
(Ed.), *Harré and his critics:essays in honour of Rom
Harré, with his commentary on them* (pp. 65–86). Oxford:
Blackwell .
Harris, R. (1996a). *The language connection: philosophy and
linguistics*. Bristol : Thoemmes.
Harris, R. (1996b). *Signs, language and communication*. London
and New York : Routledge.

Harris, R. (2004). Integrationism, language, mind and world. *Language Sciences*, **26**, 727 – 739.
Harris, R. (2005). *The semantics of science*. London : Continuum.
Harris, R. (2008). *Mindboggling: preliminaries to a science of the mind*. Luton : Pantaneto Press.
Harris, R. (2013). *Language and intelligence*. Gamlingay: Bright Pen.
Hutchins, E. (1995a). *Cognition in the wild*. Cambridge, MA : MIT Press.
Hutchins, E. (1995b). How a cockpit remembers its speeds. *Cognitive Science*, **19** (3), 265 – 288.
Hutchins, E. (2000). Distributed cognition. http://files.meetup.com/410989/DistributedCognition.pdf (accessed July 2014).
Jones, P. E. (2010). You want a piece of me? Paying your dues and getting your due in a distributed world. *AI & Society*, **25** (4), 455 – 464.
Linell, P. (2009). *Rethinking language, mind and world dialogically*. Charlotte, NC : Information Age Publishing.
Linell, P. (2013). Distributed language theory, with or without dialogue. *Language Sciences*, **40**, 168 – 173.
Love, N. (2004). Cognition and the language myth. *Language Sciences*, **26**, 525 – 544.
Menary, R. (2007). *Cognitive integration: mind and cognition unbounded*. Basingstoke : Palgrave Macmillan.
Menary, R. (Ed.) (2010a). *The extended mind* Cambridge, MA : MIT Press.
Menary, R. (2010b). Cognitive integration and extended mind. In Menary (2010a, pp. 227–244).
Melser, D. (2004). *The act of thinking*. Cambridge, MA : MIT Press.
Nardi, B. A . (2002). Coda and response to Christine Halverson. *Computer Supported Cooperative Work*, **11**, 269 – 275.

Rączaszek-Leonardi, J. (2009). Symbols as constraints: the structuring role of dynamics and self-organization in natural language. *Pragmatics and Cognition*, **17** (3), 653 – 676.

Ross, D. (2007). Introduction: science catches the will . In Don Ross, David Spurrett, Harold Kincaid, & G. Lynn Stephens (Eds.), *Distributed cognition and the will: individual volition and social context* (pp. 1 – 16). Cambridge, MA : MIT Press.

Ryle, G. (1949). *The concept of mind*. London : Hutchinson.

Sinha, C. , & Jensen De López, K. (2000). Language, culture and the embodiment of spatial cognition. *Cognitive Linguistics*, **1/2**, 17 – 41.

Spurrett, D. (2004). Distributed cognition and integrational linguistics. *Language Sciences*, **26**, 497 – 501.

Steffensen, S. V. (2009). Language, languaging and the Extended Mind Hypothesis. *Pragmatics & Cognition*, **17** (3), 677 – 697.

Steffensen, S. V. (2011). Beyond mind: an extended ecology of languaging. In S. J. Cowley (Ed.), *Distributed language* (pp. 185 – 210). Amsterdam : John Benjamins.

Sutton, J. (2004). Representation, levels, and contexts in integrational linguistics and distributed cognition. *Language Sciences*, **26**, 503 – 524.

Thibault, P. J. (2011). First-order languaging dynamics and second-order language: the distributed language view. *Ecological Psychology*, **23** (1), 1 – 36.

Uryu, M., Steffensen , S. V. , & Kramsch, C. (2014). The ecology of intercultural interaction: timescales, temporal ranges and identity dynamics. *Language Sciences*, **41**(A), 41–59.

Wheeler, M. (2004). Is language the ultimate artefact? *Language ScienceS*, **26** (6): 693 – 715.

9.

Scientism and the language sciences

Abstract
The article identifies two broad strands of scientism in modern linguistic thought. The first is that of mainstream linguistics which consists in the unwarranted scientisation of a culture-specific, second order metalinguistic discourse. The second, and the main focus of the paper, is that found in more recent naturalistic approaches to language and cognition, notably the Distributed Language Approach (DLA), which involves a dogmatic rejection of attempts to make sense of folk metalinguistic discourse. Both forms of scientism are characterised by their strong reductionism. It is argued that if enquiry into language is to be reconceived along more fruitful and humanistic lines, such scientific reductionism is to be avoided. This requires taking seriously integrational linguistics' advocacy of a lay-orientated form of enquiry.

'What, after all, have we to show for non-scientific or pre-scientific good judgment, or common sense, or the insights gained through personal experience? It is science or nothing.'
B.F. Skinner (1971:152–3)

'We are not doing natural science.' Wittgenstein (PU, p.230)

'It takes more than thousands of linguists chanting in unison "Linguistics is a science" to make it so.' Roy Harris (2005:84)

1. Introduction

The question of whether modern linguistics or any of the other academic disciplines which may fall under the indeterminate shade offered by the umbrella of the so-called and largely self-styled 'language sciences' are fittingly and intelligibly regarded as scientific is not quite the same as asking whether a science of language is possible in principle and, if so, what its requirements, limitations and uses might be. Nevertheless, it is instructive to consider both questions in conjunction since they point to a related concern, namely that of establishing the legitimacy or illegitimacy of particular forms of enquiry. The purely linguistic question of whether or not a certain discipline is labelled as a science is ultimately of secondary importance and is not one by which its academic credentials automatically stand or fall, although this is not to deny the widespread prestige which accrues to those disciplines thought of as 'genuine' sciences and the scorn often heaped upon supposed 'pseudosciences'.We are not, then, dealing here solely with matters of semantics or rhetoric. As the above quotation from Roy Harris makes clear, there is – or at least ought to be – more to being a science than simply being called or calling oneself a science. However, rhetoric may be a pointer towards more significant convictions and, as I shall argue, what is of great importance is whether the practitioners of a particular discipline regard themselves as being engaged in genuine scientific work or in some quite different type of enquiry since this is likely to have a crucial impact on the type of assumptions made, the questions asked (and indeed regarded as askable), the conceptualisation of the object of enquiry and the methods of investigation adopted.

On the face of it, it would seem both reasonable and uncontroversial to assert that a minimum requirement for a credible 'science of language' is the ability to say with certainty what language is and unambiguously identify which phenomena in the world are to count as linguistic and those which are not. Failure to do so might signal one of two things; either a humble admission that we have yet to truly or fully discover what language actually is in which case the notion of a science of language still stands as something of a promissory note, but a potentially valid one nevertheless, or the recognition that the notion of language answers to no determinate range of phenomena, thereby all but ruling out the idea of a science of language from the off. Modern mainstream linguistics, however, can hardly be accused of either of these failings. After all, its preferred approach has been to supply a very definite answer to the question, admittedly sometimes following a fair degree of definitional gymnastics, and then proceed more or less securely in the belief that linguistics simply is the science of language and that linguists are indeed scientists, while perhaps also being philosophers, sociologists, pedagogues etc. into the bargain. Unfortunately, as various authors – most notably and lucidly Roy Harris (1980, 1981, 1997) – have shown, the answers which modern linguistics has supplied have turned out to be highly inadequate, not to say downright misleading. On this alternative view, modern linguistics is a science of bogus entities and implausible metaphysical postulates. In short, it is not really a science at all.

An underlying argument advanced in this article is that the near-compulsive desire to have a science of language has, in various guises throughout the course of modern linguistic thought, all too often instead resulted in scientism and in doing so diverted attention from more fruitful and humanistic avenues of linguistic enquiry. Two broad strands of scientism can be identified in contemporary thinking on language. The first is that of mainstream or orthodox linguistics and consists primarily in the unwarranted and pernicious scientisation of a culture-specific, second-order meta-linguistic discourse (Love, 2009). That is to say it involves the misapplication of a scientific methodology and epistemological framework to the study of putative linguistic objects of dubious ontological status which it radically misconceives as *realia*. The scientism of orthodox linguistics is the relatively straightforward scientism of doing linguistics as though it were a science. Here we find a clear echo of Wittgenstein's criticism of Frazer's *The Golden Bough* in which he takes Frazer to task for doing anthropology as if it too were a science (Child, 2017). The second form of scientism, and the principal focus of this paper, is one which can be located in certain more recent epistemically naturalistic approaches to language – most notably the Distributed Language Approach (DLA) – which tend to locate themselves outside of linguistics and style themselves as instead belonging to the cognitive and/or language sciences. The scientism of such approaches consists primarily in a reductivist or eliminativist rejection of nonscientific forms of understanding and, in particular, attempts to make sense of the *explananda* of lay metalinguistic and psychological discourse (see Taylor, 2015, for an overview).

One approach which in my view avoids either form of scientism (and any resultant metaphysics) is the integrational linguistic approach most strongly associated with the work of Roy Harris. It does so by recognising that where language is concerned, the kind of determinate object required for scientific enquiry can only be obtained through reification, abstraction and by decontextualising language from the real-life communicational episodes which give rise to it in the first place. Yet, as Harris (2000: 78) notes, one cannot establish a science on the basis of abstractions. A form of linguistic enquiry conceived along such lines is not only scientifically suspect but more importantly an obstacle to the understanding of something more fundamental, namely human communication. The key to the integrationist position on both language and the possibility of a science of language is its affirmation of *the radical indeterminacy of the linguistic sign*. For integrationists, signs of any sort can only be rendered determinate in form or meaning by the contextualised sign-making activities of individuals and even then only provisionally since they are always subject to possible recontextualisation. The upshot of adopting this view is that there is then nothing open to inspection by third-party observers on which to base any science of language as a semiological phenomenon. As Harris and Hutton (2007:222–223) make clear, the consequence of such indeterminacy is that we are looking in wholly the wrong place if we expect science to provide us with fundamental insights into linguistic knowledge:

> Integrationism is committed to a 'lay-oriented' analysis of communication in the following sense: that, where language is concerned, there is no basis of knowledge or expertise other than that available to any lay member of the community. This basis is the experience acquired by participation in the process of interaction with others [...] All the metalinguistic terms and concepts used in asking and answering questions about language are ultimately derived from – and have to be explicated by reference to – someone's first-order linguistic experience. If that explanatory chain cannot be satisfactorily established, then the linguist – not the lay person – has been led astray.

2. Science or scientism in linguistic enquiry?

At this stage of the discussion, I am obviously obliged to spell out more precisely what I take scientism to be in relation to the study of language and to say what, on my understanding, distinguishes it from science 'proper'. In doing so, it would be facile of me to simply parrot dictionary definitions or those offered by other authors. In this section, I shall therefore set out in fairly broad terms what I see scientism as consisting in and also identify certain core features common to some of the admittedly quite different theoretical approaches to language which I see as incorporating elements of scientism.

It could be argued that any form of linguistic enquiry which calls itself a 'science' or claims to belong to the 'language sciences' ought automatically to be categorised as scientistic on that basis alone and indeed if one accepts the integrationist view of language and communication as radically indeterminate in terms of both what is said and what is meant, this is certainly a valid and powerful argument.[1] There can, after all, be no science of the indeterminate. Elements of such a – what one might call – rhetorical scientism can be located in both orthodox linguistics and naturalistic approaches such as the DLA. For example, in the case of the former it is commonplace, especially in introductory textbooks or books aimed at the educated non-specialist, to encounter unargued-for and unelaborated assertions, posing as uncontroversial and authoritative fact, to the effect that linguistics just is the scientific study of language, a claim readers are presumably expected to take on trust (see Evans, 2015:3, for a recent example). For a detailed discussion of the history of linguistics' rhetorical construction of itself as a science, see Harris (2005: chapter 5).

---

[1] I am grateful to an anonymous reviewer for explicitly drawing my attention to this point.

The rhetoric of science also figures prominently in the DLA's self-presentation. For example, Steffensen (2015:116) writes of 'important scientific revolutions in contemporary language sciences' in which the DLA is clearly held to be at the vanguard. Elsewhere, Cowley (2009:500) mentions the Distributed Language Group's goal of 'transforming the language sciences' and the DLA literature as a whole appears unanimous in locating the approach within or as contiguous with the cognitive sciences. Despite such rhetoric, it is my argument that the analyses of episodes of human interaction typically offered by proponents of DLA are simply not scientific but are instead interpretations based on their own individual experiences as communicating persons and are furthermore no less interesting or insightful as a result.

If one looks beyond mere surface rhetoric, however, the claim that one is engaged in a science of language can also be interpreted in a more fundamental light, namely as evidence that one has either fatally misconceived the object of enquiry or failed to understand what it is that makes a form of investigation scientific. A rhetorical scientism is therefore likely to be a pointer towards a more thoroughgoing scientism. Just as there is more to being a science than calling oneself a science, there is often more to being scientistic than wrongly or thoughtlessly calling oneself a science. Indeed, my argument is that scientism in linguistic enquiry tends also to have both onto-epistemological and methodological manifestations. One feature common to self-proclaimed 'scientific' approaches to language is their inherent reductionism in both the conceptualisation and investigation of the object of enquiry. They seek to overcome the inherent heterogeneity of language by reducing it to what is regarded as its barest elements, mechanisms or what might even be styled as its 'essence'. What that essence is of course depends on the theoretical perspective adopted and the philosophical assumptions made and these are often deeply problematic. By denying or ignoring the full heterogeneity of language, whether methodologically, rhetorically or both, reductionist approaches misrepresent language and obscure its nature as a fully integrated *semiological* phenomenon. My argument can therefore be read as an appeal against both reductionism and essentialism in linguistic enquiry, both of which are allies of scientism. Attributions of scientism must be distinguished from mere allegations of scientific error or poor scientific practice which might reside in such things as mistakes in measurement, observation or data collection etc. Scientism instead resides primarily in philosophical or conceptual error and a failure to correctly or fully identify the object of enquiry. This is a failure born chiefly of the inherent radical indeterminacy of language. The enduring obstacle confronting those seeking to establish a science of language is described by Nigel Love as follows:

> [I]t can be argued that much of what has passed for a science of language over the last 150 years has been nothing but an exercise in culture maintenance. Irrespective of what kind of science linguistics is held out to be (and different linguists have had different views on this), in so far as 'science' is those branches of study that deal with measurable and hence precisely identifiable phenomena, the perennial problem for a science of language has been to identify the phenomena that might constitute its object of study. In the words of one recent commentator, the history not just of linguistic science in the modern sense, but of linguistic thought more broadly 'can in fact be considered as a series of attempts to determine the essentially linguistic, and with each new determination a new object, claiming the name of language, is brought into focus'. (Love, 2009:31)

The trouble for those seeking to identify the 'essentially linguistic' object is, as Love goes on to observe, that 'there do not seem to be any identifiable linguistic objects for the science of language to be the scientific investigation of' (Love, 2009:39). As a result, those still seeking to establish a scientific linguistics in the absence of any ready-made linguistic object have tended to resort to metaphysics in order to manufacture one. In Saussure's case, there is the belief in telementation (Toolan, 1997) – an inheritance from a long tradition of Western linguistic thought – and *langue*, the supposedly psychologically-real, shared system of signs of which no single individual has full knowledge or even the slightest control over but which, mystically, resides fully only in the collective mind of the speech community ('la langue n'est complete dans aucun, elle n'existe parfaitement que dans la masse'). It is not my purpose here to go too much further into any critical discussion of the scientific credentials of Saussurean or Chomskyan linguistics as this has been done extensively, indeed often devastatingly, enough on numerous previous occasions by integrationists and non-integrationists alike. For in-depth critical commentaries on the metaphysical basis underlying Chomskyan linguistics and Chomsky's rationale for asserting its scientific validity, see Love (1989, 1992), Sampson (2005) and Golumbia (2015). See also Sampson (1979) for explicit reference to Chomsky's scientism. It suffices here to say that where Saussure and Chomsky's scientistic reductionism coincides is in their shared belief that the only way to have a viable science of language is to take as its object an abstract and hypostatised form of unit-based linguistic structure and ignore all else. What primarily distinguishes their respective approaches are the metaphysical rationales for arriving at a description and analysis of said structure.

One way to illustrate the scientism-science distinction is to contrast and compare the claims to scientific status of, say, articulatory or acoustic phonetics with those of phonology. While the claims of the former may be seen to have a persuasive validity on account of the fact that they are fields of enquiry which deal in the analysis and description of *measurable physical properties* of articulation, acoustics and audition (such as waveform amplitudes, vocal tract resonances, airflows, movements of the articulatory organs etc.) allowing them to be viewed as a somewhat minor subfields of both biology and physics (Pierrehumbert, 1990), the same cannot be said for phonology. Indeed, phonology essentially constitutes a psychological thesis and can be seen as incorporating both the reductionist and metaphysical elements of scientism. In fact, the reductionism of phonology stems from the metaphysical commitments underlying it. The metaphysical basis of phonology is its discipline-constitutive postulation of discrete and determinate sound systems which describe or map onto 'languages'. Yet as integrationists and many others have been arguing for years, the orthodox linguist's languages are not first-order givens (i.e. ontologically real) but second-order abstractions erroneously posing as first-order givens. As Thibault (2011:11) rightly notes: '[m]ainstream linguistics [...] has split "language" into real and abstract formal patterns (e.g. the distinction between phonetics and phonology) and focused on abstracta in constructing the theoretical object "language"'. The reductionism of phonology consists in its banishment from description and analysis those auditory elements of human communication which cannot be accommodated within the unit-based sound system of the language or lect purportedly under description. In other words, phonology describes nothing real but rather a theoretically motivated abstraction. Now, none of this is to say that second-order abstract descriptions are automatically scientistic of themselves. The phoneme principle is not scientistic purely because it does not correspond to the real nature of the phonic medium for language but rather because it thinks it does. That is to say it is generally claimed by phonologists to give rise to a real, i.e. objectively, scientifically correct, description of said phonic medium. Phonology is therefore a clear-cut instance of the scientism of the 'language myth' (Harris, 1981).

A final characteristic of scientism common to both orthodox linguistics and the naturalistic language sciences, and one which I shall expand upon in greater detail in the next section, is a notable lack of interest and in some cases hostile rejection of what are seen as non-scientific or lay forms of understanding. In the discussion which follows, my claim is that unlike in the case of, say, organic chemistry, where language is concerned this is highly problematic and can be seen as a symptom of what Wittgenstein would have called the 'scientistic attitude' which Monk (1999:66) characterises as 'the view that every intelligible question has either a scientific solution or no solution at all.'

Those unsympathetic to the position outlined above might be quick to point out that it appears to rest on little more than a highly prescriptive notion of what constitutes a science and scientific enquiry. Am I not just attempting to stake out the ground for my own preferred and no doubt prejudiced conception of what science is or ought to be? There may well be some truth in this but in response I would simply offer the following consideration. If one accepts that what are known as the natural sciences – those areas of investigation concerned with the description, prediction and comprehension of natural phenomena based on observation and empirical evidence – are uncontroversial and prototypical examples of scientific enquiry, then there are very good reasons for not regarding the study of language as belonging comfortably amongst them.[2] Indeed, there are compel-

---

[2] Harris (1987:123) makes an important observation in noting that even Saussure and Wittgenstein, whose views regarding the possibility and desirability of a scientific approach to language were sharply opposed, were in agreement as regards the question of what constitutes a science, namely a descriptive enterprise which advances empirical propositions.

ling grounds for conceiving of them as quite different forms of enquiry. My purpose then is not to advance some facile argument concerning the 'correct' or 'proper' meaning of the terms *science* or *scientific* partly for the simple reason that there are no such language-immanent meanings. Debates concerning the scientific status of linguistics or any other discipline concerned with language are primarily of interest insofar as what they reveal about the conceptualisation of the object of study, the requirements and constraints placed upon such conceptualisation and the validity thereof.

3. Distributed language and the 'naturalistic turn' in the language sciences

In a recent paper, Taylor (2015) identifies what he sees as a changing of the tide in the language sciences with the emergence of various epistemologically naturalistic research programmes exhibiting a strong commitment to empiricism and scientific method. According to Kitchener (2006:79), a hallmark and requirement of such approaches is that they countenance 'no non-naturalistic entities, non-naturalistic cognitive faculties, and no non-naturalistic methods'. One prominent and innovative area of research which has emerged in recent years and is very much in this vein is the so-called Distributed Language Approach (DLA) (e.g. Cowley, 2007, 2011b, Thibault, 2011). With its theoretical roots in Hutchins' (1995) work on *socially distributed cognition*, the DLA draws on developments in so-called '4E' (Embedded, Embodied, Enacted, Ecological) cognitive science in setting out its case for a thoroughly naturalised, anti-representationalist, non-computational ontology of language (Steffensen, 2015; see Linell, 2013, for a critical overview). Such a stance ought clearly to put the DLA at odds with orthodox linguistics which has tended to coalesce strongly around representationalist and computational theories of linguistic cognition and sure enough one sees in the DLA literature a clear and express rejection of mainstream linguistics and its misconceived attempts to scientise what Taylor (2015) calls the 'traditional *explananda* of the Western linguistic imaginary'. To this extent, the DLA shares a good deal of common ground with integrational linguistics and indeed derives the bulk of its critique of linguistics from it. Particularly influential in the DLA view of language – Steffensen (2015:106) describes them as 'seminal' – appear to have been a series of papers by Nigel Love (2004, 2007, 2009) in which he sets out in meticulous detail integrationist objections to the view that languages are, or can be coherently conceived of as, codes and draws a crucial distinction between first-order and second-order language (more on which below).

However, if one looks beyond this shared negative evaluation of orthodox linguistics, important differences are soon apparent between the distributed and integrationist approaches (see Orman, 2015, for an overview), the most significant of which being that, unlike integrationism, DLA does not reject the possibility of a scientific account of language. Indeed, a belief in that very possibility would seem to underpin the approach. Furthermore, the DLA also explicitly rejects integrationism's lay-orientation in favour of a naturalistic alternative consistent with an unapologetically scientific world-view (Cowley, 2011a:10).[3] From a naturalistic perspective, the mistake of mainstream linguistics lies not so much in its seeking a scientific account of language *per se* but in the fact that the account it offers is not remotely scientifically plausible. On this view, linguistics is not attempting the impossible but is simply a bad attempt at science that has misconceived and misidentified its proper object of study.

Interestingly, however, although the DLA clearly styles its approach as scientific and situates itself as a research tradition

---

[3] Ross et al. (2007) even go so far as to adopt the label of 'scientism' as a badge of honour in their defence of what they term a 'radically naturalized metaphysics'.

within the cognitive and language sciences, nowhere in the theoretical and metatheoretical literature is there an explicit statement either of what the language sciences are (Is there more than one language science? Is linguistics still held to be a language science despite its scientism? Does integrationism belong to the language sciences?) or any account of exactly what it is about the DLA which makes it a science. How is it then that the DLA has managed to pull off the seemingly miraculous feat of using the integrationist critique of linguistics as the basis for developing an alternative scientific approach to language? One answer lies in its (re)interpretation and elaboration of an integrationist distinction between different 'orders' of language.

4. First-order languag(e)(ing) and second-order language

Nigel Love's (1990, 2004) original distinction between a first-order and second-order of language is one which has been seized upon and run with by proponents of distributed language to the extent that it is seen as providing the basis for a coherent naturalistic science of human interactivity (Steffensen, 2015:107–108). Whether this development is one Love himself had envisaged or would necessarily endorse is open to question, to say the least. Love (2004:530) formulates the distinction as follows:

> For the integrationist, a language is a second-order cultural construct, perpetually open-ended and incomplete, arising out of the first-order activity of making and interpreting linguistic signs, which in turn is a real-time, contextually determined process of investing behaviour or the products of behaviour (vocal, gestural or other) with semiotic significance.

Steffensen (2015:109) rightly notes that the importance of Love's distinction is that it explains how the simple, even parsimonious, models of language found in, not just modern linguistic grammars, but throughout the history of linguistics, emerge from the heterogeneous verbal activities of real-life human beings in interaction with one another. In other words, "the language" that linguistic descriptions set out to explain consists of second-order constructs that in various idealized ways describe *but not determine* first-order verbal activity.

As Pablé and Hutton (2015:28) observe, for integrationists its significance also lies in the idea that individuals' actual linguistic *experience* cannot be reduced to the metalinguistic categories frequently invoked in order to comment upon, describe, explain, interpret or otherwise make sense of it. Importantly, however, they go on to note that:

[i]n calling a practice or form of analysis 'second-order' we are tacitly admitting the priority of situated communication against which the practice seems more abstract, more concerned with overt norms, and more conscious. But ultimately, integrationism sees so-called first and second-order practices as inextricably intertwined, and indeed in drawing this distinction we are assuming a particular decontextualized point of view. (Pablé and Hutton, 2015:29)

The point at which the DLA interpretation of Love's distinction begins to evolve away from the integrationist view can be traced to Thibault (2011). In this detailed exposition of the DLA, Thibault introduces as its central 'theoretical object' (p.5) the concept of 'first-order languaging[4]' which is obtained by extend-

---

[4] The concept of 'languaging' is borrowed from Maturana (1978).

ing Love's concept beyond mere vocal or gestural sign-making activity to include 'a whole range of bodily resources that are assembled and coordinated in languaging events together with external (extrabodily) aspects of situations, environmental affordances, artifacts, technologies, and so on' (p.7). First-order languaging, Thibault (2011:7) insists:

> just is whole-body sense-making activity that enables persons to engage with each other in forms of co-action and to integrate themselves with and to take part in social activities that may be performed either solo or together with other agents.

Accordingly, Steffensen (2015:110) claims that the study of first-order languaging 'must be based on a naturalised ontology'. But what sense exactly are we to make of a naturalised ontology of whole-bodied sense-making? An unacknowledged irony in all of this would seem to be that 'first-order languaging' is itself very much a second-order, i.e. metalinguistic or even metasemiological, concept. If we accept the view that first-order experience cannot be reduced to second-order categories, we might then seem to be in the paradoxical position of having to claim that first-order languaging cannot be reduced to itself. Or can first-order experience be reduced to the 'correct' second-order categories? Or does 'first-order languaging' somehow stand aloof from the first-order/second-order distinction? Or, like the metalinguistic categories and constructs of orthodox and lay linguistics, is it not also vulnerable to the criticism that it describes, in a particular idealised way, but does not determine a more fundamental order of activity? What are the implications of the fact that it seems impossible to make sense of first-order languaging without recourse to some kind of second-order discourse? What order does this form of 'sense-making activity' belong to? These are complex, potentially head-scratching questions. However, their contemplation suggests that the first-order/second-order distinction is by no means as clear-cut as the distributed account would seem to imply. Indeed, the two are integrated in complex ways. What seems to have happened is that Love's original analytical distinction intended to throw light on the scientism at the root of orthodox linguistic thought – a distinction which continues to be useful for that very fact – has been (mis)interpreted as a fundamental ontological distinction capable of throwing up a determinate, naturalistic object amenable to scientific investigation and description (see the discussion of 'wordings' below for more on this).

5. A naturalised ontology of language?

In the final section of Orman (2015), I offered an initial sketch of what I took to be some of the main theoretical differences separating integrationists and proponents of distributed language. I considered, amongst other things, the core proposition that 'language is distributed' and concluded that it held little in the way of theoretical attraction for integrationists since it appeared to offer nothing of benefit that was not already covered more effectively and lucidly by the notion of 'integrated language' (Orman, 2015:18). Especially problematic from an integrational point of view is the apparent uncoupling of language, *qua* semiological activity, from individual phenomenology which the distributed view would seem to entail. However, the main focus fell upon the issue of whether the DLA has any determinate naturalistic object of analysis on which to base its putative science. In particular, I took issue with Steffensen's (2011:205) claim that 'in order to fully grasp the complexities of human interaction and cognition, the entire extended ecology will have to become our unit of analysis' and questioned whether such an ecology is in any realistic sense determinable since it must obviously include a temporal dimension. Yet for nearly all but the very youngest humans the vast majority of one's linguistic and communicative experience is wholly irrecoverable and even if it were one is faced with the question of how to go about determining which aspects of one's previous experience are relevant in explaining the conduct of subsequent communicative encounters and, just as crucially, in what ways they are relevant. As a result ,my claim was that the notion of an 'entire extended ecology', Steffensen's term for the distributed socio-cognitive system, was far too unwieldy and indeterminable when conceived of as a unit of analysis which may be invoked to explain specific episodes of human interaction.

In his response to the article, Cowley (forthcoming) takes up some of these points by posing and proceeding to discuss the following three questions:

(1) Can there be a scientific approach to language? (2) How, if at all, can this be grounded in cognition? And: (3) If language is not based in an individual language-faculty – if a response is not "one person's" – what is *language*?

Interestingly, however, Cowley is quick to make clear that naturalists such as himself deny that 'any *concept* of language can be used to undergird the language sciences' and he also warns against ascribing any 'reality' to language. Nevertheless, according to Cowley the language sciences can apparently still be built 'on a distributed basis' by means of a 'radical and embodied view of cognition.' Such claims raise a number of questions. First, there is the mystery of how there can be a scientific approach to language if language itself has no reality. A science of the unreal would surely lead us back into the land of pseudoscience and metaphysics inhabited by traditional linguistics. Yet question (2) only arises at all if there is an affirmative answer to question (1). So it would appear that there can be a scientific approach to language – even though language is not real and we are not to have a concept of it – provided that it is grounded in a radical and embodied view of cognition. Finally, we come to question (3) –

'What is language?' – a question which on the face of it would seem to have a clear conceptual component – which we are also presumably expected to answer without proposing any concept of language while simultaneously also denying that language is 'real'. Yet one can note that Cowley is still prepared to talk of 'what language is and how it works' (Cowley and Harvey, 2016: 10) and elsewhere (Cowley, in draft), in what strikes as a surprisingly essentialist assertion, he even goes so far as to deny that writing 'captures the essence of language', all of which would seem to suggest that he does in fact have a concept of language and it is surely this concept which 'undergirds' his supposedly scientific approach to it.

What is it then about a radical and embodied view of cognition that can apparently form the basis of a science of something that is not real and cannot be conceptualised? What other sciences are constructed along such lines? One should first note that Cowley (forthcoming) rejects integrationism's much-maligned lay-orientation and toleration of 'vulgar mindspeak' (Harris, 2008) because it supposedly entails a concept of language which presupposes a concept of mind, neither of which are good naturalist entities.[5] Now, *pace* Cowley, I would argue that toleration of or even participation in folk-psychological discourse which makes mention of the 'mind' does not axiomatically commit one to the view that there are such identifiable, ontologically-real things as minds. Lay usage of the term 'mind' does not automatically amount to an empirical proposition or implicit theoretical claim about the ontological status of minds. To evaluate such usages for their 'truth value' is to fundamentally misrepresent them. However, while I am happy to concede that I do not have a mind if to claim otherwise commits me to the possession of some determinate organ or entity, I do affirm that I

---

[5] For another critical account of integrationism's lay orientation, see Sutton (2004).

have something I might choose to call a 'mental life' or 'mental activity', that is to say a more or less unceasing flow of 'inner' experiences that I would habitually describe as consisting in thoughts, beliefs, desires etc. This fact is not a product of any theory nor can it be theorised away. It is a simple and irreducible product of individual experience. Cowley claims that integrationists such as Harris 'are wrong about cognition – if defined as "that which enables flexible adaptive behaviour"'. In response, one might start by noting there are many disparate elements (social, cultural, physiological, psychological.) which enable flexible adaptive behaviour in human beings. To lump them all together under the banner of cognition is already to generate a quite unwieldy-looking concept. Yet even if we grant this definition of cognition, one would surely want to say that one of the things which facilitates flexible adaptive behaviour is mental activity or what is commonly known as 'thinking'. To say this is not to advocate any dogmatic form of mentalism or to deny the integrated nature of the mental and the physical or corporeal in human behaviour. Why is it though that for there to be a scientific account of language it apparently has to be grounded in an embodied view of cognition? The answer cannot be the reocentric surrogationalist option of stipulating that cognition *just is* embodied for there is nothing that cognition just is and there seems in any case to be a quite notable lack of consensus amongst cognitive scientists on the matter (Menary, 2010: 30). Lyon (2006) even goes so far as to claim that despite half a century or so of cognitive science we do not actually know what cognition is. Nevertheless, she argues that we still need to know 'how it works'. Cowley (2009:504) refers approvingly to this claim by Lyon and says that the same logic is to be applied to linguistic cognition. In other words, then, we still need to know how language works although we don't know what it is. One is moved here to ask just what the definitional obstacle is and how one can supposedly have a science of something that defies definition. This aspect remains mysterious.

The term 'cognition' used to and clearly still does in many domains have something to do with what we would ordinarily call 'thinking' or 'mental activity' (e.g. Harnad, 2005). However, as the failures of modern linguistics have so amply proven, such internalist views of cognition have made it impossible to deliver anything like a plausible science of language or indeed a science of the mind for they were essentially striving to be sciences of the unobservable. This much the embodied, naturalist perspective clearly recognises. The question is whether this shortcoming can be overcome simply by turning cognition inside out, externalising it and locating it in behaviour. The advantage of this move for those seeking to establish a scientific approach is clear insofar as behavioural action is observable, measurable and potentially modellable. In other words, it can be turned into data of some sort. The semiological determinacy missing from language – which even if it were present would be unobservable due to its 'mental' nature – can, it seems, finally be found by locating it in invariant aspects of physical behaviour. It looks as if we may have arrived back at a (admittedly more sophisticated) form of behaviourism albeit without the structuralism of Bloomfield and co. Indeed, Cowley (2007:577) makes the point explicitly: 'First-order language is behaviour [...] the distributed view contrasts with any form-based approach in tracing language to activity by co-acting bodies.' The problem is that this move leaves unresolved the problem of how language and mental activity are reciprocally implicated in one another. After all, even first-order language is still accompanied by and can be said to cause mental activity. Our own and other people's behaviour causes us to think, remember and believe things, as well as begetting further observable behaviour. As Olafson (2001:15) notes: 'Naturalism simply denies that there is anything distinctively mental, but leaves unanswered the question of how its account of the world can dispense with any actual experience of what the world is like'. Naturalistic approaches to language are therefore inclined to ignore or even renounce individual psychology because it seems that nothing usefully scientific can be said about it. Insofar as it is acknowledged at all, it tends to be treated at best as epiphenomenal to the determinate social cognitive system (Orman, 2015:19–21).

One can note, for instance, Cowley's apparent unease in using terms such as 'thinking'. For example, he places the term within quotation marks when he writes 'as I record my "thinking", cognitive dynamics stake out a flow.' (Cowley, forthcoming) and elsewhere he writes '[v]erbal patterns constrain bodily movements and the feeling of thinking' (Cowley, 2011b: 1–2). The curious phrase 'the feeling of thinking' is one that appears quite frequently in Cowley's writings. It appears to be derived from Harnad (2005) whose strongly mentalist view of cognition – 'Cognition is thinking.' (Harnad, 2005:501) – would seem to make him an unlikely ally for an advocate of distributed cognition. The way in which the phrase is used would seem to leave it open to a number of interpretations. Given Cowley's reluctance to give empirical weight to terms originating from folk-psychological discourse, is the idea that we are not really thinking but that it just feels like we are? Is it that the feeling is real and the thinking is not? Or is it merely an affirmation of the Nagelian notion that particular mental states, in this case thinking, supposedly 'feel like' something? Linell (2013:172) expresses similar doubts in his critical discussion of DLA when he asks '[w]hat are the implications of talk about the "feeling of thinking'? That "thinking" is "just" a sensation, of no particular importance?' Unfortunately Linell does not elaborate any further on the matter, leaving the question open. On either interpretation, though, it is still not clear what is achieved by prefixing the term 'thinking' in this way, particular when other folk-psychological or 'vulgar mindspeak' (Harris, 2008) terms (e.g. beliefs, desires, understanding etc.) which appear frequently in distributed and other naturalistic accounts are not similarly prefixed. We do not encounter any parallel talk of the 'feeling of believing' or the 'feeling of understanding', for example. This points to a serious difficulty in naturalistic accounts of both mind and language, namely the tension between the apparent desire to do away with 'unscientific' lay concepts and the need to rely on or invoke them at crucial junctures in such accounts for want of anything to supersede them. One can note in this regard that there is frequently a psychological or mental concept at one end of an explanatory chain which is either left undefined or does not undergo any technical redefinition to become a term of art. In other words, it is left to be understood in its 'ordinary' everyday sense. The reason is clear: the account on offer at some stage has to connect up with lay or common-sense understanding for it to be remotely intelligible or plausible.

A case in point is the notion of 'sense' which appears in terms such as 'sense-making' and 'sense-saturated coordination' both of which feature regularly and centrally in naturalistic accounts of language and cognition. A clear example can be found in Steffensen's (2013) paper on human interactivity and problem-solving. The central definitional claim of the paper is a seemingly simple one, namely that human interactivity is to be understood as 'sense-saturated coordination that contributes to human action'. What then is sense-saturated coordination? While 'coordination' is neatly glossed as a 'reciprocal flow of miniscule, pico-scale interbodily movements that link and lock human beings in self-organised systems' (p.197), 'sense-saturated' is defined in rather question-begging fashion as meaning 'pervaded by our species-specific capability for sense-making'. Steffensen (p.197) clarifies further by noting that '[w]e engage in sense-making as our bodies integrate present circumstances with autobiographic memories and sociocultural histories'. He also makes it quite clear that the notion of 'sense-making' is being used here in the sense of Linell (2009). However, despite being a central, frequently invoked concept in his theoretical account, the nearest Linell comes to a precise definition of 'sense-making' is the assertion that '[s]ense-making is about what is meant and made known in real-life situations, in which people make certain interpretations there and then' (Linell, 2009:253). In the end then, it seems that 'sense' means nothing more than 'meaning', 'sense-making' nothing more than 'interpretation' and 'sense-saturated coordination' as nothing more than 'meaningful coordination' or equivalent. Accordingly, we can regloss human interactivity as 'meaningful coordination that contributes to human action'. Crucially, there is no suggestion in all of this that we are to understand the term 'meaning', 'interpreration' or any of their cognates in anything other than their everyday senses. This would therefore seem to be the point at which the account on offer connects up with ordinary language.[6] Now, from an integrationist perspective, in one respect this all seems quite reasonable and uncontroversial. Attempting to understand language clearly must involve getting to grips with what it is to mean, interpret or understand something in particular communicational contexts and circumstances (Taylor, 2015). However, the question which remains wholly unanswered is how any of this can be done by assuming or insisting upon a naturalised or naturalistic ontology of language given that such concepts which originate in folk-metalinguistic or folk-psychological discourse and whose explication requires insight into the mental lives of individuals are strictly inadmissible under such an approach.

A similar baseline reliance on 'unscientific' lay concepts can also be identified in Thibault (2011). For example, we encounter mention of persons 'causally engaging with [...] dynamics so as to explore their feelings, motives, intentions, beliefs and so on' (p.11) and the claim that '[h]uman agents' actions are inform-

---

[6] Ordinary language in the non-technical sense.

ed by beliefs, reasons, and motives' (p.14). Furthermore, we are told that the asymmetry of such beliefs, reasons and motives is 'one of the drivers of interaction' (p.14). Once again, we are not given any reason to understand these terms as having specialised or technical meanings and we are therefore faced with the dilemma of how to square the apparent centrality of beliefs, reasons, motives, intentions etc. in human communication with the requirement that any analysis of it be carried out on the terms of a naturalistic ontology. It is telling, for instance, that Thibault frequently needs to invoke such concepts in making explanatory sense of his own 'pico-scale' analysis of the vocal and bodily dynamics evident in an audiovisual recording of an episode of interaction between two young boys. While Thibault provides a highly detailed description of the boys' physical movements in a series of nine so-called 'microscale events',[7] his explanatory analysis of them – indeed his interpretation – cannot but make reference, whether directly or indirectly, to aspects of the boys' mental lives (their intentions, motives, imaginations, memories etc.). Consider, for instance, the following commentary:

> In the first instance, we can say that the two boys participate in bodily based forms of intersubjective coengagement that are scaffolded by mimetic capacities. Mimetic acts such as pulling the hair, the tie, and so on, to imitate the aliens constitute and enact intersubjective engagement based on joint perception-action. A shared world is thus

---

[7] For example, microscale event 6 of 9 is described as follows: 'Boy2 leans backward and bends leftward, increasing the distance between the two while continuing to utter the low growl. His right hand is held upward and outstretched toward Boy1. Boy2's movement is in response to Boy1, who, while still holding Boy2's right ear with his left hand, takes Boy2's tie (00.00.26).' Thibault (2011:17–18).

created in imagination. The two boys exploit shared 'mimetic schemas' that serve as the basis of their coordinated engagement with each other. Thus, actions performed on familiar body parts (e.g. Boy2's hair) and items of clothing (e.g. Boy2's tie) are a part of our everyday, familiar embodied ways of acting and being in the world. These body parts and items of clothing function as intersubjective anchors because they afford nonarbitrary connections to a range of activities and modes of display that are the joint focus of attention. Such mimetic activities constitute a means of creating objects of shared attention even in the absence of the given event or object (i.e. the aliens in the present example). Mimetic activities accordingly evoke absent objects and events on the basis of potentially shareable networks of sensorimotor associations that are held in working memory in the course of the interaction. (Thibault, 2011:25)

At issue here is not so much the plausibility of the explanation Thibault offers. Rather, it is the question of how he knows or thinks he knows any of this. What is the basis for his commentary? Now, my claim is that the only possible basis is an experiential, phenomenological one, which is to say that Thibault's understanding of what is going on, indeed his own sensemaking activity in this instance, is derived from nowhere else but his own unique personal experience as a lifelong participant in communication. What he is not doing is somehow providing us with an objective report on this episode of interaction. In this sense then, despite the jargonistic terminology, there is nothing scientific or naturalistic about his analysis. What possible scientific procedure could possibly lead to or validate the conclusion that 'a shared world is thus created in imagination'? How does Thibault know this? What is a 'shared world' and what place, if any, does it have in a naturalistic ontology? Thibault

(2011:30) goes on to note that '[t]he perceiving of the interactive event has the power to evoke feelings and emotions on the basis of our experience of movement patterns'. However, slowing down the video recording and analysing it on a frame-by-frame basis does not somehow magically overcome or bypass the third-personness of the researcher or the subjectivity of his/her account of what is occurring (see Cowley et al., 2004, for a similar example of such analysis). Whatever feelings or emotions are evoked in the participants in the interactive event can only be identified via an *act of interpretation* of their physical behaviour which may or may not be accurate and is in any case always revisable. The feelings and emotions as experienced by the participants do not stand open to scientific inspection whatever the type and sophistication of the recording techniques employed.

6. Language and 'wordings'

In contrasting his position with the integrationist view, Cowley (forthcoming) writes that 'Orman thinks that, as a language-maker,[8] he knows what language is'. I do not think I would put it quite that way and I certainly do not believe there is a single, timeless, fact-of-the-matter answer to the question. However, what I would say is that if, whether as a language-maker or in any other capacity, I do not know what language is or, to put it in rather less decontextualised terms, if I am unable to satisfy myself as to what counts as language in particular circumstances and what does not (if the question ever arises outside of linguistic theorising), I very much doubt that cognitive science is going to be much help in telling me, any more that it can tell me what (and where) my personality, identity or mind are. The phenomenon of

---

[8] A reference to Roy Harris' integrationist dictum that humans are better thought of as 'language-makers' rather than the more familiar 'language users' (see Harris, 1980).

language is too diverse to have any determinate set of neural, mental or behavioural correlates. I would therefore like to turn the question back on Cowley and ask in what capacity and on what basis he knows or thinks he knows what language is. If not as a language-maker, which we can perhaps read as shorthand for 'ordinary human being', then as what? As an advocate and practitioner of cognitive science, which itself is also very much a form of – albeit highly specialised and in Cowley's own case stylistically highly distinct – language-making? The suggestion here seems to be that science has the potential to tell us what language is (and is not) where lay thinking, modern linguistics and even integrationism have failed. For instance, Cowley (2011a:10) criticises Roy Harris for relying 'on the intuition that we contextualize utterances in the circumstances'. One might counter that this insight is not a product of intuition but rather one derived from reasoned reflection on Harris's own observations and experiences as a communicating, contextualising individual. However, such 'intuitions' would seem to play a no less important role in the theoretical insights of naturalists. In fact, in an earlier paper Cowley (2001:69) actually describes language as 'an aspect of social life deriving from a capacity to contextualize experience'. Elsewhere in the same piece, he writes that 'we contextualize words[9] spoken', 'people contextualize utterances by giving voice to what they hear as "new" thoughts' and refers to the 'myriad of ways in which individuals act to contextualize experience'.

More recently, Cowley and Harvey (2016:7) write that '*wordings* [are] nonce events that are perceived and construed in relation to a person's sociocultural experience. When speech events are recognized as involving "the same" wordings, their identity relation can only be defined phenomenologically. The speaker aims, not to produce an acoustically identical sound (we never do this), but to produce a pattern that can be *treated* as "the

---

[9] Note words and not wordings.

same" as another'. While I am inclined to agree with Cowley and Harvey here that this is certainly sometimes the case (exactly when it is and when it is not is another matter) – it is essentially a reformulation of the same integrationist point regarding the uniqueness of individual contextualisation for which Cowley accuses Harris of relying on intuition! – this is plainly not an insight derived from science. How could science identify or explain a wording? What is the scientific evidence for such a claim? We can also note how its formulation relies on a number of folk-psychological terms (*recognise, construed, aims* etc.) which surely ought to be banished under a strictly naturalist ontology. Nevertheless, Cowley and Harvey here provide us with a succinct, insightful and important statement of linguistic theory. Science does not even enter the picture. Such an insight could not possibly find scientific verification. Nor does it need to. In fact, I would argue that nearly all of the most interesting and important insights of the distributed perspective – and there are many – have little to do with science but are instead heavily philosophical and the product of intelligent contemplation of human experience.

The concept of *wordings* has come to figure centrally in distributed accounts of language. 'Wordings' is the label given to phenomenologically perceived invariants in human vocalisations that evoke the familiar products of the Western metalinguistic imaginary, that is to say such things as *words, meanings, sentences* etc. Cowley (2011b:4) even goes so far as to (re)define language as "activity in which wordings play a part" and elsewhere we are told that 'the phenomenology of wordings is crucial to non-local ways of understanding' (Cowley and Harvey, 2016: 10). The more important questions which naturally follow are exactly *how* wordings play a part in linguistic activity, *how* they are crucial to understanding and whether a fully satisfactory and comprehensive definition of language can hinge on the requirement of their perception. These are questions which will be considered in the discussion which follows. However, I wish initially to focus more specifically on the ontology of wordings and in particular their initial theorisation in distributed accounts as 'second-order' which, as I shall argue, raises a number of potential difficulties and also sheds light on DLA claims to have identified a theoretical object amenable to scientific investigation.

Neuman and Cowley (2013:18) state that '[i]mportantly, in making wordings second-order, we contrast their ontology with that of languaging' while Thibault (2011:4) is also clear that wordings are 'second-order cultural patterns' which contrast with 'first-order languaging'. Elsewhere, Cowley and Harvey (2016:7) are at pains to stress that *wordings* are not the same as words. While the latter are 'strictly abstract objects, with typographic and conceptual existence', wordings are apparently 'nonce events that are perceived and construed in relation to a person's sociocultural experience'. Given this distinction, though, it is difficult to see how both phenomena can be of the same ontological order. An event, nonce or otherwise, is not an object, even less so a 'strictly abstract' one, and vice-versa. If wordings are second-order then surely must not words be third-order? However, confusion arises since later in the same article Cowley and Harvey (2016:9) claim that wordings are objects after all, indeed they are apparently '"virtual objects" or entities that are constituted by acts of perception'. So are wordings objects/entities, cultural patterns or events? They surely cannot be all three at once. Furthermore, one is led to ask in what way a virtual object is substantially different, i.e. of a different ontological order, from an abstract object? After all, abstract objects such as concepts do not exist *in any sense* until they are perceived, that is to say rendered virtual, in some way or another. If we accept the view that wordings are types of phenomenologically perceived signs,[10] the temptation to think of them as objects and hence second-order can only come about by

---

[10] The phrase is tautologous from an integrationist perspective. All semiological phenomena (signs) are made through phenomenological perception.

divorcing or abstracting them from the act of their perception. However, the making of signs cannot be divorced from their perception. It is one and the same activity. Signs are made in their perception by individual persons. Now, the question is whether such acts of perception ought to be considered first or second-order. If what distinguishes second-order phenomena is that they are abstractions of some kind, we must be clear that the act of abstracting is not the same as the thing abstracted. The act of abstraction is itself not an abstraction. Equally, the act of making the sign (its perception) is not the sign itself although it may be a metasign.

Suppose I ask someone if they would like a cup of tea by moving into their line of vision, silently lifting up the kettle in one hand and pointing at it, perhaps accompanied by an appropriately 'inquisitive' facial gesture. In response I receive what I hear as an indistinct grunt in the affirmative or at any rate not something I perceive as a 'word' with a sociocultural history and determinate visual or phonetic form. I did not hear a 'yes', 'yeah', 'yes, please', 'yep' or even 'uh-huh'. I perceived no second-order pattern, abstraction, object or entity of any sort. All I heard was a grunt-like noise which I took as a cue, indeed as a sign, to put the kettle on. My tea-desiring interlocutor, however, is in all honesty firmly convinced that she replied to my inquiry using 'proper' 'English' 'words'. As far as she is concerned, she replied by saying 'yes, please' or 'yes I would' or some broadly equivalent formulation. She heard herself say those 'words'. Now, if we accept the definition of language as activity in which wordings play a part, the question arises as to whether we have a case of language here if wordings only 'played a part' for one of the parties involved? Was it language for one person and not for the other? This is surely a conclusion any 'science of language' would want to avoid since it makes determining whether any linguistic activity occurred dependent on individual phenomenological experience, something which lies outside the bounds of scientific-empirical observation, yet it seems the only possible one given this particular definition of language. In this sense, then, science has nothing to offer in trying to answer the question of whether what occurred was language or not. The most important thing to remember in all this of course is that whether I heard a languageless grunt or a response consisting of what I perceived as 'words' may be utterly irrelevant as far as the sequence of activities integrated is concerned. Whether I was engaged in purely first-order behaviour or invoking second-order constructs may make no difference whatsoever in the here-and-now of communication. What was important was that I perceived a sign *of some sort* which served to integrate a further sequence of activities in accordance with the wishes of both parties. The question of whether what occurred was an instance of language or not only arises upon metalinguistic reflection which, although it may invoke second-order abstractions, is still very much a first-order *activity*.

Another humdrum form of indeterminacy may arise when one is unsure or has no firm view or even interest as to precisely what word(ing)s are uttered. In uttering a response to someone which might be transcribed as [dəˈnoʊ] (or any other conceivable variant thereof) what wording, if any, do I regard myself as having evoked through my first-order phonetic gesture? Was it *don't know, I don't know, dunno, I dunno, I do not know*? If, as may well be the case, I do not know or have no fixed opinion as to which, if any, of these virtual objects or cultural patterns I thought I was evoking, what then was I doing? If the same goes for my interlocutor in hearing and understanding my response, what was s/he doing? Does it make any kind of sense to suppose that I may have been evoking one of them without knowing which one? Can we even say that there was a wording here if no determinately identifiable or invariant pattern was perceived by – i.e. had no psychological reality for – either party? An important point to bear in mind is that in most cases I or my interlocutor do not need to know or be certain of whether I believed I said *don't know* or *I dunno*. Pedantic questions of this type generally do not arise. We both understand 'what was said' without having to appeal to any determinate cultural pattern or abstract object evoked by my utterance. If any doubts or concerns do crop up and there is a need to know precisely what words were said, these can be easily assuaged by means of glossing practices ("Did you say *I dunno* or *I do not know*?"). However, it may be that it is only through being confronted with metalinguistic enquiries of this sort that one is forced to entertain the notion that one used a particular linguistic formulation at all. This involves a level of reflexivity that is not always present during the original communicative act itself. Of course, on more metalinguistically self-aware occasions (e.g. very 'deliberate' speech) I might be quite certain all along as to exactly what I said. I most definitely said *I don't know* etc.

Behind all this – what no doubt might seem like – rather speculative fastidiousness, is, I think, an important theoretical point. Introspection on one's own communicative experience would seem to suggest that whether or not we perceive wordings, *qua* phenomenologically determinate cultural patterns or forms, is contextually dependent. Sometimes we do, sometimes we don't and interactionally it may not matter either way. Furthermore, we don't always know when we do and when we don't. Of course when we reflect back on particular communicative episodes we may be inclined to think that we did knowingly use specific, determinate word forms because we have been socialised to think about linguistic communication as being constituted by that very practice. However, given that individuals cannot always be relied upon to faithfully recover or recall their own past phenomenological experiences, it is not possible to definitively know whether or not one experienced a wording. At any rate, such information is certainly not available to any third-party observer. In spoken language, phenomenological perception does not always deliver a determinate semiological object/form, nor does it need to. I may not know, or more likely, may not care whether I believed you said *ugh-ugh*, *dunno* or *I don't know*. As Love (2007:707) notes, human linguistic abilities are in no way dependent on the ability to recognise linguistic units (i.e. determinate forms). The phenomenological perception of determinate forms in speech is just one possible feature or outcome of linguistic communication, not a necessary one.

The foregoing considerations are potentially problematic if one chooses to define language as 'activity in which wordings play a part'. Firstly, if wordings are second-order as Thibault, Cowley and others have claimed, then it suggests that first-order languaging requires second-order language in order to constitute itself which seems a curiously back-to-front relationship of dependence. Steffensen (2015:3), for instance, writes that '[m]y boiling an egg or preparing an omelette is hardly first-order languaging unless wordings play a part, e.g. if I recall my mother's instructions of how to make an omelette, or if I elicit my family's preferences for hard-boiled or soft-boiled eggs'. Now, while it is obviously true that cooking eggs need not involve any verbal activity whatsoever, what it very clearly must involve is semiological activity. To cook eggs, one first has to recognise and manipulate certain objects essential to the task (eggs, frying pan, cooker, oil etc.). This already presupposes a certain macrosocial proficiency. One then has to monitor the cooking process and respond accordingly (e.g. flip the omelette at the appropriate time, add salt/pepper, turn off the hob etc.). All this involves a more or less continuous flow of sign-making as one integrates the various activities necessary to the cooking process. Steffensen's rationale for denying linguistic status to his egg-cooking activities is that language involves more than just stimulus-and-response-based bodily interaction and coordination. In this, he is clearly right (see Orman, 2015 for a similar argument). However, here the integrationist and distributed positions begin to diverge. From a distributed point of view, it is wordings which take us beyond mere interaction into the realm of languaging. From an integrationist perspective, the crucial difference is between non-semiological and semiological (sign-mediated) forms of interaction whereby the latter may be constituted by any type of sign-making activity of which the verbal type (the distributors' wordings) is only one subset. By making the definition of language dependent on the presence of this restricted subset of signs and excluding other forms of semiosis if unaccompanied by them, we are left with what looks like a distinctly 'segregationist' (Harris, 1998) view of linguistic communication. Just as it is not possible to draw a sharp dividing line between the linguistic and non-linguistic in terms of traditional linguistics' forms and meanings, there is also no clear-cut line to be drawn between activity which involves or evokes wordings and that which does not. The much sought-after determinacy is once again missing in (inter)action.

As mentioned, initial distributed accounts of 'wordings' theorised them as second-order. However, things seem to have changed as it now appears that wordings have become first-order. Cowley (in draft, p.9), for instance, states that '[d]rawing on slow cultural processes, persons gain skills in using (first-order) wordings in situated and cultural events'. This is a remarkable change of ontological order for such a seemingly central concept to have undergone and appears to be a consequence of a recent shift from regarding wordings as culturally determined verbal patterns to viewing them as 'nonce events' which evoke such patterns. As far as it goes, though, this move would seem to make good sense. After all, if wordings are indeed events constituted through perception, the act of perception, as opposed to whatever it is which is perceived, must clearly be a first-order, i.e. ontologically real, phenomenon. If first-order language involves sense-making then perceiving wordings is part of sense making. The problem for distributed accounts is that by making wordings first-order, this move serves to undermine the claim that the first-order/second-order distinction can provide the basis for a viable scientific account of language. When wordings were still being theorised as second-order, Vallée-Tourangeau and Cowley (2013: 5) wrote that "[f]irst-order language is [...] *measurable* whole-bodied activity that, oddly, evokes second-order patterns'. Now, the advantage to be gained from making wordings second-order is that this enables – however justifiably or not – their perception to be separated out from the measurable physical behaviour of the individual, thereby helping to deliver a seemingly more plausible candidate as an object of scientific enquiry. However, if wordings are now first-order, this implies that they cannot be separated out from the rest of the individual's physical activity, except artificially. Yet, as phenomenological acts of semiological perception they are manifestly not measurable or quantifiable in anything like the same sense, if any sense, which basically amounts to saying that first-order language is also not measurable or quantifiable.

While it might therefore seem possible to state the general principles behind linguistic communication in broadly naturalistic terms, albeit with some recognition of the irreducible importance of individual phenomenology, the very fact of this recognition entails that the possibility of providing full accounts of specific linguistic interactions remains elusive within the naturalistic framework. Here we glimpse where the naturalistic perspective on language reaches its explanatory limit for however important bodily dynamics are in linguistic interaction and the achievement of understanding, meaning etc. – and they clearly are – such phenomena cannot be reduced to observable manifestations of behaviour. We still require insight into the mental life of individuals. Yet since we cannot observe this, other methods are required to elicit insights into it. One way – perhaps the only way – is to get people to talk about it and reflect upon it and it is precisely here where a 'lay-orientated' form of reflexive metalinguistic enquiry may be most appropriate.

While language does not reduce to the inner mental computational processes posited by traditional linguistics, it is also not reducible to embodied action. The mistake lies in trying to reduce language to anything. In this sense, then, language as a fully integrated activity eludes science. Wittgenstein's remark on philosophers therefore seems equally apt when applied to modern-day language scientists.

> Philosophers constantly see the method of science before their eyes and are irresistibly tempted to ask and answer questions in the way science does. This tendency is the real source of metaphysics, and leads the philosopher into complete darkness. I want to say here that it can never be our job to reduce anything to anything. (Wittgenstein, 1969:18)

7. Conclusion

In what now might seem like a parody of scientistic thinking, Bloomfield famously wrote that, unlike in the case of the word *salt*, linguists cannot tell us the meaning of the words *love* and *hate* because science has not yet discovered what love and hate are. The all-too-obvious rejoinder to Bloomfield here is that we know perfectly well what love and hate are for the most part and do not need any help from science in deciding. Even in cases where we might be in doubt ("Is it real love?", "You don't really hate him, do you?") it is not apparent what use science might be to us ("Your MRI scan is showing a great deal of activity in the ventromedial prefrontal cortex. Clearly you do love her after all!"). Something similar, I would argue, applies in the case of language. Bloomfield would no doubt have claimed that we did not know what language really was until his particular brand of scientific linguistics came along and told us the answer. The same applies to Chomsky and his followers. Saussure was at least shrewd and modest enough to recognise that his science of language only dealt with one part of the heterogeneous and indeterminate phenomenon that is language. Yet, whereas Saussure, Bloomfield and Chomsky quite clearly all had a distinct concept of language for the purposes of their science, those leading the naturalistic turn in linguistic theory are in the curious position of claiming to have a science of language while denying that they have any concept of language.

The idea that science alone – whether in the form of mainstream linguistics or naturalistic cognitive science – can tell us what language *really* is and how it *really* works is scientistic thinking at its most crude. More subtle forms of scientism recognise the limits of scientific enquiry but take little or no interest in what lies beyond them. In all cases, we are confronted with reductive modes of thought. If we avoid reductionism, we can recognise that science may indeed be able to tell us certain things relevant to understanding language and what it involves but that it cannot tell us everything we need to know. Where science clearly can make a contribution is in relation to what integrationists term the 'biomechanical' aspects of and constraints on linguistic behaviour. As Harris notes, Wittgenstein's unceremonious remark that 'we are not doing natural science' is too hasty a dismissal of the problem since 'there are essential aspects not only of language but of communication in general which *cannot* be investigated without "doing natural science"' (Harris, 1997:275). The major issue, however, is, as Harris immediately goes on to recognise, 'how doing these necessary bits of natural science relates to the broader semiological enterprise'. It is in taking on the challenge of elucidating and making sense of this broader semiological enterprise that science reaches its explanatory limit in relation to language. It is also the point at which an integrational linguistics as a lay-orientated form of enquiry begins.

Acknowledgements
Many thanks to Chris Hutton and Nigel Love for comments on an earlier version. I am also grateful to an anonymous reviewer for many useful criticisms and suggestions.

References

Child, William, 2017. Wittgenstein, scientism & anti-scientism in the philosophy of mind. In: Beale, Jon and Kidd, Ian James (Eds.), *Wittgenstein & Scientism*. Routledge, London.

Cowley, Stephen J., 2016. Cognition & language: one person's response. *Language and Cognition*. Available at: https://www.academia.edu/10194126/Cognition_and_Language_One_person_s_response (forthcoming).

Cowley, Stephen J. Entrenchment: a distributed perspective. In: Schmid H. J. (Ed.), *Entrenchment, Memory and Automaticity: the Psychology of Linguistic Knowledge and Language Learning*. Walter De Gruyer, Boston. (in draft).

Cowley, Stephen J., 2001. The baby, the bathwater and the "language instinct" debate. *Language Sciences* 23, 69–91.

Cowley, Stephen J., 2007. The cognitive dynamics of distributed language. *Language Sciences* 29 (5), 575–583.

Cowley, Stephen J., 2009. Distributed language and dynamics. *Pragmatics and Cognition* 17/3, 495–507.

Cowley, Stephen J., 2011a. Taking a language stance. *Ecological Psychology* 23, 1–15.

Cowley, Stephen J., 2011b. Distributed language. In: Cowley, Stephen J. (Ed.), *Distributed Language*. John Benjamins, Amsterdam/Philadelphia, pp. 1–15.

Cowley, Stephen J., Moodley, S., Fiori-Cowley, A., 2004. Grounding signs of culture: primary inter-subjectivity in social semiosis. *Mind, Culture and Activity* 11, 109–132.

Cowley, Stephen J., Harvey, Matthew, 2016. The illusion of common ground. New Ideas in Psycholology 42, 56-63 http://dx.doi.org/10.1016/j.newideapsych.2015.07.004.

Evans, Vyvyan, 2015. *The Language Myth: Why Language is Not an Instinct.* Cambridge University Press, Cambridge.

Golumbia, David, 2015. The language of science and the science of language: Chomsky's cartesianism. *Diacritics* 43 (1), 38–62.

Harnad, Steven, 2005. Distributed processes, distributed cognizers and collaborative cognition. *Pragmatics and Cognition* 13 (3), 501–514.

Harris, Roy, 1980. *The Language-makers.* Duckworth, London.

Harris, Roy, 1981. *The Language Myth.* Duckworth, London.

Harris, Roy, 1987. *The Language Machine.* Cornell University Press, Ithaca.

Harris, Roy, 1997. From an integrational point of view. In: Wolf, George, Love, Nigel (Eds.), *Linguistics inside Out: Roy Harris and his Critics.* John Benjamins, Amsterdam/Philadelphia, pp. 229–310.

Harris, Roy, 1998. Language as social interaction: integrationalism versus segregationism. In: Harris, Roy, Wolf, George (Eds.), *Integrational Linguistics: a First Reader.* Pergamon, Oxford, pp. 5–15.

Harris, Roy, 2000. Saussure for all seasons. *Semiotica* 131 (3/4), 273–287.

Harris, Roy, 2005. *The Semantics of Science.* Continuum, London.

Harris, Roy, 2008. *Mindboggling.* The Pantaneto Press, Luton.

Harris, Roy, Hutton, Christopher, 2007. *Definition in Theory and Practice. Language, Lexicography and the Law.* Bloomsbury, London.

Hutchins, Edwin, 1995. *Cognition in the Wild.* MIT Press, Cambridge, MA.

Kitchener, Richard F., 2006. Genetic epistemology: naturalistic epistemology vs. normative epistemology. In: Smith, L., Vonèche, J. (Eds.), *Norms in Human Development.* Cambridge University Press, Cambridge, pp. 77–102.

Linell, Per, 2009. *Rethinking Language, Mind and World Dialogically: Interactional and Contextual Theories of Human Sense-making.* Information Age Publishing, Charlotte.

Linell, Per, 2013. Distributed language theory, with or without dialogue. *Language Sciences* 40, 168–173.

Love, Nigel, 1989. Language and the science of the impossible. *Language and Communication* 9 (4), 269–287.

Love, Nigel, 1992. Linguistic realities. *Language and Communication* 12 (1), 79–92.

Love, Nigel, 1990. The locus of languages in a redefined linguistics. In: Davis, Hayley G., Taylor, Talbot J. (Eds.), *Redefining Linguistics.* Routledge, London, pp. 53–117.

Love, Nigel, 2004. Cognition and the language myth. *Language Sciences* 26 (6), 525–544.

Love, Nigel, 2007. Are languages digital codes? *Language Sciences* 29, 690–709.

Love, Nigel, 2009. Science, language and linguistic culture. *Language and Communication* 29, 26–46.

Lyon, Pamela, 2006. The biogenic approach to cognition. *Cognitive Processing* 7, 11–29.

Maturana, Humberto, 1978. Biology of language: the epistemology of reality. In: Miller, G.A., Lenneberg, E. (Eds.), *Psychology and Biology of Language and Thought.* Academic Press, New York, pp. 27–63.

Menary, Richard, 2010. *The Extended Mind.* MIT Press, Cambridge, MA.

Monk, Ray, July 1999. Wittgenstein and the two cultures. *Prospect*, 66–67.

Neumann, Martin, Cowley, Stephen J., 2013. Human agency and the resources of reason. In: Cowley, S.J., Vallée-Tourangeau, F. (Eds.), *Cognition beyond the Brain*. Springer, London, pp. 13–30.

Olafson, Frederik, 2001. *Naturalism and the Human Condition: Against Scientism*. Routledge, London.

Orman, Jon, 2015. Distributing mind, cognition and language: exploring the (un)common ground with integrational linguistics. *Language and Cognition* http://dx.doi.org/10.1017/langcog.2014.47.

Pablé, Adrian, Hutton, Christopher, 2015. *Signs, Meaning and Experience: Integrational Approaches to Linguistics and Semiotics*. Mouton De Gruyter, Berlin.

Pierrehumbert, Janet, 1990. Phonological and phonetic representation. *Journal of Phonetics* 18, 375–394.

Ross, Don, Ladyman, James, Spurrett, David, 2007. In defence of scientism. In: Ladyman, James, Ross, Don (Eds.), *Everything Must Go: Metaphysics Naturalized*. Oxford University Press, Oxford, pp. 1–66.

Sampson, Geoffrey, 1979. *Liberty and Language*. Oxford University Press, Oxford.

Sampson, Geoffrey, 2005. *The 'Language Instinct' Debate*. Continuum, London.

Steffensen, Sune Vork, 2011. Beyond mind: an extended ecology of languaging. In: Cowley, Stephen J. (Ed.), *Distributed Language*. John Benjamins, Amsterdam, pp. 185–210.

Steffensen, Sune Vork, 2013. Human interactivity: problem-solving, solution-probing and verbal patterns in the wild. In: Stephen J. Cowley, F. Vallée-Tourangeau, (Eds.), *Cognition beyond the Brain: Computation, Interactivity and Human Artifice*. Springer, Dordrecht, pp.195–221.

Steffensen, Sune Vork, 2015. Distributed language and dialogism: notes on non-locality, sense-making and interactivity. *Language Sciences* 50, 105–119.

Sutton, John, 2004. Representation, levels, and contexts in integrational linguistics and distributed cognition. *Language Sciences* 26, 503–524.

Taylor, Talbot J., 2015. Folk-linguistic fictions and the explananda of the language sciences. *New Ideas in Psychology* http://dx.doi.org/10.1016/j.newideapsych.2015.05.001.

Thibault, Paul J., 2011. First-order languaging dynamics and second-order language: the distributed language view. *Ecological Psychology* 23 (3), 1–36.

Toolan, Michael, 1997. A few words on telementation. *Language Sciences* 19 (1), 79–91.

Vallée-Tourangeau, Frédéric, Cowley, Stephen J., 2013. Human thinking beyond the brain. In: Cowley, Stephen J., Vallée-Tourangeau, Frédéric (Eds.), *Cognition beyond the Brain: Computation, Interactivity and Human Artifice*. Springer, Dordrecht, pp. 1–11.

Wittgenstein, Ludwig, 1969. *The Blue and Brown Books*. 2nd ed. Blackwell., Oxford.

Section III.
The Place of Theory in Linguistic Thought

10.
Explanation and theory in linguistic inquiry

Abstract

In this article, I argue that the later Wittgenstein's related conclusions regarding the importance of a non-theoretical understanding of human behaviour and the essentially therapeutic function of philosophy can be arrived at without subscribing either to the position that description and explanation are necessarily distinct activities or the idea that language is an inherently rule-based activity operating within determinate conceptual-cultural regimes. I aim to do so by bringing together two figures, A. R. Louch and Roy Harris, both of whom stand within a post-Wittgensteinian tradition, but whose kindred yet hitherto unconnected departures from the orthodoxy of that tradition render their work not only distinctive but all the more compelling for it. I shall try to exhibit the affinity between Louch and Harris by means of an expository discussion of the former's thesis regarding the role and form of explanation in the social and behavioural sciences, followed by an account of explanation in linguistic inquiry consistent with the latter's 'integrationist' philosophy of language and communication. I will also claim that the thought of both Louch and Harris points towards a form of atheoretical empiricism in the investigation of human action, as well as a broadly therapeutic conception of philosophical and linguistic inquiry respectively. However, I will suggest that such a conception is not necessarily best served by the adoption of an overtly therapeutic rhetoric.

Introduction
Some of Wittgenstein's most striking metaphilosophical pronouncements are on the subject of explanation. In the *Philosophical Investigations*, for instance, we read that '[t]here must not be anything hypothetical in our considerations. We must do away with all explanation, and description alone must take its place' (Wittgenstein [1953] 2009: 52) and '[p]hilosophy simply puts everything before us, and neither explains nor deduces anything' (Wittgenstein [1953] 2009: 55). Elsewhere, in *Zettel* Wittgenstein asks 'Why don't we just leave explaining alone?' (Wittgenstein 1967: 106–7) and 'Why do you demand explanations? If they are given you, you will once again be facing a terminus. They cannot get you any further than you are at present' (Wittgenstein 1967: 58). Probably the most well known of all is the nonchalant remark in the *PI* that '[e]xplanations come to an end somewhere' (§1). It is partly the rather abrupt and patrician manner in which Wittgenstein presents such remarks that lends them their special fascination but also, it must be said, a certain opaqueness. As Gruender (1962: 524) observes, Wittgenstein, in an impeccable self-exemplification of his position, never really explained such statements. That, after all, is the point.

Wittgenstein saw, rightly, that the issue of explanation serves as an epistemological litmus test in the study of human behaviour. How do we make sense, i.e. give an account, of what people do? As the quotations above suggest, Wittgenstein envisaged two basic, diametrically opposed options. The first is that we attempt to explain it, which implies causality, which encourages generalization, which facilitates theory, which means science but, given our unamenable – one might also say impenetrable – subject matter, this leads us only into the abyss of scientism and metaphysics. The alternative is to realize that 'we are not doing natural science' (Wittgenstein [1953] 2009: 41), drop all pretence at explanation and content ourselves with pure description. On one reading, this might be viewed as the ultimate compliment to science: only scientific-theoretical explanation is valid (assuming a causal model of explanation), we are not doing science, therefore there is nothing for us to explain. This would be a mistake though. Wittgenstein's purpose is clearly not to make a positive point about science. Rather, his point is that, unlike in the natural sciences, philosophical understanding and our understanding of human behaviour is, or at least ought to be, non-theoretical in nature. One could even say that his (meta)theory is that there is no theory to be had. Fine, one might think, but why, as a result, do away with *all* explanation? Why not ad hoc explanation? Why only description? It is in his implicit answer to this question that Wittgenstein's account arguably runs aground. Wittgenstein's position – certainly according to prominent interpreters, both favourable and hostile, such as Peter Winch and Ernest Gellner respectively – is that the concepts we employ in describing human action are in a fundamental sense self-explanatory insofar as we employ them within an already familiar cultural framework (form of life) consisting of a series of determinate, shared rules of usage for said concepts. In this sense, forms of life constitute their own explanation.

Wittgenstein, however, is not the main focus in this article. Instead, I want to argue that his related conclusions regarding the nature of philosophy and the non-theoretical understanding of human behaviour can be arrived at without subscribing either to the position that description and explanation are necessarily distinct activities or the idea that language is a rule-based activity operating within determinate conceptual-cultural regimes. I aim to do so in what may seem slightly circuitous fashion by bringing together the thought of two figures, the philosopher A. R. Louch and linguist Roy Harris, both of whom stand to varying degrees within a post-Wittgensteinian tradition but whose kindred yet hitherto unconnected departures from the orthodoxy of that tradition render their work not only distinctive but also in my view all the more compelling. I shall try to exhibit the affinity between Louch and Harris by means of an expository discussion of the former's thesis regarding the role and form of explanation in the social and behavioural sciences, followed by an account of explanation in linguistic inquiry that I take to be consistent with the latter's 'integrationist' theory of language and communication. I will also claim that the thought of both Louch and Harris point towards a form of atheoretical empiricism in the investigation of human behaviour, as well as a broadly therapeutic conception of philosophical and linguistic enquiry, respectively. However, I will suggest that such a conception is not necessarily best served by the adoption of an overtly therapeutic rhetoric.

Louch's *Explanation and Human Action*
In 1966, A. R. Louch published *Explanation and Human Action*, a book that I suggest deserves to be better and more widely remembered than is evidently the case. It must be said at the outset that Louch's book is far from unknown. In the years following its publication it was reviewed in quite a few prominent philosophy, anthropology, psychology and sociology journals on both sides of the Atlantic and it has continued to garner somewhat sporadic reference in the literature of those fields up to the present day.[1] However, as tends to be the case with anything that reeks too much of analytic philosophy, it has aroused more or less zero discussion within any area of academic linguistics despite what I hope to show are its rather obvious implications for linguistic inquiry. My speculative contention is that the reason the book – and Louch's work more generally – has remained relatively unsung and certainly underdiscussed is less to do with any defect in scholarship or argumentative rigour, but simply that its central argument is liable to be seen as so extreme and unusual, not to mention highly unfashionable, that even those not especially

---

[1] For a recent(ish) discussion of Louch's work by scholars in the sociology of education, see Hyslop-Margison and Ayaz Naseem (2007).

hostile to it may not know/have known quite what to make of it or, perhaps more to the point, quite what *use* to make of it. After all, Louch's thesis can be seen as having drastic, one might even say dire, repercussions for the form and focus of a great deal of work carried out under the banner of the social and behavioural sciences. As I shall argue below, in this respect Louch's thought bears considerable affinity to and is highly compatible with that of Roy Harris whose 'integrationist' philosophy of language entails similarly radical and what in most quarters are viewed as highly unwelcome consequences for linguistic inquiry. My purpose in this section, however, is to provide an overview of the principal features of Louch's thought by way of quotation and exegetical comment. I will not attempt simultaneously to argue for a wholesale vindication of his thesis, although I will not pretend that I do not feel a good deal of sympathy towards it.

Almost a decade after its publication, Ernest Gellner (1979) wrote a lengthy review of Louch's book entitled 'A Wittgensteinian philosophy of (or against) the social sciences'. What is striking about it is that despite disagreeing vehemently with the general thesis, Gellner's tone is highly respectful and even admiring in places. Although he describes it tellingly as an 'exceedingly strange' book, Gellner immediately goes on to note that 'it is not an unattractive one. Its attraction lies in its courage and candour'. Noting that his 'main points are breathtakingly daring and far-reaching' Gellner also admits to being impressed by the 'freshness and unpretentiousness' of Louch's manner of presentation. Anyone familiar with his work will know that such displays of generosity and appreciation towards proponents of ideas squarely opposed to his own was very much *not* Gellner's default setting, particularly when the ideas in question were so obviously in the Wittgensteinian lineage or liable to be seen as carrying any whiff of relativism. One need only turn to the blistering, trenchant review of work by Feyerabend or the sarcastic, scathing – and also very funny – evaluation of ethnomethodology that appear in the same volume for evidence.

So what are the central claims of Louch's book? An inattentive or superficial reading is maybe likely to see it merely as another typical and unremarkable piece of Ordinary Language Philosophy incorporating a standard post-Wittgensteinian critique of the scientific pretensions and what the author sees as the frequently outrageous obfuscatory pretentiousness of the social sciences in a broadly similar vein to Peter Winch's far better known *The Idea of a Social Science and Its Relation to Philosophy* (Winch 1958).[2] This, however, would render a disservice to the distinctiveness of Louch's thesis. While it does indeed contain a polemical de(con)struction of the methodological and rhetorical excesses of the social and behavioural sciences, as well as some measure of OLP-style conceptual analysis, Louch's position is, as Bernstein (1976: 74) notes, arguably far more radical than either that of Wittgenstein or Winch. Indeed, it is notable that Louch (1963: 174–79) offers an extended and forthright critique of what he sees as the quite serious shortcomings of Winch's account of human action, on which more below (see also Louch 1963).

Louch's basic argument is that a genuine scientific investigation of human action has not only not been forthcoming but is a non-starter in principle or, as he puts it, 'my main intent has been to show that the idea of a science of man or society is untenable' (1966:xviii). In Louch's view the behavioural and social sciences, notably psychology, sociology and anthropology,[3]

---

[2] At the time of writing, Winch's book has over 4800 citations listed on Google Scholar compared to just over 400 for Louch.

[3] He makes no direct mention of it but there is no doubt that Louch would have also included mainstream linguistics on his scientific roll of shame. In a later work, for instance, he speaks of the 'pseudoscience of semiotics' (Louch 1976: 175).

are instead characterized chiefly by their scientism. What distinguishes Louch's approach is that, unlike Winch, he does not attempt to make his case purely on the basis of some a priori conceptual critique of the social sciences but by means of a forceful yet elegant polemic against any appeal to generality or generalization in the explanation of human actions. Louch argues that all proper – i.e. non-trivial – explanation of human action is irredeemably context-bound and therefore necessarily ad hoc with no obligatory implications beyond the case. It therefore follows that the explanation of specific, concrete instances of human behaviour does not require the support of any general theoretical statements.

> In daily life, we succeed in accounting for our actions without recourse to general theories or statistical regularities [...] 'Behavioural scientists' (i.e. psychologists and social scientists) have put obstacles in the way of *ad hoc* explanations by demanding that any explanation lean on generalities for its support [...] these theories are often redundant and platitudinous or totally irrelevant to the behaviour they are designed to explain [...] We have, in fact, a rather rich knowledge of human nature which can only be assimilated to the generality pattern of explanation by invoking artificial and ungainly hypotheses about which we are much less secure than we are about the particular cases the generalizations are invoked to guarantee. (Louch 1966: 1–3)

To illustrate his point, Louch gives the mundane example that in order to explain the fact that it was hunger that led him to cook his dinner or Jean Valjean to steal a loaf of bread, it would be utterly superfluous to invoke the generalization that humans usually seek food when hungry. Echoing Wittgenstein's lamentation of the 'craving for generality', Louch argues, and to considerable effect, that the compulsion to generalise is the result of an 'atomistic metaphysics' and the importation of a mode of explanation based on causality and prediction from the natural sciences whereby proper explanation is held to consist either in an appeal to regularities or in bringing individual cases or events under some law. It is also quite obviously a mode of explanation which cannot tolerate any ontological indeterminacy in the phenomena within its purview. After all, natural science operates on the precisely the opposite assumption, namely the absolute determinacy of the objects under investigation (quantum theory is irrelevant here). The pernicious upshot of all this for those areas of enquiry concerned with human behaviour is, according to Louch, the fetishization of an alien methodology which both derides and obstructs genuine ad hoc explanation and results in an intellectual redundancy stemming from profound onto-epistemological confusion.

> Behavioural scientists are forced into a mistaken view of their subject matter as a result of their preoccupation with a method they take to necessary to any respectable inquiry [...] [Such a] conception of methodology has prevented sociologists and psychologists from offering significant accounts of human behaviour. [...] [M]ethodology leads only to formulae for possible theories, but not to any genuine accounts of human behaviour. A sterile scholasticism has possessed the behavioural sciences, for which philosophers with their theories about the nature of science are very much responsible. (Louch 1966: 6–7)

So far so Wittgensteinian, it might seem. However, while Wittgenstein exhorts us – at least as philosophers – to do away with all attempts at explanation and rest content with description alone, Louch sees no possibility of making such a neat division. When it comes to the description and evaluation of human behaviour, he explicitly rejects the validity of the traditional *fact/value* dichotomy arguing instead that no such separation is possible or, as he puts it, '[v]alue and fact merge'. Louch's point is that in making sense of human action there is not first a descriptive stage and then a subsequent explanatory or assessment stage. In any meaningful account of agentive human behaviour, the normative component cannot somehow be separated out from the descriptive component.

> [S]tatements ascribing desire, need, self-interest and anxiety to human agents, and role and status, function and habit to social forms and processes, arise in the context of moral appraisal. They have to do with the rules and conventions by which various kinds of human action are identified and assessed. It is the tendency among behavioural scientists to think of value as a subtle and dangerous obstacle to the business of objective description of human action. So these scientists feel that if they set their values to one side, articulate them, and isolate them in a preface all will be well. *But values do not enter descriptions of human affairs as disruptive influences; rather, they allow us to describe human behaviour in terms of action. Inasmuch as the units of examination of human behaviour are actions, they cannot be observed, identified, or isolated except through categories of assessment and appraisal.* There are not two stages, an identification of properties and qualities in nature and then an assessment of them, stages which could then become the business of different experts. There is only one stage, the delineation and description of occurrences in value terms. (Louch 1966: 56, emphasis added)

As a result, Louch claims that any explanation of human action must necessarily be what he calls 'moral explanation' since 'when we offer explanations of human behaviour, we are seeing that behaviour as justified by the circumstances in which it occurs' (Louch 1966: 4). For Louch, to identify someone as stealing a loaf of bread is both to describe and appraise their actions. There is no purely descriptive language available in which to make sense of such actions *qua* agentive behaviour. Now the rather obviously morality-laden example of theft might seem rather too easy an example on which to secure the general validity of such an argument. Applied across the board to all human actions Louch's claim might, initially at least, seem rather disconcerting. Bernstein (1976: 77), for instance, views this stronger version of Louch's thesis as 'certainly a mistake' noting that we 'can and do describe actions as voting, or signing a contract, or committing suicide'. However, Bernstein's counterargument is not especially potent and his examples seem poorly chosen. He appears to be saying that unadorned with any explicitly normative or evaluative adverbial embellishment such formulations can somehow count unproblematically as pure fact-of-the-matter descriptions of the actions in question devoid of any appraising sense. Louch's obvious response here would, I think, be to point out that all of the examples Bernstein gives are inextricably tied up with questions of intention and purpose. Indeed, for Louch intentions 'are ways of describing actions, not explaining them [...] To talk of intentions is to answer the question *what*, not *why*' (Louch 1966: 106, original emphasis). We do not first describe the act and then appeal to the intention as an explanation. For example, it would be extremely queer to say 'he committed suicide because he intended to'. To speak of someone voting or committing suicide is for the most part to assume intentionality. Furthermore, the detection of intentions is not a matter of impartial, scientific procedure but the outcome of a heterogeneous and ultimately indeterminate range of strategies for interpreting, which is to say appraising, behaviour. Such appraisal is, for Louch, necessarily moral in nature. Would we want to say that Socrates (or for that matter, Rommel) committed suicide or was murdered?[4] It rather obviously depends where our sympathies lie in each case and our moral appraisal of the actions of the relevant parties. It is not a matter to be decided by stipulating some general (social) scientifically approved definition of the concept 'suicide'. There simply is no fact of the matter. Any detection of intention necessarily involves a recognition of agency and therefore requires a moral-evaluative assessment. That so many ordinary cases of intention detection are uncontroversial perhaps blinds us to this fact, but it does not alter it.

To avoid potential misunderstanding, it is important to mention that Louch employs the term 'moral' in a somewhat extended sense. In claiming that the explanation of human behaviour is moral explanation, Louch does not mean to say that all behaviour is necessarily evaluated in accordance with some specific moral codification or any other kind of determinate framework of cultural rules. Rather, his point is that our accounts of human actions depend on how we see such actions as 'entitled' by their contexts of occurrence.

> [W]hen we offer explanations of human behaviour, we are seeing that behaviour as justified by the circumstances in which it occurs. [...] In appealing to reasons for acting, motives, purposes, intentions, desires and their cognates, which occur in both ordinary and technical discussions of human doings, we exhibit an action in the light of circumstances that are taken to entitle or warrant a person to act as he does. (Louch 1966: 4)

---

[4] See Frey (1978) for an argument that Socrates did indeed commit suicide. However, Frey arrives at his conclusion via a 'determination of the concept of suicide itself', which is to say via just the kind of a priori conceptual analysis for which Louch criticizes Winch.

One must also be careful not to conflate Louch's argument about the moral explanation of human action with the distinct and broader claim that *all* language use (and communication more generally) is an inherently moral enterprise being, as it is, a form of behaviour towards others. Louch is not claiming that all language is evaluative in the moral-appraising sense but that all accounts of agentive behaviour are necessarily so.[5] Louch maintains that the behavioural and social sciences have been led astray into redundancy, triviality and scientism by presuming to circumvent the moral dimension of explanation as evidenced by their adoption of the superficial presentational features of organized science such as prolix in-group jargon, symbolic notation, compilation of data and statistics in the form of graphs, tables and so on. The upshot is that methodology trumps relevance as the content of such investigations becomes almost wholly subordinate to their form.

Louch's position is summarized in his startlingly bold claim that 'psychology and social science are moral science. Ethics and the study of human action are one' (Louch 1966: 235). The implications of such a position are far-reaching since it entails that there is no empirical-positivist description to be had of agentive human action as opposed to, say, the movement of human bodies. There can be no naturalistic account of human behaviour when humans are viewed as moral agents. The redescription of the behaviour of humans as agents using the language and techniques of biophysical and biokinetic description which, for example, is encountered found in much contemporary work on distributed and embodied cognition, is symptomatic of the confusion Louch identifies (see Orman 2016). His point is that we

---

[5] To be clear, to make this claim is not to advocate any form of intentionalist semantics. Humans can quite obviously communicate without intending to and interpretation can take place without assuming intentionality.

are not dealing with intertranslatable idioms here.[6] One cannot be reduced to or equated with the other.

> [P]sychologists and social scientists forsake their subject matter when they suppose the proper object of their study is a description of human behaviour meeting the standards of an atomistic metaphysics or a methodology borrowed from the science. Freed from the paraphernalia of pseudo-scientific methodology it becomes apparent that what gives point to these investigations is questions about the propriety, felicity, rationality or success of human actions [...] Psychologists and social scientists, keen on achieving status among the natural sciences, have been led to suppose they could refine action-descriptions into quantitative descriptions, and so have failed to address themselves to what people do [...] [S]uch an expectation rests on conceptual confusion and bad metaphysics. It is one thing to propose a refinement of our techniques of observing muscular movements, quite another to suppose that such refinements will improve upon or replace our observation of human action. Close physical description is the first step toward a science of physiology and thus to the study of man as an organism. But such a study neither supports nor refutes the observations we make about human beings conceived as persons or human actions viewed as performances. *The view of man as an organism and man as an agent are simply totally different ways of looking at his conduct.* Psychology and social science, in different ways and to different degrees, occupy a no man's land in which the techniques for a biophysical description are applied to

---

[6] A reviewer notes that Louch's position appears to have some parallels with that of Donald Davidson.

the behaviour of men as agents. (Louch 1966: 235–36, emphasis added)

What, then, are the implications of Louch's thesis for inquiry into human behaviour? Louch does not follow Winch in arguing that theory builders in the social sciences must take their lead from philosophy in the form of a priori conceptual analysis rather than empirical investigation. This, for Louch, leads Winch into the baby and bathwater territory of rejecting the empirical simply because one has rejected the theoretical. Louch can instead be seen as endorsing a kind of atheoretical empiricism (Jarvie 1985: 46). In his dismantling of Winch's apriorism, Louch (1966: 174–82) repeatedly makes the point that any meaningful account of human actions must surely be based on observation, albeit subject to the deflationary proviso that such observation is not then seen as the basis for the construction of a generalizing or predictive theory. Louch is aware and not at all perturbed by the fact that his position might seem to cast serious doubt on the need for the social and behavioural sciences *qua* specialized, institutionalized academic pursuits. He notes for instance that:

> [T]here is no call for the specialist in the normal understanding of the social game. We are all players, and to this extent we are all, to varying degrees, experts. This seems to me the consequence of the view that language is social, that it is bound up with the actions of men, that language and act, utterance and context, cannot be separated.
> (Louch 1965: 216)

Louch's comments on anthropology are particularly noteworthy in this regard. In a move no doubt pointedly designed to scandalise the professional anthropologist who believes s/he is doing science, Louch (1966: 160) claims that 'anthropology is only a collection of traveller's tales with no particular scientific significance'. However, he is quick to make clear that he is using this obviously provocative label non-pejoratively. For Louch, travellers' tales are indeed the epistemologically appropriate form of accounting for the subject matter in such a field of inquiry axiomatically concerned with human values.

> Travellers' tales can be, as much as scientific theories, contributions to human knowledge; they can be better or worse, more or less accurate. Moreover, they are not the first and random comments that some day will be organized into a scientific theory. They are sufficient unto themselves. The pattern of explanation in anthropology is not a poor approximation of the generalizing and predictive capacities of the method of science, but moral explanation, within which instances may be judged more or less adequate. (Louch 1966: 160−61)

Louch's point is that the mark of a good anthropologist is not possession of an armoury of theoretical concepts or a science-aping methodology but, rather, acuity of observation and the skill to make what one observes intelligible to the audience to which the account is addressed. On this view, no abundance of methodological sophistication can make up for an inability to make insightful statements about the behaviour and customs of other humans. Anthropologists and the like ought consequently to be more concerned with saying something interesting than with living up to the specious requirements of methodological rigour. For Louch, it seems, anthropology would best be practised as a kind of fastidious journalism shorn of all scientistic and jargonistic excesses.

Given the extreme consequences which Louch's thesis might seem to entail for the obviously language-dependent disciplines of psychology, sociology and anthropology, it is natural to ask what implications it might also have for inquiry into language itself. This will be the focus of the next section. In fact, I will argue that Louch's thesis resonates strongly with a distinctive theoretical approach to language and communication which has arisen out of a thoroughgoing critique of mainstream academic linguistics and the philosophy of language.

Explaining language? An integrational linguistic perspective
I have already mentioned the unsurprising fact that Louch's work has garnered no attention within linguistics, that most institutionalized form of linguistic enquiry. However, a great deal of what Louch says about explanation and generalization is, I shall argue, highly compatible with and complementary to the view of language and linguistic inquiry known as integrational linguistics or integrationism, the labels associated with a defiantly non-mainstream approach to linguistic inquiry which originated in the seminal work of Roy Harris (1981, 1996, 1998). Indeed, Louch's rejection of generality in explanation coheres strongly with and may even be seen as finding expression in the integrationist principle of the *radical indeterminacy of the sign*, a principle whose recognition entails consequences for linguistic enquiry no less radical than Louch's thesis does for the sociology and anthropology. It is recognition of this fundamental semiological principle which, in a way highly analogous to Louch, leads integrationists not only to point to the absence hitherto of a *bona fide* science of language but to argue against the very possibility of such an enterprise.

Roy Harris's work comprises a profound engagement with, yet wholesale rejection of, almost all authoritative thinking pertaining to language and communication in the western intellectual tradition. According to Harris, nearly every thinker of note about language from Aristotle onwards has been in thrall to one or other version of what he memorably termed the 'language myth'. This includes Wittgenstein although his later thought gets a far more sympathetic hearing than most (e.g. Harris 1988). The language myth identified by Harris comprises two interlocking metaphysical fallacies, which he termed the 'telementational' and 'fixed-code' fallacy respectively. The telementational fallacy refers to the belief that linguistic communication involves a process of 'thought transmission' whereby mental content (conceived variously as concepts, ideas, symbolic representations, etc.) is neatly conveyed intact from the mind of one party to the other. The explanatory mechanism by which this miraculous feat is achieved is the putative fixed code, a shared inventory of signs determinate in respect of both form and meaning. This shared system of signs constitutes the language of the speech community in question. For Harris, belief in the language myth, which originates in everyday lay metalinguistic discourse, is embodied most perfectly and perniciously in the form of mainstream academic linguistics. For a discipline desperate to achieve status as a *bona fide* science, the determinacy afforded by the language myth has been a theoretical and methodological godsend for linguistics. One of its main consequences has been to allow the linguist to envisage his or her primary task as consisting in the identification of the features of the alleged abstract system underlying the language use of a community (Saussure's *langue*) thus divorcing linguistics from any concern with evaluating and otherwise making sense of the messy, piecemeal reality of actual communicative behaviour in context and indeed from social life altogether. On this account, far from advancing it, the scientism of linguistics represents a fundamental hindrance to the understanding of human communication.[7]

---

[7] It should be said of course that a great deal of contemporary work in linguistics (especially the socio and applied branches) is very much concerned with the study of actual language use in context. However, unlike integrationism, the vast majority of such work continues to operate with a Saussurean understanding of the sign (biplanar, resolutely determinate in form, although a measure of indeterminacy of meaning is sometimes conceded) and, also like Saussure, a model of communication which assumes intersubjectivity.

From an integrationist perspective, linguistic communication does not proceed on the basis of the availability of a pre-existing, shared inventory of determinate sign forms. Instead, communication is an open-ended process of *integrating* one's activities both physical and mental with those of other humans and the world around us. Such integration is made possible by the human capacity for sign-making, which includes both a productive and interpretative element. The signs we make, linguistic or otherwise, are not atemporal, impersonal invariants but are instead inextricably time- and context-bound. Their value or what we are often inclined to call their meaning is therefore determined by the activities they serve to integrate. Given the temporal uniqueness of context and the absence of any underlying system of determinate forms, signs are held to be radically indeterminate in respect of both form and meaning. From a semiological, i.e. integrational, point of view, each sign is a new sign and each context a new context. Meaning and context are also not shared in any explanatory ontological sense but are instead the product of individual phenomenological contextualization. There is accordingly no *a priori* guarantee that any two individuals will coincide in how they make sense of a particular word, utterance, stretch of discourse etc. Such indeterminacy is regarded as an inherent feature of the human communicational infrastructure.

Acknowledgment of the radical indeterminacy of language leads integrationists to reject a series of seemingly commonplace ideas that underlie authoritative mainstream academic and lay thinking about language in the western tradition. The most prominent of these include the idea that words *qua* decontextualized abstractions have meanings, that there are rules of grammar[8] and,

---

[8] Roy Harris puts it most felicitously with his observation that 'there are no rules of grammar, only grammarians' rules'.

finally, that there are languages.[9] To deny that there are languages is to say that there are no first-order, i.e. ontologically real, code-like systems which underlie and explain linguistic communication. Instead, languages are – often ideologically motivated – abstractions *from* first-order communication which themselves stand in need of explanation. The integrationist position can be neatly summarised by the claim that 'languages presuppose communication', which reverses the ontological priority enshrined in the language myth. Accordingly, the main task for linguistic inquiry from an integrational perspective is not to ascertain and report objective linguistic facts, of which there are none, but to elucidate the communicational experiences of ordinary language-users. It is in this sense that Harris's frequent advocacy of a 'lay-oriented linguistics' is to be understood.

Already certain affinities with Louch's thesis should be apparent. The integrational emphasis on the radical indeterminacy of communication clearly entails a form of the anti-generality thesis. Louch's simple observation that '[t]o generalize is to assert that some facts hold regardless of context' links up neatly with the integrationist claim that there can be no context-free or context-transcendent linguistic facts and Harris's (1996: x) observation that '[c]ontexts, like persons […] all seem to be different from one another, and thus hinder the great work of scientific generalization'. Furthermore, one can also note Harris's (1998: 106) remark in respect of linguistics that 'giving up generalizations is seen as tantamount to renouncing the possibility of "scientific" investigation of the subject'. Louch's stress on the

---

[9] Harris was not the first nor the last to deny the existence of languages. For instance, his view is echoed in Davidson's (1986: 446) famous remark that 'there is no such thing as a language, not if a language is anything like what most philosophers and linguists have supposed'. The extent to which the linguistic thought of Harris and Davidson is otherwise compatible is an interesting topic which, however, cannot be addressed here.

inherently contextual nature of meaning is another key respect in which his thought is to be distinguished from that of Winch and allied to that of Harris. For Winch, conceptual meaning resides in the determinate cultural unit and is essentially context-free. Louch, like Harris, is no cultural relativist in this sense. Instead, both Louch and Harris can be seen as propagating a kind of radically contextual, phenomenological-individualistic relativism. This crucial difference between Louch and Winch is shrewdly noted by Gellner (1979: 78) who describes Louch's relativism as 'more extreme [since] Winch is careful to limit his relativism to cultures and to deny it to individuals. Louch's knows no limits'.

Louch's profound scepticism about the academic specialist's claim to expertise where social life is concerned is echoed in Harris's iconoclastic comment that '[a] linguistic theorist speaks with no greater authority or insight about language than a baker or a bus conductor' (Harris 1997: 237). Now my purpose here is not to rediscover Louch as some integrationist *avant la lettre* nor to out Roy Harris as a closet Louchian. Harris nowhere refers to Louch's work although I find it difficult to believe that he would have been wholly unacquainted with it. While keen readers would perhaps be able to locate areas where they do not fully coincide, my focus in the following discussion is deliberately on what I take to be the far more significant aspects of concordance between Louch's and Harris's thinking. In the first place, I shall try to give an account of what from an integrationist perspective the task of explaining language might be seen to entail and some of the quandaries associated with it. As will be seen, it is an exercise which very starkly draws out the profound difficulties associated with moving towards a systematic, generality-invoking form of linguistic inquiry consistent with an integrationist view of language.

On the face of it, it would hardly seem contentious to claim that any form of linguistic inquiry worth its salt must seek to – however the term is ultimately to be understood – *explain* or at least go some way towards explaining language or the particular linguistic phenomena within its purview. Beyond this very general requirement, however, things quickly become rather murkier when the inevitable question is raised of what such explanation ought to entail. What exactly is it, after all, to explain language? To some, including most integrationists, this may already sound like a hopelessly decontextualized question and it is indeed easy enough to construe it as such. 'There is *nothing* that *it* is to explain language' might well be a reasonable response in the face of such a question. It is a question which would appear to fall comfortably into the Austinian category of 'perfectly absurd' 'pseudo-questions' (Austin 1961). What kind of question(s), then, if any, might help us to move towards a more epistemologically productive basis for linguistic inquiry? An alternative, less obviously Platonic starting point for giving expression to this concern might, I tentatively suggest, be to ask a question along the lines of 'What do we want to know about language?' In other words, what puzzles us?

What might be some likely answers to such questions? Upon contemplation, one soon sees the potential for them to ramify in multiple directions: 'How is language possible?', 'How is that specific episode of linguistic interaction X possible?', 'How am I able to write/utter these particular words on this page/in this conversation?', 'Why do human beings engage in those forms of behaviour we call language?', 'Why did A and B (and possibly also C, D [...]) engage in that particular episode of linguistic interaction?', 'Why did A and B utter those particular words and/or otherwise behave as they did in that particular episode?' The issue of whether these are equally good or even good questions can wait. Initially, a couple of things are apparent. The first is that the questions divide between *how* questions and *why* questions and, second, between questions calling for general or generalizable answers and those in respect of specific episodes and individuals. Is the answer – assuming there is one – to the general question of how humans are able to converse with one another the same as the answer to the question of how I am able to engage in conversation with person X at moment Y? In some sense, clearly it must be. If it isn't, the general answer is false. In another sense, though, it is obviously unsatisfactory since it makes no contact with the specifics of the individuals involved and the details of the particular situation. What about when the *why* version of this question is posed? Here the affirmative answer seems obviously less satisfactory. One is again reminded of Austin's (1961: 26) observation that 'it becomes very difficult to formulate any *general* question which could impose on us for a moment'.

To begin by considering the *how* and *why* questions is, though, to jump the ontological gun since there is the necessarily prior *what* question to be dealt with. If explanation presupposes description then accurate explanation presupposes accurate description. As Louch (1966: 235) notes, 'the first step to an investigation of human action, is to enquire what sort of thing men are doing'. This seems like an obvious starting point although the cause-seeking scientist will no doubt question whether an answer to this question can alone be held to fully relieve the burden of ontological explanation. After all, is one not also tempted and indeed entitled to ask the question of what else of relevance is or might be going on that can't be comfortably subsumed under the category of particular agents' doings? Isn't there always something more to be known and described, another question to be answered? While this may be true, it is this inability to stop asking questions that Wittgenstein regarded as the defining pathology of scientism, hence the famous line about justification and explanation coming to an end somewhere. Naturally, if we accept this, description must also come to an end somewhere. The question is where? For Wittgenstein it is at the point where one arrives at what he rather loftily calls *das erlösende Wort*.[10] For Louch, rather more prosaically, it is at the point where one loses interest.

> We know, surely, though research specialists do not always seem to be aware of it, that there is a great deal of information about what people do that is simply not worth knowing, information that does not add up to a coherent picture or account of a subject-matter worth teaching in schools. What generally brings facts about human doings into some coherent form is a thesis designed to explicate and clarify the nature of our actions. (Louch 1966: 237)

If description must end somewhere it must, just as importantly, also begin somewhere too. Here we can see how a looming *where* question merges almost imperceptibly with the *what* question. Given an indeterminate phenomenon, some arbitrary circumscription of the object of inquiry appears unavoidable, otherwise it seems one is faced either with having to account for *everything* or *nothing at all*.

So what sort of thing are we doing when engaging in what we call language? Is there *any* general answer to this question and, if there is, with what degree of precision does it identify and distinguish that thing? One should note that to frame the general *what* question in terms of 'doing' might already be seen to reveal some bias since there are many prestigious schools of linguistic thought for which language is in no way primarily a matter of *doing* anything, e.g. Chomskyan linguistics. However, these need not detain us here. Now integrationist theory clearly does offer a general answer to the *what* question albeit one which, tantaliz-

---

[10] Anscombe translated this rather unimaginatively as the 'key word'. However, as an alternative, Klagge (2001) suggests 'the redeeming word', i.e. whatever gets us to stop seeking further explanation.

ingly, would seem to preclude the possibility of any further general ontological statements. As mentioned, the integrationist answer runs more or less to the effect that linguistic communication involves the contextualized integration of human activities, both physical and mental, via a continuous process of creating and interpreting signs. This, then, is the integrationist explanation (or is it description? Or definition?) of what language *is* if one wishes to put it in those terms. However, what this answer does not provide is any determinate criteria for distinguishing language from other, non-linguistic forms of communication. This will no doubt fail to satisfy some but the impossibility of furnishing any such criteria constitutes one of Harris's central and most original theoretical moves. What we can say is that there is no general theoretical answer to the question of what the difference is between linguistic and non-linguistic communication. Such a question can only be answered in context and even then only in accordance with the potentially conflicting viewpoints of different participants.

Harris also supplies an impeccably definitive answer to the general *why* question, namely that unless we integrate, we die. To be alive in any worthwhile sense of the term is necessarily to engage in processes of integration.

> [The] integration of activities is something we have to take part in, whether we like it or not. It is a necessary condition of life as we know it. We are born into a world that requires us to communicate, to integrate one kind of activity with another and with the corresponding activities of other people. If we manage the integrational task successfully, we live. If not, we die. (Harris 1998: 29)

The reason these both succeed as general answers to general questions is that they are exceptionless insofar as we cannot *by definition* conceive of an instance of linguistic communication which does not involve a process of integration via the medium of signs nor any living person who does not integrate. The inclusion of a reference to signs is significant here insofar as it adds an aspect of specificity to the general answer and prevents the putative object of inquiry from being lumped together with non-semiological forms of human interaction. But is this as far as it goes? How about social relations? Isn't it a general, exceptionless feature of communication that since it always involves at least two people it establishes social relations? Let us ignore for now rather obvious counter that there are forms of self-communication which have no social aspect and suppose we answer this question in the affirmative. Communication establishes social relations. However, when elevated to the status of general truth this proposition is either false or conceals a simple circularity insofar as to communicate is necessarily to establish social relations and to establish social relations is necessarily to communicate. There can be no social relations without communication and communication cannot occur without establishing social relations. One merely becomes a disguised definition of the other. Therefore, to establish social relations is to establish social relations. Consequently, *nothing* is explained. However, if we accept the point that communication, conceived of as integration, need not necessarily involve more than one person, could we then not at least advance the general proposition that *interpersonal* communication establishes social relations? It does not take too much puzzling to see that the very same circularity results.

The trouble with any form of general(izing) explanation seeking to claim theoretical status is that unless it is exceptionless, the theory also has to explain the exceptions and given that these may vary indefinitely, it is difficult to see how it is possible for it to do so. Suppose we are inclined, as some scholars have been (e.g. Johnstone 2013: 197), to view all language as performance (in a non-Chomskyan sense). As a general claim about language we immediately encounter a problem insofar as any possibility of conceptual contrast is erased. If there is no language that is not performance, we no longer know what performance is not. What we would ordinarily think of as performances become metaperformances – the actor or singer onstage is performing performing. The actor playing a performing actor is performing performing performing and so on ad tedium. The upshot of this meta-regress is that the notion of performance is drained of any explanatory power. It no longer serves any evaluative – i.e. appraising – function in discourse. While we would want to say that all performance involves the semiological integration of activities, i.e. is communication, by also claiming the reverse, the two concepts become mutually presupposing and we find ourselves once again going around in tautologous circles: language is performance is language is performance [...] etc. When we ordinarily describe something as a performance this is because there are other things which are not performances and we wish to distinguish them from the case in question. As Louch (1966: 215) notes: 'There must be a legitimate sense in which we can speak of the person as *not* acting if there is a legitimate sense in which we speak of him *as* acting'. A general theoretical claim that language is performance either has to claim, dogmatically and opaquely, that all language is performance or, if it is not, explain on the basis of non-tautological *general criteria* which instances are not performances. However, if one accepts the integrationist point that human communication is irreducibly context-bound and open-ended, there is no way in which a theory can legislate in advance on the matter.

The obstacle that the integrationist answer to the general *what* question presents to linguistic inquiry is that it does not deliver anything like a determinate *object* of inquiry. The activities that may be integrated defy infallible and exhaustive prediction, as do the biomechanical, circumstantial and macrosocial factors that may serve to shape and constrain them. As a result, they are not activities or factors that any general theory can specify. Furthermore, the general integrationist explanations become utterly redundant as explanations when applied to specific instances. What level of insight does it provide into my morning conversation with a colleague *qua* communicative event to say that we were both integrating our respective activities by means of signs? Indeed, to do so would once again result only in tautology. After all, to identify it as a communicative situation in the first place one already has to recognize it as involving the integration of activities by means of signs. It would therefore also be utterly pointless to embark upon any kind of empirical research in an attempt to 'prove' that any semiological integration of activities took place. To invoke the general explanation would amount to claiming that this particular case of the integration of activities via signs involved the integration of activities via signs. What we want is an explanatory account of these particular activities in these particular circumstances, something which requires contextualized observation and appraisal. These are things which no theory or theory posing as methodology can supply. In this sense, even integrationist theory has no explanatory power when applied to the case. However, if one can shed the positivist mindset, this need not be seen as a weakness of the theory but can instead be regarded an essential insight of it.

An even more ludicrous result is obtained when we apply Harris's answer to the general *why* question to the specific case. Whatever else I might be doing when mundanely exchanging pleasantries in the corridor, I can hardly be said to be doing so in order not to die. Similarly, the fact that humans eat in order not to starve to death does not explain why Frenchmen eat snails or why I had a cheese and pickle sandwich and a bag of crisps for my lunch at one o'clock last Tuesday. Now there may of course be situations in which life and death hang on an ability to integrate particular activities in a particular situation – I hand the knife-wielding mugger my wallet very much in order not to die – but no *theory* of communication can have anything meaningful to say about these. Once again, integrationist theory has no explanatory power in respect of the particular case. Why, after all, should we expect or even need a theory to explain our particular uses of words any more than it should our specific choices of food or clothing?

What about the *how* question? Does this offer more potential for generality in explanation? It is notable for instance that certain prominent approaches in the contemporary 'language sciences' and biosemiotics are concerned with versions of this question. Suppose we ask a question like 'how is language possible?' or 'how does language originate?' Can such questions be answered in general terms without a general, determinate concept of language, something which integrationism denies? Harris himself might be seen as offering somewhat conflicting views on this matter. Although any talk of pursuing an alternative 'science' of language or communication had disappeared from his writings by the early 1980s, an interesting statement appears his 1997 piece 'From an integrational point of view'. Apparently drawing back slightly from the rather fundamentalist attitude encapsulated in Wittgenstein's terse dictum 'we are not doing natural science', Harris claims that:

> [T]here are essential aspects not only of language but of communication in general which cannot be investigated without 'doing natural science'. They are those which fall under the 'biomechanical scale' of inquiry. (Harris 1997: 275)

It is noteworthy and, I think, telling that despite this gesture, Harris himself – as he immediately went on to admit – never showed much interest in actually doing any such bits of science or even specifying what they might involve. The claim is also difficult to reconcile with the one made later in the same piece – namely that 'if language studies are to have any serious theoretical basis, that basis must be semiological' (1997: 304) – and another rather more unequivocal statement from a decade previous in which he wrote of:

> the misconception that advances in science will, of themselves, in time, reveal truths about language which at present lie concealed. To believe that would be absurd as supposing that future research on the brain or the human nervous system might help us understand chess any better. (Harris 1988: 127)

If scientific biomechanical investigations cannot help us understand chess any better, why is there any reason to suppose they will be able to do so where language *in general* is concerned? After all, chess involves the integration of activities. To ask this question is, though, not to endorse any kind of Wittgensteinian (or Saussurean for that matter) games metaphor. One could substitute chess for gardening, window-cleaning or telling obscene jokes to make the same point. All involve the semiological integration of activities. This then raises the twin questions of in what sense biomechanical questions can also be semiological questions and how science can assist us in answering or understanding them. For example, it clearly does not count as a scientific insight to say that in order to make some sense of the printed text of a particular book, I require a certain visual ability. The question then becomes whether there is anything of a semiological nature to be known beyond this that can be provided by a statement of general theory. Is there anything *more* specific that natural science might supply in order to give a satisfactory account of my *semiological* ability to make sense of the text? If I failed to understand you because, owing to creeping deafness, I couldn't quite hear what you were saying – a semiological, i.e integrational, failure with a biomechanical explanation – I do not need to be furnished with any pathophysiological description of my ailment or statistical data on exactly how loud your voice was or what my hearing range frequencies are in order to confirm that I did not hear you. Admittedly, some such information may embellish or enrich our ad hoc account of what happened but it in no way serves to prove or disprove the semiological explanation, an explanation which is not the product of science or any other theory.

One way of summarizing the above would be to say that integrationist theory explains or shows why specific communicative acts do not lend themselves to or require theoretical explanation. As with Wittgenstein, the theory is that there is no theory to be had. What, then, are the implications of all this for the professional linguist with integrationist sympathies? Is he or she, like Louch's anthropologist, condemned either to piecemeal, atheoretical observation or to finding another occupation altogether? It seems that from Nigel Love's integrationist perspective, the anecdote might potentially fulfil a role in linguistic inquiry analogous to the traveller's tale in Louch's conception of anthropology.

> Language is a temporally situated, ongoing *process* – the process of making and remaking signs in contextualized episodes of communicative behaviour. And if that is accepted then, apart from the provision of anecdotal accounts of the specifics of particular communicative episodes, one might be inclined to conclude that pointing this much out is where linguistics ought to stop. (Love 2007: 705)

Here Love alludes to what is typically seen as the most unappetising consequence of accepting an integrationist view of language and the reason why integrationism generally has such a dire reputation amongst those linguists acquainted with it, namely that it would seem to deny the possibility of any systematic, empirical-positivist study of linguistic data. In other words, it provides no theoretical rationale for methodology and therefore deprives the aspirant linguistic social scientist of that one thing above all else of which mastery is seen to confer professional standing and expertise. The ideological commitment to positivist methodology runs deep in linguistics, especially socio- and applied linguistics, although its ideological status is seldom acknowledged as such concealed as it often is under a rhetorical blanket of common sense or practical necessity. After all, what is the alternative? I have lost count of the number of linguists who have told me something to the effect that 'I don't (just) want to do philosophy' or 'but I love working with data' quite apart from those who have openly declared no interest in questions of theory or ontology. Could a form of linguistic anecdotalism offer an escape route for the – admittedly very rare – lapsed positivist linguist who doesn't want to do philosophy? From a Louchian point of view, there ought to be no disgrace in embracing such an approach however injurious it might be to the ego of linguists who fancy or once fancied themselves as scientists. To adapt Louch, anecdotes can be contributions to knowledge and are sufficient unto themselves. It is of course next to impossible to envisage any modern-day academic discipline content with any form of 'serious' inquiry conceived along such lines. After all, what would almost certainly come to be seen as the most urgent task of the newly institutionalized field of Anecdotology? What else, I would suggest, but a general theory of anecdotes. But not just any general theory, preferably one which requires the learning of an expert methodology for collecting, classifying and explaining them.

Conclusion: Linguistic enquiry as therapy?
Most of the dominant theories which have served to shape modern academic linguistics offer their adherents a form of satisfaction that integrationism fails to provide. Structuralist theories such as those of Chomsky and Saussure both purport to give

general explanations of language which, once accepted, relieve the jobbing linguist of any further *fundamental* explanatory burden. Indeed, linguistics could for most of its modern history happily conceive of itself as a purely descriptive enterprise because once the general explanatory mechanism was already in place, be it Universal Grammar or *langue*, no further general ontological explanation was necessary. However, as Harris and others have convincingly shown, the explanatory mechanisms of linguistics are of dubious provenance, to put it mildly. They tend either to be the result of speculative metaphysics, as in the case of Saussure and Chomsky, or, in a field such as sociolinguistics, to involve the invocation of some baseline abstraction – such as identity, performance, power, indexicality, ideology – or an explanatory chain involving several such abstractions.

The explanatory power of integrationist theory, however, resides less in its ability to explain specific episodes of linguistic behaviour than in its power to show the alleged explanatory power of other linguistic theories to be illusory. In particular, it constitutes a potent deconstruction of the metaphysics and ontological assumptions underlying theories which attempt, amongst other things, to provide general explanations of language. It does so not by replacing their explanatory mechanisms and abstractions with alternatives but by demonstrating their vacuity and incoherence. As Harris has noted, 'myths do not have alternatives'. It is on this metatheoretical level that integrationist theory reveals its explanatory potency. It is noticeable, though, and somewhat paradoxical, that a prominent weapon in Harris's rhetorical arsenal is his readiness to indulge in often sweeping generalizations in characterizing the theoretical positions of other thinkers on language.

The foregoing considerations lead us back to that recurring question with which integrationists are faced and which Harris himself never quite succeeded in providing a definitive answer to, namely: can integrationism serve any 'positive' research programme or can it only exist as a form of critical response to other metalinguistic discourses? A starker way of putting it is to ask whether there is anything for integrationists to do beyond explaining why they think others have got things wrong. If not, is there anything to recommend it to the professional academic? Again, Harris may be seen as offering conflicting answers to such questions. For instance, in what seems his most overtly Wittgensteinian moment, he wrote '[i]f an integrational linguistics is worth pursuing, it is as a pragmatics of self-understanding and a basis for lay linguistic therapy rather than as part of a university curriculum' (Harris 1997: 310). RIP the integrationist academic. Or not? It is difficult to assess just how seriously Harris intended this remark. It is, after all, notable that within little more than a year of writing it, Harris published his *Introduction to Integrational Linguistics* (1998) which, for all its many merits, seemed like nothing if not an attempt to establish an academic orthodoxy of some sort. It was also the year that saw the founding of the *International Association for the Integrational Study of Language & Communication* (*IAISLC*). In emphasizing the therapeutic potential of his thought, did Harris perhaps also glimpse the potential for talking himself and his followers into professional exile, even unemployment? After all, how much of a market is there for metalinguistic therapy?

While therapeutic is certainly not an adjective most readers would rush to apply to the tone and temperament of Harris's writing, the effect of exposure to his thought certainly can be. Whereas Wittgenstein's stated aim was to battle against the intellectual bewitchments engendered by language, one of Harris' main purposes in expounding integrationism was to liberate linguistic thought from the confusions and theoretical pseudo-problems arising from traditional western metalanguage and the misconceived attempts at its scientization. In both cases, a central concern is to identify and dissolve illegitimate, nonsensical or pathological questions. The difficulty here though is that any rival approach could claim to have therapeutic value insofar it purports to offer answers to hitherto unresolved questions or correct previously held views and if it supplies a positivist methodology to boot so much the better (at least for the academic researcher). Engaging in therapy would seem to require at the very least sufficient self-knowledge to recognize that one holds errant views, not something academics and intellectuals are conspicuously renowned for. However, even if the situation were otherwise, any views recognized as such would naturally vary from one individual to another. One person's cramping affliction is another's God's truth. Where Derrida or Chomsky might cure some, they will cause only an allergic rash in others. The same obviously goes for Wittgenstein, Louch and Harris. One cannot readily generalize about the effects of a rhetorical therapy. Here any analogy with medicinal or other forms of physical therapy begins to break down. What one thinks is a philosophical cure might also sooner or later turn out to be nothing more than a temporary placebo.

It is maybe useful here to distinguish between what one might call a therapeutic intent and a therapeutic rhetoric. While a therapeutic intent to philosophical and linguistic inquiry is both laudable and worthwhile, there is, as I think Harris himself may have seen, also a danger in adopting an overtly therapeutic rhetoric. First, of course, a therapeutic rhetoric is no guarantor of therapeutic effectiveness. Second, such rhetoric is sure to raise the hackles of those who do not regard themselves in need of therapeutic intervention, a group that would surely include most professional linguists and philosophers of language. In such cases, a more straightforwardly argumentative rhetoric seems more appropriate. Indeed, for all that their respective thought carries Wittgensteinian influences, Louch and Harris for the most part employ a combative and occasionally blistering argumentative rhetoric in staking out their respective positions. One does not find, for instance, many examples reminiscent of the kind of self-consciously therapeutic-style internal self-dialogues characteristic of Wittgenstein's later work. What the writings of both Louch and Harris show is that, if deployed effectively, polemic can achieve a successful therapeutic outcome, relieving intellectual and metaphysical cramps without indulging in the rather sanctimonious rhetoric of therapy. In doing so, they also offer a salutary reminder of the importance of argument in philosophical and linguistic inquiry.

References
Austin, J. L. (1961), 'The meaning of a word', *Journal of Symbolic Logic*, 26:1&2, pp. 23–43.
Bernstein, Richard J. (1976), *The Restructuring of Social and Political Theory*, Oxford: Basil Blackwell.
Davidson, Donald (1986), 'A nice derangement of epitaphs', in Ernest Lepore (ed.), *Truth and Interpretation: Perspectives on the Philosophy of Donald Davidson*, Oxford: Blackwell, pp. 433–46.
Frey, R. G. (1978), 'Did Socrates commit suicide?', *Philosophy*, 53:203, pp. 106–08.
Gellner, Ernest (1979), *Spectacles and Predicaments*, Cambridge: Cambridge University Press.
Gruender, David (1962), 'Wittgenstein on explanation and description', *Journal of Philosophy*, 59:19, pp. 523–30.
Harris, Roy (1981), *The Language Myth*, London: Duckworth.
Harris, Roy (1988), *Language, Saussure and Wittgenstein: How to Play Games with Words*, London: Routledge.
Harris, Roy (1996), *Signs, Language and Communication*, London and New York: Routledge.
Harris, Roy (1997), 'From an integrational point of view', in George Wolf and Nigel Love (eds), *Linguistics Inside Out: Roy Harris and his Critics*, Amsterdam: John Benjamins, pp. 229–310.

Harris, Roy (1998), *Introduction to Integrational Linguistics*, Oxford: Pergamon.
Hyslop-Margison, Emery J. and Ayaz Naseem, M. (2007), *Scientism and Education: Empirical Research as Neo-Liberal Ideology*, Dordrecht: Springer.
Jarvie, Ian C. (1986), *Thinking about Society: Theory and Practice*, Dordrecht: Springer.
Johnstone, Barbara (2013), *Speaking Pittsburghese: The Story of a Dialect*, Oxford: Oxford University Press.
Klagge, James C. (2001), *Wittgenstein in Exile*, Cambridge, MA: MIT Press.
Louch, A. R. (1963), 'The very idea of a social science', *Inquiry*, 6:1&4, pp. 273–86.
Louch, A. R. (1965), 'On misunderstanding Mr. Winch', *Inquiry*, 8:1&4, pp. 212–16.
Louch, A. R. (1966), *Explanation and Human Action*, Oxford: Basil Blackwell.
Louch, A. R. (1976), 'Criticism and theory', *New Literary History*, 8:1, pp. 171–82.
Love, Nigel (2007), 'Are languages digital codes?', *Language Sciences*, 29, pp. 690–709.
Orman, Jon (2016), 'Scientism in the language sciences', *Language & Communication*, 48, pp. 28–40.
Winch, Peter (1958), *The Idea of a Social Science and Its Relation to Philosophy*, London: Routledge & Kegan Paul.
Wittgenstein, Ludwig (1967), *Zettel* (eds G .E. M. Anscombe and G. H. von Wright), Berkeley and Los Angeles: University of California Press.
Wittgenstein, Ludwig ([1953] 2009), *Philosophical Investigations* (eds P. M. S. Hacker and J. Schulte), Malden, MA: Wiley-Blackwell.

11.

Theorising the untheorisable: Notes on integrationism and the 'Mixed-Game Model'

Abstract

In this article, I offer a critical discussion of the work of prominent dialogue theorist Edda Weigand from an integrational linguistic perspective. The discussion centres upon Weigand's 'Mixed Game Model' (MGM), a model which is claimed to constitute a holistic theory of dialogue and to describe how language is integrated in a general theory of human action. I am particularly interested in determining how much (un)common ground exists between the two approaches especially since both style themselves as 'nonorthodox' and accord considerable theoretical importance to the notion of 'integration'. In the end, I come to the conclusion that despite what turn to be some rather superficial areas of convergence, the gap between integrationist and Weigandian thought remains considerable and most likely unbridgeable. I suggest that this state of affairs can be explained by the highly divergent views concerning the nature of linguistic inquiry and the role of theory therein held by those in the respective camps.

The widespread human preference for easily applicable theories, regardless of whether they are sound or unsound, has always been one of the most formidable obstacles to intellectual progress.
(Harris 1997, 303)

1. Introduction

As an integrationist, I have found reading Edda Weigand's *Dialogue: The Mixed Game* (Weigand 2010) to be a somewhat disorientating experience. On the one hand, I have encountered numerous claims and assertions which, taken in isolation, I can construe, at least *prima facie*, so as to be largely in agreement. For instance, in the book's opening paragraph Weigand writes that "integration is the name of 'the mixed game'" and that "[i]ntegration implies rejecting traditions of reductionism and addressing complexity in a holistic approach" (2010, xi). Later on we are told that human beings are "integrational beings" (2010, 270). This might appear to offer some optimistic basis for a fruitful convergence of views. However, on further reading it emerges that these and other such statements feature as scattered assertions in an overall theoretical superstructure with which I feel a good deal less at ease.

It seems to me that the essential difference between Weigand's approach and integrationsm concerns the very nature of linguistic inquiry and in particular the burden of requirements and expectations placed upon theory. An important catalyst for my discussion is Weigand's assertion that integrational linguistics "seems to mistrust any type of theory and to virtually refuse to develop an alternative theory" (2010, 25). On one level, I am quite happy to agree. However, I reject the criticism implicit in the claim. Instead, I will argue that integrationists' reluctance to pursue theoretical accounts of specific communicative events is itself the consequence of a theoretical insight, more specifically the affirmation of the radical indeterminacy of the sign, a move which effectively precludes the possibility of nomothetic explanation or exhaustive taxonomic categorisation. In contrast to what one might call integrationism's theoretical minimalism, however, Weigand's Mixed Game Model bears witness to an excess of theoretical ambition. The attempt to theorise communicative acts down to the smallest detail or what is, for the integrationist, problematically conceived of as a 'minimal unit' seems, despite claims to the contrary, to be borne more of a methodological requirement rather than the product of any compelling (meta)theoretical insight.

For Weigand, it appears linguistic inquiry not only can, but indeed must, be scientific in orientation and science naturally entails generalisation, which means theory. The role of theory in this conception of linguistics is to give rise to a positivist methodology for investigating, taxonomising and, presumably, explaining episodes of linguistic interaction through appeal to general statements. Accordingly, she would appear to have little sympathy with the view that linguistics ought instead to be regarded as a form of philosophical inquiry. For the integrationist, precisely the opposite situation obtains. From an integrationist perspective, the notion of a 'science of language' is a chimera whose sustained pursuit inevitably results in scientism (Orman 2016). Furthermore, the philosophical dimension of linguistic inquiry is not viewed as some optional extra which one may or may not pursue at one's leisure once the serious business of methodological investigation has been completed. Instead, it is seen as inherent to the enterprise. As Harris (1990, 76) notes, for integrationists "[l]inguistics is a form of philosophy, whether we like it or not; it is that part of philosophy which seeks to elucidate how and where language fits into the general human scheme of things." As my discussion will aim to show, these opposed conceptions of linguistic inquiry lead the integrationist and the dialogue theorist down two very different, ultimately irreconcilable, paths.

Therefore, despite numerous statements suggesting some degree of common ground with integrational linguistics, Weigand's explicit pursuit of a "unified theory of language use" is a pointer towards a more profound gulf between the two approaches. I also argue that by placing such a heavy theoretical burden on scientised lay concepts such as *meaning, understanding, dialogue* etc., Weigand's approach has more in common with certain schools of orthodox linguistic thought than the revolutionary rhetoric accompanying its exposition might lead one to suppose.

2. The role and limits of theory
It is ironic that Weigand chooses a quotation from Wittgenstein's *On Certainty* to stand at the head of her Preface (2010, xi) since her theoretical enterprise turns out to be entirely antithetical to the spirit and emphasis of his later thought (*OC* was compiled from notes written just prior to his death). After all, perhaps the most defining feature of Wittgenstein's post-Tractarian philosophy is its strong aversion to theory construction of any kind when it comes to making sense of human action. It must be said though that Wittgenstein and Weigand both appear to have the same basic view of what a theory is and does. Both view it as an essentially scientific enterprise employing a causal, nomothetic model of explanation whereby individual phenomena are explained through appeal to generalities. The difference is that Weigand, like most orthodox linguists, believes that such a model can be successfully applied to language, whereas Wittgenstein does not. Wittgenstein's conception of theory also means that by rejecting it and the generalisations it licenses, his simultaneous upholding of the fact-value distinction means he is also forced to reject the possibility of explaining human action altogether. Hence his repeated insistence that philosophy must abandon all attempts at explanation and settle purely for description. Weigand too, it seems, believes that linguistic communication remains properly inexplicable without some form of generality-invoking

theory. Now for Wittgenstein to hold such a view of course suggests his adherence to some or other metatheory. In this sense, then, I would suggest that metatheory would seem inescapable even for the most theoretically disinclined which, in Weigand's view, would clearly include integrationists. In Wittgenstein's case, it might even be argued that he had more than just a metatheory and that, despite his denials and those of his subsequent Ordinary Language disciples, he did actually develop something akin to a theory of language in his later work.

It must also be conceded that Wittgenstein, due to his insistence that language is a rule-governed form of action (i.e. by generalising the notion of rule-following to all instances of language), leaves himself highly vulnerable to theoretical enterprises which take inspiration from his thought. After all, if linguistic communication is governed by rules for the use of particular word or sentence forms, it cannot then be the case that meaning is a purely contextual matter. It would make a nonsense of the idea of rules to suppose that they somehow simultaneously both emerge and determine meaning in one and the same unique context. This would reduce to the trivial and explanatorily vacuous proposition that every utterance is a product of its own one-off rule. For any semblance of cogency to attach to the idea of language as a rule-governed activity, it must the case that such rules are conceived of as context-independent invariants which may operate in particular contexts (how they do so is another question altogether). Furthermore, once one has allowed for the possibility of the same rule to operate in multiple contexts, one has opened the door to generalisation. This is one reason the later Wittgenstein's status as a champion of contextualism is a good deal less straightforward than some have supposed. So while it is highly likely that Wittgenstein would have deplored Austinian and especially Searlean excursions in Speech Act Theory as entirely at odds with the spirit of his later philosophy, the primary purpose of which was to illuminate matters supposedly obscured by theory, his own adherence to the mythology of linguistic rules serves as an encouragement to such theoretical enterprises. As Harris (1997, 278) observes, it was chiefly for this reason that Wittgenstein "was [not] entirely successful in carrying out his own admirable programme to liberate our thinking [...] from the 'bewitchment' of language." Harris goes on to make the point that integrationism is "more Wittgensteinian than Wittgenstein" insofar as it reaches similar conclusions about the nature of linguistic inquiry and the role of theory but without providing any basis for science-aping methodological enterprises (see Orman 2017b).

This, of course, is one of the main reasons why integrationism is viewed as such an unattractive option by so many linguists. This includes Weigand, who criticises Roy Harris and Michael Toolan (1996) for failing to offer "workable alternative views" (2010, 1) and pave "viable new paths" (2010, 25) respectively. This is, by now, a tediously familiar charge laid at integrationism's door (e.g. Ritzau 2014) but it is also water off an integrationist duck's back since it points to a fundamental divide concerning the purpose of theorising. From an integrationist standpoint, it is quite simply irrelevant to criticise a theory for failing to provide the empirical linguist with a satisfactory methodology. Such criticisms make no contact whatsoever with the truth claims of the theory in question. On the other hand, integrationists are very much willing to criticise methodological enterprises which they see as resting on questionable theoretical assumptions. Any integrationist would therefore be likely to happily approve Weigand's assertion that

> [T]heorizing must take precautions against a procedure which starts with methodology as is usual in traditional theorizing. [It is] a fundamental *methodological fallacy* to cut the object-of-study so that it fits methodology. Instead of distorting the natural object to make it conform with methodological restrictions, a holistic approach starts from

the attempt to achieve a first understanding of the complex whole by reflective observation and then derives methodology from it. (Weigand 2010, 3)

Elsewhere Weigand writes of her concern to arrive at "a holistic theory which does not damage the natural object because of methodological exigencies" (2010, 125). Integrationists duly applaud. However, this apparent prioritisation of theory over methodology is difficult to square with Weigand's complaint regarding the unworkability of the integrationist view. If theory is genuinely to take priority, one must surely be willing to countenance the possibility that *no* positivist methodology may be satisfactorily derived from it. To do otherwise is already to impose a methodological requirement on the activity of theorising. Furthermore, a number of Weigand's theoretical constructs and devices would seem to be clearly motivated by methodological concerns of a quite traditional nature. What else, for example, can explain the concern to identify "units" of analysis and the conjuring up of a highly abstract "object" of investigation in the form of Weigand's "competence-in-performance"? All the talk of units – especially 'autonomous units' (2010, 5) – and other objects I find extremely difficult to reconcile with the supposed commitment to holism. To my mind, despite the sales pitch, Weigand's approach seems to me uncompromisingly atomistic.

3. The Mixed Game Model (MGM): an integrational view

The central claims made on behalf of the MGM cannot be said to suffer from an excess of modesty or lack of ambition. For instance, we are immediately told that the MGM constitutes a 'completely new approach to language' (2010, xi) and that it "represents the first theory of language which starts from the complex whole of human dialogic interaction" (2010, xi). Elsewhere we are promised that the MGM makes "a fresh start by *going to the heart of language*" (2010, 1) and that it provides the basis for "a comprehensive unified typology of human dialogic interaction" (2010, 209). The stakes, then, are high. In my view, the MGM as expounded by Weigand does not live up to these lofty claims.

It is apparent that Weigand, like most orthodox linguists since Saussure, believes that she is doing science. Indeed, her claim that "[a]s a discipline, linguistics needs to specify its *scientific interest* in order to achieve a clear profile which is to some extent distinct from the profile of other disciplines that also deal with language, e.g. psychology or sociology" (2010, 4) is one which could have been written by Saussure himself since it corresponds precisely to his own rationale for attempting to set up linguistics as an autonomous academic field. I find it difficult to see how, in practice or in theory, this segregational disciplinary requirement can be squared with the 'holistic' and 'integrated' approach promised elsewhere. This is already one reason for doubting the novelty of Weigand's theoretical enterprise.

So what, then, is the central concern of Weigand's science? Here she quite reasonably departs from Saussure by insisting that the study of language cannot be reduced to the description of abstract, idealised systems. Instead, Weigand states that the "central linguistic interest is directed at describing and explaining how human beings succeed in coming to an understanding in human affairs" (2010, 4). The phrase 'coming to an understanding' appears frequently throughout the book, sometimes looking rather embarrassed between quotation marks (e.g. 2010, 141) and elsewhere unadorned. In any case, according to Weigand coming to an understanding is the "general purpose of dialogue" (2010, 59). Given the theoretical burden the notion plays in Weigand's account, we might expect to find a precise, generalisable definition of what it is to 'come to an understanding'. Unfortunately the only glosses on the phrase Weigand provides contain a glaring circularity. For example, we are told that "[c]oming to an understanding means an *understand-*

ing about a state of affairs" (2010, 53), that "'coming to an understanding' goes beyond 'understanding what is meant'" (2010, 59) and that "[i]n the process of coming to an understanding, we are confronted with divergent understanding, misunderstanding and non-understanding as an inevitable consequence of interaction among individuals" (2010, 60). Yet nowhere are we told what is meant by *understanding*. Presumably, as an extremely common item of lay metalanguage the expectation is that we all know perfectly well what it means and how to use it. This is largely the case of course. In our everyday affairs, it is perhaps only in a rather small minority of cases that we are led to question and consciously reflect on the meanings of our most common and indispensable metalinguistic terms. However, ordinary metalanguage does not deliver any kind of object amenable to the generalising practices of scientific theory. As Wittgenstein, perhaps better than any, reminded us, there is no generalisable answer to the question of what it is to understand something and by extension what it is to 'come to an understanding'. There may be 'family resemblances' but these too defy any generalising theoretical endeavour. As a lay concept, then, 'understanding' and any of its cognates are radically indeterminate.

Besides, even if acceptable unambiguous general criteria were available for defining what it means to come to an understanding, it is simply false to claim, as Weigand does, that achieving understanding is the 'general purpose' of communication if general is taken, as surely it must be, to mean 'universal'. If it is not and Weigand's claim is merely a kind of *ceteris paribus* generalisation (true except when it's not) then it is drained of all explanatory power since it leaves entirely unaccounted for all those instances of communication, which admittedly may well be in the minority, in which the achievement of understanding – whatever it is taken to mean – is very much *not* the purpose. What about cases of deliberate obfuscation, for instance, where the intention is to ensure mis- or nonunderstanding? It is no good claiming that misunderstanding or non-understanding are simply different types of understanding. Rather they suggest the absence of understanding. Now if Weigand agrees that achieving understanding is not the *universal* purpose of communication, her claim that it is nevertheless the general purpose would seem to amount to nothing more than the unexciting point that most of the time we want our interlocutors to understand what we say and write. Furthermore, this is something we surely already know without the intervention of any linguistic theorist. As a theoretical claim, then, it is entirely platitudinous. Louch (1982, 191) makes a similar point in respect of Speech Act Theory when he notes the absurdity of "appealing to the philosophers' expert testimony in order to solemnly declare that utterances can inform, impel action, or give pleasure". On the other hand, the claim that coming to an understanding is the universal purpose of communication certainly is not platitudinous since it conflicts sharply with both individual experience and common sense. The problem is that it is just not true. Either way, there seems to be no viable basis for constructing a general theory of language based upon a generalised notion of understanding that does not repeat the follies of many of the orthodox linguistic approaches from which Weigand also seems keen to distance herself. As Harris (2000, 2) puts it: "if one cannot explicate "understanding", there is no point in constructing theories in which that is viewed as the primary object of linguistic communication". Elsewhere, Nigel Love (1990, 54) makes the same point when he notes that "[t]he idea that there is a state of affairs, recurrently arising in the course of linguistic interaction, which is uncontroversially identified as 'full' or 'proper' understanding of what was said, is based on a distortedly simple concept of 'understanding' itself ".

Orthodox linguistics' solution to the problem of establishing a general definition of understanding which is then able to serve as a generalised criterion for defining linguistic communication was its recourse to the postulate of intersubjectivity which found its most iconic depiction in Saussure's 'talking heads' diagram. Saussure 'solved' the 'problem' of understanding by imposing an identity requirement and reducing it to the sharing of mental representations. If the linguistic signs produced by person A cause the same mental representations in person B as they do in person A himself, then person B has understood what person A is saying. If this matching of mental representations does not happen, understanding does not take place and, by definition, communication does not occur. In other words, according to the Saussurean metaphysic understanding and communication are one and the same process.

So what is Weigand's position on intersubjectivity? On several occasions she mentions human beings' apparent need for "intersubjective reliability" (2010, 56 and 146) and elsewhere she talks of "intersubjective validity" (2010, 226 and 232) yet no definition of either term is offered. At the very end of the book, the cat finally seems to emerge from the bag when we encounter the claims that the "position of human beings as *intersubjective beings* is a first step towards human beings as dialogic beings" (2010, 271), 'the intersubjective mind must engage in intersubjective dialogic action' and that "[h]uman beings as *social individuals* need an intersubjective mind in order to get along" (2010, 272). It is apparent from her comments (2010, 271) that Weigand regards the terms 'shared mind' and 'intersubjective mind' as synonymous. Such remarks are likely to leave most integrationists in a state of grimace. I do not suppose Weigand would approve anything as crude as Saussure's telementational speech circuit – after all, her claim of theoretical originality would be further weakened if she did – but from a theoretical perspective all this talk of a shared or intersubjective mind amounts to pretty much the same thing. In both cases, understanding, communication and social life more generally are made conditional upon the requirement of shared mental representation. It is not clear to me how the notion of intersubjectivity can be theoretically finessed in such a way as to avoid this conclusion. From a theoretical point of view, it is no solution to appeal to a kind of 'weak' intersubjectivity which allows for similarity rather than sameness of mental representation. Two things may be similar or dissimilar in an indeterminate number of ways. The notion of similarity therefore provides no basis for theoretical generalisation, an endeavour which requires determinacy in the object of investigation.

Weigand, however, believes that she finds support for her position on intersubjectivity in the latest neuroscience. She notes for instance that recent experimental research on so-called "mirror neurons" would appear to provide confirmation of human beings' "double nature" as "individuals and social beings" (2010, 3). Elsewhere she claims that her insight "integration means inter-action" has "finally been proven by neurological experiments" (2010, 58) and that "research on mirror neurons verifies the integration of human abilities [and] also their dialogic nature" (2010, 61). Weigand also claims that such research has conclusively demonstrated the untenability of the Cartesian model of mind. Now I claim no expertise whatsoever in any domain of neuroscience but it is far from clear to me that I need to do so in order to arrive confidently at the view that my own existence has both an individual and social dimension. This is a matter of personal experience that is neither proven nor disproven by any accounts of the goings-on in my brain. Intersubjectivity suggests identity of phenomenological *experience*. Just as if two individuals both simultaneously slip on a banana skin, they have not had the *same* experience, there is no way that Weigand or anyone else can prove the thesis that identity of neuronal firing – if it even makes sense to talk of such thing – entails identity of experience. Indeed, the notion of 'identity of experience' is philosophically and theoretically *obscure* and stands in need of an explanation which does not appear forthcoming. In addition, the idea that neuroscience has proven that "integration means interaction" reeks of a category mistake. If integration means interaction it is largely because these two terms have such a significant overlap in meaning that the proposition itself borders on the tautologous. Neither term serves as a useful gloss of the other. As for research on mirror neurons supposedly verifying the integration of human abilities, I simply do not know what to say in response other than I would like to know what kind of neurological findings it would take to override simple observation of behaviour and disprove the thesis that human abilities are integrated. The appeal to neuroscience is no doubt intended to boost the scientific credentials of Weigand's theorising but directed as it is towards supporting what is fundamentally a metaphysical philosophical thesis, albeit one not acknowledged as such, it falls flat and serves merely as a diversion.

Another notable feature of Weigand's thinking is that while she is more than willing to scientise ordinary metalinguistic terms such as 'understanding', 'meaning' and 'dialogue', the concept of 'the sign' fares far less well in her theoretical enterprise. Indeed, the sign is a concept which we apparently have to "leave behind" (2010, 12). Weigand sees an inconsistency in integrationism's continued talk of signs since the sign is apparently the "central concept of the code model" (2010, 25) which integrationists are forever railing against. Integrationists, it seems, are still suffering from a Saussurean hangover without perhaps realising it. I would like to suggest, however, that any inconsistency in this regard resides more with Weigand than integrationists. Weigand appears to make the elementary mistake of failing to draw any principled distinction between – indeed she conflates – the notions of a sign and a sign system. To immediately follow, as Weigand does, the quite reasonable claim that "[l]anguage use […] has nothing to do with a system of signs" with the demand that "we […] have to leave behind the concept of the sign" (2010, 12) is a simple non-sequitur. It is, *pace* Weigand, arguably the highly technical concept of the sign system – Saussure's *langue* – and not the sign which is the central concept of the code model. The sign system of course presupposes signs but the concept of the sign does not automatically presuppose a sign system. Indeed, this constitutes one of integrationism's most basic arguments, viz. that communication proceeds on the basis of sign-making but without the underlying, enabling mechanism of a determinate sign system. However, integrationists also categorically reject the Saussurean sign with its decontextualised bi-planarity, preferring to replace it with the notion of the 'integrational sign' (Davis 1997). As far as I can see, Weigand provides no clear theoretical rationale for rejecting the concept of a sign as understood by integrationists.

One of the major goals of the MGM is to facilitate the development of a typology or taxonomy of dialogic speech acts or "complex action games" to use Weigand's terminology. The taxonomy is apparently to be constructed by deriving "subtypes from a complex whole [...] which consists of all possible dialogically oriented speech acts which are interrelated as initiative and reactive acts in the minimal sequence of action and reaction" (2010, 141). What is not altogether obvious is the intellectual motivation for doing so. I therefore do not mean to be in any way facetious when I ask what inherent interest is served by devising such a taxonomy. Of course, imbued with an Aristotelian spirit linguists are inveterate categorisers and taxonimisers but it is important to make the point that a taxonomy neither explains nor provides any new information. It is, rather, an ordering device. I find that I am far better acquainted with and feel far more secure in my understanding of the particular kinds of speech acts which feature in Weigand's taxonomy pre-theoretically when not part of a taxonomic structure. Indeed, one can go further to claim that one must already have such pre-theoretical acquaintance in order to be able to make any sense of the taxonomy. The theory with its associated taxonomy and sometimes less than perspicuous terms of art therefore only becomes any clearer when applied to cases (or 'data' in the linguist's unfortunate jargon) which we are able to make sense of before its application. This calls to mind the point made by A.R. Louch (1966, 13) in respect of Parsonian sociology, namely that

> Parson applies his theoretical or taxonomic superstructure to cases which are not illuminated in any way by the application. Quite the reverse; we understand the verbiage of the superstructure a little better when we see what count as instances of his terms and rubrics. In this sense the theory has no explanatory power; and as a description is unnecessarily complex. The outrageous vocabulary clothes the essential barrenness of the theory. (Louch 1966, 13)

I find, for instance, that my own ability to offer an assurance or make an oath, as well as my understanding of what others are doing when they do so, is in no way strengthened, disrupted or otherwise embellished by Weigand's (2010, 178) assertion that assurances and oaths belong to a "declarative pattern" and serve as "a guarantee either of a representative claim to truth or of strengthening a consent after a directive speech act". Weigand's gloss would seem to offer no particular advantages over any easily available dictionary definitions of the terms in question.

Following on from her discarding of the sign, Weigand also claims that it is necessary to "reject the absolute authority of the native speaker when it comes to verifying lexical rules" (2010 12). However, it appears native speakers may exercise authority over how phrases in their native language are translated into foreign languages. For instance, Weigand writes that

> [a] native English speaker, for instance, would not consider the word *deep* as synonymous with *high*; on the contrary, these 'signs' taken in isolation seem to be antonyms. In language use however the German phrase *mit*

> *tiefem Ernst* cannot be translated literally but corresponds to English phrases such as *with high seriousness* or *with (no) great seriousness*. (2010, 12)

Now speaking as a 'native English speaker', I find that I can quite easily come up with 'acceptable' phrases in which *deep* and *high* are synonymous (deep gratitude, high gratitude, deep annoyance, high annoyance) and even more so when they are in adverbial form (e.g. deeply grateful, highly grateful, deeply annoying, highly annoying). Furthermore, I see no reason why *mit tiefem Ernst* cannot be translated 'literally' by the phrase *with deep seriousness* or *with profound seriousness*. These may well be less common alternatives to those Weigand lists but a simple Google search shows that they are far from unencountered and I also do not find that either violate my intuitions of acceptability. It is not my intention to claim any wider authority for my intuitions and judgments on these matters but it is equally not clear to me where Weigand's authority to overrule them on my behalf comes from.

4. Integrationism and theory
I turn now to offer an integrationist perspective on the activity of theorising language. It is clear from her few scattered remarks that Weigand regards integrationist thought as barely deserving of mention as a theory. She comments, for instance, that Toolan's integrationist concept of 'Total Speech' (Toolan 1996) "does not reach the status of a theory" (2010, 46). Her most interesting remark, however, is the assertion that "'Integrational Linguistics' seems to mistrust any type of theory and to virtually refuse to develop an alternative theory" (2010, 25). Now while in my view this is somewhat overstated, especially the latter claim, there is some truth in it although I do not accept the implied criticism. While integrationism offers a distinct and vigorously critical metatheoretical account (a theory of linguistic theories in other words – although I do not see any principled reason why second-

order theoretical accounts should be deemed any less theoretical than first-order theories), it is certainly the case that when it comes to providing a 'positive' account of language and communication integrationism operates with what I am inclined to call a theoretical minimalism. Importantly, though, such minimalism is itself the product of a theoretically grounded insight rather than merely some unprincipled disinclination towards theory.

Theory, I assume most will be happy to agree, entails generalisation. Now integrationism does make some general, exceptionless claims about communication, but they are very few in number and not ones which pave the way for endless vistas of methodological inquiry. For instance, integrationists argue that all human communication involves the contextualised integration of activities, both physical and mental, via processes of creating and interpreting signs (the act of interpretation is also considered a creative activity). This, essentially, is the integrationist definition of communication. For the integrationist, no process which does not involve the semiological integration of activities can be considered an instance of communication. Hence the reason integrationists are reluctant to regard as communication forms or consequences of physical interaction which operate below the level of human consciousness. If I unknowingly spilt a drink all down your back but, fortunately for me, you didn't notice me do it and never subsequently discovered the damp patch and stain on your expensive new jacket, then no signs were made of the incident and therefore communication, from an integrationist perspective, did not occur. Perhaps there was some third party who saw the whole thing take place but, anticipating the sour atmosphere likely to ensue, opted for discretion and kept quiet. In that person's case, communication did indeed occur.

So integrationism views communication as the integration of activities in context. Is this really such a novel position? Isn't Weigand essentially saying the same thing? If so, why can't integrationism give rise to similarly elaborate, theoretically inspired methodological enterprises which can keep the jobbing linguist in gainful employment? The answer lies in the integrationist recognition of the principle of *radical indeterminacy* (see Pablé 2018; Orman 2017a). Integrationism tacks on to its general definition of communication one further general feature which acts as a proviso to the methodologist, namely that signs are radically indeterminate, which is to say indeterminate in respect of both form *and* meaning. Although it is frequently overlooked, one cannot overemphasise just how central the idea of indeterminacy of form is to the integrationist understanding of communication. Those who focus solely on the indeterminacy of meaning will always fail to fully grasp the integrationist position. This failure is evident in the epic confusion of those who claim that integrationism is a form of postmodernism and broadly compatible with, say, a Derridean semiology. After all, the price Derrida imposes in order to grant himself and his acolytes the absolute freedom of interpretation required in order to embark on their onanistic deconstructionist escapades is the absolute determinacy (and hence iterability) of form, or the written form at any rate. It should also be said that the integrationist recognition of the indeterminacy of meaning neither corresponds to nor licenses any kind of postmodern interpretive free play. From an integrationist point of view, to recognise meaning as indeterminate is merely to affirm that the value or significance of any communicative act cannot be infallibly guaranteed or predicted in advance. It is a recognition of the open-endedness of communication and of human life more generally. Integrationism does not deny that our interpretations and communicative enterprises as a whole may be constrained by a wide range of factors including, importantly, our appraisal of what we think other people intend and mean by what they say and do. As an experiment, one could perhaps try living according to a strictly postmodern semiology whereby one strives to take no heed whatsoever of the purposive nature of the vast majority of other people's actions or refuse to recognise the intentionality behind most of the written texts one encounters in going about one's daily business. My guess is that life would soon become all but intolerable, not to say impossible, as one is paralysed into inaction. It certainly proved too much for Derrida himself who, as Louch (1982, 191) notes wryly, was extremely aggrieved by John Searle's supposed failure to understand his intended meanings in their famous spat. Furthermore, an integrationist would also point out that our very frequent concern to discriminate between intentional and non-intentional behaviour (or traces of behaviour) is very often fundamental to our assessment of its moral status.

Now to return to the main issue at hand, Weigand (who certainly is not a postmodernist), like many modern linguists, appears quite happy to concede at least some measure of semantic indeterminacy (e.g. 2010, 263). However, the notion of indeterminacy of form finds no mention at all in her account. One encounters the same situation in contemporary sociolinguistics. This is a telling state of affairs since determinacy of linguistic form turns out to be essential to any positivist methodological enterprise. To say that a linguistic form is determinate is basically to claim that it can exist in more than one place. In other words, it is not the product of a unique act of individual, time-bound contextualisation. The determinate form therefore has both atemporal and impersonal coordinates. The point is that as soon as one can have a form existing in two places – the same form here, the same form there – one can begin generalising beyond the specific case and embark upon theory construction. One can therefore understand most linguists' reluctance to entertain the possibility that linguistic form might be indeterminate. If they did, their theoretically grounded methodology would evaporate before their eyes.

For integrationists, however, form is no less indeterminate than meaning. What this means is simply that the forms which an individual perceives as being at play in or underlying any stretch of speech, writing etc. also cannot be guaranteed or infallibly predicted in advance and will necessarily be the result of a potentially open-ended range of time-bound, individual contextualisation practices (see Orman 2017a). Another way of putting it is that the linguistic signs which emerge in communicational episodes are not retrieved from any pre-existing inventory. Integrationism therefore rejects the contemporary sociolinguistic creed which sees individuals as being in possession of a 'repertoire of linguistic resources'. The upshot of all this is that from an integrational semiological point of view signs are not repeatable if the criterion for repetition rests upon an identity statement. As a result, they defy generalisation and theoretical explanation.

It is recognition of the radical indeterminacy of language which leads to what Weigand sees as integrationism's aversion to theory. While it is possible to make the theoretical generalisation that a particular phenomenon is indeterminate, the consequence of doing so is that any specific instantiations of said phenomenon do not then admit to further illumination by any generalising statements of theory. Hence the integrationist position that specific episodes of communication do not admit to or stand in need of theoretical explanation. This perhaps explains why, relatively speaking, so few empirical integrationist studies have been carried out. It does not stem from the fact that integrationism is somehow anti-empirical (although it can be said to be anti-positivist). If one wants to find out about how and why particular people and communities speak or otherwise communicate, it is a good idea to observe them in action. But do linguistic researchers choose their informants because they are genuinely interested in and puzzled by specific aspects of the lives of the individuals concerned or is it because they see them as convenient fodder for some theoretically informed and, one might add, ideologically motivated methodological exercise? Any language will do, it's all data in the end. The theorist-methodologist assumes an omnivorous quality. The difficulty is that once licence to invoke a theoretical explanation and generalise beyond the specific case is withdrawn many of our empirical studies simply lack interest. Not all communication is equally interesting. In fact, a great deal of it is utterly unremarkable. Some episodes puzzle us more than others. Some episodes fail to puzzle us at all. An atheoretical empirical account of any bit of communicative action whatsoever is a recipe for tedium.

It seems to me that Weigand's theory and method is not directed towards providing answers to anything that genuinely puzzles us. Instead, its motivation seems to lie in its methodological ambitions. What do we want to know about language and communication? I think this is a very good question for linguists to stop and consider. Upon reflection, and no doubt as a result of my integrationist leanings, I find it very difficult to come up with a general answer which I can conceive of as having a general solution. The kind of response one gives to such a question will, in my view, likely be a useful indicator of the place accorded to and the expectations placed upon theory in one's subsequent linguistic inquiries.

5. Conclusion

I am aware that my views as outlined in this paper are destined to be unfavourably received and liable to be seen as unhelpful, even destructive, as well as, no doubt, entirely misconceived. I am not particularly perturbed by this since I cannot share Weigand's conception of linguistic inquiry, her exalted view of theory or her taxonomic urges. Ultimately I am afraid to say that I believe the areas of common ground between integrationism and adherents of the MGM are far outweighed by the differences. This may be an uninspiring conclusion but I find it an unavoidable and an honest one.

References
Davis, Daniel R. 1997. "The three-dimensional sign." *Language Sciences* 19(1): 23–31. doi: 10.1016/0388-0001(95)00024-0
Harris, Roy. 1990. "The integrationist critique of orthodox linguistics." In *The Sixteenth LACUS Forum 198*, ed. by M. P. Jordan, 63–77. Lake Bluff, IL: LACUS.
Harris, Roy. 1997. "From an integrational point of view." In *Linguistics Inside Out: Roy Harris and his Critics*, ed. by George Wolf and Nigel Love, 229–310. Amsterdam: John Benjamins. doi: 10.1075/cilt.148.16har
Harris, Roy. 2000. *Second Thoughts on Telementation*. Unpublished manuscript.
Louch, A. R. 1966. *Explanation and Human Action*. Oxford. Blackwell.
Louch, A. R. 1982. "What is Criticism?" *Philosophy and Literature* 6(1–2): 190–195. doi: 10.1353/phl.1982.0029
Love, Nigel. 1990. "The locus of languages in a redefined linguistics." In *Redefining Linguistics*, ed. by Hayley G. Davis and Talbot J. Taylor, 53–117. London: Routledge.
Orman, Jon. 2016. "Scientism in the language sciences." *Language and Communication* 48:28–40.
Orman, Jon. 2017a. " *Indeterminacy* in sociolinguistic and integrationist theory." In *Critical Human Perspectives: The Integrational Turn in Philosophy of Language and Communication*, ed. by Adrian Pablé, 96–113. London: Routledge.
Orman, Jon. 2017b. "Explanation and theory in linguistic inquiry." *Empedocles: European Journal for the Philosophy of Communication* 8(2): 167–186.
Pablé, Adrian. 2018. "Abandoning the simple by disintegrating the sign? Semiological reflections on Edda Weigand's (meta)theory." *Language and Dialogue* 8(1): 84-101.
Ritzau, Ursula. 2014. "Learner language and polylanguaging:

How language students' ideologies relate to their written language use." *International Journal of Bilingual Education and Bilingualism* 18(6): 660–675. doi: 10.1080/13670050.2014.936822

Toolan, Michael. 1996. *Total Speech. An Integrational Linguistic Approach to Language*. Durham: Duke University Press.

Weigand, Edda. 2010. *Dialogue: The Mixed Game*. Amsterdam/Philadelphia: John Benjamins. doi: 10.1075/ds.10

12.

Some reflections on the uses and abuses of theory in linguistic thought[1]

My purpose in this piece is to offer a few brief thoughts on a series of questions with which I have become increasingly interested in recent months. Linguistics, it seems to me, is awash with theories and theoretical work of various sorts yet it is not all that often that one comes across any critical scrutiny of the theoretical enterprise itself. The basic question motivating my discussion can be put thus: why theorise language? In other words, what motivates the theoretical enterprise in relation to language and what sustains it? This sets in train a series of further questions. Why is there apparently such faith, amongst language

---

[1] This piece was published in April 2018 on the blog *History & Philosophy of the Language Sciences* (https://hiphilangsci.net/2018/04/12/theory/)

scholars at least, in theory? What does theory contribute to our understanding of a human phenomenon? Is it genuine, previously unavailable knowledge or simply a different and perhaps also professionally advantageous way of talking about it? Are theoretical enterprises generated and propelled by genuine intellectual puzzles or anomalies that challenge our settled conception of the world or more by particular ambitions? Or is it the case that where language is concerned theory tends instead to generate merely its own internal puzzles – academic questions in the most pejorative sense of the word? This raises the issue of how, why and by whom particular theories of language come to be valued which in turn potentially prompts questions which take on a more sceptical tone such as 'is it possible to theorise language without somehow giving a distorted view or misrepresenting it?' or even 'what do we lose sight of by submitting language to theoretical treatment?'

The belief that any identifiable human or social phenomenon is ripe for some kind of theoretical treatment pervades the humanities and especially the social sciences. Writing in the 1970s, the philosopher A.R. Louch spoke of the 'lust for theory' which had taken hold in literary studies. A similarly voracious and in some cases intensifying lust also exists, it seems, in many contemporary areas of scholarly inquiry concerned with language. It is fairly common, for example, to encounter the claim that a particular linguistic phenomenon, especially a recently identified one, remains 'undertheorised' – the implication being that unless we have a theoretical account of the phenomenon in question, we do not and cannot properly understand it. By way of example, Pavlenko (2007:35) claims that 'emotions remain undertheorized' in Second Language Acquisition research. Elsewhere, Elizabeth Miller (2014:4) claims that 'agency is often treated simplistically and remains undertheorized in Applied Linguistics research'. Attributions of undertheorisation therefore suggest a lack of scholarly rigour or serious treatment, whereas 'overtheorisation' tends more to be a term of lay condemnation of intellectual pretentiousness.

Underlying these considerations is a more basic question, a definitive answer to which is perhaps less forthcoming, namely 'what constitutes a theory of language?' Is any kind of reflexive contemplation or connected series of statements about a particular phenomenon automatically to be considered theoretical? How stringent a definition are we to operate with? The philosopher Eric Voegelin (1999:64), for instance, was insistent that '[t]heory is not just any opining about human existence in society. It is rather an attempt at formulating the meaning of existence by explaining the content of a definite class of experiences'. The veneration of the theorist in the Western intellectual tradition goes at least as far back as Aristotle's *Ethics* and his discussion of the figure of the *spoudaios* – often translated as the 'mature man' and which in Aristotle's thought also carries suggestions of seriousness, solemnity and moral virtue. According to Voegelin (1999: 139):

> The *spoudaios* is the man whose character has been formed by an aggregate of experiences and who has maximally actualized the potentialities of human nature, who has formed his character into habitual actualization of the dianoetic and ethical virtues, the man who at the fullest of his development is capable of the *bios theoretikos*.

Quite what the *bios theoretikos* ought to entail, however, is not always so clear. For example, in his book *Theorizing* (1973:168-9) Alan Blum provides the following Byzantine rationale for the activity of the theorist:

> Theorizing is speaking that shows the Reason of critical speaking to lie in the imperative need to re-assert itself as an instance of faithfulness to Reason itself. The success of

theorizing in the deepest sense lies in the fact that it redirects attention to the grounds of speaking by speaking so as to evoke in its very speech the ideal of addressing grounds as the Good [...] From a dialectical perspective, theorizing is the speaking which understands itself as inescapably rhetorical, and which acts upon such an understanding by preparing its very speech as an argument for the Rationality of that commitment. Theorizing then achieves its purest character when it conceives of itself as the speaking that is displaying and arguing rather than the speaking which seeks to create a unity among different arguments and displays. Whereas moderns regarded successful inquiry as that which silenced discussion by producing speech to which one must assent, dialectic treats inquiry as the re-opening of a discussion that routine usage has long covered over. Yet the arguing which theory is is not the giving of reasons, but a showing of the achievement of its authorization as a way of affirming the Rationality of that author.

I would be reluctant to take too confident a stab at trying to say what this is all supposed to mean - is Blum saying that the 'moderns' (Weber? Marx?) erred by trying to find solutions to puzzles whereas the proper role of theory is to proliferate discourse? In any case, the reader is obviously expected to agree that theorizing is a very important activity indeed and presumably one reserved only for select members of the intellectual clerisy. Further support for the theorist can be found in Edward Said (2000:210) who is emphatic in claiming that 'of course it is ridiculously foolish to argue that "the facts" or "the great texts" do not require any theoretical framework or methodology to be appreciated or read properly.' It is notable in passing that Said feels no need to place embarrassed quotation marks around the word 'properly' as he does around 'the facts'. Said would obviously feel little sympathy with Stanley Fish's claim, no doubt to be taken with a fair pinch of salt, that theory is 'an inconsequential activity'.

Peter Sloterdijk (2012:37), however, raises the prospect of a far less reverent view of the theorist when he asks:

> What if the much lauded theoretical virtues really derive from secret weaknesses? What if they're based on a questionable compensation for stubborn defects, or even the morbid inability to face the facts of life without embellishment and evasion? Does *homo theoreticus* really come from such a good background as he has assured us from his earliest days? Or is he actually a bastard trying to impress us with fake titles?

What sort of person, then, might *homo theoreticus linguae* be?

Wittgenstein and the 'anti-theory' position

The most renowned, if not entirely consistent, expression of an anti-theory position in respect of human behaviour and hence language is to be found in Wittgenstein's later work, especially in the *Philosophical Investigations* & *On Certainty*. Wittgenstein saw the urge to theorise as arising from what he called the 'craving for generality' *(das Streben nach Allgemeinheit)* and the desire to imitate the methods and secure the prestige of the natural sciences. For Wittgenstein, there was a fundamental difference between two forms of understanding which he called 'scientific' and 'philosophical'. Scientific understanding is of the theoretical or nomothetic sort – concerned with the discovery of general principles and operating with a mode of explanation based on causality and prediction whereby explanation consists either in an appeal to regularities or in bringing individual cases under some law. Philosophical understanding, however, is for Wittgenstein avowedly non-theoretical and ad hoc. He famously says that philosophical understanding 'consists in seeing connections' (*PI*, § 122). A favourite example to illustrate this point is that of what it is to understand a piece of music. Wittgenstein makes an explicit connection with language, saying that 'understanding a sentence is more akin to understanding a piece of music than one may think'. However, he goes on to make the point that the evidence for understanding in either case is 'imponderable' and therefore resistant to the generalising requirements of theory.

One slightly odd side-effect of Wittgenstein's view of the divide between science and philosophy was his insistence that by placing a prohibition on philosophers generalising from specific cases to establish general laws or principles, one therefore had to renounce the possibility of explanation and make do with pure description. Indeed, some of Wittgenstein's most resonant meta-philosophical remarks are on the issue of explanation. In the *Philosophical Investigations*, for instance, he says that '[t]here must not be anything hypothetical in our considerations. We must do away with all explanation, and description alone must take its place'(*PI*, § 109) and '[p]hilosophy simply puts everything before us, and neither explains nor deduces anything' (*PI*, § 126). Perhaps the most striking of all is to be found in the terse opening remark of the *PI*, namely '[e]xplanations come to an end somewhere' (*PI*, § 1).

Wittgenstein's repudiation of the possibility of explanation stems from his faith in what may be seen as a traditional scientific model of explanation, which involves his upholding of the fact-value distinction and the empiricist doctrine that proper explanation is a matter of exhibiting causality - causality being fundamentally a property of the movement and collision of physical matter – and hence amenable to scientific explanation through the invocation of general principles and laws. Additionally, a key feature of scientific theories is that they can be evaluated as true or false – in other words, they make realist claims about the world. It is this chain of thought which leads

Wittgenstein to reject the possibility of ad hoc or non-theoretical explanation.

Although there are strong grounds for taking issue with Wittgenstein's upholding of the fact-value dichotomy in respect of human action (see Orman, 2017), he clearly identifies the two central notions when it comes to theory, namely *generalisation* and *explanation*, or rather explanation through generalisation. It is important therefore to distinguish between two forms of generalisation: on the one hand, generalisation simply as a factual summary of individual cases (non-theoretical) and generalisation as a strategy of explanation (theoretical).

Elements of Wittgenstein's work are, however, not entirely faithful to its overall spiritual tenor. Indeed, it is significant that what are arguably the most problematic and unattractive elements of his later thought are precisely those which have received the most enthusiastic uptake within linguistics (especially pragmatics in the form of Speech Act Theory), the reason being that they provide the potential ingredients for generalising, theoretically driven methodological enterprises. Despite his aversion to science-aping theory, Wittgenstein – at least on some highly authoritative interpretations – actually succumbs to an explanatory generalisation of his own in the form of his assertion that language is a rule-governed form of action. In other words, the concept of rule-following is generalised to all instances of language, a move which, if accepted, opens the way for the kind of methodological investigation which has fortified linguistics self-image as a *bona fide* science of language.

Theory and linguistic science
This scientific conception of theory is evident in many of the key models of modern linguistics. For example, Saussure's theory of language is based upon the reductive, general, exceptionless postulate that *langue* - the determinate language system – constitutes the sole object of the linguist's investigation. If it is not *langue*,

then it falls outside the bounds and concerns of the theory and the science. So, in Saussure's reductionism, we already glimpse some recognition that key elements of language – he called them the subject matter of an external linguistics – are beyond the scope of any theoretical enterprise. It is perhaps unfortunate that Saussure did not live to develop these insights further in his promised but unrealised work on a *linguistique de la parole*.

Saussure's model of linguistic communication works on the basis of a simplistic general model operating on causal principles. In brief, A has a particular thought which triggers a corresponding sound pattern in his/her brain, the brain then transmits an impulse to the organs of phonation, sound waves travel from A's mouth to B's ear, which then triggers the corresponding psychological association of the sound pattern and concept in B's brain. This constitutes Saussure's answer to the general ontological and hence theoretical question of what communication *is*. It also provides a precise general, i.e. universal, answer to the question of what constitutes understanding – understanding is simply a case of two or more individuals matching the same mental content to the same sound patterns or signs. Under such a model, there are no grey areas or indeterminacy of comprehension – understanding either does or does not occur. Saussure therefore provides generalisable answers to the questions 'What is a language?', 'What does linguistic communication consist in?' and 'What is understanding?' – in fact these last two questions turn out to be synonymous on Saussure's account.

Now, the obvious question when confronted with a theory claiming to be the basis of science is simply "Is it true?" or perhaps more generously "How true is it?" Clearly to pass muster as science, Saussure had to maintain that his theory and its constructs constituted realist claims about entities in the world. Saussure makes the point in the *Cours* – and here he is in agreement with Wittgenstein – that a science must advance empirical propositions, yet he famously never identified a single real-life example of a *langue* as stipulated by his theory. He also offers no criteria for what would constitute empirical verification of his theory.

It is therefore interesting to reflect at this stage on the rationale for Saussure's theorising. What motivates it? It has been suggested by critics – most notably Roy Harris – that Saussure's theoretical enterprise is motivated less by a genuine intellectual puzzle or a void in knowledge but by professional ambition and the perceived necessity to set up linguistics as an autonomous science distinct from those other areas of inquiry which also deal with questions of language. It is of course true that the question of how to go about doing this generates theory-internal puzzles of its own and Saussure showed enormous ingenuity in addressing these, but in taking the course he did he arguably reduced the activity of linguistic theorising to an arid, scholastic exercise.

One theoretical approach whose accompanying rhetoric is very much focused on its alleged scientific solving of an intellectual puzzle or set of puzzles is/was Chomsky's theory of Universal Grammar. The supposed puzzle in question is that of how children are able to acquire mastery of their native language in spite of the limited data available to them – the so-called 'Poverty of the Stimulus' argument. What is of interest here is the basic form of Chomsky's explanation which allows it to claim nomothetic theoretical status. In order to explain away the puzzle, Chomsky appealed to certain postulated innate, biologically endowed, *universal* features of language. For example, the claim that all languages are organised in terms of phrases which have 'heads', 'arguments' and 'adjuncts' and that no language that was not organised thus could possibly be a natural human language.

Sociolinguistics and theory

The essential link between theory and generalisation or abstraction is also evident in sociolinguistics, a field which appears to be developing an increasingly insatiable appetite for theoretical reflection. For example, in the recent book *Sociolinguistics: Theoretical Debates,* Nikolas Coupland (2016:6) writes as follows:

> Like all theory, theory in the social sciences and sociolinguistic theory should still involve abstracting away from particular data contexts and instances. But distinctively from classical scientific theory, it might also be conceived as providing a guide to social action (the moral agenda of 'theory' returning to prominence), so that explanation may be insufficient in itself as a priority.

There are several things to say in this connection. Firstly, it points to an underlying metatheoretical assumption in which abstraction – which amounts to generalisation – is deemed to be a legitimate explanatory move in relation to language. Compare this with Deleuze's claim that 'abstractions explain nothing, they themselves have to be explained' (1995: 146). However, it seems a quite natural assumption to make for a field of inquiry such as sociolinguistics concerned as it is with the distribution and function of repeatable linguistic and other semiotic *forms*, a concern which finds theoretical expression in the materialist notion – consistent with the neo-Marxist ethic which pervades the discipline – of *linguistic resources*. The essential point here is that as soon as one has something which can exist in two places at once – the same form here, the same form there – one can begin generalising beyond the individual case and embark upon theory construction.

However, it also points to a tension at the heart of sociolinguistic theoretical endeavours, namely the twin desires to on the one hand make scientifically respectable and explanatory valid generalisations and, on the other, to pursue a particularistic socio-political, moral or, dare I say it, ideological agenda.

Problems potentially arise when the truth claims of the theory are seen to contradict or fail to provide sufficient support for the moral-ideological and - just as crucially - methodological agenda. The question, then, is which aspect takes theoretical priority? It is significant, I think, that despite its theoretical promiscuity, sociolinguistics won't just hop into bed with any old theorist or philosopher. This is not so much a question of high standards, however, – why, even Derrida still gets a look-in – as a reflection of a rather limited, ideologically determined taste. The preferred theoretical bedfellows in the case of sociolinguistics tend increasingly to be those neo-Marxist, poststructuralist thinkers who nourish its basic ideological and methodological conceit, which in turn fortifies its practitioners' claims to expertise in matters linguistic.

The foregoing considerations point to two potential dangers for theory construction in relation to language and communication, namely those of *overgeneralisation* and *imprecision*. The issue of generalisations, or statements cast in general form, which turn out to admit exceptions – in other words they turn out not to be general – is a fundamentally problematic one, albeit one that is rarely acknowledged as such, for the credibility of any *theoretical* enterprise. These are what are sometimes called – in the sciences at least – *ceteris paribus* generalisations. Essentially they are over-generalisations. A less lofty way of describing them would be statements which are true except when they're not. A simple example would be something like "People eat when they are hungry."

Probably the most well-known example from the history of linguistics of the identification of a generalisation which turned out not to be exceptionless was Grimm's Law concerning the first Germanic Sound Shift – the exception was famously noted by Karl Verner who realised that Grimm's Law was only valid when the stress fell on the root syllable of the Sanskrit cognate word. As a result, so-called Verner's Law was formulated to account for this exception in accordance with the Neogrammarian creed that 'sound change laws admit no exceptions'.

So what other kind of *ceteris paribus* generalisations can one identify in the work of linguistic theorists? Some clear examples can be found in the work of Mikhail Bakhtin, a theorist in whom there has been a surge of interest in recent years within sociolinguistics, a development which elicits sideways glances from literature colleagues for whom Bakhtin fell off the fashionable theorist radar some moons ago. However, when read as theoretical statements, some of Bakhtin's pronouncements must be classified simply as false or incoherent. The following examples are taken from his famous article *The Problem of Speech Genres* (1996).

> Neutral dictionary meanings of the words of a language ensure their common features and guarantee that all speakers of a given language will understand one another.

One might think it remarkable that someone who can make such a statement can possibly be taken seriously as a linguistic theorist at all. A more complex problem is presented by the following example:

> When selecting words, we proceed from the planned whole of our utterance, and this whole that we have planned and created is always expressive.

Bakhtin presents this piece of psychological speculation as a general statement about language, although he does not say how he arrived at the insight. If we leave aside the by no means theoretically unproblematic assumption that linguistic communication is simply a matter of selecting words, it strains credulity to suppose that we *always* plan our utterances in advance, as if everything we say follows on from some inner rehearsal process.

What about spontaneous, unplanned utterances, where we literally don't know what we are going to say until we've said it? Now if we drain Bakhtin's claim of its generality, it reduces to little more than the commonplace observation that sometimes we plan what we say. How often we do so it would appear very difficult to say.

In addition to this kind of overgeneralisation, Bakhtin's work also contains a series of what one might call open-ended generalisations. Take the following, for instance:

> A speech genre is […] a typical form of utterance; as such the genre also includes a certain typical expression that inheres in it. In the genre, the word acquires a typical expression. Genres correspond to typical situations of speech communities, typical themes, and, consequently, also to particular contacts between the meanings of words and actual concrete reality under certain typical circumstances. Hence also the possibility of typical expressions that seem to adhere to words. The typical expression (and the typical intonation that corresponds to it) does not have that force of compulsoriness that language forms have….

This whole passage hangs on the undefined term 'typical'. Bakhtin does not supply any general criteria for determining what constitutes a 'typical' utterance, expression, situation, theme, intonation etc. Nor does he provide any examples. Furthermore, the notion of typicality can be said to be theoretically enigmatic insofar as something may be typical or atypical in an indeterminate number of respects – an inherently open-ended concept. It is also a question about which people can be reasonably expected to disagree. Consensus cannot be assumed. The problem, then, is that if we are unable to definitively identify a typical utterance, word, expression etc., other than stipulatively, it then becomes impossible to identify the theoretical object, i.e. the genre, which is supposedly elucidated by appealing to it in the first place. The only way to then identify a genre is, similarly, by means of stipulation.

One further consequence of the vagueness and stipulative nature of Bakhtin's formulation is that it provides it with insulation against refutation. We cannot make the general claim that a speech genre is NOT a typical form utterance because we have no *general* criteria for saying what a typical form of utterance is. However, such insulation is bought at the price of explanatory significance. So this leads to the question: If the theory doesn't explain, what does it do?

What further sense can be made of this passage? Given its failure to specify any determinate theoretical entity, it could be read as expressing the commonplace and again, rather unexciting point that particular uses and forms of language are associated with certain types of situation. The question then becomes 'why do we need a theorist of language to tell what we surely – in some fundamental sense and however explicitly articulated – already know?' If we didn't somehow know it, we would very much be the communicatively incompetent 'social monsters' which Dell Hymes famously imagined. One answer which suggests itself – and this might be considered part of a wider postmodern rationale for theory – is that the constructs or terminology of a theory provide the basis for talking about phenomena in new, different ways. Theory then becomes, in effect, a way of redescribing in sometimes exuberant vocabulary what we either already must know or could at least conceivably come to know pretheoretically. Theory, it seems, may be a disguise for platitude.

There is an important methodological issue here too. If a theoretical claim has some high degree of generality, it becomes almost trivially easy to find instances of data which conform to it. Cue the spectre of such intellectual curiosities as Bakhtinian analyses of teenagers' text messaging and Foucauldian Facebook studies. On the other hand, if a claim is generally valid, i.e. universal, then all instances conform to it and no confirmation via individual cases is needed because the generalisation already serves to identify the phenomenon in the first place – as is clearly the case with Chomsky's universal grammar theory. for example. In this sense, then, it becomes a *formal or logical* claim.

The consequences of this were noted by the Norwegian social psychologist, Jan Smedslund (1979:9), who, noted that:

> Theories which aim at being testable and empirically valid must fit the local conditions and, hence, cannot be general. Theories which aim at being general cannot fit particular local conditions and hence cannot be testable and empirically valid. Their validity has to be purely formal. [...] This means that we must stop believing that our data are relevant for and support or refute general theories.

The only way to get around this difficulty is to treat as constants those aspects of communicational situations which, in reality, are inherently variables, in particular questions of value and meaning.

The activity of theorising may, then, become a pretext for interpretive enterprises which nevertheless often parade as empirical. A clear expression of this tendency is to be found in the work of anthropologist Clifford Geertz associated with the so-called 'hermeneutic turn' in anthropology and noted for what he called an 'interpretive theory of culture' based around the notion of Thick Description (TD) (Geertz, 1973a, 1973b) and a 'semiotic concept of culture'. Geertz takes up some curious positions. On the one hand, he is quite explicit in claiming to do science yet he asserts that for him the aim of anthropology is not to solve puzzles as such but rather to achieve 'the enlargement of the universe of human discourse' (1973a:14) – he also says elsewhere that anthropological writings are 'interpretations' and 'fictions'.

The role of theory, then, for Geertz is to make possible what he calls Cultural Interpretation. Culture with a capital 'C'. For example, he makes explicit mention of seeking to understand

Moroccan culture as a 'theoretical entity' (1973a:37). He says elsewhere that the 'essential task of theory [...] is to make thick description possible' (1973a:25), TD being 'the close-reading of a culture' with the suggestion being that 'proper' TD is not possible without theory. It is also apparent that Geertz is not especially bothered by what one might call the truth value of a theory. Instead, theories merely have to be *useful* which Geertz glosses as 'throwing up new understandings' (1973a:27). Once they stop being useful, they are presumably abandoned and one moves on to the next theory.

It is telling, then, that one of Geertz's most renowned theoretical contributions or devices comprises a metaphor, and a rather ethnocentric one at that, namely that of "CULTURE AS TEXT" which itself springs from the idea that the key to understanding culture is to apprehend the 'symbolic meaning' of social actions – a notion which Ernest Gellner (1992:30) rather nicely labelled a 'conceptual intoxicant and instrument of self-titillation'.

Now, one key characteristic of metaphors is surely that they are not straightforwardly evaluable in terms of being true or false. Rather, metaphors are more naturally assessed in terms of how illuminating, fruitful or productive they are – and this of course can only be done in relation to specific purposes. As he makes clear, Geertz's purposes are fundamentally methodological – in his case a kind of unending textualism. Texts beget texts in order to serve the stipulative goal of expanding the universe of discourse and it is in this way that his theoretical entities take on a self-justifying aspect. One significant effect of the 'culture as text' metaphor is, therefore, to reify and render culture static, as a product, a text, rather than a process, a move which obviously makes the ethnographer's task of symbolic interpretation rather easier – the methodological benefit. One of Geertz's critics, Heather Love (2013), puts it well when she talks of Geertz's 'freezing of behaviour into culture' in order to 'clear the way for interpretation and bring together data gathering and textual analysis.'

Geertz's insistence on the 'culture as text' metaphor has been described as the call sign of a 'positivist in despair' (Yoshida, 2014:57) – the idea being that if anthropology cannot be an empirical science, then it must be literature, pure interpretation, therefore *anything goes* and issues of accountability to the embarrassing notion of truth fall away. However, Geertz's hermeneutic enterprise is undermined by his linguistic metatheory which is, though, based on realist foundational claims. In perhaps the most explicit and concise statement of his philosophy of language, Geertz states that 'culture is public because meaning is' (1973a:12). In other words, Geertz subscribes to a traditional Western metaphysics of communication which regards as a fundamental requirement for communication the availability of a communal, shared linguistic code. However, this requirement cannot be coherently reconciled with a desire for endless, free interpretation because the postulation of a code implies the existence of rules, systems, determinate forms and meanings etc. which, in theory, actually do the interpretive work for us. The idea of endless interpretation due to textual indeterminacy of meaning cannot coherently be reconciled with a code-based view of language because a code is a concept which implies inherent determinacy. A code is a construct which contains its own interpretation. The code just has to be known. Or rather, to know the code is already to know its interpretation, irrespective of context.

Similar considerations can also be applied to Derrida's famous theoretical slogan 'there is nothing outside the text' – again a theoretical statement which is methodologically motivated insofar as it is seen to license the endless proliferation of interpretative enterprises. However, if one generalises the implication of Derrida's remark to all of language or even just to all written language, namely that interpretation of the intentions of the speaker or author are irrelevant to the determination of meaning, the conclusion is patently absurd. It is noticeable too that Derrida failed to live up to his own dictum and was notably upset, for instance, by John Searle's supposed misunderstanding of what he meant in their renowned disagreement. Once again, it is important to point out that Derrida's hermeneutic theory is based on a particular realist foundational claim, namely the iterability and citationality of linguistic signs which supposedly lend them their intention-flouting character. Consequently, as with all theories, any refutation of Derrida's theoretical enterprise should begin by addressing these metatheoretical issues.

Conclusion

After these mostly critical comments, I want to end by briefly outlining what might be considered a positive case against the attempted explanation of specific communicative acts by means of theory and this is tied up with a view of language as moral action and as individuals as moral agents.

Now to offer such account on principled grounds inevitably requires a particular metatheory. One of the very few theoretical generalisations that integrational linguistics makes about language and communication is that it is radically indeterminate. The paradoxical nature of this generalisation is that it is one which appears to preclude the possibility of any further ontological generalisations. As Pablé & Hutton (2015:18) note, the integrational position is that 'there is nothing in human society, psychology or biology that determines language in general.' They go on to say that 'to argue that language is indeterminate is [...] to make a general assertion about the absence of decontextual authority over what words mean' (p.19). To this one might also add the absence of any decontextual authority over what actions mean. In other words, the only determinacy which can be achieved is the unique determinacy of a particular individual's interpretation or evaluation in context. Furthermore, contexts do not submit to theoretical generalisation because:

> to generalize is to assert that some fact holds regardless of context. But our grounds for making [...] judgments as to the meaning, the significance, the purpose of an action are restricted to individual cases. For that is where meaning, significance and purpose reside. Louch (1966:215)

This might seem to suggest, as Wittgenstein held, that there is therefore no basis for explaining human action. However, this is to adhere to an inappropriate paradigm of explanation. Furthermore, it is belied by the simple observation that we usually do manage to explain people's actions to our satisfaction on an *ad hoc* basis without recourse to generalities. Indeed, following Louch, I would claim that to identify and describe an action, linguistic or otherwise, is *already* to offer an explanation of it, albeit not a theoretical one. This is on account of the fact that determining what it is people are doing – the most basic question of social inquiry – is tied up with the recognition and attribution of their motives, purposes, intentions and desires etc. and assessing their performances in the light of these. It is, for example, to distinguish between deliberate, intentional acts and involuntary or unintentional movements of the human body, a distinction which is often obscured by the catch-all term 'behaviour'. To identify an action as an action, i.e. as purposive, and then further as an action of a particular sort, is to recognise it via an act of individual, context-bound interpretation as a moral act and the individual performing it as a moral agent. When it comes to human actions, the fact/value distinction collapses and it becomes impossible even to talk about actions without recourse to evaluation and appraisal.

In his brilliant yet largely unheralded book *Explanation & Human Action* (1966), A.R. Louch makes the dramatic claim that 'psychology and social science are moral science. Ethics and the study of human action are one.' By extension and granted a view of language as action, one inference of this remark is that linguistic inquiry too might more meaningfully be conceived as a branch of ethics which places the unique, theory-defying individual at the centre of its concerns.

References

Bakhtin, M.M. 1996. The Problem of Speech Genres. *Speech Genres & Other Late Essays.* Eds. Caryl. Emerson and Michael Holquist. 60-102. University of Texas Press. Austin.

Blum, Alan. 1973. *Theorizing.* Heinemann. London.

Coupland, Nikolas. 2016. Introduction. In N. Coupland (ed.) *Sociolinguistics: Theoretical Debates.* 1-34. CUP. Cambridge.

Geertz, C. 1973a. Thick Description: Toward an Interpretive Theory of Culture. In C. Geertz *The Interpretation of Cultures,* 3-30. New York. Perseus.

Geertz, C. 1973b. Deep Play: Notes on the Balinese Cockfight. In C. Geertz *The Interpretation of Cultures,* 412-453. New York. Perseus.

Gellner, Ernest. 1992. *Postmodernism, Reason and Religion.* Routledge. London & New York.

Louch, A.R. 1966. *Explanation and Human Action.* Blackwell. Oxford.

Love, Heather. 2013. Close Reading and Thin Description. *Public Culture* 25 (3 (71)): 401-434.

Miller, Elizabeth. 2014. *The Language of Adult Immigrants: Agency in the Making.* Multilingual Matters. Bristol.

Orman, Jon. 2017. Explanation and theory in linguistic inquiry. *Empedocles: European Journal for the Philosophy of Communication,* 8 (2): 167-188.

Pablé, Adrian & Chris Hutton. 2015. *Signs, Meaning and Experience. Integrational Approaches to Linguistics and Semiotics.* Mouton De Gruyter. Berlin.

Pavlenko, Aneta. 2007. *Emotions and Multilingualism.* CUP. Cambridge.

Said, Edward. 2000. *The Edward Said Reader.* Edited by Moustafa Bayoumi and Andrew Rubin. Granta Books. London.

Sloterdijk, Peter. 2012. *The Art of Philosophy. Wisdom as a Practice.* Columbia University Press. New York.

Smedslund, Jan. 1979. Between the analytic and the arbitrary: a case study of psychological research. *Scandinavian Journal of Psychology*, 20, 1-12.

Voegelin, Eric. 1999. *Modernity Without Restraint: The Political Religions, The New Science of Politics, and Science, Politics, and Gnosticism.* University of Missouri Press. Columbia, MO.

Wittgenstein, Ludwig. 2009 (1953). *Philosophical Investigations.* (eds. PMS Hacker and J Schulte). Wiley-Blackwell. Malden, MA.

Yoshida, Kei. 2014. *Rationality and Cultural Interpretivism.* Lexington Books. New York.

13.

The linguistic thought of Ernest Gellner

Abstract
Theoretical questions concerning language and communication figure prominently throughout the work of the Czech-British social philosopher and anthropologist Ernest Gellner (1925–1995). The article traces the development of Gellner's linguistic thought from his early, controversial engagements with Ordinary Language Philosophy to his responses to Chomsky's work in linguistics and his late-career (re)assessments of Wittgenstein and particularly Malinowski whose – subsequently repudiated – view of the fundamental difference between the alleged "primitive" and "scientific" functions of language turns out to play a central explanatory role in Gellner's renowned theory of nationalism. The key to understanding Gellner's thinking on language is to grasp both his adherence to a "telementational" model of communication and his scientism. This leads him to embrace the view that modern national cultures are predicated upon an industrial-scientific mode of cognition which both requires and entails a radically distinctive metaphysics of communication, namely one which allows for the conveyance of culture transcending, "context-free" conceptual content. This, I claim, is a serious error which stems in large part from a misdiagnosis of the cognitive and communicative consequences of literacy and in particular a failure to correctly apprehend what linguist Roy Harris has termed the "autoglottic space" engendered by the availability of writing.

Introduction
Ernest Gellner (1925–1995) was known to be irritated by attempts to pigeonhole him within any particular academic discipline and was apparently fond of quoting Max Weber's famous quip "I am not a donkey and I do not have a field". Gellner's academic output was after all profoundly interdisciplinary[1] spanning and bearing upon such fields as social anthropology, sociology, ethnography and philosophy and he is a worthy holder of the respective titles typically granted to the practitioners of each of those disciplines. It might be seen to be stretching things, however, to also call him a linguist into the bargain and even more so if that designation is narrowly interpreted and held to imply any extensive engagement with the field of academic linguistics. Yet in a more profound sense Gellner was very much a linguist since ontological and epistemological questions pertaining to language and communication figured centrally throughout his work and in some cases occupied a crucial, if somewhat underacknowledged, place in his theoretical accounts. This raises a question which surprisingly appears to have received relatively little attention within the academic literature, namely that of whether Gellner had any fully formed positive theoretical position on language of his own and, if so, precisely what it entailed. The initial temptation on surveying his vast record of publications is perhaps to enter a negative answer to that question. What there does not appear to be is any fully elaborated statement or treatise on his part and there is certainly no indication of an allegiance to any particular subfield of linguistics or the philosophy of language. One reason is that Gellner, unlike most professional linguists or philosophers of

---

[1] The back-cover blurb to Gellner's final book (Gellner 1998) even mentions an, albeit unattributed, description of him as "one of the last great Central European polymath intellectuals".

language, had no interest in aridly contemplating language in isolation as some kind of splendid or curious *Ding an sich*. The kind of lexico-etymological parlour games or syntactic tree diagrams which occupied the time and attention of many of his contemporaries with a professional academic interest in language therefore held little serious intrigue or appeal. Gellner's interest in language was instead irredeemably part and also largely in the service of his wider socio-philosophical thought and indeed the two can in some sense be regarded as having co-evolved, albeit under the direction of a few seemingly ever-present philosophic convictions.

Gellner's view of language, which by the end of his life had begun to take on a broader and more explicit aspect as his social thought crystallised into an increasingly comprehensive and pellucid worldview, emerges chiefly through his evaluation of the linguistic thought of others, in particular Wittgenstein, Malinowski and Chomsky. As hinted at by the title of his last, posthumous work – *Language and Solitude*: *Wittgenstein, Malinowski and the Habsburg Dilemma* (1998) – it is Gellner's divergent responses to the linguistic thought of those two fellow Central Europeans which turn out to be a significant pointer towards grasping his own position on language, one which transpires most saliently and in fact plays a central explanatory role in his renowned theory of nationalism (Gellner 1983, 1997). Yet, while highly influential and brilliantly expounded, it is a theory which is substantially vitiated by a deeply problematic account of language and communication derived chiefly from an enthusiastic endorsement of a position first explicitly articulated by Malinowski but which Malinowski himself later came to reject. The seeds and saplings of the view of language which finally emerges in Gellner's late-career work on nationalism can however be discerned in many of his earlier writings and particularly in his assessments of Ordinary Language Philosophy (OLP) and Chomsky's work in linguistics. If one were to select a few terms which best characterise Gellner's socio-philosophical thought, *rationalism, modernism* and, more negatively, *scientism* would have strong claims to appear very near the top of the list.[2] Of the three, though, it is arguably Gellner's scientism which ultimately emerges as the most prominent feature of his thinking on language. However, it is a scientism which both springs from and serves to underpin a more fundamental(ist) rationalism, a mode of thought which for Gellner finds its most compelling socio-cultural expression in the form of the pervasive "high" cultures which come to define and index the modern phenomenon of nationalism.

While Gellner's original and distinctive theory of nationalism is both wonderfully limpid and in some respects alluringly simple, it also relies heavily a highly scientistic account of language underpinned by a mythical metaphysics of communication. The rationale for this claim is that for Gellner, the kind of scientific-literate, "high" culture necessary for the development of modern national cultures[3] entails a fundamentally different ontology of language. The basic idea, taken from Malinowski, is that under the conditions of modern scientific-literate culture linguistic communication is freed from the anchoring constraints of local action and context and becomes, in effect, a matter of decontextualised, culturally transcendent thought transmission. Indeed, Gellner (1983) insists repeatedly that modern nationalism depends upon the possibility of such "context-free communication". The problem with this account may be stated briefly thus: language is not a mirror of thought and linguistic communication,

---

[2] Gray (2011) also identifies Gellner's scientism as a defining feature of his socio-philosophical thought.

[3] A tautologous expression from Gellner's perspective. For him, nations are by definition products of modernity. For an alternative account which emphasizes the continuity of many nations with elements of pre-modern ethnocultural formations, see Smith (1987, 1998).

whether via speech or the medium of a written, codified idiom, is not, indeed cannot ever be, a process of precise, disembodied thought transmission. To suppose otherwise is to indulge in pure metaphysics, albeit a metaphysics of considerable intellectual repute in the Western tradition. There is, *pace* Gellner, also no such thing as "context-free communication". This, as I shall argue, is an illusion ensuing from a misdiagnosis of the cognitive and (meta-)communicative consequences of literacy. A further symptom of this illusion is the typical modernist-essentialist belief in standard, codified languages as communicational *realia* instead of a recognition of their true status as metalinguistically conjured objects of belief. Once this illusion is recognised for what it is, an alternative theory of communication is required to explain both the success of science and the phenomenon of nationalism.

Gellner on OLP

It might appear odd to claim that Gellner initially had an underdeveloped – or at least underelaborated – theory of language given that what first secured his reputation in academic circles and even led to his acquiring the rarefied status of public intellectual was his wholesale onslaught against the thought of the later Wittgenstein and OLP in *Words & Things* (1959). Yet there is of course no necessary reason that opposition to a theory should entail a fully developed or explicit counter-theory of one's own and there is also usually more than one way of being "anti" any particular philosophical approach. In the present case, one might argue that this is so because OLP is not, as some of its proponents – including Wittgenstein – were at pains to stress, a theory but is instead a methodology and, as such, cannot properly be assessed in terms of its being "right" or "wrong" but merely whether or not it is useful, productive etc. One could therefore say that *Words & Things* ended up being a theoretical critique of something which never claimed theoretical status in the first place.[4] Gellner, though, would not have this and was inclined to see such disavowals as little more than a deliberate smokescreen designed to obfuscate the insinuated theoretical convictions of ordinary language philosophers.

Jarvie (2005, xxiii) is quite right though when he notes of *Words & Things* that "[v]ery little is said within it about Gellner's own philosophy – of language, the world, and of philosophy". Rather than being *for* a specific view of language, the book is instead mostly a truculent, yet in places also jauntily entertaining polemic *against* one particular style of thinking about language and linguistic enquiry.[5] The most interesting and novel aspect of Gellner's account is that his most trenchant criticisms are fundamentally sociological in nature rather than language-philosophical in a more traditional sense. There is also scant mention of matters pertaining to semiology or semiotics. Gellner's preoccupation with the sociological dimension of linguistic thought is a recurring and distinctive aspect of his work which would again come strongly to the fore in his late-career (re)assessments of Malinowski and Wittgenstein. One could even formulate his position in *Words & Things* in pseudo-Wittgensteinian terms and say that Gellner viewed OLP as the product of a particular "form of life" – the socially conservative, complacent, unimaginative world of British post-war establishment academia, which to him was both personally alienating and intellectually repellent. It seems unlikely that he would have objected to this assessment but he would no doubt have been quick to retort that contrary to the claims – or what he regarded more as insinuations given the lack of explicit formulation – of the later Wittgenstein and his followers, no form of life is ever closed or absolute. Thus there could always be the

---

[4] I am grateful to an anonymous reviewer for drawing my attention to this point.
[5] For a highly critical discussion of *Words & Things,* see Uschanov (2002).

possibility of a conceptual escape route, even for the "Narodniks of North Oxford" as he memorably called them, who, for as long as they were still under the spell of Linguistic Philosophy, were nevertheless unable to see it for themselves.

While it is true that *Words & Things* gives little overt clue as to Gellner's own positive theoretical position concerning the nature of language, one can nevertheless detect the underlying presence of an idea that was to receive more explicit formulation in later years, namely that concerning the possibility of a culture-transcending language with a universal, science-enabling conceptual framework and its application to the study of human behaviour. Indeed, by the time of *Language & Solitude* Gellner identifies this as "the big question" (1998, 153). His strong inclination to answer it in the affirmative stands as a counterpoint to what he sees as the absolute cultural relativism implied by OLP and as a riposte to works inspired by Wittgenstein's later thought attacking the scientific pretensions and methodological excesses of the behavioural and social sciences (e.g. Winch 1958; Louch 1966). However, it is an opposition which in the end arguably leads Gellner too far in the other direction, which is to say into an equally resolute and untenable scientism of his own where language is concerned.

Gellner on Chomsky

Gellner's assessments of Noam Chomsky's contributions to linguistic theory, which date mainly from the late 1960s to the mid-1980s, make for illuminating reading. For one, they are conspicuous for being his only sustained engagement with any modern theorist of note from within the field of linguistics.[6] What

---

[6] Gellner did also discuss the work of, amongst others, Malinowski, Garfinkel and Quine who, however, would generally be regarded as belonging to the fields of anthropology, ethnomethodology and the philosophy of language

is also striking and somewhat uncharacteristic for Gellner is the—if not quite intoxicated, then—laudatory tone of his initial response to Chomsky's work which, over time, became more measured and circumspect. For instance, in recounting his experience of attending a lecture at University College London, Gellner (1969) speaks of Chomsky's "magic", "philosophic dynamite" and "effortless and almost diffident lucidity". Hall (2011, 211) also reports that in the early 1970s, Gellner had on more than one occasion referred to Chomsky as the "greatest living philosopher".

What is it then about Chomsky's work in the forbiddingly arcane field of syntactic theory that held such interest and appeal for Gellner the social philosopher and anthropologist? The interest would seem to lie in the fact that, as Gellner (1969, 831) himself observes, Chomsky's ideas on language "are only incidentally about language, in the sense which primarily concerns the professional linguist". It is also quite clear that Gellner shares few, if any, of these concerns. He shows little interest in the finer points of syntactic analysis and even complains of the "truly hideous notation" employed by Chomsky and other generativists, describing it as "no aid to exposition or comprehension" (1979, 115). Gellner's fascination with the Chomskyan view of linguistic competence is that it entails a more general – and also radical – view of human nature. Accordingly, he notes that Chomsky's theorizing "must profoundly affect our picture of man" (1969, 832). In a sympathetic discussion of Chomsky's revival of the theory of innate ideas, Gellner speaks of the "philosophically exciting character" of his approach and immediately goes on to note that the underlying issue driving such discussions "is really the uniqueness of man, or the uniqueness of thought, mind,

---

respectively. Not that these disciplinary distinctions count for much in the context of the present discussion.

language" (405). Some of the very biggest of the "big questions" in other words.

The interest, then, is fairly easily explained. More interesting in the present context however, and also more complex, is the question of the attraction of Chomsky's approach for Gellner. It is at this point that it becomes pertinent to highlight a fundamental metaphysical assumption – one also shared by Chomsky – which underpins all of Gellner's thinking on language and which, as will be shown, transpires most saliently in his appraisal of Malinowski and his own theory of nationalism. The key to Gellner's position is to grasp his view of the relationship between language and cognition, a view which in fact turns out to be utterly orthodox and the same pseudo-common-sense one that has long dominated the Western intellectual tradition. For Gellner, as for Aristotle, Locke, Saussure, Chomsky and numerous other illustrious names, the essential or highest purpose of language is to express and – when deployed in social interaction[7] – transmit thought. Gellner is therefore a fully paid-up subscriber to the thesis of what Reddy (1979) called the "conduit" model of language and iconoclast linguist Roy Harris (1981) termed "telementation", namely the idea that linguistic communication involves the neat transference or copying of mental content (theorised variously as impressions of the soul,[8] ideas, concepts, mental representations) from the mind of one party to another via the mechanism of a communal linguistic code. For Harris (on whom more below), the belief in telementation and languages-as-codes are two interlocking and

---

[7] For Chomsky, the essential purpose of language is to express or formulate individual thought. The sociocommunicative function of language is held to be little more than a fortuitous epiphenomenon of this more basic function and, as a result, philosophically far less interesting. However, as Carr (1997) shows, the Chomskyan generative programme is in fact also logically committed to a version of the telementation thesis.

[8] The English translation of Aristotle's *pathemata tes psyches*.

mutually reinforcing fallacies which together constitute the potent "language myth" endemic to Western linguistic thought (Harris 2002).

Now Gellner's view of the basic cognitive and communicative function of language is in itself unremarkable. Yet while his adherence to it is absolutely necessary since Chomsky's ideas would be seen to lack any kind of plausibility otherwise, it does not on its own account for the appeal which they hold for him. One can be a telementationalist without being a Chomskyan. Indeed, one can even be profoundly anti-Chomskyan while remaining fully committed to some version or other of the telementational thesis (e.g. Evans 2014). It is at this point that Gellner and Chomsky's kindred rationalism and scientism begin to figure more centrally. The basic appeal of Chomsky's thought for Gellner resides in the idea that our linguistic capacities and our conceptual apparatus are in no fundamental sense self-explanatory and cannot be satisfactorily accounted for by any empiricist model of acquisition or pseudo-therapeutic philosophising.

> Chomsky has brought home to us, more than any other man perhaps [...] that our very capacity to use language at all is not self-evident or self-explanatory, and cannot possibly be explained in terms of the repeated use of such easily accessible, introspective processes as association or its supposedly tough-minded variants, Stimulus, Response and Reinforcement. The ability to generate and recognise an infinite number of unpredictable sentences simply cannot be explained by the loose and feeble explanatory power of notions such as "analogy". To pretend otherwise is to cling to a low and infantile standard of what may count as explanation. Thus our capacity to speak, and hence to think, is rooted in our internal organisation, which is a far-away country of which we know little. (Gellner 1979, 111)

Here we see a clear statement of Gellner's essentialist view of the connection between thought and language, as well as evidence of his deep distrust of the deliverances of common sense as a resource for obtaining fundamental explanatory insights into language and mind. Gellner sees in Chomsky an ally for fighting philosophical battles on several fronts. Firstly, Chomsky's ideas could hardly be more antithetical to the common-sense-fetishism of philosophers such as G.E. Moore and the tenets of Gellner's ever-present philosophical *bête noire* – the later Wittgenstein and OLP – according to which concepts are seen as deriving all necessary explanation and justification from an exhaustive or, less favourably, microscopically pedantic analysis of their use in culture-internal "language games". Secondly, and relatedly, Gellner (1975, 83–107) endorses with enthusiasm[9] Chomsky's attack on what he sees as the "feeble" and even "bastard" empiricism of behaviourist attempts to offer an explanatory model of human conduct on the basis of low-level, "mushy" and, ultimately and ironically, mentalistic notions such as "association". So obviously correct does Gellner take Chomsky's position to be, he is even moved to ask "why is it highly intelligent men find the alleged insights and the programme of behaviourism so compulsive?" It perhaps does not need pointing out that versions of the very same question increasingly began to be asked (and no doubt still are in some quarters) in relation to Chomskyan linguistics once its halo of irrefutability inevitably started to lose its lustre.

For Gellner, as for Chomsky, something far more powerful than third-person empiricism and Senior Common Room lexicography is required to in order explain our mental powers and hence our capacity for language. This is no doubt true but

---

[9] Gellner (1975, 89) writes that Chomsky's "negative, demolition work seems to be entirely conclusive".

what exactly is it that is required? For Gellner, instinctively and emotionally at least, the answer to this problem is to be found in that ultimate manifestation of rationalism, which is to say science. But where and in what form of science? What is to be the scientific object of enquiry? What is interesting in the present context is just how readily Gellner accepts Chomsky's formulation of the terms of enquiry and the basic issues at stake. Particularly striking is his repeated parroting (Gellner 1975) of Chomsky's thoroughly reductionist-essentialist definition of what language (linguistic competence) is, namely the capacity to produce and understand an unlimited number of novel sentences. That the explanation of linguistic competence thus conceived really is the fundamental issue for a viable theory of language, Gellner does not dispute. Now it is in no way necessary to accept Chomsky's highly idiosyncratic view of language in order to identify the obvious inadequacies in the behaviourist account, although if one does it is without doubt one which draws them out very clearly. Nothing could be less behaviouristic after all. The key term in all of this turns out to be "structure". In his lengthiest discussion of Chomsky, Gellner (1975, 81–97), bee firmly in bonnet, stresses the point over and over again that "only structures ever explain anything" or "only structures are real".[10] For Gellner, this is without question "the correct view" (1975, 94). Not just any structures will do though. Where language is concerned, it is, unsurprisingly, *grammatical* structures and only grammatical structures which apparently perform all the explanatory labour. Gellner (1975, 94) quotes with approval Chomsky's claim that "language has no objective existence apart from the internalised grammar". We therefore arrive at the following equation:

---

[10] Faith in the explanatory force of structures of course also strongly informs Gellner's sociology.

mind=language=grammatical structures or in further simplified form: *mind=grammatical structures.*

What is interesting is that Gellner does not question, at least not openly, the claims to scientific status of the Chomskyan programme. Anticipating humanistic accusations of "scientism" against any impersonal form of explanation which deigns to suggest that human powers are not self-explanatory, Gellner (1975, 100–108) mounts a fascinating and impassioned defence of Chomsky's "cold", mechanistic reductionism in which he even takes the behaviourists to task for failing to live up to their own alleged toughness by not being scientistic enough, mockingly describing them as "pseudo-scientistic" and "crypto-humanist". Chomsky, it seems, is far more like the scientistic real deal although Gellner does not go quite so far as to attempt to reclaim scientism as a badge of honour. His point is rather that soft-humanist, in-principle attributions of scientism to *any* attempts to seek a scientific account of mind and language have no automatic, self-endowing validity. His main targets here are clearly the "anti-science" tendencies discernible amongst those Wittgensteinian and Austinian worshippers of ordinary language. For Gellner, the very possibility of scientific explanation cannot be ruled out a priori where language is concerned. In a powerful series of passages (Gellner 1975, 105–108), he pens a paean to "the most basic kind of humanist [...] who tries to use science itself to destroy scientism", a figure whom he sees embodied brilliantly in Arthur Koestler. This kind of humanist is claimed to be "specially and genuinely likeable" since "he does not reject science nor employ cheapjack tricks" (Gellner 1975, 106). Gellner immediately goes on to lavish further praise upon this most ideal(ised) of humanists who, it seems, may even be able to find common cause with the Chomskyan approach:

> He alone, in that camp, does not campaign against explanation and science. (He merely wants them to bring other,

more acceptable results, or is convinced that it can and will bring them.) The others invent a variety of rather repugnant, harmful, and inherently absurd dogmas, such as the self-sufficiency of common sense, the self-explanatory and ultimate nature of cultures or "forms of life", the acceptability of leaving ultimate direction to some impersonal force acting through as, and so on. To protect their world from erosion by science, they invent forces or realms which are beyond the reach of explanation. The cult of self-explanatoriness, in a variety of idioms, is their shared mark. He who would destroy "reductionism" by science itself is quite different. (And of course, it is perfectly possible, and indeed necessary to destroy *specific* reductions; but, for instance, Chomskian linguistics destroys simple models not for the sake of some carte blanche self-explanatory spiritualism, but in the pursuit of *better* models.) (Gellner 1975, 106)

It is of course a matter of divergent opinion as to whether Chomsky did indeed save linguistics from the scientism of behaviourism or instead plunge the discipline further into an even more arcane scientistic mire from which it has still to extricate itself (for arguments in support of the latter view, see Golumbia 2015; Sampson 1979, 2005; Love 1981, 1989). Gellner, without any benefit of hindsight, finds broadly and one might think rather generously in Chomsky's favour on this matter and it is not too difficult to see why. While not delivering anything approaching a finished product, Chomsky is at least seen to preserve faith in the possibility of a culture-transcending (i.e. universal), scientific account of language. It is in this still unredeemed promissory note that one can locate the fundamental appeal of the Chomskyan programme in linguistics for Gellner. Chomsky reopened the door which the later Wittgenstein was seen to not only slam shut but also, to the great relief of his many science-averse acolytes, throw away the key to. One might even say Chomsky offered Gellner exactly the kind of philosophical reassurance he was seeking, what Auden called – most fittingly in Gellner's case – the "enchantment of disenchantment".

Malinowski and the "two types of language"
While Chomsky seemed to offer the best hope of a scientifically reputable theory of linguistic structure, it is Malinowski (1923) who provided Gellner with something even more important for his own purposes, which is to say a philosophically irresistible theory of language *use*, a theory of communication in other words. That Malinowski ultimately backtracked on the very idea which Gellner so enthusiastically seized upon by reverting to an essentially Wittgensteinian position was clearly a source of disappointment to him (Gellner 1998, 151–154). The core idea which Gellner takes from Malinowski is to be found in the latter's *The Problem of Meaning in Primitive Languages* (1923). In this lengthy piece written as a supplement to Ogden and Richards' *The Meaning of Meaning*, Malinowski outlines the view that in terms of communicative and cognitive function there are essentially two types of language. The distinction is formulated as follows:

> Language, in its primitive function, is to be regarded as a *mode of action*, rather than as a *countersign of thought*. [...]

> Language, in its developed literary or scientific functions, is an instrument of thought and of the communication of thought. (Malinowski 1923, 296, 297)

While the primitive function is held to be universal in human life, Malinowski claims that the second, far rarer function only occurs under certain conditions:

> It is only in certain very special uses among a civilised community and only in its highest uses that language is employed to frame and express thoughts … In works of science and philosophy, highly developed types of speech are used to control ideas and to make them the common property of civilized mankind. (Malinowski 1923, 316)

The distinction is striking because it proposes that we are dealing with two fundamentally different metaphysics or ontologies of communication. Replete with talk of "primitive language(s)", "savage utterances", "savage psychology", "non-civilized peoples" and the like, Malinowski's paper perhaps risks being read by modern readers chiefly as a typically fusty expression of early-20th-century ethnocentrism. The validity and import of any such potential readings is a matter for debate although one ethnocentric disposition – albeit not acknowledged as such but of great appeal to Gellner who instead interpreted it in quite the opposite manner – is clearly detectable in the form of Malinowski's scientism. In the context of the present discussion, a notable aspect of Malinowski's paper is that he deems it necessary to argue at such length and in such detail the case that language (at least in its putative "primitive function") is fundamentally a form of activity, a view which would not seem to require any outlandish metaphysics or the invocation of unobservable structures or mechanisms. Yet when it comes to claiming that literate and scientific language both requires and enables the conveyance of culturally unencumbered thought – a position for which there is no direct empirical evidence and which would also seem to involve a healthy dose of speculative metaphysics – Malinowski, like Gellner after him, offers no argument in support of the claim. He simply insists it to be the case. Nor are any criteria supplied for determining when in "civilised" communities we are dealing with which particular function. How are we to know when someone is taking action in the world or instead trying to communicate pure transcendent thought? Is it merely self-evident? To claim that they are doing the latter when engaged in philosophy, science or literature etc. merely passes the definitional buck since there are no obviously determinate criteria for determining what constitutes engagement in such pursuits.

In one sense, however, one ought not to be surprised by all this. It is, after all, a remarkable feature of Western linguistic thought that theorists such as the later Wittgenstein, Malinowski (again, the later version) and Roy Harris who have each in their own way argued that language *qua* communication is *always* a matter of context-bound activity should be regarded as peddling exotic notions and as belonging to a heretic non-mainstream, while the recondite idea that language involves thought transmission is the one which carries academic respectability and can be simply assumed and asserted without much further ado. The metaphysical conundrum of how it is that literary or scientific uses of language can somehow endow it with the previously absent capacity to communicate pure, culturally untainted thought Malinowski never addresses, let alone resolves. Nor does Gellner but he at least recognises that there is an explanatory hole here. Yet he is able to offer little with which to fill it. In a somewhat desperate move, Gellner (1998, 184–186) resorts to claiming, in effect, that it just must be true because science is so very powerful and has had such profound success in transforming human life (Hall 2007, 259). How else could science possibly have accomplished all that it has? In a further dig at Wittgenstein, Gellner (1998, 183) notes of the modern rationalist-universalist "ethic of cognition" that "far from 'leaving everything as it is', it has totally transformed the world, both in content and in the spirit in which it is seen". Yet the metaphysics of the matter are left entirely unexplained. At issue here is not so much the extent or nature of the influence of scientific thought on human life. Rather it is the validity and intelligibility of the assumption that it can only have had what transformative influence it has had thanks to the mechanism of culture-transcending thought transmission, a model of communication which finds no form of verification *in* science but is instead a metaphysical article of faith. Furthermore, as Roy Harris notes, even if linguistic interaction were a matter of conveying thoughts from one party to another, there would seem to be no good reason to not regard it as undertaking action "in the world".

> It is difficult to see, in fact, why Malinowski does not count "the communication of thought" as a form of action [...] Deliberately causing something to happen is nothing if not taking action; and, in the case of A speaking B, fairly direct action with immediate effect. The question [...] is why such emphasis should be laid from the outset on the difference between the kind of action that has various other physiological or physical consequences (either instead of or in addition to the mental consequences). The answer is fairly clear. Those who think of languages in these terms, however sophisticated their terminology, are still in the grip of the telementational fallacy that mesmerized Locke and many of his predecessors in the Western tradition. (Harris 1998, 94)

While not denying that language often is what he calls "use-bound and context-linked", Gellner (1998, 147) claims that the "[s]tandardisation of conceptual currency" is a "significant element" in explaining the power of scientific thought. The fact that Gellner glimpses no other possible answer to account for the success of science stems from the tacit assumption that linguistic communication is to be explained telementationally at the level of culture. Indeed, both of the models of communication entailed by the two types of language which Gellner takes over for his purposes from Malinowski would seem to depend upon a reification and essentialisation of culture as the primary operative unit. Culture is either a communicational prison or something which has to be communicatively transcended or overcome. As Loyal and Quilley (2013, 6) note, "[f]or Gellner either cultural context *is* meaning [...] or it is not real, in which case there must be a case for 'transcultural criteria'". Thus conceived, it is a false and misleading opposition since it suggests that culture is somehow prior to communication serving as either the definitive enabler or obstacle to it. It therefore prevents one from seeing culture as a reflexive, second-order projection or rationalisation arising out of prior communication processes which necessarily remain both unexplained and inexplicable under such a model. In short, Gellner has his ontological priorities the wrong way round. It is communication which explains culture and makes it possible, not the reverse.

In his later work *Coral Gardens and their Magic*, Malinowski (1935) unambiguously renounced his belief in the "two types of language" thesis and in doing so abandoned the very position which so attracted Gellner to his thought.

> [I]n one of my previous writings, I opposed civilised and scientific to primitive speech, and argued as if the theoretical uses of words in modern philosophic and scientific writing were completely detached from their pragmatic sources. This was an error, and a serious error at that. Between the savage use of words and the most abstract and theoretical one there is only a difference of degree. Ultimately all the meaning of all words is derived from bodily experience. (Malinowski 1935, 58)

While one might think that Malinowski showed good sense in discontinuing his flirtation with the metaphysics of telementation, for Gellner this move constituted little more than a capitulation to a Wittgensteinian position and was therefore to be both lamented and rejected.

> Here we must regretfully admit and report that later in his life, Malinowski moved away from his views as outlined in his contribution to *The Meaning of Meaning*. My view is that the opinion expressed by Malinowski in that work is basically correct: there is a profound, fundamental, immensely important difference between the functional, culturally embedded use of language, and the, as it were, disembodied, abstract investigation of the world, which stands in contrast to it. Certainly, Malinowski failed to give any deep account of the nature of non-savage, genuine thought. He had indeed failed to take even the initial and most elementary steps in such a direction. [...] But, in his first important essay on the topic, he did at least uphold the recognition that this crucial difference was there, whether or not he personally advanced our understanding of the rational option [...] In a subsequent work, however, he moved away from this position. From the view point of the history of thought, or, rather, the history of the intellectual climate, what is really interesting is that he underwent a development exceedingly similar in its internal logic to that experienced by Wittgenstein. (Gellner 1998, 151)

Gellner correctly notes that Wittgenstein and Malinowski both ended up advocating similar views of language – albeit arrived at via quite different routes and styles of enquiry[11] – following the

---

[11] As Gellner (1998, 149) notes, "Wittgenstein invented his tribes while Malinowski studied them". He goes on to attribute philosophers' widespread ignorance of Malinowski's ideas, which long preceded those of Wittgenstein, to the fact that whereas "Malinowski would have sent them into the field [...] in post-

abandonment of previously held positions. However, while Malinowski might have eventually ended up getting it wrong, he did at least succeed in getting it right once unlike the hapless Wittgenstein whom, as Hall (2011, ix) notes, Gellner regarded as being "utterly wrong twice" by moving from one extreme to the other, which is to say from an absolutist affirmation of an atomistic universalism in the *Tractatus* to what he viewed as an equally autocratic cultural relativism in the *Philosophical Investigations.*

The essential features of Gellner's assessment of the linguistic thought of Wittgenstein and Malinowski can be briefly summarised as follows:

• Wittgenstein mark I (i.e. of the *Tractatus*): language as the expression of an isolated individual's thought, i.e. individual cognitive alienation.
• Wittgenstein mark II (i.e. of the *Philosophical Investigations*): language serves to regulate action using culturally bounded concepts within discrete and closed "forms of life", i.e. communal cognitive suffocation or imprisonment.
• Malinowski mark I (ca. 1923): literary-scientific languages enable communication of decontextualised, culturally transcendent ideas and concepts, i.e. cognitive liberation.
• Malinowski mark II (ca. 1935): abandonment of early position and reversion to a view resembling that of Wittgenstein mark II.

In terms of theory of communication, Gellner's position vis-a-vis Malinowski actually turns out to be distinctly conservative. When viewed within the history of the Western intellec-

---

war Oxford the study of context-bound active use of language could be carried out, far more cheaply and comfortably, on Saturday mornings".

tual tradition, Malinowski's ultimate disavowal of thought-conveyance and affirmation of the rather unexciting idea that language is *always* a form of local action, even when employed for literary and scientific purposes, actually constitutes the most radical element of his linguistic thought. However, Gellner's scientism styles it as precisely the opposite.

The place and role of language in Gellner's theory of nationalism

The influence of Malinowski's thinking on language comes strongly to the fore in Gellner's acclaimed modernist-functionalist theory of nationalism. Gellner's (1983, 1997) account of the relationship between language and nationalism runs more or less as follows. Nationalism is a phenomenon of modernity. Modernity is characterised by industrialisation. Industrialisation is greatly dependent upon and in many ways a product of science. Science is an essentially rational enterprise which imposes special cognitive requirements upon communication and therefore requires a fundamentally different type of language to the everyday, namely one which enables the transmission of impersonal, context-free messages and culture-transcending concepts via the medium of a standardised, codified idiom. The effective dissemination of such an idiom requires mass literacy which presupposes the availability of writing and an education system capable of teaching it. The existence of a shared, standardised idiom thus disseminated fosters the formation and in most cases becomes the defining feature of an associated homogenous cultural unit characterised by a high degree of social mobility (what Gellner calls "social entropy") and functional-occupational versatility amongst its members. That unit is the community which constitutes the nation. This, in essence, is the chain of reasoning which leads up to Gellner's (1983, 55) oft-cited line that "it is nationalism which engenders nations, and not the other way round".

Gellner's co-option of Malinowski's "two types of language" thesis has strong affinities with Bernstein's theory of "restricted codes" and "elaborated codes" (Bernstein 1971). For Gellner, modern nations are both defined and made possible by the availability of the latter which arise as a functional response to industrial society's non-negotiable requirement of cultural homogeneity and conceptual standardisation in public life. The reason Gellner offers for this change is that for the first time, the majority of work carried out in human society is primarily "semantic" in nature.

> Work, in industrial society, does not mean moving matter. [...] Work, in the main, is no longer the manipulation of things, but of meanings [...] Most jobs, if not actually involving work "with people", involve the control of buttons or switches or leavers which need to be *understood*, and are explicable, once again, in some standard idiom intelligible to all comers. For the first time in human history, explicit and reasonably precise communication becomes generally, pervasively used and important. In the closed local communities of the agrarian or tribal worlds, when it came to communication, context, tone, gesture, personality and situation were everything. Communication, such as it was, took place without the benefit of precise formulation, for which the locals had neither taste nor aptitude. Explicitness and the niceties of precise, rule-bound formulation were left to lawyers, theologians or ritual specialists, and were part of their mysteries. Among intimates of a close community, explicitness would have been pedantic and offensive, and is scarcely imaginable or intelligible. (Gellner 1983, 32, 33)

When viewed in a certain light, this must count as a rather extraordinary and not particularly felicitous piece of theorising on

Gellner's part for it effectively amounts to claiming that the illiterate, pre-industrial peasant could never hope to communicate in a precise or explicit manner and indeed it was neither necessary nor desirable for him to do so since meaning was somehow tacitly infused in the nebulous, folksy cultural ether. The lawyer and theologian however – perhaps both rather unfortunately chosen examples – by possessing the skills of literacy were able to give clear and unambiguous expression to their thought. What is again striking about all this is that Gellner quite openly owns up to having no real explanation for how this curious state of affairs could have ever come about. He notes for instance that:

> It is a very puzzling fact that an institution, namely human language, should have this potential for being used as an "elaborate code", in Basil Bernstein's phrase, as a formal and fairly context-free instrument, give that it had evolved in a milieu which in no way called for this development. [...] The existence of language suitable for [...] formal, context-liberated use is such a puzzle; but it is also, clearly, a fact. (Gellner 1983, 33)

Gellner's puzzlement is genuine yet also revealing since it is generated entirely by his adherence to a telementational view of communication. If one dispenses with that view, the puzzle disappears. It is only by retrospectively imposing telementational requirements on his language that the illiterate peasant can be assessed incapable of precise communication for it is not immediately clear in what sense the peasant who turns to his wife and mutters – no doubt in some barbarous local dialectal form – "These dark clouds mean rain" can be considered to have communicated in any less exact or explicit manner than the learned scribe who slips his companion a note in exquisite typescript bearing the same message. So what is the relevant difference here? One answer which suggests itself is that the peasant has not communicated by employing any formally determinate abstractions belonging to a particular written linguistic codification. Given the formal *in*determinacy of the peasant's mutterings insofar as they do not instantiate any such abstractions, it is therefore seen to follow that his corresponding thoughts must be similarly vague and indeterminate. If, as the telementational theorist assumes, words convey mental content (thoughts, concepts) then only formally determinate words can logically convey determinate, i.e. precise, mental content. However, since spoken language is inherently variable – no two utterances are ever identical – a community in which writing is not available has no medium in which to ground the formal determinacy necessary for the communication of determinate concepts. However, literate societies do have such a means at their disposal and the consequences are profound, both in terms of the communicational resources available to them and, crucially, the generalised conception of what a language is. As Love (1990, 111, 112) notes:

> [W]riting achieves the object of fixing the interpretation of utterances (in the sense of providing them with something to stand as their name) by simply laying down what it is your utterance was an utterance of. If you write it CAT, then *that* is what you said. And given the context-free, community-wide invariance of a writing system, the way is now open to the idea of a language as a context-free community-wide system of signs, the indeterminacy of whose manifestation in speech itself can be explained as a mere imperfection of the oro-aural medium. Writing thus eliminates the indeterminacy of spoken language, but only in the very general sense of eliminating, for a literate individual at least, doubts as to what abstractions he is supposed to refer what he says or hears to.

Now, as Love immediately goes on to clarify, none of this necessarily entails that there should be any determinacy of interpretation or meaning. After all, people would seem to be quite easily able to entertain the idea that their language consists of a particular inventory of linguistic forms (words) without having any unanimous agreement on what each of those words means or signifies and indeed a good deal of utterly unremarkable everyday metalinguistic discourse would seem to bear this out. This is where the adherence to a telementational model of communication again assumes such significance because it imposes as a necessary requirement on the communication process that identical meanings be attached to the "same" words by different interlocutors. If this does not happen, then according to the telementational model communication does not occur. Once the formal determinacy of the codified language is seen to correlate with a conceptual determinacy (determinacy of meaning), one is then able to glimpse how the possibility of supposed "context-free communication" acquires plausibility as communication becomes a matter simply instantiating the same form-meaning combinations. It can in fact be seen as a quasi-logical conclusion of the telementational model once it becomes applied to written language. Gellner therefore has no way of solving or dissolving his puzzle while remaining committed to the metaphysical view that the role of language is to convey thought, hence his insistence that context-free communication is an incontrovertible fact despite his complete inability to explain it.

Gellner's telementational view of communication also goes hand in hand with a typical modernist essentialism with regard to languages. For Gellner, the standardised, codified languages of modern nations are ontologically real entities. They are first-order realities which underlie and make possible the type of linguistic communication necessary for their emergence and perpetuation. These communal codes which enable telementation form the basis of the shared national culture. If telementation is real, then the mechanism which facilitates it – the linguistic code – must also be equally real. Such languages are consequently presented as the cultural givens out of which national identities are constructed. Gellner's theory of nationalism can therefore be seen to rely on the very essence of the "language myth" which Roy Harris (1981, 2002) spent more than three decades debunking while developing and expounding his profoundly non-essentialist "integrational" school of linguistic thought. In a discussion of that other prominent modernist theorist of nationalism, Benedict Anderson, John Joseph (2005, 138) makes the shrewd point that "an essentialist outlook on languages […] seems a bargain to the sociologist or political scientist, to whom it brings explanatory simplicity (not to mention ease)" although it is only fair to point out that it has also seemed like just as much of a snip to many a linguist over the years. Gellner's basic mistake lies in the fact that he takes linguistic codification at face value and conflates discursively articulated claims to common culture for common culture as a first-order communicative reality. Yet despite appearances, codification does not make a language, *qua* communicative system, into a communal code capable of conveying decontextualized mental content or indeed into a code of any other sort. All communication presupposes a context of some kind. It therefore cannot be the case that a precondition for the emergence of national cultures is the possibility of such communication because that is not what human communication is or can ever be. It is simply not possible for humans to communicate thus and yet nations (and science) flourish nevertheless.

However, where Gellner, like Malinowski before him, is at least partially right is in glimpsing that literacy has important communicative and cognitive consequences. Yet he is wrong in his diagnosis of exactly what those consequences are. Writing is indeed a technology which "restructures thought", in Ong's memorable phrase, albeit just not in the way Gellner claims.[12] In particular, Gellner fails to see what Roy Harris calls the "auto-glottic space" (Harris 1989) created by the availability of writing for what it is. It is not the case that writing somehow – and miraculously – makes contextless communication possible but that it "prises open a conceptual gap between sentence and utterance" by offering a form of "unsponsored language which is not limited to particular categories of speech act or verbal practice" (Harris 1989, 104). It is the existence of such "unsponsored language" which facilitates the cognitive feat of decontextualizing words and sentences which in turn helps to foster the illusion that literate communication consists in the conveyance of context-transcendent conceptual content.

> [I]n a literate culture it is relatively less difficult than in a primary oral culture to distinguish consistently what is said and what is meant from the person who said it and the occasion on which it was said. In a primary oral culture there are no genuinely autological forms of verbal knowledge because there is no technology by means of which words and their relationships can be decontextualized at will. Writing constitutes such a technology: it thereby introduces a level of verbal conceptualization which detaches words from their human sponsors. It is the availability of this level of conceptualization which makes it possible for Socrates to ask questions like "What is justice?" (Harris 1989, 104)

Gellner arguably conflates "context-free communication" with what is better and certain less misleadingly described as non-face-to-face or even anonymous communication, the possibility of

---

[12] Neither, for that matter, if one accepts Roy Harris's (1989) account, does writing restructure thought in quite the way Ong claims.

which is very much a distinguishing feature of literate societies. Far from decontextualizing communication, however, writing vastly increases the possibility of new forms of contextualisation as it leads to a historically unprecedented expansion of the communicational universe. One new form of contextualisation resides in the possibility of formulating non-ephemeral messages that can be received and interpreted by an indefinite number of unknown parties at unknown points in time for as long the message remains legible and accessible. Such parties may likewise also be faced with the task of contextualising messages about which they know nothing of the circumstances and moment of production. Yet at no point are the participants in any literate communicational episode relieved of the burden of contextual interpretation.

Likewise, nations do not have whatever existence they have because their members, the overwhelmingly majority of whom are and always will be utterly anonymous to all other members, can communicate decontextualised thoughts to one another via a written code. Yet the possibility of pervasive anonymous, spatio-temporally remote communication is clearly of fundamental importance for the development of the nation as an "imagined community" (Anderson 1983), which is to say a discursively produced and maintained identity community. As Schirmer (2002, xviii) observes: "[t]he citizens of a nation-state are members of an organizational framework that transcends the *hic et nunc* of face-to-face communication and spans remarkable distances in time and space". Any such "organisational-communicational framework" is inconceivable without the technology of writing and the "autoglottic space" engendered by it. Modern nations are very much a socio-political consequence of literate forms of communication but this is in no small measure due to the illusions about language and linguistic communities which those very forms serve to propagate and institutionalise. In expounding his theory of nationalism, Gellner falls victim to one of the most powerful and enduring of these illusions.

Conclusion

My purpose here has not been to single out Gellner for having a uniquely erroneous theory of language, which is far from the case. Indeed, in terms of its basic features, there is very little which is genuinely original about it. The more interesting aspect is how Gellner weaves his rather unexceptional ideas about language into a highly distinctive and comprehensive sociological-philosophical worldview. One rather self-indulgent motivation for writing on Gellner is that it affords the sheer pleasure of reading and rereading him. Yet one does not always have to agree with him to delight in the quality of the writing – especially the gags and put-downs – the frequent jocularity of which cannot conceal the depth and seriousness of thought behind it. However, proclivities of scholarly temperament and style aside, there are more fundamental reasons for attending to Gellner's linguistic thought. Firstly, as I have attempted to show, there is a philosophic and intellectual unity to it discernible throughout its gradual development and elaboration and this alone is of interest when it concerns a thinker of such influence and renown. In this sense, analysis of it brings the features of Gellner's wider and extremely powerful social philosophy into even sharper focus. Secondly, the case of Gellner is a highly instructive example of just how centrally a theory of language and communication can serve to underpin and even determine essential features of other, broader theoretical accounts of human behaviour, cognition and society. Another blunter way of putting it is that problematic theories of language make for problematic theories of human life more generally.

References

Anderson, Benedict. 1983. *Imagined Communities: Reflections on the Origin and Spread of Nationalism*. London: Verso.

Bernstein, Basil. 1971. *Class, Codes and Control: Theoretical Studies towards a Sociology of Language*. London: Routledge & Kegan Paul.

Carr, Philip. 1997. "Telementation and Generative Linguistics." In *Linguistics Inside Out: Roy Harris and His Critics*, edited by George Wolf and Nigel Love, 65–83. Amsterdam: John Benjamins.
Evans, Vyvyan. 2014. *The Language Myth: Why Language is Not an Instinct*. Cambridge: CUP.
Gellner, Ernest. 1959. *Words and Things*. London: V. Gollancz.
Gellner, Ernest. 1969. "On Chomsky." *New Society* 13 (348): 831–833.
Gellner, Ernest. 1975. *Legitimation of Belief*. Cambridge: CUP.
Gellner, Ernest. 1979. *Spectacles and Predicaments: Essays in Social Theory*. Cambridge: CUP.
Gellner, Ernest. 1983. *Nations and Nationalism*. London: Blackwell.
Gellner, Ernest. 1997. *Nationalism*. New York: NYU Press.
Gellner, Ernest. 1998. *Language and Solitude: Wittgenstein, Malinowski and the Habsburg Dilemma*. Cambridge: CUP.
Golumbia, David. 2015. "The Language of Science and the Science of Language: Chomsky's Cartesianism." *Diacritics* 43(1): 38–62.
Gray, John. 2011. "The Free-floater." *New Republic* 242 (2): 30–33.
Hall, John A. 2007. "Gellner's Metaphysic." In *Ernest Gellner and Contemporary Social Thought*, edited by Siniša Malešević and Mark Haugaard, 253–270. Cambridge: CUP.
Hall, John A. 2011. *Ernest Gellner: An Intellectual Biography*. London: Verso.
Harris, Roy. 1981. *The Language Myth*. London: Duckworth.
Harris, Roy. 1989. "How Does Writing Restructure Thought?" *Language & Communication* 9 (2–3): 99–106.
Harris, Roy. 1998. *Introduction to Integrational Linguistics*. Oxford: Pergamon.

Harris, Roy, ed. 2002. *The Language Myth in Western Culture*. London: Routledge.
Jarvie, Ian. 2005. "Preface to the Routledge Classics Edition." In *Words and Things*, edited by Ernest Gellner, xv–xxiv. London: Routledge.
Joseph, John E. 2005. "'The Grammatical Being Called a Nation': History and the Construction of Political and Linguistic Nationalism." In *Language and History: Integrationist Perspectives*, edited by Nigel Love, 120–141. Oxford: Routledge.
Louch, Alfred R. 1966. *Explanation and Human Action*. London: Basil Blackwell.
Love, Nigel. 1981. "Making Sense of Chomsky's Revolution." *Language & Communication* 1 (2–3): 275–287.
Love, Nigel. 1989. "Language and the Science of the Impossible." *Language & Communication* 9 (4): 269–287.
Love, Nigel. 1990. "The Locus of Languages in a Redefined Linguistics." In *Redefining Linguistics*, edited by Hayley G. Davis and Talbot J. Taylor, 53–117. London: Routledge.
Loyal, Steven, and Stephen Quilley. 2013. "Wittgenstein, Gellner, and Elias: From the Philosophy of Language Games to a Figurational Sociology of Knowledge." *Human Figurations* 2 (2): 2–9.
Malinowski, Bronisław. 1923. "The Problem of Meaning in Primitive Languages." In *The Meaning of Meaning*, edited by C. K. Ogden and I. A. Richards, 296–336. London: Routledge and Kegan Paul.
Malinowski, Bronisław. 1935. *Coral Gardens and Their Magic*. New York: American Book Co.
Reddy, Michael J. 1979. "The Conduit Metaphor – A Case of Frame Conflict in Our Language about Language." In *Metaphor and Thought*, edited by A. Ortony, 284–310. Cambridge: CUP.

Sampson, Geoffrey. 1979. *Liberty and Language*. Oxford: OUP.
Sampson, Geoffrey. 2005. *The 'Language Instinct' Debate*. London: Continuum.
Schirmer, Dietmar. 2002. "Introduction." In *Identity and Intolerance: Nationalism, Racism, and Xenophobia in Germany and the United States*, edited by Norbert Finzsch and Dietmar Schirmer, xi–xxv. Cambridge: CUP.
Smith, Anthony D. 1987. *The Ethnic Origins of Nations*. Oxford: Wiley.
Smith, Anthony D. 1998. *Nationalism and Modernism*. London: Routledge.
Uschanov, T. P. 2002. "Ernest Gellner's Criticisms of Wittgenstein and Ordinary Language Philosophy." In *Marx and Wittgenstein: Knowledge, Morality and Politics*, edited by Gavin Kitching and Nigel Pleasants. London: Routledge.
Winch, Peter. 1958. *The Idea of a Social Science*. London: Routledge and Kegan Paul.

14.

Theorised to Death: Diagnosing the Social Pseudosciences.
Re-reading of A.R. Louch, *Explanation and Human Action*
(Basil Blackwell, 1966).

Philosophers who openly reject the very possibility of the academic disciplines they philosophise about are something of a rarity. It is also not surprising that their arguments tend either to be ignored or all too conveniently sidestepped by the vast majority of dutiful practitioners of the disciplines in question. Excommunication is often an easier fate to which to condemn the intellectual heretic or arch-sceptic than decisive refutation. To reject the possibility of a discipline is, however, not necessarily to deny the existence of its basic subject matter nor even to disclaim the propriety of an interest in it. The philosopher here is not quite in the same position as the man in the street who thinks palmistry and horoscopes are a load of old cobblers, which is not to say that there may not be people who regard themselves as philosophers of such pursuits. It is more a case of taking issue with the onto-epistemological assumptions—i.e., the theory—which underlie the programmes and methodologies typically formulated and deemed formulable in order to give an account of the subject matter in question. For instance, it is notable that what are seen as some of the most radical—and in some quarters even scandalous — theories to have emerged from those fields of inquiry concerned with human doings and society are those which reject the possibility of a scientific account of their subject matter. It hardly needs saying that this situation is not mirrored in the natural sciences. We do not find organic chemists falling into disrepute or controversy for advocating the superiority of lay or *ad hoc* accounts of photosynthesis for the simple reason that there are not, at least as far as I am aware, any making such claims. Furthermore, it does not require too much of us to see why such claims would be absurd. Chemists and the like are therefore generally not forced to expend much effort guarding against humanistic or common-sense encroachments on their turf. In the humanities and what are presumptuously called the social sciences, though, the wrongheadedness of attempting scientific accounts of human action is generally something which has to be forcibly argued for and, depending on the specific discipline in question, sometimes to the distinct professional disadvantage of those doing the arguing. To point out this asymmetry is not so much to bemoan it as to invite attempts at understanding and explanation. My purpose in this piece is to revisit a work which sought, amongst other things, to do just that.

That certain works and thinkers do not necessarily gain the attention or have the influence one thinks they ought to is a fairly unremarkable aspect of intellectual life. If one were to conduct a poll seeking nominations for the most influential philosophical treatment of the social sciences in the post-Wittgensteinian tradition, a safe bet for top answer would be Peter Winch's *The*

Idea of a Social Science and its Relation to Philosophy (1958). Rather fewer, I feel sure, would propose A.R. Louch's *Explanation and Human Action* (1966), a book which, however, advances a thesis and a consequent view of social inquiry not only more distinctive and radical than that of either Winch or Wittgenstein but which, I would like to suggest, is also more cogent and powerful as a result. However, it is a thesis whose radical originality —Ernest Gellner (1979: 66) in a critical yet admiring review described it as 'breathtakingly daring and far-reaching'—is some-what belied, and endearingly so, by the resolute unpretentiousness, intellectual honesty and sobriety of its presentation. While Louch's work is certainly not unknown, having been reviewed by various prominent names in the years following its publication, its overall impact has been somewhat modest and judging by the scientistic tendencies of so much contemporary work in the humanities and social sciences its central message remains largely unheeded. This state of affairs is, to put it rather mildly, a pity. I would therefore like to suggest that there is much to be gained from revisiting the definitive statement of Louch's thought, even if some of the most important lessons to be drawn from it might be rather disconcerting and unwelcome, to say the least, for certain tribes of professional academic.

Louch wastes little time in signalling the drastic ambition of his project, albeit in rather unassuming fashion. In the Preface, he outlines to his aim to undermine several fundamental tenets of social scientific and philosophical orthodoxy. Louch in fact makes the most devastating claim imaginable about the social and behavioural sciences, namely that they are impossible. His argument is not simply that they have so far conspicuously failed to offer coherent scientific accounts of their subject matter but that any aspiration to do so is fundamentally mistaken: 'My main intent has been to show that the idea of a science of man or society is untenable' (p. viii). How is this to be done? By no less a measure than attempting to overturn one of the most sacred of modern philosophical dichotomies—the fact-value distinction—at least as applied to the study of human behaviour.

> I should claim as my own the attempt to outline a view of the nature of explanation and description of human action which brings together questions of fact and value. I believe that a coherent account of human action cannot be given by separating these interests, though much of epistemology and ethical theory has had the effect of dividing them irrevocably. (p.vii)

Louch's attempted dismantling of what he sees as the bogus and ideologically pernicious scientific pretensions of the social and behavioural sciences is accomplished primarily through his expounding of a highly original and polemical account of explanation in respect of human action. This takes the form of a rejection of any explanation of agentive behaviour—as opposed to physiological movements—which rests on an appeal to generalities or generalisations. One way of summarising Louch's thesis is that human actions do not require or admit to theoretical or nomothetic forms of explanation. The mild irony of course is that it takes a theoretical insight of some considerable sophistication to arrive at the view that there is no theory to be had. Instead, Louch argues, as far as human action is concerned, the appropriate [1] mode of explanation is unavoidably *ad hoc* and irredeemably context-bound without any necessary implications beyond the individual case. In his own words:

> In daily life we succeed in accounting for our actions without recourse to general theories or statistical regulari-

---

[1] Louch also notes that it is our customary mode of explanation although he is careful to make clear that it is not appropriate because it is customary.

ties [...] A student in my office reaches for a cigarette and matches, he strikes a match and lights the cigarette, inhales and exhales the smoke. It would not occur to me to accompany this set of observations of his actions with further comments designed to explain what he did. If I had to do so, I should appeal to his reaching for a cigarette as indicating a desire to smoke, and the rest of his actions as contributing to the same end. It would not occur to me or to my interlocutors to offer or demand general laws from which this action can be shown to follow, or regularities of which the connexion of this action and its motive would be an instance. (p. 1)

A further example offered by Louch is his observation that it would be irrelevant and superfluous to explain the fact of his cooking his dinner via an appeal to the generalisation that men generally seek out nourishment when hungry. Any number of similarly mundane examples could be called upon to illustrate this quite simple point. For instance, in what sense does the observation that humans generally seek to conserve energy explain why I take the train to work instead of cycling or getting up at 5 am, swimming across Victoria Harbour and walking the remaining distance? Equally, what are we to make of the fact that there are plenty who eschew public transport and make their way to the office under their own steam? The generalisation is therefore either trivial or false when applied to the case. One might be forgiven at this point for wondering what all the fuss is about. Is there anything surprising in all this, let alone radical? The rub, as they say, lies in the fact that, as Louch (p. 2) observes, most philosophers and social scientists are 'inveterate generalizers and criterion-mongers'. A defining characteristic of the approach of many renowned authorities engaged in the academic study of man and society – Louch's chief targets are sociologists, psychologists and (some) anthropologists although I have no doubt he would also have regarded most linguists and semioticians as ripe for similar treatment—is in fact a deep suspicion of and dissatisfaction with *ad hoc* explanation. Displaying all the symptoms of what Wittgenstein mournfully termed the 'craving for generality', such scholars are, according to Louch, beholden to a Humean atomistic metaphysics and a consequent mode of explanation imported wholesale and uncritically from the natural sciences which seeks to extend the account beyond the specific case through an appeal to regularities or by subsuming an event under a law and thereby lending it predictive force. It is the pursuit of generality in explanation which, Louch claims, has led the social and behavioural sciences astray and into a fixation with methodological form at the expense of content, thereby resulting in explanatory impotence.

> Behavioural scientists are forced into a mistaken view of their subject-matter as a result of their preoccupation with a method they take to be necessary to any respectable inquiry. (p.5)

> [...] conception of methodology has prevented sociologists and psychologists from offering significant accounts of human behaviour [...M]ethodology leads only to formulae for possible theories, but not to any genuine accounts of human behaviour. A sterile scholasticism has possessed the behavioural sciences, for which philosophers with their theories about the nature of science are very much responsible. (p. 6)

> [...] redundancy and platitude are the consequences of typical attempts to apply wholesale the techniques of the natural sciences to explanation of human behaviour. (p.39)

To redundancy and platitude one might also add triviality and obfuscation. Louch has few difficulties and no small fun in showing how some of the grandiloquent theoretical statements, definitions and mathematics-aping formulas proposed by some of the leading sociologists of his day amount to little more than addled banalities. He is particularly devastating in respect of George Homans and Talcott Parsons. The thrust of Louch's argument is that much work in positivist sociology and psychology peddles obfuscated tautology posing as fresh scientific insight. Louch shows how Homans' numerous attempts in *The Human Group* (1950) to establish laws expressing functional relationships between activity types and psychological factors rely exclusively on a 'series of tautologies masquerading as empirical generalizations' (1960: 15). Lest one is inclined to suppose that modern social scientific research has progressed beyond such failings, the same criticism can also be brought to bear on a far more recent case study published in the *Journal of Social & Clinical Psychology* (Ryan et al., 2010) in which the authors detail their unsurprising finding that people generally appear to be in a better mood at the weekends during their time off (the so-called 'weekend effect') than they are on Mondays when back at work. The primary explanation proffered to explain this state of affairs is that they are apparently freer to do as they please when not working. These are not quite the terms in which the authors put it however. Instead, their - inevitably confirmed - hypothesis was that 'both weekends and non-working times would be associated with enhanced well-being, and that these relations would be mediated by greater satisfaction of autonomy and relatedness needs' (Ryan et al., 2010: 95). A further hypothesis was that 'much of the weekend effect would be accounted for by the work versus non-work contrast, given that work activities are expected to be associated with a lower sense of autonomy and relatedness than nonwork activities' (ibid.). Once one has dispersed the fog of jargon, what this appears to be saying is that the state of being in a better mood and the state of not working are both characterised by a greater freedom to do what one wants. In other words, they basically amount to the same thing or can at least be said to overlap significantly. To not be engaged in work is therefore by definition to be in a better mood and vice-versa. Another way of putting it would be that greater freedom of action is correlated with greater freedom of action. Operating with such a glaring circularity, the study cannot fail to 'prove' its hypothesis although in this case such proof consists in dressing up something that we either arguably already know or may even see fit to dispute in a barrage of statistics, path diagrams and less than perspicuous terminology. Either way, nothing is explained. How does such triviality come about? The answer lies in the fact that, as Louch himself noted in respect of Homans' work, the authors insist on a measurable, behavioural criterion for mood in order to facilitate empirical generalisation. However, when presented as an explanation, such generalisation results in blatant falsehood since it is quite clearly not a law of human life that one is always in a better mood—if understood in the ordinary psychological sense—when not working. Who, after all, has not had the odd grumpy day off moping around at a loose end followed by a more cheerful few days while busily engaged in the office, workshop or classroom? The generalisation therefore only acquires any plausibility when expressed as a concealed tautology and by scientising the concept of 'mood'.

In Parsons' case, Louch singles out the following passage:

> [...] when the structure of the larger system is undergoing a relatively continuous process of change in the direction of increasing differentiation, the mechanisms involved in this change will, under certain circumstances, operate to dichotomize the population of units receiving the primary 'real' output of the focal system of reference and to pro-

duce an orderly alternation of relative predominance of the two nearly equal parts. (cited in Louch, 1966: 11)

Observing how the 'outrageous vocabulary clothes the essential barrenness of the theory', Louch glosses Parsons' passage as follows: 'given social change in a democratic society parties in power will tend to swing from liberal to conservative and back again' (p. 14). He then immediately adds: 'I do not know why such simpler formulations will not do in place of the bewildering complexity, unless it is that the terminological display clouds the paucity of information.' Louch makes the point that if the purpose of theories is to help us understand events and phenomena better, then those of social scientists such as Parsons fail utterly since the reverse is often the case. Instead it is often only through our ordinary, pre-theoretical acquaintance with such events and phenomena that we are finally able to gain any grasp of the theory.

> Parsons applies his theoretical or taxonomic superstructure to cases which are not illuminated in any way by the application. Quite the reverse: we understand the verbiage of the superstructure a little better when we see what counts as instances of his terms and rubrics. In this sense the theory has no explanatory power; and as a description is unnecessarily complex. (p. 13)

Now Louch was neither the first nor the last to level these kinds of criticism against Parsons and sociologists of a similar orientation. What is of particular interest here, though, is how he integrates them into the service of his broader argument, employing them to highlight the banalities and absurdities which result when theorists go to such extreme lengths in order to avoid capitulation to the layman's (social-)scientifically disreputable strategy of *ad hoc* explanation. It is in the marriage of his insistence on the propriety of *ad hoc* explanation and his rejection of the fact-value distinction that Louch's thesis acquires its potent originality. Whereas Wittgenstein laid great stress on upholding the distinction in his repeated demand that philosophy do away with all attempts at explanation and concern itself solely with description, Louch contends that such an aspiration rests on mistaken premisses where human action is concerned. His argument is not that description and appraisal of human behaviour are impossible but that they are not distinct activities. To describe a person's action is also to offer a value judgment as to what type of thing the person is doing. In offering an account of agentive human behaviour, there is no purely descriptive stage followed by an appraising or explanatory stage. As Louch puts it: 'The man or situation is not seen and then appraised, or appraised and then seen in distortion; it is seen morally. Value and fact merge' (p. 54). These considerations prompt Louch to advance the view that any explanation of human action is necessarily what he terms 'moral explanation', for which he provides the following rationale:

> When we appeal to desires, pleasures, emotions, motives, purposes and reasons we are offering what I shall call moral explanation [...A] man whose actions are guided by his assessments, and his understanding of his own and others' actions by the grounds he finds for those actions in the situation of the actor, is looking at behaviour morally. So long as he describes his own and others' conduct as doing things well or poorly, effectively or clumsily, appropriately or mistakenly, he is a moral agent or observer. It may be that the grounds he discovers as the end products of his diagnoses shock or offend various moral sensibilities; but this is relatively unimportant. The point is, he thinks in terms of grounds. He acts or describes action, not by seeking temporal antecedents or functional dependencies, but deciding that the situation entitles a man to act in the way he did or is likely to do. (p. 51)

The point here is that human actions can only be identified by means of an evaluative concept which blends a descriptive and appraising component. To harbour the aspiration for sociology, psychology and even philosophy to be value-free pursuits is on Louch's view to fundamentally misconceive their subject matter. This is not to say that any account offered under the aegis of such disciplines must necessarily be soaked in bias or prejudicial ideology which pays no heed to any standards concerning acuity of observation or argumentative rigour. It is rather that such disciplines cannot even get off the ground without the application of moral concepts to human behaviour. Attempts to scientise moral concepts such as intelligence or paranoia through the stipulation of context-free, positivist-empirical criteria by which they can supposedly be identified and measured stand as a denial or in ignorance of this—what for the aspiring positivist social scientist is an admittedly inconvenient—insight.

> [...] statements ascribing desire, need, self-interest and anxiety to human agents, and role and status, function and habit to social forms and processes, arise in the context of moral appraisal. They have to do with the rules and conventions by which various kinds of human action are identified and assessed. It is the tendency among behavioural scientists to think of value as a subtle and dangerous obstacle to the business of objective description of human action. So these scientists feel that if they set their values to one side, articulate them, and isolate them in a preface all will be well. But values do not enter descriptions of human affairs as disruptive influences; rather, they allow us to describe human behaviour in terms of action. Inasmuch as the units of examination of human behaviour are actions, they cannot be observed, identified, or isolated except through categories of assessment and appraisal. There are not two stages, an identification of properties

and qualities in nature and then an assessment of them, stages which could then become the business of different experts. There is only one stage, the delineation and description of occurrences in value terms. (p. 56)

It is worth emphasising just how radical a position this amounts to and the drastic consequences which its acceptance would entail for the positivist social sciences. These are summarised in Louch's iconoclastic claim that 'psychology and social science are moral science. Ethics and the study of human action are one' (p. 235). Sociology, anthropology, ethnography, psychology, linguistics—for Louch, properly conceived, all branches of ethics. It must be said though that Louch does not offer much in the way of disciplinary agenda-setting insofar as he gives little indication as to what work in these fields might look like once reconceived as fields of ethical inquiry. However, this might be interpreted less as an omission on his part than as a recognition that intellectual inquiry is best driven by a desire to investigate aspects of the world which genuinely puzzle us rather than by any set of professional ambitions. The identities and details of such puzzles are of course very much in the eye of the beholder. Accordingly, ethical fields of inquiry are to be conceived as inherently open-ended and unamenable to programmatic delineation.

It is in respect of any such potential disciplinary realignments that Louch's thought begins to diverge most significantly from that of Winch and indeed it is the point at which Louch's forceful and somewhat sorrowful critique of Winch takes off. Winch's far better known polemic against the social sciences is based on a form of a priori conceptual critique which he develops by extrapolating, not altogether uncontroversially, from Wittgenstein's idea of a 'form of life'. Winch's basic premise is that human action is shaped and constrained by the concepts used to describe it. Accordingly, to understand the actions is necessarily to understand the concepts and to understand the concepts is to know the rule- and convention-determined possibilities for their deployment within the language of the community in question. The major disciplinary and methodological consequence of this view is to throw out the empirical entirely and recast social inquiry as a wholly conceptual enterprise. In other words, social science becomes a dominion of philosophy. Far from fulfilling the humble underlabourer or handmaiden role, the Winchian philosopher is now promoted, by himself at least, to oracle of the social game.

Despite their shared Wittgensteinian heritage, Louch rejects utterly Winch's conception of the philosopher's role vis-à-vis social inquiry. His two principal, and I think quite devastating, objections to Winch's thesis are '(1) it leaves out of account the manner in which conventions are deciphered and (2) it gives the impression that the sociologist or anthropologist is concerned only with intra-cultural or intraconventional actions' (p. 164). The first objection disputes the idea that conceptual meaning can somehow be context-free and identified in ignorance of the specifics of particular communicative situations and participants. In other words, Winch assumes determinacy of meaning or what has been called a 'fixed code' view of language, which itself entails a generality thesis of the sort to which Louch is opposed. The second objection is related to the first and contests the assumption that such determinate meanings are intersubjectively shared and to be located at the level of—an inevitably reified—cultural membership, a view which provides the basis for what Gellner (1979: 70) aptly terms Winch's 'claustrophilic' form of cultural relativism which leaves him at a loss to explain intercultural conduct.

Now Louch is quite prepared to concede that his own thesis also leads to relativism, albeit one of a quite different sort to that of Winch and which somehow manages to be both more radical and more pragmatic. Whereas Winch's relativism is collective and decontextualised, Louch's is individualistic and context-bound. For Louch, relativism means that actions can only be judged in context and [...] there happens to be no universal context. Explanation of human action is context-bound. This should not be surprising. Human conduct is a response to an incalculable variety of situations. (p. 207).

What I take this as saying is that the meaning of actions and concepts can only be determined by an individual's contextualised interpretation of them. This introduces an element of inherent indeterminacy missing from Winch's highly deterministic account insofar as no two individuals can be guaranteed in advance to interpret an action in the same way (i.e., conventionality cannot be assumed *a priori*), nor can any one individual be guaranteed to interpret an action in the same way at two different points in time. In this respect, Louch's thought bears striking similarities to that of iconoclast linguistic theorist Roy Harris whose 'integrationist' philosophy of communication is based on a recognition of the 'radical indeterminacy' of the sign (Orman, 2018). Gellner (1979: 78) was therefore quite right in noting—despite deploring the fact —that Louch's relativism 'knows no limits'.

The radical distinctiveness of Louch's thesis can be drawn out most clearly when one considers its consequences for philosophical and social inquiry. Louch's rejection of the positivist metaphysics driving generality-seeking empirical work in the social sciences does not lead him to embrace Winch's professionally self-serving view according to which sociology, properly conceived, reduces to analytic philosophy. Instead Louch retains a more modest view of the philosopher's role and arguably one more in line with the spirit of Wittgenstein's later work, choosing to remain an

> unregenerate underlaborer, looking at philosophy as a heterogeneous collection of strategies designed to remove discomfort and positive misery occasioned by the balky

places in any kind of human inquiry. I see no reason to suppose that there is some special object for philosophical investigation. It may be that nowadays there is a great deal more misery and balkiness in social studies than elsewhere, and so one might expect gadflies to swarm over the swamp. But to elevate this accidental swarm into a discipline, to spell philosophy, as it were, with a capital P, is a bit of pretense which more humble underlaborers may be afforded the recreation of deflating. (Louch, 1965: 216)

So if social inquiry is neither science nor philosophy, what is it? Louch's position can best be seen pointing towards a form of what one might call atheoretical empiricism. Indeed, he stresses the point on a number of occasions that a great deal of our knowledge of human behaviour and society is necessarily arrived at through observation, noting, for instance, that 'it is a matter of empirical discovery that people talk certain ways, for it is only in the context of the talk that we can claim to understand what they are doing and why they are doing it' (p. 175) and that 'there are many significant statements that depend upon observation other than those of a statistical or theoretical nature, and that these constitute the bulk of our non-scientific knowledge of the world and of human affairs' (p. 181). The enemy for Louch is not observation per se but observation serving as a basis for explanatory generalisation and theory construction. Where does such an emasculating stipulation leave the social sciences qua academic disciplines and the social scientist qua expert practitioner? Louch's answer, which he formulates with provocative clarity and without perturbation, is unequivocal.

> [...] there is no call for the specialist in the normal understanding of the social game. We are all players, and to this extent we are all, to varying degrees, experts. This seems to me the consequence of the view that language is social,

> that it is bound up with the actions of men, that language and act, utterance and context, cannot be separated. (Louch, 1965: 216)

This links up with the observation elsewhere that there are many features about human conduct which 'do not require study by social scientists' or afford 'a particularly significant body of information about behaviour requiring university instruction' (1966, p. 224). Instead, the kind of *ad hoc*, piecemeal, context-bound information which typically provokes and sates our interest in specific groups and instances of human action would seem to call more for a kind of scrupulous journalism than any stringent, science-aping methodology forming the basis of an institutionalised academic discipline. Perhaps the most inflammatory claim in the entire book is Louch's somewhat nonchalant suggestion that a lot of anthropology is little more than shoddy travel writing or, as he puts it, 'anthropology is only a collection of traveller's tales with no particular scientific significance' (p. 160). Yet for Louch travellers' tales are exactly what anthropology should consist in, which is to say the furnishing of interesting accounts about the customs, habits and beliefs of groups of people (often vastly) different to one's own based on the meticulous and insightful observation of said groups. Such accounts are not somehow deficient in virtue of their not being scientific but are instead epistemologically appropriate to the - irreducibly moral - subject matter in question.

> Travellers' tales can be, as much as scientific theories, contributions to human knowledge; they can be better or worse, more or less accurate. Moreover, they are not the first and random comments that some day will be organized into a scientific theory. They are sufficient unto themselves. The pattern of explanation in anthropology is not a poor approximation of the generalizing and predic-

tive capacities of the method of science, but moral explanation, within which instances may be judged more or less adequate. (pp. 160–161)

If anthropology is bad travel writing, it arguably points to an even more dire judgment in respect of sociology. Travel writing, however bad, at least tells us about places and peoples with which we are largely unfamiliar. We still perhaps learn something new. However, sociology is more like bad in-house journalism, telling us what we already know albeit often in an idiom in which we feel anything but at home.

> The sociologist tells us in a formidable barrage of terminology and theory a good many things about our various roles which we must know about in order for the sociologist to have observed us playing them. We are able to do so as a result of instruction and example, and it is thus that we come to act as merchants or teachers or fathers or friends. For a sociologist to tell us about this with the air of novel discovery strikes us as redundant, not to say insulting [...] Social practice is much like playing games. The rules must be known to play, and playing is to understand what you are doing. (p. 180)

The committed positivist sociologist will no doubt claim that this constitutes a gross parody of the discipline and its working practices. This is certainly one thrust of Ernest Gellner's critical response to Louch's thesis. Gellner's lengthy review which constitutes by far the most in-depth and high-profile engagement with Louch's thought makes for absorbing reading. Although Gellner, the self-declared 'enlightenment rationalist fundamentalist', was, unsurprisingly, quite overtly hostile to Louch's overall thesis, it is clear that he was also highly stimulated by it, calling *E&HA* an 'exceedingly strange book' yet praising Louch for the openness and candour of his approach. Gellner's critique has a number of aspects, the lengthiest of which consists in a feisty and at times exasperated defence of the generalising tendency in social inquiry. While agreeing with Louch about the 'appalling pretentiousness and verbosity of recent [sociological] "theory"' (Gellner, 1979: 64), Gellner accuses him of exaggerating the failures of social science. Gellner (1979: 84) claims that '[w]e do have some general knowledge' although he adduces no examples in support. Gellner further develops his argument against Louch by insisting on a distinction, derived from a view of language first articulated by Malinowski, between two separate and opposed cognitive modes which he calls the Generalising/Scientific (GS) and the Traditional/Primitive (TP). In Gellner's view, Louch fails to see that in modern, scientific-literate cultures communication is no longer irredeemably local and context-bound. Instead, Gellner argues, mass access to a codified, communal idiom facilitated by near-universal literacy makes the possibility of context-transcendent communication and, by consequence, general(isable) forms of public knowledge a mundane, if inexplicable, reality. For Gellner, Louch's thesis rests on a model of communication which only obtains universally in pre-scientific societies. This is not the place for an in-depth discussion of Gellner's linguistic thought, suffice it to say that perhaps one reason Louch (and many others) failed to appreciate Gellner's distinction is that it does not constitute a particularly compelling piece of theorising on his part, incorporating as it does a profound misdiagnosis of the cognitive and communicative consequences of literacy.[2] It is worth noting that even Malinowski himself later came to unambiguously reject it, a move Gellner, in his desperation to establish a scientific basis for rationality, could only lament.

---

[2] See Orman 2017 for an extensive critical discussion of Gellner's linguistic thought.

A second prong of Gellner's critique concerns what he describes as Louch's own 'substantive pieces of moralising' (1979: 93). Now it is certainly true that Louch's thesis is undergirded and to some extent propelled by an anti-universalist ethical viewpoint which Gellner quite accurately describes as consisting in a rejection of both nomothetic sociology and moral Kantianism. Here we see how Louch's moral philosophy merges with his advocacy of atheoretical empiricism in social inquiry.

> A universal moral principle presupposes a common life, which our differences of occupation, age, sex, and income deny [...] It could emerge only if men truly shared a common life in which distinctions of employment, wealth and status have disappeared. The changes in society envisaged to achieve that end are messianic, whether this messianic hope is Christian or Marxist. And perhaps this suggests that moral agreement is not worth the price of such uniformity [...] And so the only moral recommendations, as the only recommendations for the empirical study of man, come to the same thing—a move here, a move there, zig and zag, after the manner of Aristotle's recommendations with regard to the Mean, everything tentative and subject to change. (pp. 207–208)

Louch might also have said that a universal moral principle presupposes a common life which his—admittedly somewhat implicit—theory of communication denies. Where Gellner seeks to derive his faith in a universalist rationalist morality from a context-transcendent model of communication, Louch does the very opposite. Given his conception of sociology as a branch of ethics, it would be correct to say that Louch's rejection of positivist methodology in social inquiry is of a piece with—indeed is the same thing as—his rejection of any context-transcendent moral code. No linguistic code, no moral code. Communicational relativism leads to moral relativism.

Louch sees the generalising tendency in social inquiry as not only conceptually and epistemologically confused but also as promoting a pernicious, dehumanised view of man and society, albeit one cloaked in a justificatory rhetoric of progress and material improvement. In Louch's view, the scientism of the social and behavioural sciences leads to the adoption and propagation of what he calls an 'engineering attitude' according to which successful practice is a matter of exercising ever greater control over human or animal subjects. For Louch, this engineering attitude finds near diabolical expression in the work of B.F. Skinner. The moral direction of a society in thrall to such an attitude is, Louch claims, irredeemably dogmatic and authoritarian because it does not allow for any re-examination or revision of aims. In the realm of politics and social policy, scientific methodologies with their univocal conception of truth cannot countenance leaving open or unanswered the questions of moral value upon which they bear. A scientifically prescribed good life can take only one form at a time. Louch concludes his book with following dystopian lament.

> Totalitarianism is too weak a word and too inefficient an instrument to describe the perfect scientific society. For in the totalitarian regimes known to us, one is still conscious of coercion and thus of alternatives, however disastrous to the individual such alternatives may be. In the engineers' society, perhaps unwittingly promoted by psychologists and sociologists bent on being scientists, we should have to give up the concept of an open or civil society which, however inefficiently, serves as the prop for a social order based on respect for men as persons or autonomous agents. A programme having such ultimate consequences cries out for refutation. (p. 239)

It is on this score that Gellner believes he wins the day over Louch insofar as he accuses him of fearing that which he has devoted an entire book to refuting, namely the possibility of social science. If, as Louch claims, human conduct is not subject to general laws of explanation, then surely there is nothing to dread in the social engineers' hopelessly misguided programmes which cannot possibly succeed. Gellner moves in for what he thinks is the kill by noting of Louch that '[i]f what he fears is even a possibility, then what he asserts elsewhere is not true' (Gellner, 1979: 95). It is curious that Gellner regards this as such a decisive blow against Louch's thesis for if one were to seek a general principle informing his argument, something Gellner surely would not object to, it would seem to amount to the claim that something is either true, in which case all well and good, or, if not true, then harmless. It would also seem to contradict Gellner's own well-known, irascible assessments of Wittgenstein's later thought and the tradition of Ordinary Language Philosophy (OLP) which it inspired (e.g., Gellner, 1959; 1998). Now while Gellner clearly regarded OLP as false, he can hardly be said to have regarded it as harmless since the principal purpose of his withering and largely sociological assessment of the movement seems to have been to draw attention to what he saw as its pernicious—and also obfuscated—ideological tendencies. Louch makes a similar point in his reply to Gellner's review of *E&HA* (Louch, 1977). In his case, the ideology in question is scientism.

> [...] my fears about applied social research are not founded on the expectation that social science's long-awaited Galileo will appear, making possible, by his lawmaking, a host of technical solutions to human problems. Those expectations, I believe, are incoherent, and rest upon an incoherent methodology. But I fear the methodology nonetheless, for its effectiveness has to do with ideology, and not with scientific results. [...] But suppose the expertise

is a sham. What is left is an ideology called the methodology of science. Its elements are the components of an attitude towards men and nature. (Louch, 1977: 249–250).

So, why reread Louch now? Well, several reasons. First, for the intellectual reward of reading a supreme articulation of a distinctive philosophical position. Louch's work constitutes the most coherent exposition of the antitheoretical stance more famously associated with the later Wittgenstein. One might even say that Louch out-Wittgensteins Wittgenstein. After all, one notable irony in Wittgenstein's case is that his later work actually went on to serve as inspiration for various scientific theoretical and taxonomic enterprises, most notably Speech Act Theory. However, while he would have no doubt been appalled at such developments, Wittgenstein must shoulder some of the blame on account of his overgeneralisation of the notion of rule-following and his upholding of the fact/value distinction. With his highly original dissolving of that distinction by way of the notion of moral explanation, it is arguably Louch who offers what is perhaps Wittgenstein's most topographagnostic fly the clearest escape route from the bottle.

A second, more urgent reason to read Louch is that the ideology against which he writes, namely scientism, has not only not gone away, it flourishes. The scientistic humanities thrive, relatively speaking, against the lingering and somewhat paradoxical backdrop of a now highly familiar trope whereby the humanities as a whole are depicted as suffering a crisis of inexorable decline. The scientistic humanities fulfil their role as dutiful servants of the corporate university, bringing in research grants, scholarships, funded graduate positions, funds for teaching relief (which in turn fuels the increasing adjunctification of teaching staff) while churning out all manner of methodologically intricate projects of moot intellectual value which nevertheless manage to attract such rich support because they are deemed to align with nebulously defined institutional buzzword values ('impact' is a current favourite) which never become any more perspicuous or concretely intelligible despite their incessant, mantra-like incantations. Explaining the intellectual crisis in the humanities is no doubt a complex and contested matter with both internal and external forces at play. But to what extent are the humanities complicit in their own intellectual enfeeblement? Could it be that in coveting the prestigious trappings of their scientific colleagues, large swathes of the humanities have ideologised and methodologised themselves into irrelevance and redundancy? In a book review written some two decades after *E&HA*, Louch wrote of the 'lean and indigestible banquet' to which positivists in the human sciences extend an invitation. Nevertheless, argues Louch, despite its nutritional deficiencies an appetite for such a banquet

> can easily be revived by the promise of Nobel prizes, fat research grants, and more abstruse questions on the blackboard—or more honestly, at the spectacle of a generation's abdication of intellectual responsibility, pursuing false or ephemeral gods. (Louch 1989: 361)

Anyone surveying the lie of the land in contemporary academia can hardly fail to conclude that such an appetite has not only been revived (if it was ever indeed sated) but has come to assume a ravenous quality in many quarters. An invitation to (re)read Louch is an invitation to understand and debate both the intellectual roots and persistence of this dismal state of affairs. Who knows, it might even prompt some to try and do something about it.

References
Gellner, Ernest. 1959. *Words and Things*. Victor Gollancz. London.

Gellner, Ernest. 1979. *Spectacles and Predicaments*. CUP. Cambridge.
Gellner, Ernest. 1998. *Language and Solitude: Wittgenstein, Malinowski and the Habsburg Dilemma.* CUP. Cambridge.
Homans, George C. 1950. *The Human Group*. New York. Harcourt. Brace & Co.
Louch, A.R. 1965. 'On Misunderstanding Mr. Winch.' *Inquiry*, 8 (1-4): 212–216.
Louch, A.R. 1966. *Explanation and Human Action*. Basil Blackwell. Oxford.
Louch, A.R. 1977. 'A Discourse on Methodology: A reply to Ernest Gellner.' *Philosophy of the Social Sciences*, 7: 239–250.
Louch, A.R. 1989. 'Review of "*The Rhetoric of the Human Sciences. Language and Argument in Public Affairs*" by John S. Nelson.' History and Theory, 28 (3): 357–366.
Orman, Jon. 2017. 'The Linguistic Thought of Ernest Gellner.' *Social Epistemology*, 31(4): 387–399.
Orman, Jon. 2018. 'Explanation and Theory in Linguistic Inquiry.' *Empedocles: European Journal for the Philosophy of Communication*, 8 (2): 167–186.
Ryan, Richard M., Bernstein, Jessey H., & Brown, Kirk Warren. 2010. 'Weekends, Work, and Well-Being: Psychological Need Satisfactions and Day of the Week Effects on Mood, Vitality, and Physical Symptoms.' *Journal of Social and Clinical Psychology*, 29 (1): 95–122.
Winch, Peter. 1958. *The Idea of a Social Science and its Relation to Philosophy*. London. Routledge & Kegan Paul.

Section IV.
Language, Migration and Identity in Post-Apartheid South Africa

15.
Language and 'new' African migration to South Africa

Abstract
This article examines the phenomenon of African migration to post-apartheid South Africa from a language-sociological perspective. Although the subject has been one largely neglected by language scholars, the handful of studies which have addressed the issue have yielded ethnographic data and raised questions of considerable significance for the development of theoretical perspectives on the sociolinguistic consequences of geographical and social mobility. In the case of African migrants to South Africa, mobility is often seen to entail a reductive reordering and re-evaluation of their linguistic repertoires which serve to both index and be partly constitutive of their unequal social status. In the final section of the paper, I argue that conventional language planning approaches, and in particular those which place an emphasis on various forms of language rights, are epistemologically disinclined and therefore ultimately theoretically unable to meaningfully address certain types of language-related problems which may arise as a consequence of mobility. Indeed, it is doubtful whether such problems may be amenable to resolution through any form of planned intervention. Such an insight serves as an important brake on ambition in terms of what can be formulated as realistic expected outcomes of language planning measures aimed at tackling sources of social inequality.

Introduction
This paper looks at the language-sociological dimension of 'new' African migration[1] to post-apartheid South Africa. The primary aim is to provide an overview of the subject area and a survey of the limited but often highly insightful previous literature on the topic, upon which this contribution seeks to build. Of particular interest are the types of language-related problems encountered by migrants as a consequence of their condition as mobile, often displaced beings and the ways in which these contribute towards both the production and indexing of various forms of social inequality which commonly accompany migrant status in South Africa. As will emerge in the course of the discussion, such problems cannot simply be reduced to a question of 'not knowing the local language(s) (well enough)'.

Building on this foundation, the article moves on to consider the aforementioned issues from the perspective of language policy and planning. The central question and doubt motivating the discussion is whether certain of the language-related problems experienced by migrants as a result of their relocation are amenable to alleviation or resolution through any form of planned

---

[1] In referring to 'new' African migration to South Africa, I am following the example and rationale of Crush and McDonald (2002) and Maharaj and Moodley (2002). Although, as the aforementioned authors also acknowledge, South Africa has a long and well documented history of hosting migrants from other African countries, most notably contract mine workers from neighbouring countries such as Lesotho, Zimbabwe and Mozambique, the post-apartheid era has seen an unprecedented increase in the volume and diversity of African migration to the country. Therefore, while in no way suggesting a total historical discontinuity, the realisation that, as Crush and McDonald (2002:4) note, 'South Africa is increasingly host to a truly pan-African and global constituency of legal and undocumented migrants', as well as the fact that contemporary flows include many more women and long-term migrants than was previously the case, enables one to locate meaningful elements of 'newness' in post-apartheid African migration patterns.

intervention. I argue that traditional language planning approaches and especially those which focus upon the attribution and implementation of linguistic (human) rights are epistemologically averse and by consequence theoretically unable to effectively address such issues. It is also doubtful whether hitherto attempts to move beyond the rights-based paradigm in language planning, most notably the notion of 'linguistic citizenship' (Stroud 2000, 2001; Stroud and Heugh 2003) which articulates a view of language as a resource and emphasises grassroots agency in planning processes, offers a sufficiently substantial or communicable basis for arriving at successful planning outcomes with respect to such problems. As a result, it is argued that expectations to combat particular sources of language-related social inequality via language planning measures would do best to remain modest in scope.

African migration to post-apartheid South Africa as a field of sociolinguistic/ language-sociological enquiry

Although the post-apartheid period has witnessed a proliferation of interest in matters of language and society and language politics from within traditional sociolinguistic/language-sociological domains of enquiry and the issue of African migration to the 'new' South Africa has quite naturally been the subject of extensive attention in various related fields such as sociology and political studies, the academic literature documenting the linguistic dimension of African migrants'[2] experiences of and adaptations to life in South Africa is notable primarily for its scarcity. The sociolinguistic aspect of African migration to South Africa, when understood as an instance or indeed multiple individual instances of transnational mobility underpinned by processes and effects of globalisation with the migrants themselves constituting

---

[2] I use the term 'migrant' broadly to also include refugees, asylum seekers and foreigners present illegally in the country.

an 'ethnoscape' of globalisation (Appadurai 1996), therefore remains underdocumented and, as a consequence, largely undertheorised.

While there have been a handful of insightful studies carried out on the language practices and attitudes of sub-Saharan African (im)migrants in South Africa which provide us with a varied if ultimately incomplete (both in terms of breadth and depth) view of a number of relevant issues and which will be discussed in the course of this article, the overriding silence on or disregard for the subject, particularly in terms of an integral thematic treatment, would seem to require some attempt at explanation. We perhaps should not be overly surprised at the lack of attention to linguistic matters from outside specialist language-focused fields. After all, despite some more recent attempts to correct the perception (see, for example, Kymlicka and Patten edited volume from 2003), it has by now become a familiar complaint from linguists that insufficient regard is generally paid to matters of language by sociologists and political theorists or at least that language, when addressed, is mostly treated in overly simplistic or unproblematic terms within such fields. However, at the risk of succumbing to the linguistic solipsism which Spolsky (2004:ix) has termed 'linguicentrism', this general disregard for language matters in an otherwise abundant and varied sociological and political literature on the subject of African migrants in post-apartheid South Africa ought to invoke at least some measure of reflexivity on the part of linguists insofar as it leads us to reflect upon and question the centrality of language or linguistic issues in the lives of migrants in South Africa and, in particular, in their experience of difference and inequality. After all, there are clearly a great many factors impacting upon and outcomes generated by processes of migration which are beyond the remit of sociolinguistic or language-sociological analysis. This question, amongst others, will be taken up in greater depth elsewhere in the course of the article.

However, to return to the main thrust of the discussion here, what might explain the relative lack of coverage from within sociolinguistics and the sociology of language of the linguistic practices of African migrants to South Africa, who have been estimated to comprise 3–4 % of the total population in the country (McKinney and Soudien 2010:4), and the linguistic ideologies which operate within and impact upon the social spaces occupied by them? Blommaert (2007:9) rightly notes that 'language policies are very often very bad empirical indicators of the sociolinguistic landscape as there are usually far more languages spoken in a territory than the ones specified in language policies'. He goes on to support his argument by citing the example of Ethnologue which lists more than 30 language names as being spoken in South Africa, while only 11 named varieties enjoy (admittedly with varying degrees of enjoyment) official status under the constitution. However, if one consults the Ethnologue page on South Africa it soon becomes apparent that this too provides an incomplete depiction of the empirical sociolinguistic reality of the country. While most of the indigenous and colonial varieties spoken in South Africa are mentioned (including extinct ones such as |Xam and ||Xegwi), along with varieties spoken by older immigrant communities (e.g. Hindi, Greek and Gujarati), many of those spoken by more recent arrivals remain undocumented. Apart from a mention of 18,000 Shona speakers in the country which seems a gross underestimate given that the number of Zimbabweans in South Africa has been estimated at more than two million, no mention is made of the varieties spoken by the numerous post-apartheid (im)migrant populations from elsewhere in Africa such as the DRC and Nigeria, many of which have a clearly visible and audible presence and particularly in certain areas of larger cities such as Johannesburg and Cape Town.[3]

---

[3] The issue of whether post-apartheid migration has yet resulted in the formation of diaspora communities is open to question. While many Zimbabweans in

Vigouroux (2009:238), for example, writes that the presence of African migrants in Cape Town has 'manifestly been transforming [the city's] linguistic landscape'.

Blommaert's point about language policies could be equally applied to the vast majority of the sociolinguistic and language-policy literature on South Africa, including, it must be said, the present author's own work on language policy in the post-apartheid era (Orman 2008). To illustrate this point further, the past decade has seen two books published with title *Language in South Africa* (Mesthrie (ed.), 2002 and Webb 2002), although the emphases of the two books do differ somewhat, the aim of Mesthrie's edited volume being to provide 'a comprehensive and wide-ranging guide to language and society in South Africa' and Webb's volume constituting a discussion of language policy and planning in the context of national transformation and development. Yet, other than a brief acknowledgement from Mesthrie (2002:12) that the post-apartheid era has seen an influx of refugees and professional migrants bringing with them various 'new' African languages and African varieties of French and Portuguese to South Africa, neither book makes any further reference to the presence of sub-Saharan African (im)migrants in the country. Elsewhere, in 2004 a special issue of the journal

---

South Africa seem clearly to regard themselves as part of a diaspora, as evidenced by the holding of the Zimbabwean Diaspora International Conference in Johannesburg in April 2007, it may not necessarily be the case with other migrant communities. The answer one gives to this question naturally depends on how one goes about defining a diaspora. Bakewell (2008:8), in an incisive article highlighting the relative lack of attention to African diasporas within Africa, notes that the term is increasingly used in a loose sense as 'little more than a synonym for migrants' and suggests that it might be more beneficial to adopt a more rigorous definition of the term. He also goes on to sound the important warning that 'in looking for diasporas within Africa, we may help to "invent" diasporas by naming them' (2008:15). I am grateful to an anonymous reviewer for drawing my attention to this issue.

Language Problems and Language Planning (Volume 28, Number 2) was published on multilingualism in South Africa but not one of its contributions addressed the subject of migration. Kamwangamalu's (2004:198–213) 'Language Profile of South Africa', while mentioning many of the older, but numerically very small European immigrant languages in South Africa, again makes no mention of more recent African immigrants and their linguistic repertoires. The highlighting of these omissions should not be read so much as a criticism of the individual works in question as they are wholly unremarkable in this respect, but it rather serves to highlight the fact that many prominent and influential sociolinguistic descriptions and subsequent analyses of South Africa are empirically incomplete to some degree (although whether a temporally and spatially anchored text can ever achieve full empirical completeness is doubtful) and the extent to which African (im)migrants have been repeatedly rendered invisible and inaudible by even the most well-intentioned of sociolinguistic and language-sociological work.

In seeking to find a satisfactory explanation for the relative silence on the language-sociological dimension of African migration to South Africa and particularly from within the subfield of language policy and planning, we need to consider the prevailing historical and ideological context in which most recent work on language and society in South Africa has been undertaken. The title of one of the first and still very few works to address the issue of African migrants from a language-policy perspective - *Silenced by Nation-Building* (Reitzes and Crawhall 1997) - eloquently summarises perhaps the principal reason behind the initial and, indeed, continuing lack of attention to the subject in the post-apartheid era. In recent years, language-sociological theory, in certain circles at least, has witnessed a gradual move away from an analysis and reading of sociolinguistic phenomena in terms of static, essentialist categorisations of language and identity with a predominant focus on the (nation-)state as the highest level of contextual scale towards a more nuanced, dynamic understanding of such phenomena in relation to the multifarious social and geographic instances of mobility linked to the sociological realities of transnationalism and globalisation (Blommaert 2003, 2007, 2010; Pennycook 2006, 2007a; Fairclough 2006). However, the theory and practice of language policy and planning in South Africa over the past two decades or so has remained predominantly situated within a strongly modernist, nationalist framework.[4] This has seen a dominant emphasis placed on securing societal development and transformation through the institutionalisation and implementation of constitutionally defined language rights (essentially tied to the ethnolinguistic categorisations of the apartheid era) and a complementary process of identity construction or 'nation-building'. Despite some less optimistic voices (e.g. Orman 2008), the South African 'national question' has generally been approached by linguists, one thinks in particular of the prominent work of Neville Alexander (1989, 2002, 2004) and Vic Webb (2002, 2004) espousing a positive belief, albeit one not seemingly based on any appropriate historical precedent, in the potential of language policy and planning to effect meaningful sociolinguistic change in the direction intended by those formulating and implementing it. However, this focus on nation-building does not in and of itself explain the absence of reference to migrant communities in language policy debates in South Africa. After all, issues of language and immigration form a central component of

---

[4]This is of course not to ignore the work of organisations undertaking language planning or management efforts which are not primarily focused on issues of nation and statehood. Examples here would include the South African based Commission for the Promotion and Protection of Cultural, Religious and Linguistic Community Rights and African Academy of Languages (ACALAN) which has its headquarters in Bamako, Mali and is concerned with transregional language management in the form of promoting 'vehicular cross-border languages.'

debates concerning national identity in other parts of the world such as the USA and many countries in Western Europe. We need then to look at some of the particularities of the South African situation. The most important observation to make in respect of the government-led nation-building project is that regarding its relative recentness. In terms of national-identity formation, the two decades or so since the dismantlement of apartheid is not very long at all. During a period in which the form and content (racial, cultural, linguistic etc.) of South African national identity have been and to a considerable extent still are a matter of frequently intense contestation from within the body of citizens, coupled with the deep and enduring levels of socio-economic marginalisation which afflict large sections of the citizen population and which have often been shown to correlate with or be partly explained in terms of unequal access to linguistic resources, it is maybe not altogether surprising to find (im)migrants relegated to or beyond the periphery of discussions on language and nation-building. The arrival of significant numbers of African migrants in South Africa is therefore a phenomenon which has coincided with a vigorous prevailing nationalist emphasis in government discourse and much scholarly work with a focus on language policy and planning. While a good deal of this work has admittedly been highly critical of and unaligned with government policy mainly as a result of the perceived gap between stated policy commitments and actual practices, it has still nevertheless been very much framed by a normative nationalist perspective. This has entailed a concerted focus on the role and responsibility of government institutions to deliver or facilitate solutions to language-related social problems in line with the commitments to multilingualism as articulated in the constitution amongst a putative national community defined in terms of citizenship. Indeed, for most treatises on language-political issues in South Africa, citizenship appears to be the qualifying criterion, however unknowingly or implicitly, for inclusion within the scope of discussion. The notion of citizenship is of course a notoriously complex and contested issue and it is therefore necessary to gain a nuanced appreciation of what the term denotes in the South African context and in particular the rhetorical and material mechanisms by which the boundaries of citizenship are drawn. In his extremely insightful and persuasive monograph dealing with issues of xenophobia, citizenship and identity politics in post-apartheid society, Neocosmos (2006) argues that the promotion of a notion of citizenship reduced to indigeneity and autochtony which sees the trumpeting of the superior rights of 'natives' vis-à-vis 'foreigners' has been a central component of state discourse in the post-apartheid period and represents one of the leading explanations for the virulent xenophobia which has frequently characterised discourse on and physical interactions with foreign migrants and in particular black Africans from outside of South Africa. Nationalism alone cannot be held to account for the type and scale of xenophobia witnessed since the end of apartheid, but rather a nationalism based upon a particular conception of citizenship and relationship between state and society.

> Exclusion from community means exclusion from citizenship, its rights and duties, as it is the latter which defines community membership of the nation in particular. Xenophobia is thus intimately connected to citizenship, in other words to the fact of belonging or not belonging to a community [...] Xenophobia is about the denial of social rights and entitlements to strangers, people considered to be strangers to the community (village, ethnic group as well as nation) not just to 'foreigners' as conceived by the law. It is thus about a certain conception of the community as founded on indigeneity/community from which follows that this conception of community is necessarily essentialist and ahistorical and is visualised as unchanging. [...] [I]t is the outcome of power relations between state and

society. Finally, in hegemonic (state) discourse, citizenship is reduced to passive citizenship and nationhood is reduced to indigeneity. (Neocosmos 2006:16–17)

The next section examines the linguistic dimension of xenophobia against African migrants in the South African context. See also Wee (2011: chapter 6) for an exploration of how migration and global mobility impact upon and problematise notions of citizenship and language rights.

Xenophobia, difference and linguistic conspicuousness
Xenophobia is the issue *par excellence* which frames the reporting on and study of African migrants in post-apartheid South Africa. A survey undertaken by the Southern African Migration Project (SAMP) in 2006 led it to conclude that 'South Africa exhibits levels of intolerance and hostility to outsiders unlike virtually anything seen in other parts of the world' (SAMP 2008:1). Descriptive accounts abound in both popular and academic literature of widespread instances of violence and discrimination, primarily directed against black African migrants (Harris 2002; Crush and Pendleton 2004; Wa Kabwe-Segatti 2008; Dodson 2010). There appears, however, to be a lack of consensus regarding the cause(s) of such hostility. Neocosmos (2006:4), for example, influenced by the work of Alain Badiou, claims that most popular and academic attempts at accounting for the phenomenon have been deficient, relying too heavily on superficial, depoliticised explanations such as its being an expression of frustration at a form of 'relative deprivation' experienced by the South African population at large or an inability to tolerate difference due to the continuing socio-psychological effects of the apartheid years. See Dodson (2010) for a detailed overview of explanations of xenophobia in the South African context.

On the surface at least, language features prominently in accounts and discussions of xenophobia. Language is, as one would expect, one of the most salient indexicals[5] of otherness by which foreigners can be identified as such. For example, there is a good deal of anecdotal and more concrete evidence of shibboleths being used to identify non-South Africans (Harris 2002: 5–6). The most commonly heard example is that of suspected migrants being asked the Zulu word for body parts such as the toes, little finger or elbow with those failing to come up with the correct answers ('ucikicane', 'inzonzwane' and 'indololwane' respectively) sometimes falling victim to violent assault (*Mail and Guardian*, 24th May 2008; *The Times*, 30th July 2008).[6] Language would seem to have the simultaneous potential to frequently render migrants both visible/audible and silent. For instance, a number of Kamuangu's (2006) interviewees in his study of the 'family language policies' of DRC immigrants in Johannesburg talk of a reluctance to speak their homeland languages in public situations for fear of violent or abusive reactions from South African citizens, preferring instead to either not speak at all or speak only English which, as they acknowledge, still often gives them away due to their accent (Kamuangu 2006:118). Vigouroux (2009:239) describes similar findings amongst DRC migrants in Cape Town, noting that 'migrants themselves have made conscious decisions to remain as inconspicuous as possible in Black townships in order to avoid being targeted by segments of the indigenous population that don't appreciate their presence. The migrants' strategies [...] range from remaining silent on the streets or in public transportation to

---

[5] Other means of identification reported by the Internal Tracing Unit of the South African Police Service include clothing, hairstyles, skin tone or, in the case of Mozambicans, yellow fever vaccination scars on the left forearm (Minaar and Hough 1996:166–167).

[6] The veracity of this story has been disputed. One writer claims it to be an urban legend that dates back to the 1980s when Zulus were reported to be using the same method to identify Xhosas, the Xhosa word for elbow being *ingqiniba*. (*The Sunday Times*, 8th June 2008).

adopting the local sartorial style.' According to Vigouroux, very few migrants make an effort to learn Xhosa or Afrikaans on account of their perceived limited economic value and because both languages apparently index categories of speakers with whom migrants are highly reluctant to identify as a result of their often negative experiences as Black Africans in Cape Town.

In another study, De Kadt and Ige (2005:142) mention how their Nigerian interviewees in Durban report experiencing social exclusion and being made to feel 'inhuman and un-African' by local South Africans on account of their inability to understand or speak Zulu. Given this inability and the ineffectiveness of Nigerian languages as a means of out-group communication in South Africa—examples of what Blommaert et al. (2005:205) term 'low-mobility resources'—English (Nigerian English) remains the only option available to them for communicating with South Africans. As De Kadt and Ige (2005:143) note: 'Nigerians are substantially restricted in the number and the quality of languages available for daily use, and the "space" available to these languages'. Elsewhere, Mbong (2006), in her study of Cameroonian migrants in Cape Town, also reports how English has come to feature more centrally in their linguistic repertoires, with reduced socio-functional spaces for French and Cameroonian Pidgin English. However, this functional expansion would not always seem to result in an (self-perceived) increased proficiency in English. One of Mbong's interviewees even reports a deterioration in the quality of his English since arriving in South Africa due to his frequent interactions with Xhosa-speaking workplace colleagues who struggle to express themselves in the language, requiring him to 'patch up the English in a way that it would be understandable to them' (2006:72).

Blommaert (2003:613) reminds us that mobility, understood as a movement across social and geographical spaces, nearly always entails a functional reordering and re-evaluation of individuals' linguistic repertoires. Some form of linguistic adaptation would therefore seem to be an inherent dimension of migration and particularly that which involves the crossing of social-identity boundaries (cultural, ethnic, linguistic etc.). However, what the examples discussed above demonstrate is that the hostility perceived and experienced by, one assumes very many, African migrants on account of their foreignness leads them to make certain reductive adjustments in their linguistic behaviour *which they might otherwise not make* and which are presumably not necessary for more 'prestigious' (i.e. white[7]) migrants. Such adjustments are therefore simultaneously both partly productive and reflective of the inequality which pervades the social life of African migrants in South Africa. As far as establishing any form of linkage between the two is concerned, we can venture so far as to say that language appears to be implicated in xenophobia as both a vehicle for its overt expression (the propagation of xenophobic ideas through discourse and the use of language to directly perpetrate acts of xenophobia) and as a form of behaviour which is altered in some way (e.g. reordered, reduced repertoires or avoidance of speaking in certain situations) by virtue of the phenomenon. Furthermore, the possession of xenophobic sentiments would, in some cases, also appear to have an effect on the communicative behaviour of local citizens insofar as it may result in a refusal to assign meaning or recognition to the content of migrants' utterances, instead focusing on the indexical significance of the form of their speech (see quotation from De Kadt and Ige in the next section). One ought to bear in mind, however, that the conclusions reached thus far, although they may seem intuitive and reasonable, are based on a quite small amount of data and are therefore necessarily somewhat provisional in terms of their application beyond the specific case studies in question. In order to arrive at a more complete and

---

[7] It has been noted, for instance, that only black Zimbabweans have been subjected to xenophobic attacks. (*The Zim Diaspora*, 2nd May 2010).

detailed inventory of the types of linguistic adjustments made by migrants as a result of xenophobic-type prejudice, there is a clear need for further research. However, the current trend is not especially encouraging. Apart from Vigouroux (2008, 2009), the last five or so years have unfortunately yielded virtually nothing in the way of new published research on the sociolinguistics of African migration to South Africa.

Indexicality, re-evaluated repertoires and inequality
In the discussion of xenophobia above, it was noted that migration tends to result in a mostly reductive reordering of the functions of the many elements which make up migrants' linguistic repertoires and that this reordering *inter alia* generally reflects the social inequality which accompanies immigrant status. The linguistic basis for the inequality and disadvantage experienced by many African migrants[8] resides not only in their lack of competence in African South African languages (Boullion 1996:10) and the often drastically reduced functionality of their homeland languages, but also in the reception and evaluation of the varieties of English spoken by them in the South African context. While the ability of African migrants to communicate in English varies substantially from one individual to another and is most likely dependent to varying degrees on a combination of factors such as country of origin (Anglophone, Francophone or Lusophone Africa?), socio-economic status and level of education in the home country, time spent in South Africa or other countries

---

[8] Of course, many migrants from neighbouring countries such as Botswana, Mozambique, Zimbabwe, Swaziland and Lesotho do indeed speak versions of those transborder varieties also spoken in South Africa (e.g. Setswana, Shangaan/Tsonga, Ndebele, Swati and Sotho) and some migrants from elsewhere in Africa also do acquire competence in local African languages, for example Vigouroux's (2009) interviewee from the DRC who had learnt Xhosa.

where English is spoken, gender[9] etc., a good number of migrants undoubtedly possess a proficiency in English which is broadly comparable or even superior to many South Africans. As De Kadt and Ige (2005: 140) note: 'The well-developed education system in Nigeria does mean that many Nigerian (im)migrants speak English with some fluency; the need to negotiate substantial domains of life in English does not immediately silence them'. However, as they go on to observe, this fluency frequently fails to achieve the intended communicative aims in terms of audience reception and response as the anticipated or desired uptake of meaning may be impeded by negative stereotyping, thereby having a 'silencing' effect on their attempts at communication.

> In interactions between local inhabitants and immigrants, however, the former tend to respond by no longer acknowledging the full range of meanings expressed in the language of immigrants. In recognising (im)migrants as such, referential content may be devalued and possibly ignored. Instead, the language variety or accent used will be interpreted as the main signifier in what has been said and, moreover, simply equated with an available stereotype. The complexity of discourse is reduced to a social statement, simplistically interpreted on the terms of the local speaker. In this way, the one language remaining to the (im)migrant, too, becomes voided of its rich complexity and largely reduced to a one-dimensional shell, to which stereotypical meaning can be simply assigned by those with power. (As is the case of these Nigerians, this stereotype may often have little to do with the actual

---

[9] Many of Kamuangu's (2006) female interviewees from the DRC report and exhibit a weaker command of English in comparison to their husbands. This is explained on account of their being homebound mothers and a 'woman's traditional role as a carrier-conveyor of ethnic values' (2006:254).

variety spoken.) In this way, in spite of fluency in this language, (im)migrants may be substantially threatened with silencing. (De Kadt and Ige 2005:141).

In other words, such migrants can be seen as having a problem of 'voice' (Wee 2011:131). While they may be able to speak, they encounter greater difficulty in being 'heard' and making themselves understood, something which constitutes just as critical a component of the communicative (semiotic) process. This brings to mind Bourdieu's (1977:651) assertion that '[d]iscourse is a symbolic asset which can receive different values depending on the market on which it is offered'. Whereas in Nigeria knowledge and use of local varieties of English which approximate some form of internationally valid 'standard' English [10] confer considerable social prestige and advantage (Adegbite 2004), the relocation of these varieties to, in this case, the South African context sees them undergo a substantial devaluation and stigmatisation, an example of what Blommaert (2003: 613), inspired by the work of Dell Hymes, terms the 'relative value of semiotic resources'. The English spoken by such migrants would in effect seem to contain the potential for a double stigmatisation. Firstly, in most cases the Englishes spoken by Nigerians and other African migrants differ saliently from those forms of English which function as elite or high-prestige varieties in the South African context. In some cases, they may only differ perceptibly in terms of accent but this is still nevertheless sufficient to index a meaningful otherness and therefore become a potential catalyst for differential or unequal treatment. Secondly, the otherness of their English, in combination with

---

[10] This does not include Nigerian Pidgin. However, this should not be read as an endorsement of 'creole exceptionalism' (Degraff 2005) or even as an attempt to enter the ultimately unresolvable debate on what counts or ought to count as 'English' (Mufwene 1994, 1998; Pennycook 2007b).

other non-linguistic indexical factors of course, can lead to migrants being identified not merely as speakers of low-prestige varieties, but also specifically as Nigerians, Zimbabweans, Mozambicans etc. and then subjected to the respective stereotyping. Although, as De Kadt and Ige (2005:134–135) report in the case of their Nigerian interviewees, migrants' nationalities are not always immediately identifiable from their accent, the detection of difference, of non-South Africanness in their speech can often lead to enquiries as to their country of origin.[11]

A further example of the downward re-evaluation of elements of linguistic repertoires which can result from migration is mentioned by Vigouroux (2005:240). She reports that many of her interviewees from the DRC arrived in South Africa expecting to be able to exploit their knowledge of French, the language of highest social prestige in their home country, by working as translators, teachers and tour guides etc. only to experience the disillusioning disappointment of discovering that French provided them with little benefit on the local job market. And yet, as Vigouroux (2005:245) goes on to emphasise, a knowledge of English also does not necessarily increase employment chances as this is often negatively outweighed by their status as black African migrants. As she notes: 'Command of a local language does not necessarily result in professional insertion in the host country [...] Such facts obviously invalidate the usual and highly politicized assumption that command of the 'host language' is a sufficient condition or at least a prerequisite for migrants to be "integrated" in the host country' (2005:246). Once again, we see mobility exercising a restrictive effect on communicative repertoires which may be experienced as traumatic in both psycho-

---

[11] Raj Mesthrie (personal communication) reports anecdotal evidence suggesting that some Xhosa speakers are able to broadly differentiate between West African and East African migrants, although there are of course most likely more than just linguistic factors involved here.

logical and economic terms. The contributions of Vigouroux (2005, 2008, 2009) on the language practices of Francophone[12] Black African migrants in Cape Town, although not directly engaging with issues of language policy, represent the most sustained and in-depth ethnographic engagement with the subject area to be published thus far. A particular focus in her work has been on the 'identity displays' and 'identity dynamics' supposedly instantiated in the linguistic behaviour of migrants.[13] Emphasising the notions of 'space' and 'territoriality', an important, foundational point which emerges strongly in the work of Vigouroux is that linguistic repertoires should not be conceived of in static terms as they too are subject to constant realignment and revaluation as a result of individuals' geographical and social mobility (2005:253).

The point to be drawn from the preceding discussion, then, is that the difficulties which face many African migrants in attempting to integrate into and participate in South African society on something approaching equal terms do not lie simply in acquiring spoken proficiency in one or more South African languages, although this can indeed be regarded as a necessary condition. In fact, many already possess such proficiency prior to their arrival in the country or acquire it to a greater or lesser degree soon after. Owing to its indexical significance, language

---

[12] Vigouroux (2008:422) herself acknowledges that the ascription of a 'Francophone' identity to such migrants is by no means unproblematic or uncontested.

[13] It is not my intention in this article to enter too far into discussions of migrant identity issues. While the subject of language and migration clearly provides very fertile ground for an exploration of questions of social identity, there are in my view particular epistemological and methodological issues which require addressing and, in particular, the question of whether retrospective analysis of linguistic 'data' by the researcher can deliver coherent insights into the way in which identity is experienced as a first-order phenomenon (see Pablé et al. 2010). To address such questions here would be beyond the scope of this paper.

may frequently be used as a pretext or signal for discrimination, but it is questionable to what extent the ultimate root of such discrimination can be said to be linguistically motivated. In their study of conflict between South Africans and immigrants in the township of Mizamoyethu[14] near the Cape Town suburb of Hout Bay, Dodson and Oelofse (2002:126) attribute a more material cause:

> Although social and cultural differences play a role, the roots of the conflict are primarily material: "locals" and "foreigners" compete for scarce employment, for housing, services, and facilities; and for simple physical space. This local conflict is also grounded within a xenophobic national discourse on immigration – a discourse which both fuels, and is fuelled by, incidents of violence between South Africans and immigrants. "Illegal aliens" have been accused of "taking the jobs of locals, lowering wages, increasing crime and spreading diseases", and, as a consequence, have become targets of resentment, hostility and verbal and physical abuse.

B. Harris (2002:174) notes that the 'biological-cultural' factors which index the otherness of white or Asian foreigners in the country do not entail the same risk of violence or prejudice as those which mark out black Africans, perhaps suggesting a more elemental cause, namely a rejection of their presence as black Africans in South Africa. It is obviously difficult, on the basis of the evidence available, to make any firm conclusions about the specific significance of language as a motivating factor in xenophobic discrimination. However, if it could be compellingly demonstrated that linguistic issues are mostly of non-primary importance as causes of discrimination against black African

---

[14] Now generally known as Imizamo Yethu.

migrants, while certainly not serving to dismiss the linguistic dimension as unimportant or unworthy of study it would, in my view, have serious implications for any claims, whether of a theoretical or more practical nature, which might be advanced on behalf of a language policy and planning approach as representing a possible means of effectively addressing certain of the language-related problems with which they are confronted in South Africa.

African migration to South Africa: a language policy and planning perspective

The intention in this section is to provide a brief overview of what little previous research exists on language policy and planning and African migrants in the post-apartheid period and to identify some of the more significant questions raised or implied by such work. The principal argument which emerges in the remainder of this article is that the phenomenon of African migration to South Africa can help to shed additional light on many of the theoretical shortcomings and troublesome epistemological conceptualisations underlying previous 'positivist' approaches to language policy and planning (Canagarajah 2006:154; Johnson 2009:72). It also points to some more fundamental limitations of language policy and planning as a theoretically informed practice and discipline.

As intimated previously, in terms of work on African migration from a language-policy perspective, the cupboard is extremely bare. The study by Reitzes and Crawhall (1997) on 'African immigrants and language policy in the new South Africa' is still the only published work on the subject and furthermore the only one of the South African Migration Project's[15] more than fifty research documents published thus far to specifi-

---

[15] A 'research programme designed to facilitate the formulation and implementation of new initiatives on cross-border population migration in the region' (www.queensu.ca/samp/).

cally address language matters. Although the research on which the study was based was undertaken well over a decade ago, many of Reitzes and Crawhall's empirical findings undoubtedly still hold good today. For example, they note the absence of a coherent or explicit government language policy in respect of immigrants and a widespread tendency amongst state officials and government departments to violate, often as a result of ignorance or confusion, the supposedly constitutionally guaranteed language rights of non-citizens. They conclude that this absence of explicit policy and related planning measures 'contributes to an overall governmental silence about the legitimate linguistic and cultural presence of other Africans in South Africa... [which] has the potential to obscure real and potential human rights abuses by government, civil society and South African citizens' (1997:3). They also report on the lack of interpreters for non-South African languages which frequently lead to delays in court proceedings, a number of common misconceptions held by state officials in relation to immigrants, e.g. that all West Africans, including Nigerians, speak French, and an abundance of anecdotal evidence of xenophobia which they attribute to the 'ambiguity of nation-building' (1997:2). Their research leads them to identify the emergence of an exclusive national identity based upon a linguistic hierarchy in which 'immigrant African languages, including those which are not recognised as official languages, are in a sub-class off the scale, and out of the realm of policy' (1997:6). Although the singular lack of any follow-up research makes it difficult to determine precisely to what extent Reitzes and Crawhall's findings are still valid today, given the prevailing political and socioeconomic climate which provides little in the way of psychological or material succour for most black African immigrants there would seem to be little reason to suppose that anything significant of a fundamental nature has changed in the intervening years since their study was carried out. As far as governmental or academic publications on language policy and planning in South Africa are concerned, African (im)migrants certainly continue to remain very much beyond the scope of discussion or even reference.

While Reitzes and Crawhall's empirical findings from the late 1990s still have considerable currency, their attempts to formulate prescriptions and policy recommendations for addressing the problems which they identify are, admittedly when considered with a good deal of hindsight, less successful. Although their focus on language policy and African immigrants makes the study highly exceptional even 14 years on, the work is very much a product of its time in terms of its emphasis on the promotion of linguistic (human) rights (with the essentialist notions of language and identity which tend to underpin such discourse (Stroud and Heugh 2003)) and a belief in the work of official bodies such as PanSALB as representing solutions or at least part-solutions to the issues under consideration. However, the fine details of any such solutions seem to be lacking from their recommendations. There is frequent use of vague, unglossed phrasings which essentially function as descriptions of ideal-type or at least more desirable situations and do little to illustrate how might arrive at such situations, e.g. 'PanSALB should make immigrant and migrant languages more visible', 'Victims of language rights violations should know where to take their complaints for investigation', 'Conditions need to be created...', 'There needs to be support...' (1997:26–27). This kind of language has by now become quite a familiar feature of work on language policy and planning issues and is symptomatic of the acute difficulty in moving from diagnosis to remedial prescription. To be fair, as Reitzes and Crawhall themselves note, they were hampered by a profound lack of information, both statistical and ethnographic, which makes the formulation of concrete and effective language planning measures a more onerous task than it already is. This absence of reliable information on migrants and language still very much persists. Other than a handful of postgraduate ethnographic studies (Kamuangu 2006; Mbong 2006) which provide some interesting and potentially useful data but little in the way of profound analysis and the work of Vigouroux and De Kadt & Ige, very little beyond anecdotal information or relatively superficial press reporting is known about the linguistic lives of African migrants in South Africa. The forthcoming 2011 census is also unlikely to deliver much in the way of useful linguistic data as the only language-related question asks which of the eleven official languages the respondent speaks as a home language; any other languages are simply recorded as 'Other', thereby denying the possibility of an affirmative linguistic self-representation to many non-citizens within the framework of the census.

The shortage of relevant information on migrants' language repertoires and their uses constitutes a practical inconvenience which ought to be readily surmountable provided there is the required motivation and competence to gather it. Language policy discussions therefore need not be eternally handicapped by a shortage of qualitative or quantitative data. Once a useful amount data has been collected, however, the question which then arises for engaged language planners becomes one with a combination of practical and, crucially, theoretical implications, essentially asking what language policy and planning can do to address and remedy the linguistic dimension(s) of inequality in the lives of migrants. This is where the discussion unfortunately acquires a more pessimistic tone. Much of the difficulty lies in expectation. The perspective which regards language-related problems, conceived as causes and outcomes of sociolinguistic inequality, as both theoretically and practically amenable to successful intervention in the form of a positivist, rational planning approach would seem to naturally entail the view that such problems can in many cases be explained in terms of planning/management failure or the successful implementation of policy which is inherently inequitable. In other words, language planning as a discipline is validated as a domain of discourse and action in which meaningful sociolinguistic change or prevention of change can be accomplished. The position taken by Reitzes and Crawhall, namely that much of the language-related discrimination experienced by African migrants originates in a refusal or failure to acknowledge and respect their linguistic and other human rights under the constitution and could be remedied by better implementation of policy, clearly reflects just such a positivist view of language policy and planning. It is not the intention here to retread old ground and provide yet another intricate critique and deconstruction of traditional language policy and planning approaches incorporating, amongst other things, elements of language rights and/or Linguistic Human Rights (LHR) discourse and the implied or explicit linguistic ontologies contained therein as this has been done more than competently on numerous previous occasions (e.g. Blommaert 2001; Stroud 2001; Stroud and Heugh 2003). Suffice it to recap that the most targeted areas of criticism have been the overreliance on static and essentialist understandings of language and identity coupled with frequent use of ecological and biological metaphors, the positing of bounded, ontological entities called 'languages' (Pennycook 2006:66–67) with a concomitant overlooking of internal inequalities within such languages and a view of the state level as constituting the ultimate site of linguistic inequality. The essential argument in the discussion which follows is that certain of these criticisms are brought into focus and validated by an understanding of some of the types of language-related issues faced by migrants as discussed in this article.

Firstly, we can note that in certain cases the problems which confront migrants are of a sort which is generally not addressed by traditional policy actors and it is here that some of the limits of language policy and planning, when conceived of as a discipline of praxis aimed at solving or easing 'language problems', are revealed. By way of example, let us return to the issue of the indexical significance of forms of linguistic variation such as accent. While certain individuals' social visibility as a result of their accent may frequently be experienced as problematic or even traumatic due to ensuing hostile or prejudicial treatment,[16] it has generally been the case, as Blommaert (2009: 244) reminds us, that the hitherto leading actor in the field of language policy and planning, the state and its institutions, has shown little interest in attempting to plan and control supposedly peripherally significant elements such as accent and even less so, one might add, in order to enable or compel immigrants to integrate into the host society. Peripheral, that is, to the central focus of such policies—putative objects called 'languages' and their social and geographical distribution. One might well argue that this lack of concern is not simply a case of omission or oversight but is instead for good reason, namely that accent is not a feature which lends itself to successful planned intervention, other than perhaps in the most formal and punitive of early learning environments. However, as Blommaert's (2009) article on internet courses in accent reduction or elimination (in this case, 'reducing' foreign-sounding English to the normative benchmark of standard American English) shows, forms of accent planning and the associated normative complexes are being marketed with some vigour by certain private enterprise actors. Despite the glowing testimonials on such websites, it is of course difficult to ascertain to what extent such programmes actually achieve their stated aims or claimed results, although one cannot help but be highly sceptical. Indeed, as Lippi-Green (1997:50–51)

---

[16] I am not referring just to the more overt instances of institutional accent discrimination which may be remedied or countered by the implementation of anti-discrimination legislation or suchlike, but more particularly the way in which individuals may be unthinkingly judged or classified to their disadvantage on the basis of accent in everyday situations of interpersonal communication.

observes, significant or complete accent adjustment or 'reduction'/'removal' is a highly improbable prospect for most people beyond the language acquisition stage and something upon which intelligence or application would seem to have minimal bearing. Another important consideration in this regard of course is that we are not dealing here with a pathology on the part of the language user which requires therapeutic intervention, but a pathology of society which in this particular context renders significant elements of the language user's repertoire as markers of an unequal social status, namely that of an unwelcome foreigner. Or, as Blommaert et al. (2005:198) put it, we are dealing here not with 'a problem *of* the speaker, but [...] a problem *for* the speaker, lodged not in individual forms of deficit or inability but in the connection between individual communicative potential and requirements produced by the environment'. The general point I am seeking to make here, though, is that the state's usual lack of concern for accent planning is most likely the result of some ideological or pragmatic tolerance of certain forms of intra-language diversity and a view of accent as being a feature of peripheral or negligible importance rather than any recognition on its part of the severe unlikelihood of registering successful planning outcomes (Harris 1998:130). It is perhaps just good fortune that the ideological disinclination and/or epistemological and theoretical shortcomings which have often blinded traditional language policy and planning approaches to the role of communicationally significant aspects such as accent in the production, consolidation and reflection of certain forms of social inequality have generally meant that ill-conceived attempts to address such issues directly through planned intervention have not been undertaken.

Central to the argument being pursued here is the notion of mobility and its role in the production of inequality. More specifically, we can observe that mobility across different normative regimes of language use and valuation may render certain linguistic repertoire elements problematic which would not otherwise be so. It is therefore clear that any viable language planning approach aimed at in some way addressing such problems would need to not only incorporate an acknowledgement and understanding of the potential sociolinguistic significance of such mobility within its theoretical framework, but also devise some method of manipulating its outcomes to desired effect. Again, this last point is where the difficulty lies as it would seem to involve nothing less than attempting to plan away a sociolinguistic truism. An understanding of migrants as mobile, transnational beings, sometimes with only a transient or interrupted presence in the host country, often in possession of highly fragmented linguistic repertoires—'bits of languages' (Blommaert (2010:118)—and without any politically effective, institutionally organised community structure to call on for support certainly reveals the inappropriateness of, for example, a static, 'in situ' rights-based approach whereby *de jure* or normatively postulated rights are bound to and dependent upon the national or ethnolinguistic community of origin which in turn presupposes the possession and command of particular discrete, named languages (Stroud 2001). As Wee (2011:129) notes, the concept of language rights does not 'fare well' in circumstances which involve mixed or hybridised language repertoires. Furthermore, language rights, which invariably focus on the right of persons to speak or be spoken to in a particular way, appear to be quite unable to get to grips with the problem of 'voice' mentioned in Sect. "Xenophobia, difference and linguistic conspicuousness".

> Speaking without being heard merely increases the sense of frustration on the part of the speaker, but the problem with the notion of language rights is that it focuses on the right to speak, assuming that this coincides with the 'right' to be heard or understood. But if the latter is absent, then it

is not clear what purpose is served by making claims regarding the former. (Wee 2011:131).

It should of course be acknowledged that there have been attempts made to transcend the theoretical limitations of the right-based paradigm, the most prominent of which is the development of the notion of 'linguistic citizenship' (Stroud 2000, 2001, 2003; Stroud and Heugh 2003; see also Makoni 2011). Linguistic citizenship is styled as a 'post-liberal' paradigm which views language as a resource for societal development and rejects the essentialist epistemologies which underpin most rights-based approaches. Linguistic citizenship also moves away from a view of the state and its institutions as the primary actor in language planning processes, instead emphasising the importance of grass-roots agency and struggle. According to Stroud (2001:353):

> Linguistic citizenship denotes the situation where speakers themselves exercise control over their language, deciding what languages are, and what they may mean, and where language issues (especially in educational sites) are discursively tied to a range of social issues – policy issues and questions of equity. [...] The concept of linguistic citizenship permits multiple (democratic, participatory) approaches to citizenship issues based on an idea of languages as a political and economic 'site of struggle', on respect for language diversity and difference and on the deconstruction of essentialist understanding of language and identity.

While the deconstruction of such essentialist notions is to be welcomed and represents progress in terms of academic theorising, the immediate question which arises is how situations in which speakers, often highly marginalised and disempowered, are able 'to exercise control over their language' are to be brought about in the first place. This would seem to require social policies and social change well beyond the scope of language planning enterprises. There is also the crucial question of how the notion of linguistic citizenship, one articulated at quite a high level of theoretical abstraction and with considerable intellectual sophistication, is to be made available and accessible to the individuals and communities it aims to empower. For example, Stroud (2003: 18) states that 'both policy making and implementation need to be opened up to extensive democratic participation of grassroots organisations'—a sentiment with which it is difficult to disagree but there is little in the way of suggestion as to how this might actually be achieved. This caveat would seem particularly relevant to migrants living on or beyond the periphery of dominant social and educational systems often with little in the way of community structures to call upon and whose socio-political status is after all invariably defined by a *lack* of citizenship as conventionally conceived in the South African context. Although it is claimed that linguistic citizenship 'pertains to a view of language as a symbolic, material, intimate and global resource in the service of participatory governance' (Stroud and Heugh 2003: 18), the matter of how migrants fit into mainstream or politically dominant discourses on citizenship is what is of material relevance here. We can again also observe the difficulty in moving beyond theoretical diagnosis and formulating concrete recommendations for policy and planning measures. While linguistic citizenship functions effectively as a potent critique of the essentialist and frequently counterproductive thinking underlying the linguistic rights paradigm and importantly emphasises the need to move beyond analysis solely of the formal, state-sanctioned sphere in consideration of the linguistic resources available to society, it is doubtful whether, in its present articulation, it provides a sufficient basis for material action to achieve successful planning outcomes either on behalf of or by disparate and fractured population groups. However, as an orientation in highlighting the structural obstacles to grassroots linguistic empowerment, linguistic citizenship may well serve as a useful starting point from which to bring about future theoretical and practical advancement in the discipline of language policy and planning, although this remains to be seen.

Concluding remarks
By way of conclusion, I am aware that this discussion may be seen to have entered into territory somewhat removed from the subject of language and African migration to post-apartheid South Africa. It might also appear that I am unfairly focusing criticism or scepticism on language planning based on the consideration of a subject in relation to which any discussion of policy and planning remains mostly hypothetical given the almost total lack of attention to it in governmental, NGO or academic circles. In response, I would counter that the type of issues, *qua* sociolinguistic phenomena, which are brought to light by consideration of the situation and experiences of African migrants in South Africa as documented thus far invite us to question some of the foundations upon which current prevailing notions of language planning are based. In particular, it is my claim that deficient conceptualisation, particularly that underlying traditional, positivist approaches to language planning and as exposed in certain measure by the phenomenon of migration and the empirically verifiable sociolinguistic consequences of mobility, goes some way to explaining the often overly optimistic assessment of the potential of the discipline. A more sustainably reasoned conceptualisation of language and its relation to social life leads, perhaps regrettably, to the conclusion that language-related problems of the type discussed above are not suitable targets for intervention in the form of language planning. Furthermore, the thanklessness of embarking upon a traditionally conceived language policy and planning approach in respect of migrant communities in South Africa (and no doubt elsewhere) is further compounded by more

practical considerations, namely the wholly unfavourable ideological climate, exemplified by an often highly salient xenophobia, and an absence of effective political will to allow African migrants to claim a legitimate space in South African society.

In order to avoid misunderstanding and/or accusations of overemphasis, let it be stated that I am not claiming that the language-related problems which emerge as a consequence of mobility and the resultant differential indexicalities which are thereby invoked are the only type of language problem or issue worthy of attention, but that they are of significance and we would therefore do well to take account of them in our analyses. The more traditional policy concerns such as acquisition, literacy, the functional use and allocation of official and non-official forms in both public and private domains are clearly still of acute relevance and continue to represent legitimate topics of discussion from a policy standpoint. However, an acknowledgement of the role of mobility in producing and maintaining sites of language-focused inequality allows one to introduce an important refinement into the analysis, albeit one which suggests that the resolution of such states of affairs lies beyond both the theoretical and practical capacity of a language-planning approach, especially as commonly conceived. Could reconceptualisation offer some measure of rehabilitation for the notion of language planning? Perhaps, but it would seem to require a relaxing of entry criteria as regards which communicational elements are admitted within the definitional scope of language, something which 'orthodox' linguistic approaches have traditionally been extremely reluctant to permit. After all, there are clearly certain elements of the semiotic environment, or landscape if one prefers, which are intuitively more amenable to a planning or management approach. For example, publicly or officially produced written (and/or pictorial) material. However, if our approach to language planning remains reduced to attempting to influence the formal properties of verbal behaviour then its subsequent failure would seem to invite preordination.

The fundamental inadequacy of the essentialist approach for arriving at an understanding of language has been well documented, most cogently and certainly most scathingly from an integrationist perspective (e.g. Harris 1981, 1990, 1998). This is not the place to revisit these arguments in detail here, suffice it to say that if one accepts the idea that the reality and totality of human linguistic behaviour in no way corresponds with these things called languages which have no discernible or discoverable ontological status and are merely second-order cultural-ideological constructs, the notion of somehow being able to plan such behaviour based upon these constructs, as well as its evaluation by other speakers, largely dissolves away with them. As Pennycook (2006:69) observes, once this view of language has been undermined it brings into question various concepts such as language rights, mother tongues and multilingualism which are largely parasitic upon the idea of discrete languages with neatly corresponding identities. Furthermore, such concepts represent some of the foundational theoretical cornerstones upon which approaches to language policy and planning have been and continue to be based. Indeed, it is perhaps this 'artefactual' view of language (Seargeant 2010:4), one which regards it as an essentially passive object which can be used, adapted or have rights attached to it etc., rather than a form of communicative behaviour which is continuously created anew and whose apparent systematicity is an effect of temporary sedimentation rather than of the existence of a fixed, underlying structure (Hopper 1998), which in some measure encourages the conviction that it can be manipulated through rational, planned intervention.

References

Adegbite, W. (2004). Enlightenment and attitudes of the Nigerian elite on the roles of languages in Nigeria. In M. J. Muthwii & A. N. Kioko (Eds.), *New language bearings in Africa: A fresh quest* (pp. 89–100). Clevedon: Multilingual Matters.

Alexander, N. (1989). *Language policy and national unity in South Africa/Azania.* Cape Town: Buchu Books.

Alexander, N. (2002). *An ordinary country: Issues in the transition from apartheid to democracy in South Africa.* Pietermaritzburg: University of Natal Press.

Alexander, N. (2004). The politics of language planning in post-apartheid South Africa. *Language Problems & Language Planning,* 28(2), 113–130.

Appadurai, A. (1996). *Modernity at large: Cultural dimensions of globalization.* Minneapolis: University of Minnesota Press.

Bakewell, O. (2008). In search of the Diasporas within Africa. *African Diasporas,* 1(1), 5–27.

Blommaert, J. (2001). The Asmara Declaration as a sociolinguistic problem: Reflections on scholarship and linguistic rights. *Journal of Sociolinguistics,* 5(1), 131–142.

Blommaert, J. (2003). Commentary: A sociolinguistics of globalization. *Journal of Sociolinguistics,* 7(4), 607–623.

Blommaert, J. (2007). Sociolinguistic scales. *Intercultural Pragmatics,* 4(1), 1–19.

Blommaert, J. (2009). A market of accents. *Language Policy,* 8(3), 243–259.

Blommaert, J. (2010). *The sociolinguistics of globalization.* Cambridge: Cambridge University Press.

Blommaert, J., Collins, J., & Slembrouck, S. (2005). Spaces of multilingualism. *Language & Communication,* 25, 197–216.

Boullion, A. (1996). 'New' African immigration to South Africa. Unpublished paper presented at the Conference of the South African Sociological Association, Durban, 7–11 July.
Bourdieu, P. (1977). The economics of linguistic exchanges. *Social Science Information*, 16(6), 645–668.
Canagarajah, S. (2006). Ethnographic methods in language policy. In T. Ricento (Ed.), *An Introduction to language policy: Theory and method* (pp. 153–169). London: Blackwell.
Crush, J., & McDonald, D. A. (2002). Transnationalism and new migrant spaces. In J. Crush & D. A. McDonald (Eds.), *Transnationalism and New African Migration to South Africa* (pp. 1–19). Cape Town: South African Migration Project.
Crush, J., & Pendleton, W. (2004). *Regionalizing xenophobia? Citizen attitudes to immigration and refugee policy in Southern Africa*. Cape Town: South African Migration Project.
De Kadt, E., & Ige, B. O. (2005). Finding ''Space'' in South Africa: Constructing identity as a Nigerian. In R. Finlayson & S. Slabbert (Eds.), *Languages and identities in a postcolony* (pp. 121–146). Frankfurt am Main: P. Lang.
Degraff, M. (2005). Linguists' most dangerous myth: the fallacy of Creole exceptionalism. *Language in Society*, 34, 533–591.
Dodson, B. (2010). Locating xenophobia: Debate, discourse and everyday experience in Cape Town, South Africa. *Africa Today*, 56(3), 2–22.
Dodson, B., & Oelofse, C. (2002). Shades of xenophobia: In-migrants and immigrants in Mizamoyetho, Cape Town. In J. Crush & D. A. McDonald (Eds.), *Transnationalism and New African Migration to South Africa* (pp. 124–148). Cape Town: South African Migration Project.

Fairclough, N. (2006). *Language and globalization*. London and New York: Routledge.
Harris, B. (2002). Xenophobia: A new pathology for a new South Africa? In D. Hook & G. Eagle (Eds.), P*sychopathology and social prejudice* (pp. 169–184). Cape Town: University of Cape Town Press.
Harris, R. (1981). *The language myth*. London: Duckworth.
Harris, R. (1990). On redefining linguistics. In H. G. Davis & T. J. Taylor (Eds.), *Redefining linguistics* (pp. 18–52). London: Routledge.
Harris, R. (1998). *Introduction to integrational linguistics*. London: Pergamon Press.
Hopper, P. (1998). Emergent grammar. In M. Tomasello (Ed.), *The new psychology of language* (pp. 155–175). Mahwah, NJ: Lawrence Erlbaum.
Johnson, D. C. (2009). The relationship between applied linguistic research and language policy for bilingual education. *Applied Linguistics*, 31(1), 72–93.
Kamuangu, G. K. (2006). *Language, immigration and ethnicity: The choice of language in DRC immigrant families*. Unpublished PhD dissertation, University of the Witwatersrand.
Kamwangamalu, N. M. (2004). The language planning situation in South Africa. In R. B. Baldauf & R. B. Kaplan (Eds.), *Language planning and policy in Africa* (pp. 197–281). Clevedon: Multilingual Matters.
Kymlicka, W., & Patten, A. (Eds.). (2003). *Language rights and political theory*. Oxford: Oxford University Press.
Lippi-Green, R. (1997). *English with an accent: Language, ideology and discrimination in the United States*. London and New York: Routledge.
Maharaj, B., & Moodley, V. (2002). New African immigration to the Durban Region. In J. Crush & D. A. McDonald (Eds.), *Transnationalism and New African Migration to South*

Africa (pp. 149–160). Cape Town: South African Migration Project.
Makoni, S. B. (2011). Language and human rights discourses in Africa: Lessons from the African experience. *Journal of Multicultural Discourses*, 1, 1–20.
Mbong, M. M. (2006). *Assessing patterns of language use and identity among Cameroonian migrants in Cape Town.* Unpublished M.A. dissertation, University of the Western Cape.
McKinney, C., & Soudien, C. (2010). *IALEI country report: Multicultural education in South Africa.* http://www.intlalliance.org/fileadmin/user_upload/docume nts/Conference_2010/NP-SA.pdf. Date accessed: 18th March 2011.
Mesthrie, R. (Ed.). (2002). *Language in South Africa.* Cambridge: Cambridge University Press.
Minaar, A., & Hough, M. (1996). *Causes, extent and impact of clandestine migration in selected Southern African countries with specific reference to South Africa.* Pretoria: Human Sciences Research Council.
Mufwene, S. (1994). New Englishes and criteria for naming them. *World Englishes*, 13(1), 21–31.
Mufwene, S. (1998). Native speaker, proficient speaker and norms. In R. Singh (Ed.), *The native speaker: Multilingual perspectives* (pp. 111–123). New Delhi: Sage.
Neocosmos, M. (2006). *From "Foreign Natives" to "Native Foreigners", explaining xenophobia in postapartheid South Africa: Citizenship and nationalism, identity and politics.* Dakar: CODESRIA.
Orman, J. (2008). *Language policy and nation-building in post-apartheid South Africa.* Dordrecht: Springer.
Pablé, A., Haas, M., & Christe, N. (2010). Language and social identity: An integrationist critique. *Language Sciences*, 32, 671–676.

Pennycook, A. (2006). Language policy and postmodernism. In T. Ricento (Ed.), *An Introduction to language policy: Theory and method* (pp. 60–76). London: Blackwell.
Pennycook, A. (2007a). The myth of English as an international language. In S. Makoni & A. Pennycook (Eds.), *Disinventing and reconstituting languages* (pp. 90–115). Clevedon: Multilingual Matters.
Pennycook, A. (2007b). *Global Englishes and transcultural flows*. London and New York: Routledge.
Reitzes, M., & Crawhall, N. (1997). *Silenced by Nation-Building: African Immigrants and Language Policy in the New South Africa*. Cape Town: South African Migration Project.
Seargeant, P. (2010). The historical ontology of language. *Language Sciences*, 32, 1–13.
South African Migration Project (SAMP). (2008). *The perfect storm: The realities of xenophobia in contemporary South Africa*. Cape Town: South African Migration Project.
Spolsky, B. (2004). *Language policy*. Cambridge: Cambridge University Press.
Stroud, C. (2000). Language and democracy: The notion of linguistic citizenship and mother tongue programmes. In K. Legère (Ed.), *Language and democracy*. Windhoek: Macmillan.
Stroud, C. (2001). African mother-tongue programmes and the politics of language: Linguistic citizenship versus linguistic human rights. *Journal of Multilingual and Multicultural Development*, 22, 339–355.
Stroud, C. (2003). Postmodernist perspectives on local languages: African mother-tongue education in times of globalisation. *International Journal of Bilingual Education and Bilingualism*, 6(1), 17–36.
Stroud, C., & Heugh, K. (2003). Language rights and linguistic citizenship. In J. Freeland & D. Patrick (Eds.), *Language*

rights and language survival: Sociolinguistic and sociocultural perspectives. Manchester: St. Jerome Publishing.

Vigouroux, C. B. (2005). 'There are no Whites in Africa': Territoriality, language, and identity among Francophone Africans in Cape Town. *Language & Communication*, 25, 237–255.

Vigouroux, C. B. (2008). "The smuggling of La Francophonie": Francophone Africans in Anglophone Cape Town (South Africa). *Language in Society*, 37(3), 415–434.

Vigouroux, C. B. (2009). From Africa to Africa: migration, globalization and language vitality. In C. B. Vigouroux & S. S. Mufwene (Eds.), *Globalization and language vitality: Perspectives from Africa* (pp. 229–254). London: Continuum Press.

Wa Kabwe-Segatti, A. (2008). 'Clandestins' et 'makwerekwere' dans l'Afrique du Sud post-apartheid: production de categories, pratiques administrative et xe´nophobie. *Social Science Information*, 47(4), 661–680.

Webb, V. N. (2002). *Language in South Africa: The role of language in National Transformation, reconstruction and development*. New York and Amsterdam: John Benjamins Publishing Company.

Webb, V. N. (2004). African languages as media of instruction in South Africa: Stating the case. *Language Problems & Language Planning*, 28(2), 146–173.

Wee, L. (2011). *Language without rights*. Oxford: Oxford University Press.

16.

Language policy and identity conflict in relation to Afrikaans in the post-apartheid era

South Africa bears witness to a long and varied colonial and post-colonial history of contact between various language groups and, by almost inevitable consequence, also one of social conflict around matters of language and linguistic policy. This is particularly so in relation to Afrikaans (still known officially as Dutch until 1925), itself an example *par excellence* of a language that can trace its current and historical population of speakers as well as some of its most distinctive structural and lexical features to the consequences of linguistic contact between groups of highly divergent origins (Roberge 2002). The predominant focus in this paper, however, will remain limited to only a small part of this aforementioned history, namely the 17 or so years of the post-apartheid period up to the time of writing.

In terms of official language policy, the post-apartheid era signalled a radical departure from the strict bilingualism of the previous dispensation with the introduction of an 11-language policy which has seen nine African languages acquire official and nominal equal status alongside English and Afrikaans (Orman 2008:91). While this policy was heralded in some quarters as an innovative and progressive development in the domain of state language policy, it is generally acknowledged, at least by those familiar with the language-political situation in South Africa, that the policy in fact constituted a quite shrewd measure of conflict avoidance on the part of the ANC. As Heugh (2002a:460) notes, the policy was the result of an 'eleventh-hour compromise' designed to appease the concerns of Afrikaners that Afrikaans would be marginalised or even removed from public life in the new era as the language issue had become the major sticking point in the negotiations between the National Party and ANC which preceded the transition to democratic rule. A pragmatic retrospective interpretation of the policy necessarily leads one to the conclusion that rather than signalling any genuine and novel ideological commitment to the multilingual implications of the new constitution, the elevation to official status of nine African languages instead merely enabled the ANC to neutralise the previously privileged position of Afrikaans without Afrikaners being able to claim that their language had been downgraded, at least not in a *de jure* sense.

Despite there now being a policy in place under which all official languages possess a theoretical equality (as if the abstractions which we call languages could ever be equal when their speakers manifestly are not), Afrikaans is the only language which has experienced a signifcant decline in use in public/ official functions in the post-apartheid period, a development which can be regarded as the flip side of the artificially elevated position the language enjoyed during apartheid. It has been said that post-apartheid language policy has seen Afrikaans "reduced to an equality" although this claim is somewhat misleading when viewed from a *de facto* perspective. In practice, Afrikaans occupies a position equal neither to that of English nor the nine African languages. It instead occupies something of an intermediate position. While English clearly inhabits a seemingly unassailable position at the top of the country's linguistic hierarchy, Afrikaans still certainly has a greater nationwide presence as a public language and is far more widespread in higher, prestige domains (particularly education) than any of the African languages. That said, the position of Afrikaans as a public language has manifestly weakened since the ANC's assumption of power in 1994, hence Mesthrie's (2008: 327) claim that it might be more apposite to talk of Afrikaans having been 'reduced to an inequality'. Although the compromise solution of the 11-language policy initially sufficed to placate mainstream Afrikaner concerns regarding language at least, the existence of a language policy "gap", that is, a discrepancy or contradiction between stated official policy and *de facto* practices, which has resulted in South African public life becoming ever more monolingual-English in character, combined with lingering historical tensions and suspicions, has ensured the continuation of a historical identity conflict between certain Afrikaner elements and advocates of the ANC's approach to the 'national question'. In the words of Alexander (2000: 29):

> Many right-wing and not so right-wing Afrikaners have frequently expressed their frustration at what they see as government tactics to bring about the anglicisation of South Africa via the gradual but ineluctable scaling down of Afrikaans and of other South African languages.

We therefore see that a conflict which was traditionally played out around issues of racial identity has to some extent shifted focus, in public discourse at least, to the seemingly more "politically correct" question of language. However, it would be mistaken to underestimate the continuing and frequently central relevance of racialised thinking in the persistence of post-apartheid identity conflict. One area of national interest in which racial tensions have often been notably present is the sporting domain. The imposition of so-called "quotas" requiring provincial and national teams (particularly in cricket and rugby union) to select a stipulated number of "players of colour" has been the subject of considerable controversy and discontent amongst sections of the white community as a whole (i.e. both English and Afrikaans speakers) and has even led to a sizeable number of high-profile athletes leaving South Africa to pursue professional careers overseas. In addition, one can also note a recent shift towards a more explicitly racialised rhetoric emanating from within ANC circles, with particular attention focused on the figure of Julius Malema, leader of the ANC Youth League (see conclusion for further discussion). While not wholly congruent with and in some way more contained than the domain of racial conflict, the language issue in relation to Afrikaans is still nevertheless one which dovetails and intersects with it to an appreciable extent.

A further point to be made and one which will emerge more saliently during the course of this paper is the fact that the implicit linguistic ideology and language practices of the ANC have a negative material and symbolic impact upon not only white Afrikaans speakers but more particularly upon the many highly marginalised non-white speakers of the language and all African-language communities. Previous studies have amply demonstrated the pernicious effects of *de facto* ANC language policy insofar as it acts as a barrier to the equitable integration of socio-economically and culturally marginalised citizens into the national system (Alexander 2002, 2004; Heugh 2002b; Orman 2008; Webb 2002a). It is also my argument that due to its overwhelmingly ethnocentric and middle-class character, contemporary Afrikaans language activism is in its present form both disinclined and unable to effectively address questions pertaining to the potential of the language to serve a transformational agenda through the empowerment of its most marginalised speakers who, for the most part, happen not to be Afrikaners.

Characterising the conflict
A first point to emphasise is that for historical reasons which are well known but cannot be discussed in any depth here, attitudes towards Afrikaans have generally borne a strong emotional content amongst certain significant sections of the South African population. One can note the existence of two views of the language with a diametrically opposed emotional character which provide a pertinent indication of why there still exists such conflict potential around the language. Admittedly, the views as presented below are done so in a somewhat caricatured fashion and are best conceived as representing positive and negative ends of an affective continuum along which any number of intermediate individual positions may be identifiable.

On the one hand, there are the strongly ethnonationalist Afrikaner elements with their fierce and renowned *taalliefde* ('love of the language') who have frequently depicted their relationship with the language as constituting one of what I have elsewhere described as 'critical symbiosis' (Orman, 2008: 110), that is to say based on the conviction that without Afrikaans there would be no Afrikaner *volk* and vice-versa (Zietsman, 1992: 1), an ideologically-laden view which effectively equates Afrikaans solely with *Algemeen Beskaafde Afrikaans*, the white standardised version of the language and overlooks the fact that Afrikaans is also the name given, although admittedly sometimes preceded by a qualifying adjective, to the variety spoken as a primary language by the majority of so-called "coloured" South Africans. This racialised standardisation of Afrikaans clearly makes a mockery of the well-known nationalist slogan, borrowed and adapted from Flemish nationalists, *Die taal is gans die volk* – "The language is the entire people".

On the other side, there is the negative view held amongst sections of the black population of Afrikaans as the language of the oppressor, as Afrikaans is widely associated with apartheid oppression and the deeply unpopular education policies of the era (Giliomee, 2003: 578-580). In addition, the apartheid-era denigration of non-standard — that is, non-white — forms of Afrikaans as crude, coarse or uncivilised (Nienaber 1942; Esterhuyse 1986; Orman 2008) has led to somewhat ambivalent attitudes towards the language amongst much of the so-called coloured population and arguably contributed towards the entrenchment of a sense of linguistic inferiority and alienation from the standard language. One notable consequence of the coloured community's somewhat equivocal relationship with Afrikaans, when combined with the social and economic allure held by the English language, has been a long-term language shift away from Afrikaans which is especially salient in the larger urban areas of the Western Cape (Alexander 1989: 57).

The path of modern South African history has led to a contemporary state of affairs whereby contrastive and frequently antagonistic attitudes towards Afrikaans have become potentially politically significant elements in the identities of various competing social and ethnic groups. It therefore follows that any initiatives to promote, marginalise or restrict the language through the implementation or non-implementation of language policy or planning measures are experienced as threats to the material and/or symbolic vitality of one identity group or another and hence become causes or sites of conflict. For instance, attempts on the part of Afrikaner interests to promote or defend Afrikaans are frequently interpreted as being parochial, particularistic, divisive and in full contradiction with the model of national integration being pursued by the ANC which purports to claim a kind of de-ethnicised universality, shorn of all ethnic bias, for the content of the national identity which it endorses. Of course, claims as to the existence of wholly non-ethnic nations must be seen as aspirational discourses stemming from an ideology of civic or political nationalism rather than assertions based on empirical sociological analysis (Oakes and Warren 2007: 13; Orman 2008: 13-19). The ANC elite and those wedded to its nationalist project can be equally regarded as constituting a separate ethnic group since their group identity, which happens also to pose as the sole legitimate South African national identity, also displays elements of ethnic-type attributes, such as a belief in common myths of origin (although not necessarily biological) and struggle, a shared historical experience and a *de facto* common-language ideology.

Conversely, efforts by the ANC government to restrict or downgrade Afrikaans via policy implementation or inaction, whether finding their origin in active enmity or mere indifference towards the language and/or its speakers, are experienced by some as a severe assault on the central, defining element of Afrikaner identity and contribute towards the sense of psychological insecurity and unwelcomeness which many Afrikaners claim to be experiencing in the new South Africa. The current perceived threat to Afrikaans serves very much as a reinforcement of the traditional, insular nationalist reading of Afrikaner history which centres upon the recurrent theme of a battle for ethnocultural survival in response to out-group persecution. The *Taalstryd* or "language struggle" has invariably been a central feature of such efforts. A key point to take into account then is that the continuation of this identity conflict in a certain sense sees actors on both sides in familiar antipathetic territory, therefore acting as a psychological reinforcement of the historical group identities, thereby strengthening their antagonistic nature and opening up the conflict to potential political exploitation by enabling political opportunists on both sides to recruit large-scale grassroots support without recourse to rational argument. And indeed, this leads us on to perhaps the most pernicious consequence of the vigorous emotionality which frequently characterises the conflict (as well as popular debates on language matters more generally), namely that it endows it with a strong measure of intractability, causing actors in the conflict to be less inclined to seek or accept compromise solutions.

A prominent dimension of the conflict and debate around Afrikaans is the language activism which both accompanies and to a considerable extent sustains it. Much of the significance of language activism on behalf of Afrikaans insofar as it contributes towards the perpetuation of the identity conflict under discussion here can only be grasped when one considers the state of language activism in South Africa as a whole. The most notable feature of language activism in South Africa is its highly uneven, predominantly Afrikaner-centric nature (Du Plessis 2004, 2008; Orman 2008: 149-157; Kriel 2010a). By this is meant that it has been and continues to be predominantly white Afrikaans speakers, through their traditional cultural organisations (for example the Afrikanerbond, FAK, AKTV[1]) and media channels (news-papers such as *Beeld*, *Die Burger* and *Die Volksblad*), who have contested ANC linguistic policy most vigorously. The extent and organisational sophistication of language activism on behalf of Afrikaans finds no comparable counterpart in any African-language community in South Africa. And indeed, this is indicative of two important and related facts, namely that the Afrikaner community has a far larger middle-class than most African-language communities and that ethnocentric language activism in general tends to be predominantly middle-class in character (Orman 2008: 155). This insight is certainly reflected in Afrikaans language activism, which appears to be conducted chiefly by academics, lawyers, journalists and nationalist politicians with

---

[1] Federasie van Afrikaanse Kultuurvereniginge (Federation of Afrikaans Cultural Associations) and the Afrikaanse Taal- en Kultuurvereniging (Afrikaans Language and Cultural Association).

a strong focus on securing language rights for Afrikaners at the group level. The comparative underdevelopment of language activism in other communities has the effect of creating a more prominent profile for Afrikaner/Afrikaans activism and to some extent feeds the perception that discontent with ANC language policy resides to a significant degree only within the Afrikaner community, which in turn lends force to ANC claims that Afrikaans language activism merely serves a narrow, ethno-nationalist interest.

The blanket designation of contemporary Afrikaans-based activism as nationalist or ethnocentric in focus has become a matter of some contestation in certain activist circles. Indeed, there have been some ostensible rhetorical attempts from more "moderate" Afrikaner voices to uncouple language activism on behalf of Afrikaans from an Afrikaner nationalist agenda and promote the notion of a single, non-racial "Afrikaanse" culture. Kriel (2010a: 278) draws attention to the fact that in the September 2005 edition of *Die Vrye Afrikaan*[2], some prominent Afrikaans language activists even went so far as to proclaim Afrikaner nationalism as dead, proceeding to identify themselves as "post-nationalist" Afrikaners and styling themselves as a mere cultural group. However, as Kriel's article goes on to demonstrate, closer inspection of the rhetoric and actions of certain of these supposedly "reformed" nationalists points to their serving of quite clear ethnocentric agendas or at least elements thereof. And certainly, understandable suspicions remain that efforts to downplay or deny the ethnic character of Afrikaans language activism are merely intended to provide a veneer of socio-political legitimacy for what, from the ANC's perspective, constitute continuing and unacceptable tendencies towards ethnocentric particularity. Of course, in the more radical pastures of Afrikaans activism there are no such suspicions as the protagonists are quite open

---

[2] A journal published by the FAK.

about their nationalist, even secessionist, aims and explicit rejection of both the desirability and possibility of a common South African identity. Falling into this category would be figures such as Dan Roodt, head of the Pro-Afrikaans Action Group (PRAAG), a "non-party political movement which fights for the continued existence of Afrikaans and the Afrikaner in South Africa[3]" (my translation), and the so-called "volkstaaters"[4].

In order to mitigate the risk of overemphasising the extent and salience of the conflict in South African society at large, it is important to highlight a further feature of Afrikaans language activism and the so-called *taaldebat* in general, namely the fact that, as Brink (2006:1) observes:

> [T]he majority of South Africans are unaware of it. This is because the debate *about* Afrikaans has been conducted almost exclusively *within* Afrikaans. Thus, whatever the merits or demerits of the various arguments may be, and whatever lessons may be learnt for our other indigenous languages, or higher education, or nation-building, it *cannot be heard by all.*

---

[3] http://www.praag.org/

[4] Advocates of a separate ethnically-based state for Afrikaners within South African territory. Examples include the *Afrikaner Volksparty* (www.afrikanervolksparty.org) which refuses to recognise the legitimacy of and hence participate in national elections and the Orania Movement (www.orania.co.za) which describes itself as 'an Afrikaans cultural movement with the aim to restore Afrikaner freedom in an independent, democratic Republic based on Christian values and a healthy balance between independence and cooperation with surrounding areas.' The town of Orania in the Northern Cape, the population of which consists entirely of Afrikaners, has even issued its own currency, the Ora, although it is not recognised by the South African Reserve Bank.

Therefore, despite its wider significance in relation to issues of national integration and public multilingualism, the expressive manifestation(s) of the conflict in relation to Afrikaans remains a largely niched phenomenon which may only sporadically come to the attention of a wider national audience. Even the few works published in English on the subject have tended to be specialist academic texts with quite limited readerships. This in turn leads us to what one might cautiously propose as a universal characteristic of debates or conflicts of this type, namely that they are inherently variable in terms of their intensity and salience and may even pass through periods of apparent latency.

Having outlined some of the defining features of the conflict as a whole, the discussion now moves on to consider the two most prominent domains of conflict in relation to Afrikaans, those of university medium-of-instruction policy and ANC renaming policy.

ANC language policy and the Historically Afrikaans Universities (HAUs)

The most controversial and complex question pertaining to Afrikaans in the post-apartheid period has undoubtedly been that regarding its continuing use as a medium of instruction at tertiary education institutions. It is certainly the issue which has aroused most anxiety amongst Afrikaans language activists and to some extent is the part which has become emblematic of the language conflict as a whole. The root of the conflict lies in the fact that the five single-medium Afrikaans universities of the apartheid era — the University of Stellenbosch, the University of Pretoria, the University of the Free State, North-West University (formerly the Potchefstroom University for Christian Higher Education) and the University of Johannesburg (formerly the Rand Afrikaans University) — have come under increasing political pressure from above to use English as a medium of instruction alongside, in addition to (dual or parallel-medium) or even instead of Afrikaans at the undergraduate and postgraduate level in order to cater to the supposed language preferences of non-white students, as it has been an unyielding and explicit demand of the ANC that previously white-only universities open their doors to students from all previously disadvantaged groups and that language not serve as means of exclusion.

The ANC justifies the increased use of English as medium of instruction on the basis of 'accessibility' arguments and the need to alter the racial profile of the universities in question in order to make them more representative of the South African demographic as a whole. Such arguments, which posit English as the language of educational inclusion, of course have a strong politico-ideological motivation and are essentially only valid at the middle-class level. Whatever the ANC rhetoric to the contrary, given the current linguistic demography of the country the displacement of Afrikaans by English at university level necessarily serves the cause of increasing the ideological and material accessibility of educational resources and services for the thin, but growing stratum of the black middle-class elite. We can note therefore that, in its present form, the conflict around the university medium-of-instruction issue is still dominated by middle-class interests on both sides. In addition to overlooking entirely the possible role of African languages as media of instruction at the tertiary level, this also has the effect of sidelining arguments concerning the potential of Afrikaans to function as a medium of educational inclusion for the Afrikaans-speaking coloured community which is the largest population group in the Western Cape and by some accounts the most educationally disadvantaged community in the whole country (Schlemmer and Giliomee 2001: 121).

In most cases, the universities appear to have towed the ANC line to the point where only Stellenbosch University and the Potchefstroom campus of the North-West University can now be considered predominantly Afrikaans universities. Recent figures indicate that still the majority of students at these institutions report having Afrikaans as their first language although a downward trend can nevertheless be noted (Van der Walt, 2008: 217; Pienaar, 2006: 30). The University of Pretoria has even gone so far as to affirm an official language policy recognising 'the right of every individual to receive tuition via the language of his or her choice' although of course in reality this choice remains limited to Afrikaans or English. Elsewhere, Beukes (2010: 205) notes that the University of Johannesburg has been largely unsuccessful in implementing its envisaged policy of "functional multilingualism" and that it has consequently been criticised for "neglecting its historic constituency by failing to provide an academic home for Afrikaans-speaking students". This overall situation has created widespread displeasure and anxiety amongst numerous Afrikaans-speaking academics and student bodies fearful that the trend towards the Anglicisation of the HAUs spells the beginning of the end for Afrikaans as a language of higher education. Fears have also been expressed that the quality of English-language education at certain of these institutions may often be inferior due to some Afrikaans-speaking staff members not being sufficiently proficient in English to lecture in it (Webb 2002b: 50). The university language issue is one which is rarely absent from the letters pages and opinion columns of the Afrikaans newspapers (both print and online versions) which of course have a strong commercial interest in keeping the issue alive and, as a corollary, ensuring the continued vitality of the language itself. Entire books devoted to the issue have been published, most notably by Chris Brink (2006), former vice-chancellor of Stellenbosch University which, as that most iconic of Afrikaner universities, has very much become the central locus and focus of the *taaldebat* (see also Giliomee 2006). In another, earlier volume on the subject (available only in Afrikaans), Schlemmer and Giliomee (2001: 118) articulate a pervasive fear held by Afrikaans activists in relation to the medium-of-instruction issue, namely that of Afrikaans' relegation to the status of a medium of mere grassroots cultural interaction and identity:

> The single greatest danger for Afrikaans, however, is that if it should weaken or disappear as a university language, this would signal the decline of Afrikaans as a language of science, as a professional language, as a language of intellectual discourse and eventually also a literary language. [...] There is also little doubt that Afrikaans is going to survive in sports stadiums, pubs, cafes, living rooms and bedrooms. But who is going to take it seriously if it is not present at an intellectual and professional level? Just like other native African languages, Afrikaans would be decapitated [*onthoofd*] in such a case.

The universities have found themselves in the midst of a dilemma, caught between the desire to maintain their Afrikaans character and thereby not alienate their core constituency of students and benefactors and yet fall in line with new, non-negotiable commitments to facilitate accessibility to education, promote non-racialism and achieve a more demographically representative student body. Indeed, it is a predicament shared by certain more moderate Afrikaans activists and organisations in general, one which amounts to performing a fine balancing act between advocating on behalf of the interests of Afrikaans speakers without being seen to promote an ethnocentric agenda and in doing so further perpetuate conflict and ANC intransigence with regard to granting concessions on language matters. The question which remains to be answered definitively is whether, given the actors involved, such a balancing act is feasible on either a theoretical or practical level, although there seem few grounds for deviating too far from a generally sceptical outlook in this regard.

The medium-of-instruction question (and indeed the language debate more generally) has not only been a source of conflict between Afrikaner interests and the ANC government, it has also spawned additional conflicts and discords within the Afrikaner community as individuals and organisations have adopted varying positions on the issue. While a fairly broad spectrum of standpoints can be identified, a somewhat crude binary distinction has sometimes been drawn between the so-called *taalglyers* and the *taalstryders* or *taalblyers*[5] (*Rapport* 17 June 2007; *Die Burger* 29 October 2009). At one end, there are those who have been willing to compromise and concede ground to government demands, a position taken by most of the universities as a matter of pragmatic necessity and which has on occasion resulted in sizeable demonstrations against them by their own students. Chris Brink, who explicitly rejected the notion of Stellenbosch as "the kind of 'Afrikaans university' envisaged by the *taalstryders*"[6] (Brink 2006: 164), became a highly polarising figure during his term as vice-chancellor in which he oversaw the implementation of a far-reaching "transformation agenda" at the university. Brink has been accused variously of "wanting to turn Stellenbosch black", "displaying a shocking lack of critical analysis of the current South African dispensation"[7] and of being "an enemy of Afrikaans" (*Die Burger* 10 March 2005). Occupying the middle ground, if indeed it is appropriate to use such a formulation given the Manichean terms in which the interests at stake in the language conflict tend to be presented, are what might be termed the moderate Afrikaner nationalists, those whose rhetoric is not explicitly racialised or as overtly confrontational as that of the more 'extremist' activists, but for whom the Afrikaner

---

[5] The "language slide-aways" versus the "language fighters" or "language loyalists".
[6] http://www.praag.org/rubriek268d.htm
[7] http://www.oulitnet.co.za/taaldebat/rossouw_brink.asp

nation as a group entity is still plainly the primary unit of concern. There has therefore by no means been a monolithic response to the issue from within the Afrikaner community, nor is one able to talk of a firm consensus of opinion. At most, one can note the formation of fuzzily definable and sometimes shifting factions and it is the various ideological gaps which may appear in between such factions which give rise to the potential for inter-community conflict. Furthermore, far from exercising the entire community, it should be noted that there are some, indeed possibly many, white Afrikaans speakers for whom the *taaldebat* and related issues are of little or no active concern and who may not even self-identify as Afrikaners. For example, Mesthrie (2008: 330) cites a newspaper article from August 2004 by Max du Preez, a prominent Afrikaans-speaking political journalist, who writes that:

> There is probably no other public issue in South African national life that elicits so much heated drivel, falsehoods, pretentiousness and wasted emotion than the issue of the Afrikaans language. I am bored to the depths of my soul with the Afrikaans debate.

It is apparent then that not all those who identify as white Afrikaans speakers/Afrikaners perceive themselves to be in a conflict situation as regards the language. The singular communal psycho-emotional "realities" sometimes projected, however sincerely, by activists in the promotion and self-justification of their cause can instead be seen as rhetorically intended strategies designed to lend weight to their arguments. As such, the manifestation and intensification of conflict can in some measure be regarded as the product of the activism itself. After all, the rhetoric of language activism thrives on the experience or perception of some form of conflict. It would therefore seem naive to regard language activism merely as a reflection of pre-existing conflict. We can instead seek to determine how conflict manifests itself through the actions and pronouncements of activists, adopting a critical posture as regards the extent to which such activism resonates with the attitudes and experiences of the community members it claims to represent.

ANC renaming policy
The second major domain of language-related conflict between Afrikaner interests and the ANC in recent years has been that relating to the ANC's renaming policy and in particular with regard to its renaming of numerous settlements with Afrikaans or Afrikaner names. The issue is of interest from a conflict-analysis perspective in that it constitutes a wholly symbolic — but no less emotive — domain of conflict which might instinctively appear more amenable to a conflict-management approach, but which is instead neatly illustrative of how conflict may be knowingly pursued or at least tolerated as part of a policy aimed at asserting a measure of symbolic-ideological hegemony. The changing of place names (*pleknaamverandering* in Afrikaans) is not a recent phenomenon in South Africa. As Lubbe's (2007) historical survey shows, various waves of settlement renaming have occurred with varying degrees of systematicity throughout its colonial history reflecting the changing socio-political fortunes of the various indigenous and settler population groups present in the country. The apartheid government also pursued such a policy, most notoriously in the case of the Johannesburg suburb of *Sophiatown* which in 1963 was renamed *Triomf* following the forced removal of the black population to Soweto. The name *Sophiatown* was officially restored in 2006 in yet another reflection of politico-ideological change. The ANC's current renaming policy only began to take on a systematic character following Mbeki's succession of Mandela as president in 1999, which signaled a move away from an era of symbolic reconciliation between the ANC and Afrikaners (most famously embodied by Mandela's

wearing of the Springbok rugby jersey at the 1995 World Cup Final) towards an explicit policy of transformation and Africanisation, one with far clearer conflict potential.

The settlement renaming policy has been focused primarily in the north of the country and especially in the province of Limpopo (formerly the Northern Province) where all but two towns (Burgersfort and Groblersdal) with Afrikaans/Afrikaner names have been officially renamed. Examples include the provincial capital, formerly known as Pietersburg but now renamed as Polokwane and the towns of Potgietersrus and Nylstroom which have become Mokopane and Modimolle respectively (Orman 2008: 125). Elsewhere, Nelspruit, the capital of the Mpumulanga province (formerly Eastern Transvaal), has been renamed as Mbombela and the town of Lydenburg had its official name changed to Mashishing in 2006. The most high-profile cases have been that of Pretoria, the country's administrative capital, and to a lesser extent Potchefstroom, a university city of around 125 000 inhabitants located in the North-West Province. In 2005, a proposal to change the name of Pretoria to Tshwane met with huge opposition from Afrikaner organisations and civil-rights groups and a compromise was eventually reached whereby the name Pretoria was retained for the city itself while the metropolitan area became known as the City of Tswhane (Truter 2005; Labuschagne 2006). A similar compromise also materialised in the case of Potchefstroom following substantial protests with the city's name remaining unchanged but the municipality being renamed as Tlokwe (*Mail and Guardian* 18 June 2007).

ANC renaming policy has not only been concerned with the renaming of towns and cities but has also targeted street names and public buildings such as airports, hospitals, libraries and sports stadiums, with the most notable example being the renaming of Johannesburg International Airport, known as Jan Smuts Airport until 1994, as O.R. Tambo Airport in honour of the former ANC president. In another case predestined to arouse Afrikaner sensitivities, Bloemfontein's *Voortrekkerstraat* was renamed as *Nelson Mandela Drive* (Lubbe 2007: 71-74).

ANC figures have explained the rationale behind the renaming policy as being part of initiatives aimed at ridding the country of supposedly offensive, colonial-era names reminiscent of past injustices and oppression (Orman 2008: 126). The policy has often been styled as signalling the advent of a cathartic decolonisation process. The following quotation is taken from the first annual report of the South African Geographical Names Council, the body charged with overseeing the implementation of the renaming policy:

> Liberation has been achieved, it is now time for the people of South Africa to play their role in changing our country to be what we fought for [...] We should soon change the face of our country and not to be seen as part of Europe in Africa [...] It is then incumbent upon all South Africans to see to it that this (changing of names) is done and achieved, as this will be a major mark that will show change in our country.

However, when the policy does not just target those names which are quite clearly offensive, such as *Kaffirspruit*, *Kaffirskraal* and the numerous streets named after Verwoerd or Vorster[8], but also places such as *Naboomspruit*, named after the local pro-

---

[8] Incidentally, there are still a fair number of H.F. Verwoerd streets and others named after apartheid-era nationalist politicians throughout the country which remain unchanged to this day. In central Cape Town, there was, until late 2011, still an Oswald Pirow Street. Pirow was a far-right nationalist politician who served as Minister of Justice and Defence in the 1930s and was an open admirer of Hitler and the Nazi regime. The renaming policy has therefore been far from comprehensive.

fusion of euphorbia trees, or *Warmbad* (Warmbaths), it is difficult to escape the conclusion frequently articulated by Afrikaner activists and politicians, as well as numerous "ordinary" Afrikaans speakers in the letters pages of newspapers etc., that many of these names have been deemed offensive and thus illegitimate solely on account of their being Afrikaans. Afrikaner sensitivities in relation to the issue have been further heightened by the fact that place names which bear quite explicit reference to British colonial heritage, examples of which include Grahamstown, Cradock King William's Town, Port Elizabeth (Eastern Cape), Caledon and Wellington (Western Cape), have escaped relatively unscathed.

The ANC's general unwillingness to compromise on the renaming issue, acting on the whole as if a place or building could only ever have one name in blatant contradiction of the multilingual implications of the constitution[9], can be quite unproblematically interpreted as an attempt to extend and consolidate its measure of semio-ideological hegemony. It is furthermore apparent that it is also willing to tolerate a degree of identity-based conflict in order to do so. After all, it is not too difficult to envisage what form a compromise solution might take in such a case, namely an additive naming policy whereby the settlements or buildings in question possess official names in two (or more where necessary) languages. In most cases, this would not seem to require much more than the production of bi- or multilingual signs, letterheads etc. In 2005, a correspondent to an Afrikaans newspaper asked, presumably rhetorically: "Can we trust that the present government, in the spirit of constitutional loyalty, will make a contribution towards positive nation-building through

---

[9] Cases such as Cape Town which, in line with the Western Cape's policy of having three official languages in the province, is also known as *Kaapstad* (Afrikaans) and iKapa (Xhosa) clearly depart from the general ideological tendency of the ANC.

inclusive place name additions instead of replacements?" (*Die Volksblad*, 26 November 2005). Any such faith continues to be misplaced. The effect of the ANC's overwhelmingly subtractive approach to this matter (and others) has been to symbolically alienate Afrikaner elements from its nation-building discourse through its styling of meaningful elements of Afrikaner history and cultural identity as fundamentally incompatible with the "new" South African national identity over which it claims executive ownership (Orman 2008: 128-129). It is primarily in this sense, then, that one can talk of an identity conflict in relation to Afrikaans.

Wider consequences of the identity conflict in terms of the national question
The South African case points to the innate conflict potential of an ideologically hegemonic, non-conciliatory model of national integration. In terms of linguistic policy, ANC hegemony makes itself felt at both the instrumental, material level and the symbolic, emotional level, although to varying degrees amongst different sections of the South African population. The ANC's privileging of English and apparent lack of concern for Afrikaans[10] is preventing a sizeable number of Afrikaans speakers from enjoying a sense of sentimental attachment to the current government and state apparatus, in addition to the fact that more extreme Afrikaner elements are quite unable to reconcile themselves to the fact that the new rulers of the country are mostly black (and English-speaking for good measure).

---

[10] In perhaps an overestimation of the ANC's interest in matters linguistic, the more vigorous Afrikaner nationalist elements naturally tend to advance the idea of a deliberate plot against Afrikaans. As Brink (2006: 99) notes: "A strong thread running through the *taaldebat* has been the notion that Afrikaans is endangered because it has powerful enemies (italics in original).

There is something of an irony to be detected in the ANC's policy in relation to Afrikaans insofar as its pursuit of what amounts to a conflict strategy has the effect of stimulating an ethnonationalist response on the part various Afrikaner elements (Kriel 2010a). The irony resides in the ANC's traditional repugnance for and rejection of what it conceives as ethnic politics. Indeed, as mentioned previously, such is the ANC's ideological aversion to expressions of ethnicity, it is even unable to acknowledge the manifestly ethnic nature of certain of the elements constitutive of the South African identity it promotes. The difficulty here when viewed from a perspective favouring a non-hegemonic, inclusive approach to national integration, which given the nature of South African society must necessarily involve some measure of conflict management, is that when two identities are styled and perceived as incompatible or even dialectically opposed the more primordial ties are invariably likely to be stronger and more mobilising. In other words, it would seem quite unrealistic to expect white Afrikaans speakers to take up membership *en masse* in the ANC-endorsed national community at the price of renouncing their Afrikaner identity. In a more concise formulation, we can say that the persistence of salient inter-ethnic conflict inhibits the development of a common, state-bounded national identity.

A second, arguably more pernicious effect of the conflict relates to the potential of Afrikaans to serve as a language of empowerment and social advancement for its genuinely materially marginalised speakers. As long as the main social issue pertaining to the language continues to be perceived in terms of an identity conflict between Afrikaners and the ANC government, attention and resources are likely to remain diverted from engagement with questions with genuinely transformational implications. Perhaps the most telling irony of all in the whole debate concerning Afrikaans is that, besides so-called "native" speakers of English, it is the white middle-class Afrikaners who most vigorously defend their language that are generally best able to function in English when required to do so. The following remarks by Schlemmer and Giliomee (2001: 132) in relation to the university language issue could be equally applied to various social domains:

> If Afrikaans is forced out at the university level, the young white middle-class Afrikaners will be able to move into English language institutions, here or abroad, comparatively easily. The case for the maintenance of Afrikaans is much more about the needs of the academically underdeveloped coloured (and white, as well as some black) Afrikaans-speaking communities.

When considered from this angle, one could say that what is currently taking place is really the wrong type of conflict in relation to Afrikaans, that is to say one centred upon matters of ethnic identity rather than a class-based conflict focused on issues of socio-economic inequality and restricted access to cultural goods. If the fully-inclusive, democratic incorporation of all South African citizens into the national system is to be the motivating aim, which in no way can be taken for granted, it is quite evident that ANC linguistic policy needs to be challenged and hence some form of conflict initiated. In this view, conflict *per se* need not be regarded as a necessarily negative phenomenon. Indeed, one might argue that the initiation of conflict is a positive and necessary step in challenging the social order. However, in South Africa's case, if the predominant social conflicts around matters of language continue to be conducted almost exclusively by middle-class elites intent on staking out a symbolic identity-bound territory through the acquisition of group rights at the level of the ethnolinguistic community, the prospect of the meaningful linguistic empowerment of the country's most marginalised citizens cannot but remain dim.

One organisation which has explicitly sought to advance the cause of an inclusive, non-racial Afrikaans community, consisting of so-called *Afrikaanses*, is the *Stigting vir Bemagtiging deur Afrikaans*[11] (SBA). Described by Kriel (2010b: 59) as the "only mainstream Afrikaans organisation with a 'brown' leader", the main thrust of the SBA's work is to promote literacy in Afrikaans amongst both primary and secondary school pupils and contribute towards community development and socio-economic empowerment (*Rapport* 1 January 2006). This has manifested itself in, amongst other activities, a number of reading projects for schoolchildren in various age-groups, literacy and language policy workshops for teachers and school-management bodies and language skills training for school leavers and unemployed adults. However, given the deep schisms which still persist between white and non-white speakers of Afrikaans insofar as their attitudes and relationship to the language is concerned, it still remains to be seen whether any firm material realisation can be given to the notion of a single language community, although a default scepticism in this regard is perhaps advisable.

Some concluding remarks: towards a general theory of language-based conflict?
Given the varying extent and nature in which language may be implicated in particular social conflicts, combined with other case-specific historical and circumstantial factors which may play a central role in determining key features of the conflict situation, it is doubtful whether anything other than a very general descriptive or predictive theory of language-based conflict could be feasibly developed. In any case, a useful and perhaps rather obvious starting point would be the so-called "Nelde's law", which states that there can be no language contact without language conflict (Nelde 1998). While the formulation of the law

---

[11] Foundation for Empowerment through Afrikaans (www.afrikaans.com).

may contain a degree of rhetorical overstatement, it does point us in the direction of an important and foundational insight, namely that conflict or tension in some form or another concerning language is to be regarded as unexceptional, ongoing and essentially as the default situation in multilingual, multi-ethnic societies and even more so in those characterised by salient inequalities between competing groups. Very rarely is language an entirely uncontested domain. As a result, in policy terms it would certainly seem more realistic to approach such conflicts, whatever their fluctuating degree of latency or salience, in terms of management, rather than definitive resolution or prevention.

A further important consideration in relation to inter-ethnic conflicts and one which has a potentially limiting effect on ambitions in language policy and planning, is that language issues may form only one aspect of the conflict in question and that the conflict, which at root is fundamentally more about identity than language *per se*, may furthermore shift in focus or emphasis and relocate beyond the domain of language policy. This obviously makes a language policy response aimed at addressing or resolving the conflict as a whole an improbable prospect, amounting in effect to a *pars pro toto* approach. Indeed, of late one can note just such a shift of focus away from language matters in the Afrikaner-ANC conflict and a return towards a more explicit focus on questions of race. The most prominent instantiation of such a shift can be observed in the response to the actions and rhetoric of Julius Malema, leader of the ANC Youth League (ANCYL), who had a court case brought against him by Afriforum, an Afrikaner civil rights organisation, for his public singing of an anti-apartheid struggle song with the lyric "Dubula ibhunu" ("Shoot the Boer"). In May 2011, the South Gauteng High Court declared Malema's actions as incitement to murder. Malema, who has also advocated forced removal of land from whites and made various other inflammatory remarks with strongly racialised overtones, rapidly became something of an obsession in the Afrikaans press, with opinion pieces and letters concerning or making reference to him published on an almost daily basis. Rather ironically, a fair number of such letters complained about the supposedly excessive coverage afforded him. The key point to grasp for the purposes of this discussion, however, is merely that such developments clearly relocate the identity conflict beyond the domain of language policy.

The case study discussed in this article also shows how the existence and propagation of language conflict, up to a certain level of salience and intensity, may serve various political and activist agendas on all sides. One cannot therefore assume that language policy will be formulated and implemented with a conflict-management approach in mind, nor is conflict necessarily to be regarded as an accidental by-product of policy. Indeed, conflict may be knowingly and actively pursued via policy or at least have some in-built allowance for it in order to further political and individual agendas. If language policy is to serve as a means of conflict management then it appears axiomatic that any such initiatives must chime with the self-perceived interests of the parties involved, something which cannot be assumed *a priori*. Moreover, depending on one's preferences and convictions, it may not necessarily be desirable as conflict avoidance at any social price is clearly not a universally satisfactory approach. This can then lead us towards a more affirmative view of language-based conflict, albeit conflict of a certain type and with a particular social emphasis, as representing a necessary strategy in countering hegemonic political and cultural forces.

References
Alexander, Neville. 1989. *Language Policy and National Unity in South Africa/Azania*. Cape Town: Creda Press.
Alexander, Neville. 2000. "Manuell Castells and the New South Africa". *Social Dynamics* 26(1): 18-36.

Alexander, Neville. 2002. *An Ordinary Country: Issues in the Transition from Apartheid to Democracy in South Africa.* Pietermaritzburg: University of Natal Press.
Alexander, Neville. 2004. "The politics of language planning in post-apartheid South Africa". *Language Problems & Language Planning* 28(2): 113-130.
Beukes, Anne-Marie. 2010. "'Opening the doors of education': Language policy at the University of Johannesburg". *Language Matters* 41(2): 193-213.
Brink, Chris. 2006. *No Lesser Place: The Taaldebat at Stellenbosch.* Stellenbosch: Sun Press.
Du Plessis, L. Theodorus. 2004. "Afrikaans en taalactivisme [Afrikaans and language activism]" In F.I.J. van Rensburg (ed.), *Afrikaans: lewende taal van miljoene.* Pretoria: Van Schaik: 169-182.
Du Plessis, L. Theodorus. 2006. "Language activism in South Africa". In G. Sica (ed.), *Open Problems in Linguistics and Lexicography.* Monza: Polimetrica: 69-89.
Esterhuyse, J. 1986. *Taalapartheid en skoolafrikaans* [Linguistic apartheid and school Afrikaans]. Goodwood: Taurus.
Giliomee, Hermann. 2003. *The Afrikaners: Biography of a People.* Parl: Tafelberg.
Giliomee, Hermann. 2006. *'N Vaste Plek Vir Afrikaans* [A permanent place for Afrikans]. Stellenbosch: Sun Press.
Heugh, Kathleen. 2002. "Recovering multilingualism". In Rajend Mesthrie (ed.), *Language in South Africa.* Cambridge: Cambridge OUiversity 9ress: 449-475.
Heugh, Kathleen. 2002b. "The case against bilingual and multilingual education in South Africa: Laying bare the myths". *Perspectives in Education* 20(1): 171-196.
Kriel, Mariana.2010a. "Towards an alternative take on language Activism: A South African case study". *Language Matters* 41(2): 278-293.

Kriel, Mariana. 2010b. *South African Language Rights Monitor 2006*. Bloemfontein: Sun Press.
Labuschagne, P. 2006. "Pretoria or Tshwane? The politics of name changes". *Journal for Contemporary History* 31(1): 49-61.
Lubbe, Johan. 2007. "Pleknaamverandering in Suid-Afrika: 'n historiese oorsig [The changing of place names in South Africa: a historical overview]". *Acta Academia Supplementum* 1: 54-82.
Mesthrie, Rajend. 2008. "South Africa0 The rocky road to nation building". In Andrew Simpson (ed.), *Language and Rational Identity in Africa*. Oxford: Oxford University Press: 314-338.
Nelde, Peter H. 1998. "Language conflict". In Florian Coulmas (ed.), *The Handbook of Sociolinguistics*. London: Blackwell: 285-300.
Nienaber, G.S. 1942. *Afrikaans tot 1860* [Afrikaans until 1860]. Johannesburg: Voortrekkerpers.
Oakes, Leigh and Warren, Jane. 2007. *Language, Citizenship and Identity in Quebec*. Basingstoke: Palgrave Macmillan.
Orman, Jon. 2008. *Language Policy and Nation Building in Post-Apartheid South Africa*. Dordrecht: Springer.
Pienaar, M. 2006. "Simultaneous interpreting as an aid in parallel-medium tertiary education". *Stellenbosch Papers in Linguistics PLOS* Volume 33:27-41.
Roberge, Paul T. 2002. "Afrikaans: considering origins". In Rajend Mesthrie (ed.), *Language in South Africa*. Cambridge: Cambridge University Press: 79-103.
Schlemmer, Lawrence and Giliomee, Hermann. 2001. "Afrikaans by die kruispad [Afrikaans at the crossroads]". In Hermann Giliomee and Lawrence Schlemmer (eds.), *Kruispad: Die Toekoms van Afrikaans as Openbare Taal* [Crossroads: The Future of Afrikaans as a Public Language]. Paarl: Tafelberg: 115-135.

Truter, E.J.J. 2005. "Die polemiek rondom die voorgestelde naamsverandering van Pretoria na Tshwane soos weerspiël in die gedrukte media [The polemic concerning the proposed name change of Pretoria to Tswhane as reflected in the printed media]". *Nomina Africana* 19(2): 81-118.

Van der Walt, Christa. 2008. "University Students' Attitudes Towards and Experiences of Bilingual Classrooms". In Anthony Liddicoat and Richard B. Baldauf Jr. (eds.), *Language Planning in Local Contexts*. Clevedon: Multilingual Matters

Webb, Vic. 20021. *Language in South Africa: The Role of Language in National Transformation, Reconstruction and Development*. New York and Amsterdam: John Benjamins Publishing Company.

Webb, Vic. 2002b. "English as a second language in South Africa's tertiary institutions: A case study at the University of Pretoria". *World Englishes* 21(1): 49-61.

Zietsman, P.H. 1992. *Die Taal is Gans die Volk* [The Language is the Entire People]. Pretoria: University of South Africa.

www.ingramcontent.com/pod-product-compliance
Lightning Source LLC
Chambersburg PA
CBHW052203090526
44583CB00015BA/1103